WHISPERING
PINES

ALSO BY JASON SCHNEIDER

3,000 Miles

Have Not Been The Same: The CanRock Renaissance
(with Michael Barclay and Ian A.D. Jack)

WHISPERING PINES

THE NORTHERN ROOTS OF AMERICAN MUSIC FROM HANK SNOW TO THE BAND

JASON SCHNEIDER

ECW PRESS

Published by ECW Press, 2120 Queen Street East, Suite 200,
Toronto, Ontario, Canada M4E 1E2 / 416.694.3348 / info@ecwpress.com

LIBRARY AND ARCHIVES CANADA CATALOGUING IN PUBLICATION

Schneider, Jason, 1971-
Whispering pines : the northern roots of American music from Hank Snow
to the Band / Jason Schneider.

ISBN-13: 978-1-55022-874-8 / ISBN-10: 1-55022-874-9

1. Popular music — Writing and publishing — Canada — History.
2. Musicians — Canada — Interviews. i. Title.

ML3484.S359 2009   782.42164'13   C2008-907564-1

Editor for the press: Michael Holmes
Cover: type set in Cheap Stealer, © Billy Argel
Text design: Tania Craan
Typesetting: Mary Bowness

Photo section: image of Wilf Carter courtesy Whyte Museum of the Canadian
Rockies (V225 accn. 6068); image of Bob Dylan's Rolling Thunder Revue ©
Bettmann / Corbis. All other images courtesy Showtime Music Archives (Toronto).

Printing: Friesens   1   2   3   4   5
This book is printed on paper made of 100% post-consumer waste content.

The publication of *Whispering Pines* has been generously supported by the
Canada Council for the Arts, which last year invested $20.1 million in writing and
publishing throughout Canada, by the Ontario Arts Council, by the Government
of Ontario through Ontario Book Publishing Tax Credit, by the OMDC Book
Fund, an initiative of the Ontario Media Development Corporation, and
by the Government of Canada through the Book Publishing Industry
Development Program (BPIDP).

Canada Council   Conseil des Arts   ONTARIO ARTS COUNCIL
for the Arts   du Canada   Canada   CONSEIL DES ARTS DE L'ONTARIO

PRINTED AND BOUND IN CANADA

ECW PRESS
ecwpress.com

To my parents

There were new lands.
His heart lifted.

— Thomas Wolfe, *Look Homeward, Angel*

TABLE OF CONTENTS

PART THREE: DESERTER'S SONGS

THE LAST WALTZ

"WHAT NOW?"

Robbie Robertson leaves the question hanging in the air each time someone asks. Keeping his attention focused on the vast crew assembled to document this occasion both on film and on record has taken a toll. He's done with it for now, and besides, with the crucial performance and all it involved finally behind him, he's got other things on his mind. For the last several weeks — time that passed with the speed of the universe collapsing in on itself — he has been the place where the buck stops for everyone involved. It was his idea to bring an end to The Band in this way; the final night is yet another manifestation of the leadership role Robertson had acquired by not entirely democratic means. He had long ago come to grips with the fact that the breadth of his ambitions outstripped that of the others, and no longer felt guilty about it. His aspirations had gone from the basic desires that came with being a rock and roll guitar player to simply surviving within a business that had left scars of one sort or another on everyone around him. No matter what the rest of the group thought of this scripted *coup de grâce*, it did benefit them all. Hard knocks had made Robertson believe that there were no happy endings in rock and roll, yet he was intent on giving this the appearance of one.

Others marking the occasion with The Band had also travelled long roads, conceptually and geographically, to

Winterland, the former San Francisco ice skating rink done up for the event in Old World operatic splendour. (Whether over-the-top set design or ironic comment on the performers' over-inflated egos, the choice had been made: it would look good on film and that's all that mattered.) The guests all stood for the kind of dedication that made their hosts so revered: satisfying the music fan's never-ending search for something to believe in, without compromising themselves in the process. They came from places like Hibbing, Minnesota, crossroads towns in Arkansas, Mississippi, and Louisiana, the south side of Chicago, the suburbs of England and Ireland — locations that in spite of vast differences had nonetheless spawned artists drawn together that night by their musical commonalities.

There were as many on the stage whose origins had given them far less, raised in austere Ontario towns as colonial as their names — London, Stratford, and Simcoe, and the barren prairie fortresses of Winnipeg, Manitoba and Saskatoon, Saskatchewan. Their maps of musical tradition were of little use; they took what they could get and fashioned an identity out of it, ending up on trails that often crossed or ran parallel before converging at Winterland that night. The audience contained at least some who had come by similar routes. After five thousand turkey dinners were served in recognition of the day's quintessentially American holiday, Thanksgiving, a few small contingents proudly waved the Maple Leaf as the lights went down. This was their moment. When the artists caught a glimpse of their homeland's banner, there was a flash in each of them. They had not only cleared the trail, they had paved the road.

Ronnie Hawkins, the man who had originally brought The Band together, struts on stage and tears into a song that, when they first recorded it together, made him realize these boys had something the shit-kickers back home didn't: a desire to prove themselves in a world that seemed beyond their reach. Until, that is, The Hawk miraculously landed in their backyard, with his con man's eye for conquest, and an eager young drumming charge in tow. He knew soon after he arrived that what he'd found couldn't be much better. Roaring the song up to full speed, he yells to the unseen promoter in the casual good old boy manner that carried him through many lean years, an aside meant for all — "Big time Bill, BIG TIME. . . ." Eyes lovingly fixated on his onetime protege guitarist, his every move painfully acknowledges that the next few minutes are likely the end not just of his old backup group, but of his own rock and roll dream.

Next, a gaunt troubadour comes to the microphone, a figure who could as easily be taken for a Vietnam vet wandering in off Mission Street to infiltrate the festivities. With one nostril bearing the powdery remnants of backstage preparation, Neil Young smiles broadly and embraces the adoring crowd with a slurred yet heartfelt greeting, "It's one of the great pleasures of my life to be on stage with these people tonight." The number he sings sentimentalizes his upbringing, a spare reflection longing for memories only a northerner knows, which according to the song, can never truly be recaptured.

Staying off stage to sing backup on "Helpless," Joni Mitchell later adds "Coyote," a more personal and explicit account of what she and Young both found after finally arriving in this promised land, California. Poised and pristine, she was his natural foil through the many traits they shared, including the search to replace the desolation that had formed, and still motivated, so much of their artistic sensibilities. Now, though, the terms of the search had changed.

A little over a year later, The Sex Pistols, an anarchy-fuelled conglomeration who ignited a cultural revolution in their own country, would play their last show at Winterland as well, definitively completing the sea change that The Last Waltz began.

November 4, 2006, almost thirty years to the day since The Last Waltz, Robbie Robertson sits in the gallery of the National Arts Centre in Ottawa, along with other recipients of the Governor General's Performing Arts Lifetime Achievement Awards. The year's only other honouree with a household name is *Saturday Night Live* producer Lorne Michaels, and it's doubtful many in attendance are regular viewers of his work. Robertson seems comfortable here, shoulder to shoulder with Canada's cultural elite. His looks betray more of his aboriginal heritage than when he was younger, when his dark skin, high cheekbones, and hooded eyes made him alluring not because of interest in first peoples or multiculturalism, but because he was a rock star. While many of his contemporaries had long since given up exploring new musical territory, in recent times Robertson recorded albums inspired by his Mohawk lineage, 1994's *Music for The Native Americans*, and 1998's *Contact from the Underworld of RedBoy*, with the latter containing a track based on a taped phone conversation with imprisoned American native activist Leonard Peltier, advocating for his release.

Asking Buffy Sainte-Marie to give the introductory speech further accentuated the importance of the aboriginal element of Robertson's work in relation to the award. A Cree, she is his contemporary insofar as their international success extends, and, as inventor of the Native American pop star activist, is the only suitable speaker for this stilted affair. He takes in her words with the dignified aura he has perfected ever since he decided The Last Waltz would be more than a concert documentary. The film allowed him the chance to ruminate — at the expense of his band mates — on his disillusionment with rock and roll.

At the gala show, an R & B band — the modern, utterly soulless kind — takes the stage for a rendition of Robertson's greatest composition, "The Weight." The singer tries to employ the vocal tricks of more able women who covered the song right after its original release, like Aretha Franklin — perhaps an even more meaningful honour bestowed by the Queen of Soul long before the tribute tonight, on behalf of the Queen of England. This singer is no Mavis Staples either, and the song is rendered impotent, its verses rearranged at will in the process. The television camera frequently cuts back to gauge Robertson's reaction. He is at ease through what may have been an excruciatingly familiar ordeal, after forty years of similar ham-fisted versions in theatres, bars, and beer halls across the world. It was still his song, however haunted by innumerable ghosts of himself and others, and behind the cool facade he was the only person who knew how many.

Backstage in San Francisco, piano player Richard Manuel seems adrift as well as drunk. Dressed in a gaudy plaid suit, he's an easy target for illicit gifts to either calm his nerves or wind him up. Rick Danko, the genial bass player, acts as if this were just another gig. Organist Garth Hudson is the most introverted of them all; he graciously accepts compliments on his performance and is the most uneasy when the music ends. Levon Helm, the uncharacteristically outgoing drummer, still simmers over his marginalization, coolly and consciously staying out of the way of certain others. And Robertson, once Helm's trusted partner? He wants to be relieved but can't be yet, since there is still much to be sorted out, as is always the case in this business. He loves these guys like his family, as members of any great rock and roll band have to, but, like all families, the burden of their shared experiences had caused some irreparable rifts.

This familial burden wasn't the same as the burden they had sung about every night on stage, how you can put your weight onto the back of someone willing to take it. That tune had been written at a perfect moment for people to instinctively pick up on its meaning, 1968, when the nation The Band were mostly foreigners to was in need of a new way to accept the burdens of all her citizens. Almost immediately after writing "The Weight," Robertson was thrust into the ranks of songwriters he had admired across the border (and some he didn't), opening more doors than he could ever have imagined.

What now?

It had been a long night full of drama, tension, exhilaration, and drugs. It needed to be wrapped, and it was up to all of them to finish on their own terms, to go out like they started — playing straight up rock and roll songs unencumbered by the many coded messages imposed by critics ever since they'd been producing their own music. A decision on how to end it had to be made fast, as the cameras rolled and the director, in true directorial fashion, was on the verge of a nervous breakdown. They settle on "Don't Do It," the early Marvin Gaye track they picked up as it climbed the charts over a decade ago, back when a white bar band needed to play black hits to ensure the night would end with a little bit of money. The song had stuck with them, probably because its gospel swing was so natural for them to play, and because of a power in the subject's persistent plea, that transcended race and nation, to save an intimate relationship.

My biggest mistake was loving you too much . . .

Everyone lights fresh cigarettes and Robertson abandons his pinstripe suit jacket and silk scarf for a hooded zip sweatshirt and a fedora that hasn't been a mandatory accoutrement since the days when the father he never knew was running numbers around the family's working-class Toronto neighbourhood. Once everyone is in place, the crowd briefly settles. Taking his cue, Robertson musters the strength to announce, "We're gonna do one more song, and that's it." Helm kicks it off and Danko lays down one of his trademark idiosyncratic grooves before the rest of them jump in, not so conscious that this is the last time they will play together in public as this is the last time they will play this song.

Now ya got me where ya want me, and you won't let me go . . .

A few short minutes later, Robertson thanks the audience with a simple, "Goodnight . . . Goodbye."

From there, it's a blurry scene of shaking hands, pats on the back, and more blow shoved in their faces than most can imagine consuming in a lifetime. Everyone is in a good mood, confident in the night's success. Not perfect, but they were never that anyway. It was supposed to be — scripted to be — about the magic that happened when the five of them played together, and the fact that that was now gone. Robertson heads for the limousine that will take him back to the hotel, where this once-improbable scenario will continue to consume his thoughts amid the raging party.

Had this been a night about Canadian music? Robertson said back then there was no such thing, that it was all North American, although now he concedes that Canada has always been a great breeding ground for talented artists. Why? The question rankles endlessly, spawning reams of commentary, especially north of the border. One suspects Robertson has been asked this same thing too many times, but his answer makes as much sense as any that have been arrived at so far: "Must be something in the water," he says definitively.

PART ONE

WHEN FIRST
UNTO THIS COUNTRY

CHAPTER ONE

BRAND ON MY HEART

THERE'S A DIFFERENCE BETWEEN GROWING UP POOR in the north and growing up poor in the south. Whenever someone criticized Hank Snow for affecting a Tennessee drawl, what they were in fact hearing were traces of an accent particular to Lunenburg County, Nova Scotia, where Snow was born. Hank was Clarence back then, Jack to his friends and family. He had holes in his shoes and the cold North Atlantic wind blew through the walls of the shack they called a house, where he slept on a mattress stuffed with old rags, endured regular beatings, and longed to escape. When he went to sea at age twelve, he spent the money he earned not on shoes, and not on a train ticket out. He laid it down on the T. Eaton mail order counter and bought himself a guitar.

The hardships Snow had overcome to get to Nashville and embark on a career "beyond his wildest dreams" would be told and retold, as is the lore of so many country music stars. His rags-to-riches story culminates during his first few months at the *Grand Ole Opry* when his future there was uncertain after the lukewarm reception of his one weak U.S. chart showing, "Marriage Vow," written by country song peddler Jenny Lou Carson and foisted on him by his record company, RCA. Their initial goal was to pattern his sound after the enormously successful schmaltz of Eddy Arnold, before they switched tacks and instead targeted the massive audience that had been mesmerized by his *Opry* contemporary, Hank Williams.

Having been refused once already, Snow was finally permitted by RCA's Artists and Repertoire (A & R) man, Steve Sholes, to record "I'm Movin' On." When it began to climb the charts, the 'Opry suits' that were ready to sack him suddenly suggested that Snow buy a house.

It's tempting to say that the woman Hank leaves behind in "I'm Movin' On" is Canada, or at least someone who lived there, since he'd found "a pretty mama in Tennessee." There certainly was no shortage of them in the audience at the fabled Ryman Auditorium each Saturday night when the Opry took to the airwaves. He had many friends there, too, like Ernest Tubb, The Carter Family, Hank Williams, and a young man who would soon take Sholes' attention away from producing hits for Snow — Elvis Presley.

Decades later, and it's difficult to conceive such a storyline: A scrawny thirty-six-year-old wearing a bad toupee, and with fifteen years of beating his head against the wall in Canada already behind him wouldn't have a hope in hell in Nashville, no matter who his friends were. It wasn't even "I'm Movin' On" that got Snow there, but it was the one that meant he could stay. It had been a long, long road, and he damn sure wasn't going to turn back. Becoming a U.S. citizen in 1958 was, he said, not to sell out Canada, but part of the basic practicality of being a citizen of the country in which you live. But even though Snow may have reached the proverbial end of the rainbow in Nashville, he never stopped being Canadian.

In spite of Snow's achievements, if you spend time with Nova Scotia country music fans today, it quickly becomes apparent that there is no middle ground when it comes to comparing him with the province's other significant contribution to the genre, Wilf Carter. Those who support Carter chiefly admire his common touch and family values, and chastise Hank Snow for his naked ambition and unspoken philandering. Conversely, Snow fans regard him as one of the most influential figures in all of country music and cite his triumph over personal adversity as inspiration to face their own struggles. To them, Wilf Carter is merely a charming relic.

The gap between the two singers was already ingrained in the rest of the country in 1971, as the pair embarked together on another Canadian tour, a semi-regular occurrence since the early sixties, when Snow's career was at its apex and Carter's was fading. For this reason, Snow could — and did — always insist on closing every show, even though each possessed a presence that illustrated their unique appeal to their audience, a segment of the population that still thought of rock and roll as a figment of society's collective imagination.

Backstage at Toronto's Massey Hall during that tour, Snow sported a glittering country music uniform as always. Made by his friend Nudie Cohn, it was covered in rhinestones and a grape motif inspired by Revelation 14 *("Anyone who worships the beast or its image, or accepts its mark on forehead or hand, will also drink the wine of God's fury…")*. He was swamped by the crowd after the show, signing a never-ending stream of programs and photographs as is the custom for country artists. An unexpected face jockeying for position near Snow was Ken Thomson, newspaper mogul, fine art connoisseur, and one of the wealthiest people in the world. Here was a unique glimpse of two men who chased their dreams in a country that, during their youth, had little to offer in terms of fulfilling them. Their shared experience, along with deep mutual respect for each other's success made Snow's earliest records Thomson's personal "Rosebud" — that is, if Orson Welles had based *Citizen Kane* on him instead of William Randolph Hearst. After a brief conversation, and likely an invitation to dine later, Thomson gracefully left Snow to the other waiting fans.

By contrast, Carter was every inch the robust working cowboy he set out to be back in the thirties, which, when combined with his early fascination with yodelling, had unexpectedly started earning him a more than respectable living. Not the drinker Snow was purported to be, he did allow himself at least enough luxury to imbibe his beverage of choice, pink champagne, from a refrigerator specially designed for his car. His stage dress bore no concessions to Nashville finery; Carter could be seen in his white Stetson, conservative western-cut suit, and boots on any given day. Moreover, as the man who at the start of the fifties had made more records than anyone else on the planet (it was claimed), Carter bore no grudge over Snow's desire to be the star of the show. Each had his own definition of stardom, and Carter's was still bound to a time when that word was not in the lexicon of Canadian musicians.

Popular music was a highbrow art form in the early twenties when Carter began performing out of an honest desire to amuse himself, and those close to him. Soon after that, "hillbilly music" became the latest craze and by the time Snow was ready to take up similar pursuits, there were real possibilities to make money, and chase the wild show business fantasies many kids of the era had about escaping dire poverty. All one needed for proof was to look at how in 1925 a light opera singer named Marion Slaughter adopted the names of two Texas towns, Vernon Dalhart, and had the first million-selling 78 rpm record in the new genre with "The Wreck of the Old 97" b/w "The Prisoner's Song," both seminal works that Snow and many others later recorded.

Yet, another artist would come to define hillbilly music: Jimmie Rodgers, a former railway worker from Meridian, Mississippi. Also known as "The Singing Brakeman," Rodgers' haunting "blue yodel" became the manifestation of the sadness and isolation felt by so many who allowed themselves the relatively cheap decadence of gramophone records. Rodgers had come close to perfecting his yodel when he got word of open auditions being held in Bristol, Tennessee, in late July 1927. Victor Records sponsored the auditions, hoping to find anyone capable of competing with rival labels that were just beginning to tap into this new-found market. Within a year, Rodgers' records were selling as much as Victor's top pop acts. Even with the 1929 stock market crash, his overall sales exceeded six million copies. Unfortunately, the prolific star could already see the fast-approaching end, having suffered throughout his career with tuberculosis. He kept up a strenuous touring and recording schedule in order to reap the benefits of his fame in the short time he knew he had left.

With each new release, the blue yodel slowly found its way to all corners of North America, although to some it was merely a twist on a sound that was already a part of their immediate surroundings. In fact, it was not Rodgers' yodel that had captivated Wilf Carter, but a more ancient version that directly stemmed from its origins as a method of alpine communication. Fewer things could have sounded as exotic to a young boy growing up in a tiny Nova Scotia town at the dawn of the twentieth century.

Carter had experienced several of these towns up until he discovered yodelling in his early teens, starting with Port Hilford, in the northeastern corner of the province, where he was born on December 18, 1904. Wilfred was the sixth of nine children conceived by the Reverend Henry Carter and his wife Rose (née Stone). Born in Sarnham, England, in 1864, the elder Carter had devoted his life to the service of God at an early age, and the need for his own congregation brought him and his young fiancée to Nova Scotia in 1889. Not long after their marriage, Henry heard of an opportunity to do missionary work in Australia, a further two-year commitment, but one that made him a fully ordained Baptist minister in 1893, upon completion of his formal training in Springfield, Prince Edward Island. Carter led several congregations in that smallest of provinces before being posted to Port Hilford. Still, every four months or so, his growing family was forced to move to other tiny locales around Nova Scotia that required a pastor, such as Clementsport, Pereau, and River Hebert, making education a challenge for all of the children. Young Wilf was forced to become more adept at fighting than the three Rs.

The family's survival was a matter of even greater importance, and all of the Carter children had to find work on neighbouring farms. Indeed, manpower was at a premium by the time Wilf turned ten and the First World War engulfed Europe. His oldest brother, Alva, had enlisted, not so much out of duty as for the soldier's pay. Those much-needed funds were abruptly cut off in 1917 when he was reported missing in action in France. Wilf continued working during those summers, driving a team of oxen, which earned him a healthy monthly wage. Such responsibility inevitably caused Wilf to begin questioning the relevance of his father's profession, and that rift deepened the moment Wilf witnessed the event that changed his life.

It happened during their stay in Pereau. Wilf was taking a load of apples to the nearby Annapolis Valley town of Canning when he noticed a poster for an upcoming performance of *Uncle Tom's Cabin* at the town hall. But it was the added attraction that caught his attention, someone simply known as "The Yodelling Fool," an apt moniker, in his father's estimation, when Wilf asked for permission to see the show. Predictably, he was denied, but using his own money Wilf defied his parents with the full knowledge of the painful consequences that would ensue. From that point on, Wilf became obsessive about mastering the yodel. He could be heard all day in the fields and at home when he was out of earshot of his father. He eventually began to miss his father's services, and soon after the family's last relocation, to Point de Bute, just over the New Brunswick border, in 1920, Reverend Carter banished his wayward son from the household.

Wilf had already found work in the area's prosperous logging industry, but the long days were tempered after he met a young church organist and was accepted into her family. Their bond was strong enough to allow him to join their move to Massachusetts in 1921, where he worked for her father's construction business. When that and a subsequent relationship with another young lady ended badly, Carter was forced back to the New Brunswick lumber mills in the winter of 1922. He sought any alternative, and found one the following summer when an opportunity arose to work in the vast Alberta wheat fields. Although the conditions weren't much of an improvement, Carter loved being around horses and learning the tricks of the cowboy trade. The friendship the men shared was something new for Carter as well, and they all enjoyed his yodelling. He sang at informal gatherings at first, but by 1925 he was the main attraction at the weekly dances held in the schoolhouses and church halls that served as meeting places for the farmhands. For Carter, Alberta was now home.

Yodelling had, in fact, been a popular singing style in North America for many decades before Carter first encountered it. It was heard in minstrel shows dating back to the mid-nineteenth century, as well as on some of the first Edison wax cylinder recordings. Yodelling records in the traditional "Tyrolean" style maintained their popularity through the first two decades of the twentieth century, and this was the sound that first captivated Carter, as it would many young, promising singers of the era, whose primary aim was often merely to push their vocal cords to the limit. The marriage between yodelling and the mythological Old West had yet to occur. Only in the years following Carter's arrival in Alberta would he have possibly heard, as Jimmie Rodgers did, the mournful sound of Riley Puckett's 1924 Columbia recording of "Sleep Baby Sleep," which Rodgers, in turn, recorded during the Bristol sessions.

Carter had not even started playing guitar to accompany his yodelling when cowboy singers began attaining widespread popularity. This came in the wake of Chicago radio station WLS introducing its *National Barn Dance*, an all–"hillbilly music" program, in 1924, or Carl T. Sprague's "When the Work's All Done This Fall," the first in a series of hit songs the Texas ranch hand recorded the following year that effectively set off the "singing cowboy" craze. In any case, these factors suddenly brought Carter's future into sharp focus. All of the elements were suddenly there before him: a guitar, his voice, and the cowboy life.

Yet Carter was rejected at his initial radio audition, for Calgary station CFAC, in 1926. This prompted him to try to make a living in the rodeo circuit. After a couple of harrowing seasons as a broncobuster and chuckwagon racer, he befriended Calgary Stampede champion Pete Knight. Born in Crossfield, Alberta, Knight began as a bronco rider during the war, and became one of the first widely celebrated rodeo stars after winning nearly every competition in North America. Carter was determined to learn Knight's techniques, but after several failed attempts, Knight persuaded Carter to stick to music before a likely injury prevented him from playing guitar. Nevertheless, the two remained admirers of each other's talents, and through their friendship Carter found the inspiration for two of his earliest songwriting attempts, "Sway Back Pinto Pete," and "Pete Knight, King of the Cowboys."

They were songs he thought he could record, but in 1928 there were few options to do so in Canada, even though the market for recorded music had developed concurrently with its American counterpart. The first Canadian demonstration of Thomas Edison's phonograph took place on May 17, 1878, for the benefit of the Governor General at Rideau Hall in Ottawa. Edison had only just patented the invention, mere months ahead of Emile Berliner's prototype for the gramophone, which he had created through the patronage of Alexander Graham Bell. By the time Berliner got his first gramophone company established in 1893, patent lawsuits raged between Edison and other upstart phonograph companies (including what would become Columbia Records). Almost immediately, Berliner Gram-O-Phone Co. faced its own battles over licensing and manufacturing rights for its unique flat shellac discs, battles that were compounded when other companies marketing already obsolete wax cylinder technology jumped in with further patent challenges to the gramophone.

When the dust settled, Berliner was left with no choice but to sell his U.S. interests to his manufacturing partner, Eldridge Johnson, in 1899. Berliner then set up shop in the greener pastures of Montreal, where he still held the Canadian patents for his invention. The E. Berliner Co.'s retail outlet opened that year at 2315 Sainte-Catherine Street, and, along with gramophones, sold exclusive recordings produced in the United States by Johnson's company, Victor Talking Machine. It was also the year that Victor adopted its logo, derived from a painting Berliner had found, entitled "His Master's Voice," by French artist François Barraud. The painting depicted a dog named Nipper cocking its ear toward a gramophone horn.

As sales of gramophones and records increased in Canada, Berliner's company built its own recording studio on Peel Street in 1905 to keep up with the demand for discs. The first

Canadian artist the company recorded was baritone Joseph Saucier, and other vocalists and instrumentalists were thereafter invited to use the facility. The market for homegrown folk music in Quebec proved particularly lucrative, as traditional fiddlers such as J.B. Roy had been recorded by 1918, four years before the first American fiddle record, Eck Robertson and Henry Gilliland's "Sallie Goodin" b/w "Arkansas Traveler."

But while hillbilly music had penetrated north of the border by the late twenties, it had not inspired the English-Canadian labels to follow suit with their own homegrown discoveries. However, the growing infiltration of U.S. radio programs (WSM Nashville's *Grand Ole Opry* debuted in 1925) forced Canadian stations to compete by airing their own shows featuring local musicians. George Wade & His Cornhuskers (a square-dance band) hit the air on Toronto's CFRB in 1928, and fiddler Don Messer's iconic career began at Saint John, New Brunswick's CFBO in 1929. Messer would staunchly reject being labelled a hillbilly artist, preferring the term "folk artist" instead.

In the fall of 1930, buoyed by performances at the Calgary Stampede that came on the heels of a desperate hand-to-mouth period riding the rails to Vancouver and back, Wilf Carter was given a slot during Calgary radio station CFCN's Friday night hillbilly program, *The Old Timers*. The response to Carter steadily grew in the following weeks and months, as letters of support trickled in from far-flung areas of Alberta and Saskatchewan. America had its popular cowboy singers in Jules Verne Allen and Ken Maynard, among others. In Wilf Carter, Canada now potentially had hers, and some immediately saw the potential in that.

John Murray Gibbon was always looking for new ways to use music as a means to promote his company. As the publicity agent for the Canadian Pacific Railway (CPR) and all of its connected tourism businesses, he noticed early in the twenties how folk-based music could attract a diverse clientele. He staged a number of annual festivals at CPR-owned hotels during the decade, but when he heard about Carter, Gibbon pegged him for a more specific job. Each summer, Trail Riders of the Canadian Rockies attempted to give campers the full cowboy experience, and Gibbon surmised that involving Carter would be the icing on the cake — an actual singing cowboy, just like in the movies. Carter didn't hesitate to take the job, since it beat the physical toll of the Stampede, and he got along well with those he sang for around the campfire during his first two expeditions in 1932 and 1933. The reaction to Carter was so positive that the bosses at the CPR booked him to entertain on the company's new cruise liner, the SS *Empress of Britain*, during its maiden voyage, in the winter of 1933, to the West Indies. Life was good, almost good enough to make Carter forget his desire to make a record. But on his way to New York that December to board the ship, Carter remembered what someone had told him on the trail about making a record for RCA-Victor in Montreal. When the train stopped there, Carter got off and decided to see if this was indeed possible.

It had been a difficult few years for the company that Emile Berliner had started. Victor Talking Machine bought out Berliner Gram-O-Phone in 1924, and the old man himself died in 1929. That same year, with the domination of radio driving down record sales, Victor caved in and merged with the Radio Corporation of America (RCA). The move proved fortuitous, as the record business was one of the first to be ravaged by the Great Depression. The battle to stay afloat resulted in the resignation of Emile's heir, Edgar, as president of RCA-Victor Canada in 1930, severing the Berliner family's last ties with the company. The task of guiding its future was now left to others.

Berliner had hired Hugh A. Joseph, born May 25, 1896, in Quebec City, as a chemist in 1923. In 1927, he was promoted to general manager of the recording department. Although most of his work kept him occupied in the classical field, he was fully aware of the rise of hillbilly music underway in the U.S. Yet, following the resignation of Edgar Berliner, the staggering decline of overall sales throughout 1930–32 prevented Joseph from exploiting the music's popularity. Once the industry stabilized somewhat in 1933, RCA-Victor started the Bluebird subsidiary label, aimed at competing with discount labels that were selling records at the more than half-price rate of twenty-five cents apiece. What Joseph sought most for Bluebird Canada was homegrown English talent based on the unwavering strength of traditional folk music in Quebec. In Wilf Carter, he got everything he could have hoped for.

Although Joseph was immediately taken by Carter's yodelling style, what sealed their subsequent partnership was Carter's cache of original material, which Joseph described later as possessing "a 'homey' quality — a sense of sincerity and undertaking — that appealed to people of all walks of life." Such were the values that needed to be reinforced during the darkest days of the early thirties. And with the death of Jimmie Rodgers on May 26, 1933 (two days after his final TB-hampered recording session), still foremost in the minds of his fans, there was a gaping hole that needed to be filled. For his first hastily arranged session, in Montreal on December 20, Carter, alone with his guitar, recorded two original songs. The first was "My Swiss Moonlight Lullaby," its sole purpose being merely to showcase what became known as Carter's "three-in-one" yodelling technique, an astonishing approximation of the sound heard those nights on the mountain trails, as his voice echoed down into valley.

The second song Carter recorded was "The Capture of Albert Johnson," a cowboy ballad with a distinctively Canadian angle. In early January 1931, an unidentified man shot and killed an RCMP officer in the Northwest Territories and escaped into the Mackenzie Valley. What followed was the largest manhunt in Canada to that point, and for the next several weeks stories spread of the "Mad Trapper" on the loose. On February 26, police found an emaciated and frostbitten body west of the Richardson Mountains in the Yukon and positively identified it as their suspect, a man they called Albert Johnson. Although no one was able to confirm that this man was indeed the culprit, the story reinforced the RCMP's well-known mission to "always get their man," as Carter reinforced in the song's final verse.★

★Future examinations of the case led to Johnson being viewed as a renegade anti-hero, best shown by how the story was depicted half a century later in the film *Death Hunt*, starring Charles Bronson.

Without question, Joseph knew that both songs held strong appeal. He pressed the record while, aboard the *SS Empress of Britain*, Carter's yodel intermingled with the warm winds of the Caribbean, a place that, for him, must have been paradise.

Young Jack Snow did not get to taste any Caribbean winds during his days at sea, only the bone-chilling, salty Atlantic gales he had known while growing up within a cluster of outposts on Nova Scotia's south shore, two hours by train from Halifax. He entered the world as Clarence Eugene Snow on May 9, 1914, in the town of Brooklyn, the first male child of George Lewis Snow and Marie Alice Boutlier to survive infancy. Given the nickname Jack for reasons that remain unknown, he was doted on by his two sisters, while learning the value of music through his mother, who supplemented the family's income by playing piano in the town's silent movie house, or as accompaniment for the local blackface minstrel troupe.

There is little evidence that Jack ever formed a lasting bond with his father though. When he was not away working in lumber camps in New Brunswick and Maine, George Snow showed little affection toward his frail son, and the two would rarely speak to each other again following George and Marie's divorce, a highly unusual occurrence for the time that forever traumatized the eight-year-old Jack.

In the wake of the divorce, a court deemed Marie unable to financially support her children, and Jack was placed in the custody of his paternal grandmother. For the next several years, he weathered her resentment over being forced to raise him. When Marie found housekeeping work two miles away in Liverpool, Jack frequently walked the distance just to hear her sing or play piano. Following these brief encounters, he would choose to spend the night in the Liverpool train station rather than face the wrath of his grandmother. Marie continued to regain her life as best she could by taking up with a fisherman named Charlie Tanner, and her children reunited in his house in Blue Rocks, a tiny outcrop from which he would launch his boat every morning into the misty Atlantic. It was not always fish that

Tanner and his cohorts were after, though. Prohibition meant that anyone with the means to transport liquor could turn a quick buck, and Tanner was not a man to question the morality of law. Marie endured the harsh conditions for the sake of the relationship, and turned a blind eye to the verbal and physical abuse Tanner meted out to Jack, whose physical shortcomings once again made him easy prey. "I was treated by him, mildly speaking, like a dog," Snow said many years later. "I took many beatings from him and still carry the scars across my body that were left by his ham-like hands."

Marie's only response was to encourage Jack's interest in a Hawaiian guitar she had ordered from a catalogue in lieu of owning a piano. Jack displayed a natural ability to sing, but this did little to change Tanner's attitude toward him. When Tanner and Marie finally married, it permanently dashed any hopes the twelve-year-old held that the relationship was just a nightmare, and left him with the terrible choice to leave home. He had heard that jobs were available for young boys on the large fishing trawlers that sailed out of the nearby port of Lunenburg. These crewmembers were known as flunkies, doing the bidding of both the captain and the cook. But Jack would be away from Tanner, and that's all that mattered. He was hired the next day, and was out at sea the following Monday.

From that first excursion in 1926, Snow became adept at surviving on the high seas, but never grew accustomed to the lifestyle. A close brush with death during a late summer hurricane in 1930 finally swore him off the boats for good, although the Depression had erased most other opportunities for work on land. He turned to bootlegging, just as Tanner had, but also tended horses for a delivery business, and even peddled lobsters door-to-door. But once he received his new guitar purchased from the Eaton's catalogue, he became a familiar sight performing for money on the streets of Lunenberg. His sister Lillian and her husband Wilbert Rissert boarded him there, and during this time he was asked to take part in a blackface minstrel show coming to the neighbouring town of Bridgewater. Snow had no reservations about blackening his face for the chance to sing just one number.

It was undoubtedly a Jimmie Rodgers song, since the presence of his records in both his mother's and sister's homes had made Snow an unwavering devotee. A particular favourite was "Moonlight and Skies," a haunting prisoner's lament, with the expected yodel replaced by a Hawaiian slide guitar. The only other record he played as often was Vernon Dalhart's "Wreck of the Old '97," which naturally appealed to Snow's love of trains. Armed with this material, Snow was determined to get on the radio in the spring of 1933. His destination was CHNS in Halifax, but his first written request was rejected. A few months later, in May, he went in person and was granted an audition. He was allowed to sing two Rodgers songs on the air that night, "The Yodelling Cowboy" and "My Blue-Eyed Jane," which led to a weekly Saturday night appearance. Sometimes introduced as "the Cowboy Blue Yodeller," or as "Clarence Snow and his guitar," he always eagerly turned up, even though he was not paid for his performances. The trade-off was that, by the summer of 1934, Snow was popular enough to start regularly booking himself into small halls around Halifax, accompanied by a friend, Jack Faulkner. That fall, CHNS instituted its own hillbilly program, *Down on the Farm*, with Snow as its star. To mark the occasion, Snow agreed to announcer Cecil Landry's suggestion that he change his name to the more rugged Hank, with Snow himself adding "the Yodelling Ranger," in a tribute to Rodgers.

At the same time, Snow could already see the trail being blazed by Carter, who had been urged to return to Montreal for more recording sessions immediately after the *Empress of Britain* completed her voyage. Hugh Joseph was so excited about the prospect that he sent a limousine to pick Carter up at the train station, a gesture the singer instinctively refused under the assumption that he would have to pay for it himself. Carter went on to cut fourteen sides over two days, January 11 and 12, 1934, among them his first passes at songs that would eventually cement his reputation as a cowboy singer: "He Rode the Strawberry Roan," and "My Little Grey-Haired Mother in the West." Carter returned to Calgary to discover his first record was on the radio, and by April he had come to the attention of Toronto music publisher Gordon V. Thompson.

Born August 9, 1888, in what is now Port Colborne, Ontario, Thompson got into the business at an early age, using his brother's print shop to make sheet music that, in turn, funded his university education. He made even more money writing his own patriotic ditties during the First World War, and acquiring the rights to songs like "For King and Country," which sold upwards of 100,000 copies. However, in spite of becoming the founding president of the Authors and Composers Association of Canada in 1918, his company, Gordon V. Thompson Ltd., seemed as destined to be wiped out by radio at the outset of the thirties as the record labels were. Stumbling upon Carter, therefore, proved to be a godsend, as Thompson stated in a 1951 *Maclean's* article: "I published a folio of Wilf's songs, about fourteen of them, and after three months I totalled up his royalties. He'd already made seven hundred and fifty dollars."

Carter's mass appeal was later driven home when Thompson published the first Irving Berlin songbook concurrently with a new Carter collection. Initial orders for the Carter book sur-passed those for Berlin's by more than a five-to-one margin. By the last half of the thirties, Carter sheet music such as *Cowboy Songs* and its four similarly titled sequels were all selling around 60,000 copies annually. Thompson would find Hank Snow to be a similar sure-fire seller upon publishing Snow's first songbook in 1938.

The year of Carter's national breakthrough, 1934, also saw another Canadian songwriter emerge, albeit on a much differ-ent stage. Clarence Robert Nobles was born on April 13, 1908, in Winnipeg, Manitoba, to Flora and Harry Nobles, although this information would be listed differently on documents throughout his life. What is known is that he became Clarence Nolan when the family moved to Tucson, Arizona, in 1921, where the isolation of the desert kindled a creative spark within his young mind. In 1929 he became Robert "Bob" Nolan upon heading to California in search of a career as a singing cowboy, and for the next two years he bounced around every amateur night and radio gig he could find, running into others with similar aspirations along the way.

One of those was Leonard Slye, born on November 5, 1911, in Cincinnati, Ohio. Knowing that Nolan wrote his own material, Slye contacted him, along with another budding singer-songwriter, Texan Tim Spencer, in 1933 to form a group they called The Pioneer Trio. With impeccable harmony as their calling card, they became The Sons of the Pioneers in 1934, upon signing with Decca Records. Their recording career was launched with two of Nolan's songs, "Cool Water" and "Tumblin' Tumbleweeds," both vivid snapshots of the mythical Old West and tailor-made for the B-grade westerns Hollywood was churning out at this time. The studios soon took notice. Nolan got his first movie job later in 1934, dubbing his voice over Ken Maynard's image on the opening song of *In Old Santa Fe*, but it was Slye who would ultimately bring the group national fame.

As The Sons of the Pioneers continued to write songs and perform in dozens of serials, Slye was singled out as the star of the trio, having changed his name to the more suitable Roy Rogers. By the early forties, Rogers was America's favourite cowboy, and although the others were there for his early success on film, by the end of the decade both Nolan and Spencer could no longer keep up with the demands of the group's schedule. But although Nolan rarely sought the spotlight again until his death on June 16, 1980, he could always find solace in the fact that, in "Cool Water" and "Tumbleweeds," he had written two of the few songs that outlived the era, and which, like the films of John Ford, came to best represent for succeeding generations a vision of the American west that inspired pride in an uniquely American way of life, even though it never truly existed.

It was, in fact, a good time for any outsiders wishing to shape American culture according to their own specific visions. The throngs of immigrants who established Hollywood, as well as the New York songwriting factories that collectively became known as Tin Pan Alley, were slowly repairing the covenant that the Civil War had nearly destroyed. Most who worked in the latter, like Irving Berlin, unabashedly used their output to celebrate the freedom they never forgot was their constitutional right. In this respect, Nolan was no different, although his songs penetrated in a much subtler way, setting the pattern for Canadians to draw from the aspects of America they most identified with. These, inevitably, could not include the burden of fashioning "the city on a hill," an idea of the country ingrained in the psyche of every American-born citizen. What Nolan did instead was no less remarkable; he created what amounted to great American art that bore no traces of that burden, and could therefore never be restrained by the shackles of history.

Despite his growing fame in Canada, Wilf Carter still had to earn a living on the Rocky Mountain trails in the summer of 1934. One greenhorn he befriended during that year's expedition was G.B. Mitchell, an American millionaire at a time when such a description truly meant something. Perhaps it was while they settled around the campfire one night that Mitchell mentioned how his friends in the radio business in New York would be interested in a guy like Carter. It might have taken another drink or two for Mitchell to commit to arranging an audition, and for Carter to convince him that he would actually follow through by making the trip. Carter was already committed to further recording sessions in Montreal in October, during which he cut a remarkable twenty-six sides in four days, nearly all of them original cowboy-themed compositions, but made plans to go to New York before the start of 1935.

Mitchell had arranged auditions at three major radio networks, with CBS ultimately taking the plunge. Once his publisher had secured a work visa, Carter was heard on 250 affiliate stations within weeks. His debut didn't come off without a hitch, however. Before the broadcast, a secretary was typing out the lyrics to his latest Canadian hit, "The Cowboy's High-Toned Dance," and asked what name she should put on it. In the tension of the moment, Carter reflexively answered, "Anything will do." Taken aback, the secretary looked Carter over and typed "Montana Slim," the name that would stick with him throughout the United States after announcer Bert Parks introduced him that night. Montana Slim remained a fixture on the network for the next two years, during which time he made the bulk of his recordings at RCA-Victor's New York studios. Under this new moniker, along with Tex Ritter and others, he helped instigate a brief infatuation between the Big Apple and cowboy culture. Carter later said he didn't care what he was called, as long as he was paid.

Hank Snow, meanwhile, was still looking for a way out of Nova Scotia in 1935. His local reputation had attracted a wife, Minnie Blanche Aalders, and the following year she gave birth to what would be their only child, a son who, without hesitation, was christened Jimmie Rodgers Snow. Hank still had to take jobs, like selling Fuller brushes, before briefly going on government assistance, but his radio career received an unexpected boost when CHNS offered a daily fifteen-minute spot sponsored by Crazy Water Crystals. The Texas-based company, whose product was said to cure everything from arthritis to acne despite being nothing more than a common laxative, had raised its profile by sponsoring U.S. broadcasts of the Monroe Brothers, the Blue Sky Boys, and others. The makers would later face scores of false advertising charges and go out of business in the forties. But, for the time being, the partnership was exactly what Snow had been waiting for, and it helped him land a three-month tour of the Maritimes with a pop and western swing band called The Mountain Boys. Snow was given a solo spot each night, with the real benefit coming through the band's regular nationally broadcast appearances on the CBC.

Emboldened by both this and Wilf Carter's success, Snow wrote to Hugh Joseph in Montreal about making a record, but, as with his initial radio enquiries, this was rejected. After several more requests, Snow was granted an audition if he could make it to Montreal. In late October 1936 Snow showed up at Joseph's office, broke and nervous. Joseph made it clear that he was only interested in original material, and Snow bluffed that he had two songs ready to record. Joseph agreed to a session the next day at the new RCA-Victor studio, a converted church on Lenoir Street, and Snow wrote the two songs that night in his hotel room, both of which predictably bore a strong resemblance to songs by others in his repertoire. In spite of this, both "The Prisoned Cowboy" and "Lonesome Blue Yodel" were strong efforts, made even more affecting by Snow's voice, a much more rough-hewn instrument then Carter's. The eventual record, credited to "Hank 'The Yodelling Ranger,'" sold poorly, leaving him thankful that he still had his radio slot, and also his sideline business giving guitar lessons in the style of one of his other main musical inspirations, Karl Farr, who accompanied The Sons of the Pioneers. But Joseph acquiesced to another session when Snow — overjoyed at receiving his $1.96 in royalties — wrote to say he had new songs to record. Snow cut eight sides between November 6 and 9, 1937, this time accompanied by steel guitarist Eugene "Johnny" Beaudoin. The label released them sporadically throughout 1938, the biggest seller being "The Blue Velvet Band," for which Snow earned $150.

It was the breakthrough Snow had been dreaming of, although he still lagged behind Carter, whose own sales were consistently rising due to his U.S. radio exposure.★

With fans demanding to hear more, Carter's releases had fallen into a consistent pattern of B-movie sentimentality ("Cowboy's Mother"), pure yodelling ("The Hobo's Yodel"), and ballads based on current events ("The Hindenburg Disaster"; "The Rescue From Moose River Gold Mine"). But in 1937 came a song he surely never imagined he would write, "Pete Knight's Last Ride." On May 23, Carter's old rodeo mentor was competing in Hayward, California, when he was killed while his wife, baby daughter, and 5,000 fans looked on. He was buried with the highest honours the rodeo world could bestow, and Carter's song solidified Knight's legend outside of that small community. This heartfelt tribute was among the few instances that hinted at what Carter later enigmatically called his

★Carter's shows included regular endorsements for Lucky Strike cigarettes, an unfortunate sponsor considering he didn't smoke.

battle with the "Dark Angel" emerging in his music. Given the circumstances of his upbringing, it's easy to assume, by modern standards, that depression and other demons were a constant presence in his life. However, in the age of the cowboy hero those things had to go unspoken, and Carter went to great lengths to maintain an overwhelmingly positive persona throughout his life.

That task became easier after he fell in love with Bobbie Bryan, a nurse and fellow tenant in his New York apartment building. She became the inspiration for many of his best-known songs from that point on, including "There's a Love-Knot in My Lariat," but following their marriage, later in 1937, Carter was keen to build a new family home back in Alberta. In 1938 they moved onto a 320-acre cattle ranch near Calgary, near what would become the Spruce Meadows show jumping grounds. There they raised their daughters, Sheila and Carol, as Carter continued to tour North America and make radio appearances. A sample of a CBC programming day from that year showed him on the air from 11:15 to 11:30 p.m., following the day's last news and weather report. The schedule also listed music from Glenn Miller, an episode of the soap opera *The Guiding Light*, and a speech by Neville Chamberlain entitled "Peace for Europe."

Indeed, the gathering storm also foreshadowed the demise of the yodelling cowboy; heroes would soon come in a different form. Until then, Carter still had a substantial following among those citizens of the United States who couldn't find Germany on a map, and he wasn't about to ignore them. But, as many country stars who came after him would discover, life on the road was not without risk. On April 30, 1940, Carter and his wife were driving back to Alberta from New York when an oncoming vehicle containing another married couple struck their car near Shelby, Montana. A passing laundry truck took the four people involved to the nearest hospital, but one of them, Mrs. A.D. Banker, died en route. Carter himself suffered a severe back injury that kept him laid up at the ranch for over a year. Although RCA-Victor had enough recordings in the can to keep Carter's regular release schedule up, when he did venture back into the studio, in New York on December 16, 1941 — two weeks after Pearl Harbor — much of the old spark was missing.

Carter, even if he cared to, could not alter his image any more than his fellow singing cowboys could. Hank Snow, however, ever prepared to go to any lengths to expand his audience, recognized the coming changes on the country music horizon. Although he had joined the Canadian Army Reserve at age eighteen, Snow had been disqualified for full military service due to a childhood lung ailment, another side effect of this being a deepening of his voice that forced him to phase out yodelling. Now billed as "Hank 'The Singing Ranger,'" Snow and his small band still clung tightly to the cowboy motif that endeared them to so many. They continued to play almost every small town and radio station in the Maritimes (hauling their gear in a customized trailer), on top of the annual trips to Montreal for recording sessions. Hugh Joseph had urged Snow to stockpile material due to the looming American Federation of Musicians strike, which virtually halted record production from 1942–43. This hectic period yielded another hit to rival "The Blue Velvet Band" in 1942, the energetic "Wanderin' On." Snow's hopes of breaking into the U.S. rose with each subsequent release, especially after a Philadelphia promoter named Jack Howard invited him to play a string of War Bond fundraising shows.

These appearances were only a taste of what Snow felt was his next logical step: being heard on the powerful Wheeling, West Virginia, station wwva, which had a clear signal throughout eastern Canada. Snow's entrée proved to be one of the station's regular performers, Big Slim, whose song, "We'll Never Say Goodbye, Just Say So Long" was part of Snow's marathon May 1943 strike session in Montreal. When he informed Slim (born Harry McAuliffe, in 1903, of Cherokee descent) that he had done the song, Snow received, in return, an invitation to come to West Virginia. While Snow did not perform on that initial visit, Slim promised to get him an audition at the station whenever he was able to return. That didn't occur until after another intense four-day Montreal recording session just before Christmas 1944. Among the eighteen songs recorded then were the subsequent hits "The Soldier's Last Letter" and "You Played Love on the Strings of My Heart." With Joseph satisfied that there was now enough material stockpiled to ride out the strike, Snow confidently went back to Wheeling in early 1945 and won a regular slot on WWVA's *Jamboree*, a Saturday night fixture for thousands of listeners. Performing on such a large stage sent Snow's imagination into overdrive, and, on the advice of Big Slim, he purchased a trained horse, Shawnee, to incorporate into his live show. With Shawnee able to execute such feats as sitting down for breakfast with Snow, whispering in his ear, and pulling a blanket over the two of them as they lay down to sleep, it was an undeniably charming combination, enough for Snow to, for the first time, entertain realistic thoughts of going to Hollywood.

To get there, he contacted an acquaintance, Allen Erwin, a singing cowboy who had achieved a modicum of success as "The Calgary Kid," but who nevertheless knew all the right people. Snow's stint at WWVA ran out at the start of 1946. Days later he drove by himself, in his tan Cadillac, to Los Angeles to meet Erwin, who promptly took Snow to Republic Pictures, home studio of The Sons of the Pioneers, as well as other cowboy stars such as Randolph Scott and Gabby Hayes. Later, they went to see the popular western swing bandleader Spade Cooley, who, after meeting Snow, invited him on stage for a song. Such a gesture clearly touched something deep within Snow, as he would always consider Cooley a close friend, despite the circumstances that would later mar his reputation forever.★

Cooley was a prime example of what Hollywood's dark side could conjure, and while Snow's closely guarded reputation as a womanizer could have easily drawn him into that world, the

★Cooley had beaten a rape charge in 1945, and would go on to be convicted of the brutal killing of his wife in 1961. Snow continually petitioned California state officials to show mercy for this crime, and saw his efforts pay off on November 23, 1969, when Cooley was given a temporary release to perform a police association benefit concert in Oakland. Incredibly, Cooley suffered a fatal heart attack during the show.

dying days of the cowboy star held few opportunities for Snow to remain in California. Instead, Snow set about mounting a large-scale road show to tour eastern Canada in the summer of 1946, featuring himself, along with Big Slim and all of their trick ponies. It was an extremely ambitious idea, given that Snow was personally bearing all of the financial liabilities, and as the miles — and bills — piled up over the next year, it became increasingly imperative for him to somehow start selling records in America. He tried knocking on doors in Hollywood one more time, and while the movie studios assured Snow that cowboys were out of fashion, he was welcomed by Julian and Jean Auerbach, whose company, Hill and Range Songs Inc., was the first predominantly folk-based music publisher that also offered a fifty-fifty split on performance royalties with its artists.

If that wasn't enough, Snow also received word that "Brand on My Heart," a song he had recorded in December 1945, had hit the top of the chart at Dallas radio station KRLD. Up until then, Snow's fans from all over North America had been mounting crusades to get his records played in the U.S., often personally mailing copies to radio stations. The breakthrough in Dallas came largely as the result of a local newspaper columnist, Bea Terry, getting on the bandwagon and plugging Snow's music to her contacts. The airplay provided Snow with the motivation to go to New York and plead with RCA-Victor president Frank Walker to pick up his catalogue, which included several releases that had hit the 50,000 sales mark at home. Walker, perhaps not surprisingly, had no idea who this aggressive Canadian was. Snow later said, "What they would tell me, which I found ridiculous [was], 'Well, before we release any records you do some personal appearances and get around and get known.' Well hell, that's what I wanted records for, to get known. So I think it was just a brush-off."

Angry and bewildered, Snow headed to Dallas, where his name meant something. For the remainder of 1948, he frequently appeared at the Roundup Club, and later the Silver Spur, owned by Jack Ruby, who also showed Snow around the after-hours joints he ran. Snow temporarily settled in a small apartment on Lovett Street, where his wife and son joined him at the start of 1949.

It wasn't long before financial desperation set in again, and Snow was forced to reach out to anyone for help, his idols included. Years before, he had sent records to Ernest Tubb, a like-minded Rodgers devotee who became one of the first stars of the *Grand Ole Opry*. Tubb had responded favourably, so when Snow got the chance to appear with him on a package show in Fort Worth called the "Cowtown Jamboree," meeting the man became more important than the twenty-five dollars Snow earned for singing "Brand on My Heart." Tubb let him play one of Rodgers' guitars, which he now owned, and reassured Snow that his future lay in Nashville. He added that he would try to get Snow a shot at the *Opry*, but it would not be easy with his records not widely available in America. That all changed early in 1949, when RCA-Victor's new head of A & R, Steve Sholes, bowed to pressure from Hugh Joseph to give Snow a new contract and a much-needed advance. Sholes requested a four-song recording session in Chicago, and Snow came prepared with a tune he thought was ideal for the occasion.

Sholes and the rest of the staff, however, did not appreciate "I'm Movin' On," as Snow naturally assumed they would. It was not a country song as the style of the time dictated; built upon the strong beat and chord structure of rhythm and blues — as well as the western swing he'd encountered in Hollywood — and decorated by rapid-fire, defiant lyrics that barely masked the frustration Snow had endured for his entire life, the song was a defining triumph of the sort every artist desires. But it would have to wait until Sholes got what he wanted: a record that presented Snow as a country crooner similar to one of the label's biggest sellers, Eddy Arnold, a.k.a. "The Tennessee Plow-boy," whose hits up until then included "Bouquet of Roses" and the old minstrel show standard "Anytime." On March 8, 1949, Snow and his hired band recorded what became his first U.S. RCA-Victor release — and first release simply as "Hank Snow" — "Marriage Vow" b/w "Star-Spangled Waltz."

Disheartened that Sholes had passed on "I'm Movin' On,"

and with little confidence in his latest recording, Snow returned to his homeland. He tried the fresh pastures of British Columbia first, playing in and around Vancouver for several months before an extended stay in Winnipeg later that summer. He fulfilled another goal, that of playing in Newfoundland, before landing back in Nova Scotia. By then he could clearly see that country music, and his own career, were both entering a new era.

It was an era that would not readily welcome Wilf Carter as he mounted his comeback following the car crash. He had never had the inclination to follow his peers into B-movies (he refused to do anything onscreen that a normal cowboy wouldn't do), but now the days of simple songs about the love between a man and his mother, his horse, or the open prairie, seemed finally over. Taking their place were songs with far less noble sentiments, songs of guilt and regret, and songs as coarse and rowdy as the rhythms on which they were based. Hank Williams (born September 17, 1923, near Greenville, Alabama) began recording his own songs in this style, a style that also drew heavily from blues, in 1947, with modest success. But just as Snow completed his first U.S. recording session, Williams' recording of "Lovesick Blues," a yodelling song with an arrangement that could be traced back to Emmett Miller, the influential minstrel show performer, began its slow climb up the *Billboard* country and western chart. It reached number one a week before Williams made his *Grand Ole Opry* debut on June 11, 1949. It was a night when, after an unprecedented number of encores, all had to concede that he was Jimmie Rodgers' natural heir. Would-be stars immediately scrambled to follow suit, while established cowboy singers searched out new avenues, specifically television, to stave off their inevitable descent into obscurity.

Snow did not become fully aware of Williams' ascendance until the conclusion of his Canadian tour that summer, when he was invited back to Texas to participate in a show in Corpus Christi that Williams was headlining. The two Hanks hit it off that day, with Williams offering Snow a guest spot on his *Louisiana Hayride* radio appearance a week later. But Snow's real dream of making it to the *Opry*, as Williams had, still seemed unattainable. That is, until Ernest Tubb lived up to his word and arranged an audition near the end of the year.

Snow made his *Grand Ole Opry* debut on January 7, 1950, singing "Brand on My Heart," backed by Tubb's band, the Texas Troubadours. "I don't mind telling you I bombed," Snow told country music historian Charles K. Wolfe. "The people just sat there while I sang. And sat. No applause, no nothing. Almost. Just sat." Nevertheless, this achievement led Sholes to arrange a session in Nashville on March 28, giving Snow another shot at laying down "I'm Movin' On," along with three other tracks. Perhaps it was a Williams influence that Sholes heard in the song that changed his mind about it, but, in any case, Sholes needed something hard-edged to compete with the string of hits Williams (who had been signed by MGM) had put together in the wake of "Lovesick Blues," specifically the proto-rockabilly number "Move It On Over." The decision paid off, as three months later "I'm Movin' On" began its remarkable twenty-one-week reign atop *Billboard*'s Best Selling Country and Western chart, and remained in the Top 10 a further twenty-three weeks.

As was often the case, however, the impact of this revolution in Nashville was slow to arrive in Canada, where Wilf Carter's popularity had not diminished, despite an obvious dearth of quality material by the end of the forties. He reached back for the odd Klondike folk song, "When the Ice Worm Nests Again," written by poet Robert Service in 1939. The song retained its specific appeal to Canadian sensibilities, as did "The Blue Canadian Rockies," written by Cindy Walker, whose vast output also provided hits for Bob Wills, Gene Autry, and Ernest Tubb. Around this time, Carter also became the artist most Canadians associated with "You Are My Sunshine," the song that helped put another one-time Jimmie Rodgers devotee, Jimmie Davis, in the Louisiana governor's mansion in 1944. There were plenty of attempts at novelty, too, but songs like "Goodbye Maria (I'm Off to Korea)," "Hot Foot Boogie," and the intriguingly titled "What Cigarette Is Best" didn't linger very long.

Carter's last great success turned out to be a song that a Vancouver nurse had written in 1947 for the enjoyment of the children in her ward. When friends started spreading word of Elizabeth Clarke's "(There's a) Bluebird on Your Windowsill," she was asked to sing it on Vancouver station CKNW. The station's house band, the Rhythm Pals, subsequently recorded it in response to overwhelming demand from listeners. Carter brought the song to Steve Sholes' attention, but was turned down just as Snow had been with "I'm Movin' On." Undeterred, Carter paid for a recording session himself, and managed to convince RCA to release it as the B-side to "All I Need Is Some More Lovin'." "Bluebird" was given more exposure soon after through Tex Williams's version, and continued to turn up everywhere throughout the fifties, crossing over to the pop charts thanks first to the Andrews Sisters, then Doris Day and Bing Crosby. As the royalties poured in, Clarke donated every cent to children's hospitals across Canada until she died in July 1960 at age forty-nine.

Carter's 1950 "welcome back" concerts, on the strength of "Bluebird," at Toronto's Canadian National Exhibition, drew a then-record 50,000 fans. He followed these up with his first-ever concerts in the Maritimes, where he was given a hero's welcome. But, while he felt a genuine obligation to those at home who had stuck by him, he was equally eager to reclaim his audience in the U.S., where several imitators using the name Montana Slim had cropped up in his absence, and many fans even presumed he was dead. Carter moved his family to new digs in Clinton, New Jersey, and began touring under the banner "The Family Show With the Folks You Know," with his daughters taking their turns in the spotlight. It proved to be a tough grind, and in 1952 Carter attempted to break from the music business by purchasing a plot of land in Maitland, Florida, and building the Wilf Carter Motor Lodge. It marked the beginning of a new career he felt would be a natural transition from his years on the road. However, dealing with the whims of guests was something he did not have experience in, and within two years Carter was resigned to the fact that he still needed to perform for a living.

He signed a new deal with Decca, which brought him to Nashville. There, he re-recorded many of his old hits, backed by the likes of guitarist Chet Atkins. It became a fertile period creatively for Carter, resulting in three albums: *I'm Ragged But I'm Right*, *The Dynamite Trail*, and *The Wilf Carter Souvenir Album*. But even the occasional cursory nod to rock and roll prior to his leaving the label in 1958 couldn't overcome the fact that most of the fifties belonged to Hank Snow and his fellow honky-tonk heroes. It was music that embodied the tough-minded spirit of an American working class that had consistently triumphed over everything the world had thrown at it, and even though Wilf Carter belonged to this generation, his music still leaned too heavily on the innocence that had long since been wiped away by the Second World War.

Snow followed up "I'm Movin' On" with two more rhythm-heavy, self-penned number-one hits, "The Golden Rocket" and "The Rhumba Boogie." He was now headlining his own shows with his full-time band, the Rainbow Ranch Boys, a name he also gave to the permanent home he purchased outside Nashville, in Madison, Tennessee. After years of relying on favours from others, Snow was beginning to gain control over his career. It allowed the generous aspects of his nature to emerge, starting with a 1952 trip to perform for troops in Korea. Then, along with Tubb, he successfully initiated the construction of a Jimmie Rodgers memorial. He undertook these projects on top of the many hours he devoted to children's aid charities, a cause that stemmed directly from his upbringing. More practically, his status as the most popular country music performer of 1953 (Hank Williams had died New Year's Day en route to a concert in Canton, Ohio) gave Snow first choice of prime material like "A Fool Such As I," and "I Don't Hurt Anymore," two more songs that would forever bear his stamp. In fact, Snow's ear for popular material was as much a key to his success as his own writing ability. While still in the Maritimes, he had even created his "Silver Star Song Club" through which, for a one dollar annual membership, fans were allowed to submit two of their own songs for regular contests that Snow judged himself. The winner would indeed receive prizes, but it was also an efficient way for Snow to pad his catalogue while making a small profit in the process.

Once established in Nashville, Snow's natural instinct to maximize his returns on all of his ventures — an instinct honed through bitter experience — came to dominate his way of thinking even more. With this goal in mind, and eager to revamp his touring regimen, Snow reached out to a variety of different booking agents in 1954. Eventually, he came across Eddy Arnold's former manager, a man who called himself Colonel Tom Parker. Parker was, in fact, Andreas Van Kuijk, a Dutch immigrant and former carnival hustler who had drifted into the music business after promoting shows in Florida by country stars Gene Austin, Roy Acuff, and Tom Mix. He quickly saw that the real money was in artist management, and Arnold was the first to take Parker's bait after the two met at a show in 1944. The partnership proved extremely fruitful for both sides until 1953, when their increasing personality clashes finally brought it to an end.

Snow did not bother to ask how things were ultimately settled between Parker and Arnold as he sat in the former's office, situated in a corner of his garage, which happened to be just down the road from Snow's Rainbow Ranch. What Snow heard, instead, was how Parker had recently formed a new agency called Jamboree Attractions, and was already working with *Grand Ole Opry* stars Minnie Pearl and Cowboy Copas. Parker proposed that Snow would be his main act, should he sign on, and even offered to rename the company Hank Snow Enterprises–Jamboree Attractions. It was exactly what Parker knew Snow — as Nashville's current top dog — wanted to hear; although, unbeknownst to both of them, the partnership would end up changing popular culture forever.

That process began with the *Grand Ole Opry* broadcast on October 2, 1954, when a barely known Elvis Presley was thrust upon the *Opry*'s hallowed stage. Sam Phillips, through his Memphis-based Sun label, had turned Presley into a regional phenomenon after only one single, and he was determined to use the *Opry*'s national audience as the next logical step in terms of exposure. Snow, who had never heard of Presley before being asked to introduce him that night, was courteous, but thought nothing more of the kid until Parker mentioned him a few months later as someone who would make a smart addition to their stable of clients. What Snow was not aware of was that Parker had already made overtures to Presley's manager, Bob Neal, to include Presley in one of Jamboree's upcoming package tours, slated for the early spring of 1955. From the moment Neal agreed to put Presley on the bill, Parker pulled out all of his guns to take command of the situation. First, he planted the seed that Presley needed to record for RCA-Victor, the label that had made both Snow and Arnold stars, and that he, Parker, could place him there. Snow reinforced the advantages of this idea with Presley during their subsequent travels together, and also recommended him to Steve Sholes, perhaps seeking to repay the kindness that Ernest Tubb and others had shown him.

But as the saying goes, no good deed goes unpunished. Snow endured being upstaged by Presley at every show they did in 1955 (some of these also featured Bill Haley & The Comets) with the knowledge that all the screaming was translating into money in his pocket. In early 1956, Parker completed the next stage of his plan by mediating a buyout of Presley's Sun Records contract by RCA-Victor for $40,000. Snow simultaneously brought his publisher, Hill and Range Songs Inc., into the picture on Presley's behalf. The last piece of the puzzle, Snow assumed, was signing Presley to Hank Snow Enterprises–Jamboree Attractions, since Presley's management contract with Neal had by then expired. But when Snow finally questioned Parker about this, a few days after Presley's March 24 appearance on the Dorsey Brothers television show, he was bluntly told that Elvis Presley was under exclusive contract to Colonel Tom Parker, and that their company should be dissolved immediately. This was accomplished without much opposition from Snow considering that, much to his attorney's dismay, there were no formal papers of incorporation. As Jimmie Rodgers Snow, who was also a close friend of Presley's during this period, later tried to explain in the most sympathetic of terms: "I don't think that my dad realized at that time what had happened."

Indeed, it is nearly impossible to imagine a more complete betrayal, and not just because of Parker's actions. With Presley leading the rock and roll insurgence, Snow's status was immediately diminished as his audience was undercut by a previously unacknowledged generation gap. This forced Snow and other established country and western artists to circle their wagons around Nashville, thereby isolating themselves even further from the music business hubs on the east and west coasts. Fortunately, many of these artists were saved thanks to the increased marketability of the long-playing record (LP), which allowed hits to be conveniently packaged, while simultaneously giving artists more flexibility in the recording studio. This usually led to theme-based albums, and Snow produced many memorable ones, including 1958's *When Tragedy Struck*, 1959's *Sings Jimmie Rodgers Songs*, 1963's *Railroad Man*, and 1965's tribute to The Sons of the Pioneers, *Heartbreak Trail*. These projects would come to play a significant role in Snow's career, especially when changing commercial tastes brought an abrupt end to his run of hit singles in the fall of 1963 after "I've Been Everywhere," written by Australian Geoff Mack, and "Ninety Miles an Hour (Down a Dead End Street)," a Don Robertson–Hal Blair song.

A major factor in this last string of hits was Chet Atkins, now an RCA staff producer, whose slickly orchestrated "Nashville Sound" became a timely response to the stream of pop chart-toppers being churned out of the Brill Building and Motown. Snow and Atkins worked well together, even recording many guitar duets — a reminder of Snow's underrated talent in that regard. But Snow's motivation to write original material was on the wane, a trend compounded by the assembly-line studio demands Atkins had instigated. Instead, Snow became one of the first artists to construct a home studio, in order to work at his leisure, despite the fact that such a retreat distanced him from

Nashville's sonic transformation.

Conversely, Snow still managed to retain a partial foothold in rock and roll, even as his son, who, upon being called by God had abandoned his own music career in 1958, preached its wickedness. Ray Charles recorded "I'm Movin' On" in 1959, his first experiment in what would become a groundbreaking crossover into country music. The Rolling Stones exploited the song's raw energy, as well, including a frantic live version on 1965's *December's Children*. Even Presley belatedly tipped his cap to his old friend by recording it as part of his landmark *From Elvis In Memphis* sessions in 1969.

"I'm Movin' On" would continue to provide the stability that Hank Snow had sought his entire life, but just as becoming a member of the *Grand Ole Opry* gave him the surrogate family he never truly had, his unshakeable position within the Nashville establishment also proved to be a curse. By remaining loyal to what was perceived to be an ultra-conservative institution in the late sixties, Snow was pushed further to the margins, even within Nashville itself, which by then had attracted its share of denim-clad, dope-smoking songwriters. The world was spinning out of control; Snow's unwavering support for the armed forces was put to the test when he performed for troops in Vietnam, while his tacit involvement in his son's ministry throughout the seventies caused others to scratch their heads, especially after the younger Snow appeared to tarnish his father's heartfelt tribute to his musical inspiration by changing the spelling of his name from "Jimmie" to "Jimmy."

However, the *coup de grâce* was saved for 1981; RCA dropped Snow from its roster, when, after many years of questioning the label's accounting practices, Snow went ahead with an audit of his royalties. The outcome left him at his lowest point. Unable to draw nearly the same audience numbers he once did, even Snow's requests to perform at fairs in Nova Scotia that year were denied. He would not play in his home province again until finding a backer in Irving Oil, which went as far as to include concert tickets with the purchase of a tank of gas. When he toured western Canada that year with Wilf Carter, Snow emphatically ordered that a listing of all of his awards and nominations be a part of his introduction.

When asked what he thought of his own collection of awards, Carter said, "You can't eat 'em." Just two years beforehand, he was named grand marshal of the Calgary Stampede, an honour he said he appreciated more than any music industry accolade he had ever received. The truth was that Carter had never let such concerns worry him, in contrast to Snow, whose opinions of his treatment by the industry in the eighties often caused his tongue to slip in conversation. Snow would not record again, except at the behest of Willie Nelson, who extended a hand of gratitude with the 1985 duet album *Brand on My Heart*, released on Nelson's label, Columbia Records. Few other artists besides Nelson were in a position to make such a gesture then, which drove home the point that being a member of the *Grand Ole Opry* in the eighties was the equivalent of being in a museum.

Conversely, while sales of Carter's RCA LPs, which began appearing on a regular basis in 1963, certainly helped him during a time when he needed it, his music career from then on came down to what it had essentially always been, singing for the people who enjoyed listening to him, even if it meant playing nursing homes. On one of these occasions, an old timer, unaware of who this cowboy was, said, "You know, you're a good singer, but you know who could really sing a song? Wilf Carter." Carter laughed louder than anyone else in the room.

For Snow, it was much harder to accept such a reality. After the 1981 tour, nearly in his seventies, he hit the road again, playing nothing but the old hits. He did his final tour of Canada in the summer of 1989, playing the last show at a high school gymnasium in Owen Sound, Ontario, on September 24. He continued to make regular *Grand Ole Opry* appearances until 1993, a point at which Wilf Carter was conceding that he could no longer tour, either.

Having gone his entire career without a manager, Carter had once barked at Snow backstage, "You gotta tell 'em what you want, don't let them flunkies tell ya." But, at the same time, Carter admired Snow's resiliency, leading him to bequeath his old broncobusting saddle to the younger man. Snow would treasure that gift over the ensuing years, and never more so than on December 5, 1996, when word came that Carter had succumbed to stomach cancer at his home in Scottsdale, Arizona.

On December 20, 1999, Hank Snow died in Nashville, content in the knowledge that he would be given a funeral on the *Grand Ole Opry* stage that had meant so much to him, right until the very end. Although he would no longer be heard on those Saturday night broadcasts, those who had tuned in to hear Snow over the preceding half-century would never forget that voice — brimming with equal parts unwavering conviction and down-home charm — especially the countless numbers who would later forge their own musical paths from all over North America to Nashville and beyond.

CHAPTER TWO

WHO DO YOU LOVE

Sic transit Gloria, GLORY FADES.

General George Patton put it this way: "All glory is fleeting." But he was merely paraphrasing Napoleon Bonaparte's more thorough, "All glory is fleeting, but obscurity is forever." From whom he stole these words is unknown.

Addressing a woman he spotted in the front row in 2006, Ronnie Hawkins said, "Honey, if you come backstage, I'll fuck you so many ways, you're bound to like one of 'em."

If rock and roll is, in fact, the never-ending war it often appears to be for those participating in it, then it stands to reason that Ronnie Hawkins' greatest triumph on the battlefield was too fleeting to be remembered by anyone outside the few who saw it occur on stages in the early sixties. But, like all great generals, it took the courage and loyalty he inspired in the men he led to transform that brief moment into something that would truly be remembered. In spite of himself, Ronnie Hawkins introduced rock and roll to an entire nation, and that kind of glory evidently does not fade quickly.

When countries around the world started getting a whiff of rock and roll in the late fifties, the rush was on for local kids to be the first on their home charts with versions of Sun Records owner Sam Phillips' dream of white boys who sounded like black boys. England had Cliff Richard and Billy Fury; France had Johnny Hallyday. Canada had no one of consequence, and perhaps didn't want anyone, based on reactions to Elvis Presley bringing his brand new Nudie-tailored gold lamé suit to Toronto on April 2, 1957 ("All Too Plainly Visible Elvis Is Barely Audible," declared the *Toronto Star*), Ottawa the next night ("Convent Suspends Eight Elvis Fans," boasted the *Ottawa Citizen*), and, later, Vancouver on August 31. Although these would be his only concerts ever outside the United States, at that point, nothing could prevent the seeds of revolution within Presley's records from taking root, be it in Canada or anywhere else. Presley was the product of an American musical culture that had already existed for at least a decade, one that did not reach Canada until its arrival was announced by "Heartbreak Hotel" in early 1956, or, slightly prior to that, by Bill Haley & The Comets' "Rock Around the Clock." Kids were still translating these foreign messages by the time their authors started heading north in search of new territory to plunder.

That new territory held extra importance for those who had come late to the original party, and were left to pick over the scraps discarded by Presley, Jerry Lee Lewis, and Carl Perkins. Then again, some of them weren't invited to the party to begin with, mostly because the further the sound disseminated from Memphis, where an unspoken social code among musicians allowed the crucial marriage between black and white styles to be consummated, the more it was instilled with isolated, unmanageable backwoods aggression. John Tolleson, a local rockabilly hero from Fayetteville, Arkansas, stated flatly, "People today don't realize the impact that music had. It was like somebody put a wall down. The old music stopped here. The new music started here."

Harold Jenkins and Jimmy Ray Paulman were among dozens of other Arkansas boys who, like Tolleson, were ignited by Presley in 1956. With their band, The Rock Housers, they went further, following the by then well-trodden path to Sun, where they cut a demo that November that Sam Phillips ultimately rejected. However, their signature song, "Rock House," was passed on to Roy Orbison, who recorded his own version. Jenkins changed his name to Conway Twitty (perhaps following Vernon Dalhart's example by combining the names of two towns he noticed on an Arkansas/Texas road map), and found new interest from Mercury Records, a label in need of Presley sound-alikes. "I Need Your Lovin'" b/w "Born to Sing the Blues," was released on April 20, 1957, followed on July 15 by "Shake It Up" b/w "Maybe Baby." Both records generated little interest, but they got The Rock Housers out of the south that summer. Yet the further north they went, the cooler the reception for their unpolished act became, and when a scheduled extended run in Washington, D.C., was cut short after three days, the band's manager, Don Seat, desperately called on any promoter within a five-hundred-mile radius to help them earn enough money to get home.

"The clubs in those days would book acts sight unseen, and that's what happened with Conway. He wasn't able to draw, so they fired him." If anyone can speak with authority on how nightclubs operated in the fifties, it's Harold Kudlats. Born in Glasgow, Scotland, with the surname Kudlatz, he moved with his family to Hamilton, Ontario, at the age of eight. In 1946, he took a job managing The Forum on Barton Street, a 4,000-capacity venue that operated as an ice rink in the winter and a roller rink in the summer. In July 1947, some Toronto promoters wanted the Glenn Miller Orchestra to play there, a request Kudlats shrewdly refused until he got a piece of the action. Not long after, the introduction of provincial liquor licenses allowed him to expand his new booking enterprise to several other venues around town. Jazz was in demand, and he worked with the best: Duke Ellington, Stan Kenton, Tommy Dorsey, and Jack Teagarden, although his greatest triumph was bringing Louis Armstrong to the Dundas Arena in May 1951. From his office in the Royal Connaught Hotel, Kudlats earned a reputation as an honest businessman who respected musicians, so when the plea came to rescue The Rock Housers, he didn't hesitate to book them into the Flamingo Lounge, where the Hamilton Place Theatre now stands. "Little did Conway or I know at the time that it was going to change both our lives," Kudlats says. "Conway did such gangbuster business here, it made me ask him if there were any other bands back in Arkansas that he could recommend."

Upon The Rock Housers' return to the Flamingo in the fall of 1957, Kudlats also had Sun artist Billy Lee Riley — known for the classic "Flying Saucers Rock 'N' Roll" — playing at the Golden Rail, two blocks away, at the intersection of King and John streets. The friendly competition between the two bands soon turned nasty, as some of The Rock Housers, including guitarist Paulman, saw Riley as the faster rising star. In the midst of this tension, Twitty composed a soaring ballad, called "It's Only Make Believe," one night between sets at the Flamingo. Twitty went on to record it in early 1958 for MGM, and from then on few would ever believe that he once sang rockabilly.

For Paulman, the dream of making it with Riley didn't pan out, and at the end of 1957 he was back in Arkansas trying to put a new band together. All he needed was a singer, one that had to be crazier than Twitty and Riley combined. Paulman knew exactly who to call.

Ronald Cornett Hawkins was born on January 10, 1935, in Huntsville, Arkansas, the second surviving child of Jasper Hawkins and his wife Flora. That day, in Tupelo, Mississippi, Gladys Presley held her newborn son, Elvis, while his father, Vernon, buried the baby's stillborn twin brother. In 1944, the Hawkins family moved to Fayetteville, home of the University of Arkansas, where Jasper worked as a barber, and Flora as a schoolteacher. Young Ronnie had been introduced to music at a young age through several relatives, most notably his guitar-playing uncle Delmar, who ventured to California in the forties, finding work backing up The Sons of the Pioneers, among others, before meeting his end in a house fire. But what firmly set Hawkins on his path was encountering Dixieland jazz musician Buddy Hayes, who would rehearse his band behind Jasper Hawkins' shop. Listening to Hayes and his nephews, pianist Bob "Pint" Thompson and drummer Clifford "Half Pint" Thompson, Hawkins discovered the forbidden black rhythms that were rockabilly's catalyst.

Few things, it seemed, were ever forbidden to Hawkins. He reputedly (and with Hawkins, every aspect of his life is reputed) first learned how to drive at age twelve, later turning that skill into a three-hundred-dollar-per-week job, more than triple his father's wages, running whisky in a Model A Ford from Missouri to Oklahoma, which did not officially repeal Prohibition until 1959. He managed to keep up his studies (for his mother's sake), graduating from high school in 1952, and spent that summer hanging around the music scene in Memphis. But, unlike most of the budding rockabillies, Hawkins could not be bothered to learn how to play an instrument. He was instead fascinated by the tricks he noticed Hayes and his nephews utilize to make their money when they played on the street, and, in particular, a move they called the "camel walk," one not dissimilar from the "moon walk" Michael Jackson would employ to startling effect thirty-two years later. Once Hawkins mastered the move himself, his passable voice, and, more importantly, his irrepressible personality, easily won him many friends whenever he showed up for a gig or jam session.

Still, music remained only one of many possible avenues for Hawkins. He enrolled in university and dropped out, enlisted in the National Guard and was discharged. He even tried to go legit by running his own nightclubs, using older friends as fronts until he turned twenty-one and could serve his own liquor. With all of these distractions, there was little time left for Hawkins to fully absorb what was going on at Sun and elsewhere during the tumultuous years 1954–56. He wasn't even aware that his own cousin, Dale Hawkins, Delmar's son, had struck gold in early 1957 with "Suzie Q," based around a stinging riff by his writing partner, a young Louisiana guitarist named James Burton. Granted, by then Hawkins was in the army in a bid to do his duty before another war came. The plan proved to be a typically savvy one, as there were not many responsibilities placed upon Fort Sill, Oklahoma, where Hawkins was stationed after his basic training. Weekends were spent at a nearby club, where his ease with popular rhythm and blues numbers led to a full-time gig fronting the black house band, which thereafter became known as The Black Hawks.

Hawkins' stint in the service was over by the time Jimmy Ray Paulman tracked him down to see if stories of the singer's

49

unhinged performances were accurate. In fact, Hawkins' reputation already rivalled those of more accomplished local musicians like John Tolleson (who would test the waters in southern Ontario himself not long after Twitty) and Hawkins' time fronting The Black Hawks had only deepened his knowledge of black music. The most obvious example was Hawkins' grasp of the Bo Diddley beat, the primal, pseudo-African rhythm first put forth by an eccentric guitarist named Ellas McDaniel and almost instantly adopted by every musician who heard it. Under the name Bo Diddley, he recorded the song, "Bo Diddley" for Chicago's Chess Records in 1955, firmly laying another cornerstone in the foundation of rock and roll. Furthermore, McDaniel illustrated how it was possible to raise oneself to mythical status in the new post-war pop culture universe; in song after song, Bo Diddley's exploits grew increasingly outlandish.

Hawkins accepted Paulman's offer without hesitation, joining Paulman's piano-playing cousin, Willard "Pop" Jones, and seventeen-year-old drummer Lavon Helm in the new group.

Mark Lavon Helm was the second child and first son of Diamond and Nell Helm, born May 26, 1940, in Elaine, Arkansas. Shortly after his birth, the family moved onto a parcel of land between the towns of Turkey Scratch and Marvell, twenty miles west of Helena. He grew up immersed in the music of the area, witnessing Bill Monroe & His Bluegrass Boys, as well as blues harmonica player Sonny Boy Williamson whose daily "King Biscuit Time" show on Helena radio station KFFA had made him a local star. By age nine, Helm was playing guitar and performing in public with his sister Linda. He saw Presley in Helena in 1954, and again in early 1955, when drummer D.J. Fontana was added to Presley's group, which then consisted of guitarist Scotty Moore and bassist Bill Black. Helm was captivated by what the drums added to the sound, but continued to accompany his sister on guitar. The siblings shared a bill with The Rock Housers at a grocery store grand opening in 1956. The following year, the duo of Lavon & Linda expanded to become The Jungle Bush Beaters, with second guitarist Thurlow Brown and an untrained rhythm section that lived up to the band's name. For Helm, the music was now a lifestyle, and during one hazy night in Forrest City, spurred on by the bottle of bourbon in his pocket, Helm got behind the drum kit during a jam session instigated by Paulman and his friends and naturally fell into a Bo Diddley beat. From then on, he was branded a drummer.

Hawkins and Helm formed an instant bond after their first rehearsal together, with the twenty-two-year-old singer (already the spitting image of the campus dope dealer played by John Drew Barrymore in the 1958 film *High School Confidential*) eager to pass on his wealth of illicit knowledge to the kid. Throughout the spring of 1958, the Ron Hawkins Quartet barnstormed around the south, honing its act until Helm finished high school that May, and the group could head to where Paulman told them the real money was, Canada. The guitarist had already arranged dates with Harold Kudlats, and they played their first show at the Golden Rail in Hamilton, ostensibly as an audition. "Conway's start was okay at first, and he built from that, but Hawkins's start was a disaster," Kudlats recalls. "Audiences had never heard anything like that, and during the afternoon rehearsal they drove the customers out, and the bartenders threatened to quit if we didn't cancel the act. We didn't, of course." However, it didn't take long for those audiences, many comprised of Hamilton steelworkers, to come around. "There was nothing like that kind of music in Canada. That's why Conway exploded when he got here, because it was music we had never heard before. The big factor, both with Conway's group and Hawkins' group, is that they were both from the south, and the accent and all that was a big thing back then. Also, there was no dancing allowed, so all the lounge groups had to be good musicians and good entertainers. I was more concerned about Levon, though, who looked like he was twelve years old. Back then, the liquor board was pretty strict on the age, twenty-one, and I figured that there was no way he was going to be allowed to work. But we had Levon wear sunglasses whenever he was on a break or in the dressing room, and we got away with it."

Hawkins and his band played out the week in Hamilton before heading west to London for three weeks at the Brass Rail, then back east to Toronto for a month at Le Coq d'Or, on Yonge Street. In feeding off the hunger of every nascent rock and roll fan, Hawkins had found the perfect situation to let his fantasies run wild, and he did so every night, both on stage and off, acquiring the nickname "Rompin' Ronnie" in the process. Perhaps the moniker was too quaintly Canadian, considering that he and the band were spending most of their pay on women, booze, and pills.

The excitement did indeed light a fire within the emerging recording industry. The first label interest came during the group's Toronto residency, when a Quality Records' A & R man, Dan Bass, offered to cut a single before the band went back to the States. Quality had established itself in Toronto in 1950, under George Keane, as an independent record manufacturer for the Canadian market, and later became an exclusive distributor for MGM and its affiliated labels. Working with Hawkins was certainly a coup, since Canada had made only peripheral contributions to rock and roll up until then. One of these was the Toronto vocal group The Crew-Cuts, whose whitewashed treatment of doo-wop group The Chords's "Sh-Boom" became a surprise hit across North America in 1954. Another was Ottawa's Paul Anka, whose 1957 smash debut "Diana" foreshadowed the wave of puppy-love crooners that would soon usurp the original rockers on the U.S. charts.

The man who should have been Canada's first homegrown rock and roll star unfortunately only resided in the country until the age of ten. Jack Scott, born Giovanni Scafone, Jr., on January 24, 1936 in Windsor, Ontario, learned to play guitar from his father, and was fronting his own band by age eighteen, long after his family had moved across the river to Detroit. In 1957, he signed his first of a series of record deals, wich nonetheless led to a string of hit singles over the next two years, including the rockabilly standard, "The Way I Walk." After a brief stint in the army in 1959, Scott turned to country music with even more success, highlighted by the smashes "What In The World's Come Over

You," and "Burning Bridges." If not for The Beatles, Scott would hold the record for the greatest amount of chart-placing singles (nineteen) within the shortest span of time (forty-one months).

It would be left, then, for Hawkins to make the first true rock and roll recording in Canada, at Quality's makeshift studio on Kingston Road in Toronto, in the late summer of 1958. Of the four songs laid down that day (with Gordon Josie added on bass), two were staples of the live show: "Hey Bo Diddley," the 1957 update of the original "Bo Diddley," and Chuck Berry's "Thirty Days," the September 1955 follow-up to his first single, "Maybellene." The others were Hawkins originals, a weak Buddy Holly-esque ballad called "Love Me Like You Can," and "Horace," a potent rocker written in Hamilton. With its ridiculous quasi-female vocals, "Horace" was the clearest example of the extremes Hawkins' performing capabilities could reach. Seeking balance, Quality opted for "Hey Bo Diddley" b/w "Love Me Like You Can" as the single, released only in Canada in early 1959. Despite being a vivid document capturing the moment of Hawkins' arrival, it could hardly be described as a masterpiece. And with an initial pressing of five hundred copies, Hawkins himself treated it as a novelty, since there was no chance of it being released south of the border.

However, Kudlats was drawing on all of his resources to get the band work there so they could remain busy between their Canadian engagements. One of his New York contacts, Larry Bennett of Associated Bookings, brought the quartet south in the spring of 1959 for a run of club dates along the Jersey Shore. News that authentic rockabilly still existed soon floated across the river, making even Columbia's sober A & R head, Mitch Miller, curious. But when Hawkins was told of interest from Morris Levy, of Roulette Records, he knew it was an offer he couldn't refuse. "I kept telling Larry, I've got a helluva band here and we've got to get some kind of connection with a record company," Kudlats says. "Larry was hooked up with Morris Levy and got us an audition. So I took the band down to New York and they were rehearsing at four o'clock in the afternoon when Morris Levy came in. He flipped, never heard anything

like it. Six o'clock that night he says we're going to start recording an album, and that was unheard of. Morris loved the band;
he figured they would take over because Elvis was in the army.
But we had no idea the connections that Morris had."

It was common knowledge in the music business that with
Levy on your side, anything was possible. Having already made
a fortune, bankrolled by associates who chose to remain anonymous, in the New York jazz scene, and later with doo-wop
groups such as The Crows and Frankie Lymon & The Teenagers,
Levy turned to rock and roll in 1956. He started Roulette in
partnership with Alan Freed, the man lauded as the first white
DJ outside the south to play black records, and through their
combined efforts, illicit and otherwise, they pushed Roulette's
second release, "Party Doll," by Buddy Knox, to the top of the
Billboard chart in April 1957.

Levy and Hawkins certainly did share an understanding of
the world that most others didn't, and neither was about to
hedge their bets. If Levy truly saw Hawkins as the man to fill
Presley's shoes, the singer was prepared to use every trick at his
disposal to keep his boss shelling out for luxury hotel rooms and
steak dinners, even if those bills would eventually come back to
haunt him. Hawkins, Helm (now formally known as Levon),
Paulman, and Jones, augmented by jazz bassist George Duvivier,
renowned Atlantic Records house saxophonist Sam Taylor, and
a black chorus, set up in New York's Bell Sound studio on April
13, 1959, to record "Ruby Baby" and "Forty Days," the former a
straight copy of The Drifters' song of the same name, and the
latter a none-too-subtle rearrangement of "Thirty Days."
Although it was not altered enough to avoid paying royalties to
Chuck Berry (who himself was unknowingly forced to share
credit with Alan Freed on "Maybellene" as a kickback for airplay), "Ruby Baby" and most of Hawkins' other Roulette
recordings were credited to "Hawkins-Magill," that is, Jacqueline
Magill, Morris Levy's girlfriend. Moreover, Levy controlled all
publishing rights through his company, Patricia Music, named in
honour of his mother.

The band was in the studio again two days later, recording

an even wilder version of "Horace," along with "One of These Days," another mongrel doo-wop number that was chosen as the B-side for the first single, "Forty Days," which, over the course of eight weeks, would barely scrape into the *Billboard* Top 50. On April 29, just prior to its release on May 4, they undertook a final marathon session, laying down eight songs to fill up an LP. Most of these, like "Red Hot" and "Dizzy Miss Lizzy," were already part of the lexicon of Arkansas rockabillies. A few of Hawkins' more heavy-handed sexual fantasies were also thrown in, such as "Odessa," inspired by one of his favourite Helena whores, and the self-explanatory "Wild Little Willie." But the standout of the session proved to be "Mary Lou," written and originally recorded by Obediah Jessie (a.k.a. Young Jessie) in 1955 for the Bihari brothers' L.A.-based label, Modern. Jessie entered the music business with his classmate Richard Berry, composer of "Louie Louie," and spent time in The Coasters, as well as other vocal groups. His 1956 New York session, which also featured saxophonist Sam Taylor, produced the overlooked rocker "Hit, Git, and Split." Further recordings for Atlantic and Mercury throughout the sixties failed to generate much interest, outside of a few die-hard rhythm and blues fans.

However, the sordid tale of "Mary Lou" would from then on be Hawkins' signature song after its release in early August 1959. It rose into the *Billboard* Top 30, and landed the group on *American Bandstand* on August 17, where they performed it along with "Forty Days." Kudlats recalls, "We were in Morris's office and he picks up the phone to his secretary and says, get me Dick Clark, get me Steve Allen, and two other people who had big shows. I mean, for anybody else, if you got someone like that on the line, you'd plead with them. Morris said, 'We've signed a new act. I want them on your next show' — *I want*, y'know? We looked at each other and figured this guy's nuts."

Now billed as Ronnie Hawkins & The Hawks, with Conway Twitty's one-time bassist, Jimmy Evans, as a permanent fixture, the band wore out their Cadillacs driving between Arkansas and Ontario during the summer of 1959, still able to ride high on the lingering aftershock of rock and roll's original big bang.

But Levy's hopes for Hawkins were already waning when the album *Ronnie Hawkins* was released in September, with everything about it telling the world who the star of the show was. The fees had increased, and Hawkins took his cut at the expense of the rest of the band. Jones was the first to leave as a result of this, with Paulman following by year's end. Fred Carter, Jr. replaced him, lured away from Dale Hawkins' band when the cousins were reunited for a show in New Jersey that fall. The brief twin-guitar lineup of Paulman and Carter did make one appearance in the studio, an eight-song session in New York on September 16 with producer Henry Glover, best known as the composer of the Ray Charles soul classic "Drown in My Own Tears," and for his work at King Records, Cincinnati's pioneering R & B label. The intention, it seemed, was to cut tracks for one of Roulette's instrumental compilations (Hawkins only appears on "Cathy Jean"), but nothing immediately significant would become of these songs. At the start of October, the Hawks were back for an extended run in Toronto, and awaiting their arrival was a kid who was eager to climb aboard the gravy train.

While a large part of Hawkins's appeal in Canada lay in the more exotic and dangerous aspects of his music, his shows in Toronto, especially, attracted many from poorer neighbourhoods who naturally accepted rockabilly as a soundtrack to their hard-scrabble lives. Not all had talent or the desire to escape like Hank Snow, so in Hawkins they finally had a role model who, although he was in many ways a mere carpetbagger, was at least willing to establish some common ground with them. What Hawkins inherently understood was that rock and roll could only thrive when it engaged audiences on a primal level, and it didn't take long for him to seduce Canadians with his reality of what it meant to be American.

Like all major northeastern cities, Toronto's rapid expansion throughout the first half of the twentieth century was only achieved through a diverse influx of immigrants. As the new arrivals earned their meagre wages, they were relegated to the specific areas of the city that could sustain them. Parliament

Street had been named, with the noblest of intentions, in 1794 as the trail that extended north from the site of the first seat of government for Upper Canada. But as other grand thorough-fares and structures emerged around it, the balance of power quietly shifted, until Parliament was no different than any other street. To the residents of Parliament Street who settled in the aftermath of that power shift, it was much worse. The predom-inantly Irish population, concentrated within the east-west boundary of Parliament and the Don River and the north-south boundary of Gerrard and Queen streets, first prompted outsiders to call it Cork Town. As conditions deteriorated during the Depression, those living there were often left with no recourse but to grow their own food in small gardens, caus-ing observers to rename the neighbourhood Cabbagetown. The low rents attracted both slumlords and common criminals, heightening its nasty reputation by the forties.

It is not known what attracted Rosemarie Chrysler to such an area. She was of predominantly Mohawk descent, and had grown up on the Six Nations Reserve an hour's drive southwest of Toronto, near Brantford. She moved in with an aunt some-time after the start of the Second World War, and was soon seduced by a neighbourhood Jewish gambler named Alexander David Klegerman. From an early age, Klegerman had naturally drifted into the highly organized network of bookmaking rings centred in and around Cabbagetown. Many of these were con-trolled by notorious gambling boss Maxwell "Maxie Bluestein" Baker, who based his operation at the Lakeview Athletic Club, in the west-end suburb of Etobicoke. Although there is little evidence that Klegerman ever got involved in large-scale crim-inal activities, in the coming years his brother Nathan, or "Natie," would become a major figure in loan sharking, extor-tion, and diamond fraud, at the same time as he earned a Ph.D. in philosophy.

In this setting, Rosemarie gave birth to a son, Jaime Robert Klegerman, on July 5, 1943. Even less is known about whether becoming a father changed Alexander Klegerman's lifestyle, because he did not live long enough to find out himself. He was struck and killed in a hit and run when his car broke down on the Queen Elizabeth Way, the highway connecting Toronto and Hamilton. Jaime would instead become the adopted son of the man Rosemarie soon married, James Patrick Robertson, whom she met at the jewellery-plating factory where they both worked. With their earnings, they provided stable homes for Jaime at several Toronto locales, including Bloor Street, across from the well-known discount store Honest Ed's, and near the Scarborough Bluffs. Rosemarie did not want her son to know of the Klegermans if she could help it, although echoes of Jaime's Jewish roots haunted him later in life, long after he'd taken his adopted father's surname. "My great-grandfather came to this country, he was a scholar from Israel," Robertson said. "When he got here, all he studied was meaningless. He was capable of nothing but reading and intellectualizing. He became a ragman, not an unusual thing at the time. He had a horse and a wagon and he would go up and down the lanes singing this song, 'Rags, bones, and old used clothes.' It's a chant that stuck in my head. The image. I never saw him doing it, but the legacy carried on. When I was a kid, I would see the ragman and it was a frightening symbol to me. The chant would never leave my mind."

Instead, his mother wanted him to be accepted by her family, and this entailed spending large portions of summer vacations at the Six Nations reserve, where Robertson was introduced to all manner of relatives during their annual gatherings. He came to admire an older cousin, Herb Myke, who, along with his brother Freddy and their dad Waddy, entertained everyone by playing songs by Hank Williams and other country stars. "He was a very quiet kid who noticed a lot," Herb says. "He used to sit right in front of my knees and watch me. I'd show him something on guitar and he'd try it out." Robertson demanded to learn more once back home, and his mother found a teacher who advertised Hawaiian guitar lessons. But the lap-slide technique was not what the kid had in mind, forcing him to wait patiently for future visits to the reserve. Myke added, "To be the best wasn't difficult, because there weren't too many guitarists around at the time. We had a big family, and we played a lot because there was no television, and we didn't have a radio."

However, Robertson did have a radio, and he quickly made a connection between what his cousins were teaching him and the strange sounds he heard every night when he spun the dial. When the weather was clear, he could get John R.'s blues show from WLAC Nashville, but the most reliable was George "Hound Dog" Lorenz, broadcasting from WKBW, just across Lake Ontario in Buffalo, New York. Lorenz's program was mandatory for every Ontario kid who was into rock and roll between 1955 and 1958, until it vanished when the station switched to a Top 40 format. Still, those few years were crucial in spreading the rock and roll gospel, and there wasn't a more devoted convert than Robertson. Rosemarie could not deny her son's passion for the music, and likewise could not oppose his desire to join a band once he became proficient on his first cheap electric guitar.

The first band that would have him was Little Caesar & The Consuls, formed in 1956 by pianist/vocalist Bruce Morshead and guitarist Gene MacLellan, who later achieved fame as the composer of "Snowbird." Robertson, now going by the more befitting rock and roll moniker of Robbie, joined in 1957, and remained for close to a year, playing current hits at Toronto teen dances until he felt confident enough to form his own band. His partner became guitarist and all-around gearhead Pete "Thumper" Traynor, who would go on to start the Traynor amplifier company, which later became Yorkville Sound. Their first band together was The Rhythm Chords, which changed to Robbie & The Robots after they saw the movie *Forbidden Planet*, and like most hip teenagers, became fans of the film's main character, Robbie the Robot. Traynor even went so far as to customize Robertson's guitar with space-age trappings to get the point across. Next came the short-lived Thumper & The Trombones (or Trambones, depending on what mood they were in), before Robertson and Traynor found pianist Scott Cushnie in 1959 and became The Suedes.

It was this band that brought Robertson and Ronnie Hawkins together. Hawkins was present on October 5, when The Suedes performed at Toronto station CHUM's Hi Fi Club on Merton Street, and joined them for a couple of numbers. Immediately afterward, Robertson started shadowing Hawkins, making the most of every opportunity to show off his talent. The singer was indeed impressed by the sixteen-year-old's guitar playing, but what firmly caught his ear were the original songs in The Suede's repertoire, some of which, like "Hey Boba Lou" and "Someone Like You," were written with Cushnie.★

The timing proved ideal for Robertson, as Hawkins had a recording session scheduled with Henry Glover at Bell Sound on October 26 and needed material. Taking things a step further, Hawkins thought of giving Robertson the final say over which songs would appeal most to kids, and, upon getting Rosemarie's approval, took him to New York.

Whatever influence Robertson may have had on the end result of *Mr. Dynamo*, released in January 1960, it was in name only, as was nearly everything that had to do with Roulette Records. Songs were once again credited with little regard to their actual sources, the most egregious being "You Cheated (You Lied)," which bore Helm's name despite being a Top 20 hit by The Shields in the fall of 1958. It was more believable that Helm co-wrote "Baby Jean," one of the few songs that contained sufficient energy to live up to the album title. But it's difficult to imagine famed Brill Building writers like Doc Pomus and Otis Blackwell agreeing with Hawkins' view that Robertson would be the next big thing after hearing "Hey Boba Lou," a strange minor-key rhumba, or "Someone Like You," a pale Rick Nelson imitation. Even Morris Levy seemed indifferent to the final product, allowing its first single, the unnerving, organ-dominated "Southern Love," to stall at the bottom of *Billboard*'s Hot 100. Instead, Levy pointed Hawkins toward England, where a legion of ignored rockabilly fans beckoned.

A round of uneasy shows back in Arkansas signalled the end of the all-American Hawks, just prior to Hawkins going over-

---

★Cushnie would eventually have his own brief stint with Hawkins and go on to a session career, which included appearances on several of Aerosmith's early albums.

seas, with Helm along for the ride, as usual. Paulman was out, and Fred Carter, Jr. had given Hawkins three months' notice. When Jimmy Evans suddenly quit, Hawkins gave Robertson his break, summoning him to Fayetteville to play bass. Once he had proved his dedication in this capacity, Robertson begged Hawkins to give him Carter's gig. Hawkins responded by handing over one hundred dollars and telling Robertson to learn everything he could from Carter while Hawkins was in England. "Fred Carter took me over to Memphis from West Helena, and I spent my whole first paycheck on records from that store [Reuben Cherry's] Home Of The Blues," Robertson recalled. "I wanted every record in that store. And that was *really* my schooling. On the same first trip into Memphis, we went over to Sun Records, and Jerry Lee Lewis was recording. And I just thought, 'I'm here, I made it.' I was a little kid realizing this dream. And everything — the smell of the air, the movement of the river, the way people talked — it all worked perfectly for me."

When Hawkins returned and heard the kid playing the trademark riffs of the great Memphis blues guitarists Hubert Sumlin, Willie Johnson, Matt Murphy, and Pat Hare, he once again felt, momentarily, that he had the world in the palm of his hand. However, Robertson remained on bass into the spring of 1960, when Carter's final departure heralded the new Hawks lineup, featuring Lewis-inspired pianist Stan Szelest and bassist Rebel Paine, both hijacked from The Tremblers, a Buffalo-based band. If rockabilly was dead in North America, then this Hawks lineup aimed to put the final nail in the coffin.

In spite of the band's potency, Hawkins still knew that it wasn't enough to get him back on the radio. The first hint that folk music had the potential to break into the mainstream came in 1958, when The Kingston Trio — college boys who harmonized while strumming banjos — had a surprise hit with "Tom Dooley," based on the nineteenth-century murder ballad sometimes listed as "Tom Dula." Almost immediately, it heralded the mainstream breakthrough of a "folk revival" that had been gathering strength among the political left in response to the U.S.

government's anti-communist hysteria, which ran throughout the decade. Still, all Hawkins wanted was a hit to maintain his growing list of investment properties, mostly clubs in Arkansas. He had already flirted with the folk ballad form at the onset of his fame in May 1959 by recording (but not releasing) "The Death of Floyd Collins," a song first done by Vernon Dalhart in 1925, about the well-publicized demise of a real-life cave explorer.

Now, almost a year later, Hawkins was growing desperate. Scanning the headlines, he stumbled upon the story of Caryl Chessman, convicted in 1948 as California's "Red Light Bandit," and scheduled to be executed on February 19, 1960, despite mounting pressure to commute his sentence. Hawkins hastily summarized the story in "The Ballad of Caryl Chessman" — punctuated by a chorus that pleaded, "Let him live" — and recorded it in New York on February 2 with a simple banjo and string bass–led ensemble. Roulette rushed it out as a single, with "The Death of Floyd Collins" as the B-side, by which time Chessman's execution had been stayed until early May. Unfortunately, the song died on the charts the same moment Chessman died in the gas chamber. Even still, Hawkins forged ahead with more folk-friendly material. The album *Folk Ballads of Ronnie Hawkins*, containing such songs as "I Gave My Love a Cherry" and "John Henry," was completed in Nashville. The still-green Robertson was the only regular band member not to participate. Released at the end of May, the album, predictably, confused many of Hawkins' fans, especially those who still packed clubs in southern Ontario to see him during the summer of 1960.

Still unsure about handing all of the guitar duties to Robertson, Hawkins didn't hesitate to hire Roy Buchanan. Although an Arkansas native, Buchanan had grown up in California, playing guitar in Pentecostal tent meetings before bouncing around the South with his band, The Heartbeats, starting in 1955. In 1958, he took a gig with Dale Hawkins, easily handling the riffs that James Burton had made famous. That had run its course by 1960, and Buchanan sought out Ronnie in Toronto, briefly becoming a

Hawk that summer. Buchanan's later status as arguably the best rock guitarist in the world from 1972 (when his first solo album was released) until his death in 1988 was richly deserved, but until then his biggest impact would be indirectly inspiring Robertson's playing to new heights. Fred Carter's playing was one thing, but Buchanan tore into the strings with the ease of a man truly possessed, something that was also reflected in his brooding disposition. Robertson took detailed notes of everything.

Before his disposition got Buchanan kicked out of the band, The Hawks continued to flaunt life at the top in Canada. As Hawkins saw more and more young bands emerge, he even began to envision himself as the ruler of his own separate Canadian rock and roll dominion, one that was nonetheless built on Kudlats's connections. "Hawkins and Conway, they opened so many doors for me that I wouldn't have gotten into otherwise," Kudlats says. "If you had a band that was breaking, doing good business in Hamilton or Toronto, somehow through the grapevine every club in Ontario knew about it, so there was really no selling involved. It turned into if they wanted Conway or Hawkins, they'd have to buy some other groups I had. If I couldn't keep a group working forty or so weeks a year, they were no good to me. That's the way it was, but I treated the musicians like human beings. Never had a contract with anybody."

Hawkins therefore scrutinized every opening act: in Port Dover, there was that kid who played and sang like Ray Charles; over in Simcoe there was that gangly, juiced-up kid who was a show all by himself; then there was that strange kid from down near Detroit who could play just about anything you put in front of him. *Man, put all those cats together somehow, and now you've got a band.*

But Hawkins couldn't dwell too long on such notions while he still had business to take care of with Roulette. The label, and Levy in particular, had been under investigation since the start of 1960 over payola charges; that is, the long-accepted practice of record companies paying DJs to play specific records. The scandal had publicly ruined Alan Freed's reputation, but Levy seemed nonplussed, as he had the support of his unnamed partners to fall back on. But he must have been distracted by something when Hawkins told him he wanted to record an album of Hank Williams songs. The sessions took place in October 1960 in Nashville, with Helm the only Hawks regular present among seasoned country veterans like Owen Bradley. "Cold Cold Heart" was a minor hit in Canada, but the album's disappointing reception made it clear that, much like the folk world, the country music world wanted nothing to do with Ronnie Hawkins, either.

As 1961 unfolded, The Hawks' lineup remained in flux, with Helm and Robertson the only constants. Now fully committed to staying in Canada, Hawkins determined to build a stable band to keep a steady stream of money flowing.

Richard Clare Danko was born on December 29, 1943 (most sources incorrectly cite 1942 as his year of birth), in the town of Green's Corner, near Simcoe, Ontario. He was the third of four sons fathered by Maurice Danko, who built his farm in Simcoe after leaving the one settled by his father, a Ukrainian immigrant, in Manitoba. The Danko home did not have electricity until Rick turned ten, forcing the tight-knit family to entertain themselves with whatever means were at hand. Rick became adept at guitar and fiddle, and developed a unique singing style through his attempts at harmonizing with the country songs that commonly filled the house. By fourteen, he and his brothers, Maurice Jr., Dennis, and Terry, were putting on country and western shows locally under various names, until Rick, feeling the need to strike out on his own, quit school and took a job as an apprentice butcher.

Danko had his revelatory moment when he saw The Hawks for the first time, at the Simcoe Arena in late 1960. When the band returned the following May, Danko ensured that his own group had the opening slot. A few nights later, when they shared the bill at Pop Ivy's in Port Dover, Hawkins made Danko an offer on the spot to play rhythm guitar, with the intent of taking up the bass upon newlywed Rebel Paine's impending departure. Local historian John Cardiff recalls: "Rick worked in the Simcoe Meat Market next to my father's drug store, Cardiff

Pharmacy. He and his co-workers were always in there talking to girls and browsing the magazine rack, or any other excuse that allowed them to stretch their legs when business was slow. One day, just at store closing, Rick asked Dad if they could talk. Rick said he had a chance to join a rock and roll band, and wanted to bounce the idea off Dad. To this day I suspect what Rick really wanted was a chance to practice telling his folks that farming and butchering weren't for him."

By midsummer, Danko had become proficient on bass, mostly through studying Stan Szelest's left hand on the piano, and was able to take over for Paine. Szelest's days as a Hawk were numbered, as well, since he had been splitting his time with the Bill Black Combo (led by Elvis Presley's former bassist). This time, however, Hawkins already had someone waiting in the wings. Richard George Manuel was born on April 3, 1944, in Stratford, Ontario, the hub of a large farming community east of London, and, appropriately, home to the largest Shakespeare festival in Canada. His parents, James Edwin and Gladys (née Haviland) Manuel had three other sons, Jim, Allan, and Donald, all of whom faithfully attended Ontario Street Baptist Church each Sunday. Richard sang in the choir before starting piano lessons at age nine, but was soon converted to rhythm and blues through the radio.

He also discovered that a friend from church, David Priest, was a more advanced pianist, and after each service Manuel would pry new techniques out of Priest until he could sufficiently play by ear. At fourteen, Manuel was working on songs with a guitar-playing friend, John Till, and a year later they had formed The Revols (short for Revolutions), with bassist Ken Kalmusky, singer Doug Rhodes, and drummer Jim Winkler. Priest vividly recalls the moment he knew he had nothing more to show Manuel: "One time I was over at the Manuels' when Richard was rehearsing in their living room with a group he'd put together. The band was doing all the current chart tunes, practicing for school dances all over the place, as well as a ton of other gigs. This particular time, the tune they were working on was 'In The Still of the Night' by The Five Satins and Richard's piano part was exactly the way it was on the record. Even though he had mastered a whole lot of licks and phrases, which he *could* have played, he instead kept his part true to the original."

The Revols were a hometown sensation, and aimed to take the next step by sharing bills with The Hawks. They got their first chance at Pop Ivy's in the summer of 1960, and Hawkins immediately noticed the passion of the jittery piano player with the dark, French-Canadian features, whose friends mercilessly called him "Beak," due to his disproportionate nose. Their paths would cross again the following spring, when The Revols headlined over The Hawks before a hometown crowd at the Stratford Coliseum. That night, it was Manuel's solo turn on "Georgia on My Mind," a still-current hit by Ray Charles, that made Hawkins see dollar signs. He decided not to steal Manuel for his own band, but instead offered to become The Revols' manager, to which they readily agreed. His first move was to send them to play one of his clubs in Fayetteville, the Rockwood, that summer for "seasoning." Upon arrival, the band of sixteen-year-olds had to drive one of Hawkins' Cadillacs to Memphis to straighten out their immigration papers. They spent a day in jail until they could prove the car wasn't stolen. Despite this traumatic introduction to the United States, The Revols thrived in their new surroundings, with Manuel taking advantage of the wide range of temptations, willing young females in particular, which earned him a new nickname, "The Gobbler." But it wasn't long after their triumphant return home that Hawkins reluctantly had to call on Manuel, when Stan Szelest was fired for breaking Hawkins's unwritten rule: he got married. With the rest of The Revols' blessings, Manuel met The Hawks in Tulsa, and spent most of the fall of 1961 playing around the South.

It was there that rock and roll still breathed in America in the early sixties, where black R & B stars were heroes to hard-partying white college kids. As Robertson told music critic and author Greil Marcus, "[These were] places where people got wild, got seriously fucked up. It seemed like whenever we got to one of those places, Hank Ballard And The Midnighters had just left. We had to follow them, and they had a routine where for an extra thousand dollars they'd play naked. Maybe with little gold jockstraps. We had to follow that."

Just prior to recruiting Manuel for the fall tour, in mid-September, the band recorded three sessions in New York that yielded Hawkins' next single, "Come Love" b/w "I Feel Good." The sound was a calculated return to rock and roll, largely due to the confidence Hawkins now had in Robertson's abilities. Other tracks they laid down were generally highlights of the live show, from Carl Perkins' "Matchbox" to Hank Ballard's "Sexy Ways." Hawkins even allowed Helm to take over lead vocals on tough, prowling takes of Bobby Blue Bland's "Further On Up The Road" and Muddy Waters' "She's Nineteen Years Old," where Robertson's fire can first be truly heard. Conversely, a third Helm vocal, on a song called "What a Party," which he wrote during the sessions with Henry Glover, appeared deigned to be a pop single, with clever lyrics describing a gathering catered by a who's who of R & B, including Sam the Cook(e) and Jerry the Butler. However, the tune was discarded and caused much confusion for decades to come when Hawkins' final Roulette album, 1964's hastily assembled *Mojo Man*, included "She's Nineteen Years Old" mislabelled as "What a Party."

Although The Hawks' piano seat had stabilized with Manuel's arrival, Hawkins still kept an invitation open to a kid from London whom Helm and Robertson had said was the best all-around musician they'd ever seen. Eric Garth Hudson was the only child of Fred James Hudson and Olive Louella (née Pentland), born on August 2, 1937, in Windsor, Ontario. By the time Garth was five, they had moved east to London — home of big band leader Guy Lombardo — when Fred (a First World War pilot) became a government farm inspector. Olive came from a musical background, and Fred played a little saxophone, so they had few qualms about putting Garth in piano lessons at an early age. At the same time, he was performing country songs on the accordion, and sometimes played hymns on the organ at his church or his uncle's funeral parlour. A love of jazz was stoked at the age of thirteen by Jack Wingate, who ran the Heintzman Piano Store, which also doubled as a record shop, before Hudson was sent to Toronto for a full classical music education. That was all but ignored by age sixteen, when he discovered rhythm and blues via Alan Freed's *Moondog Matinee*, broadcast from Cleveland.

In 1956, Hudson, singer Paul Hutchins, and some other friends from London formed The Silhouettes, and found steady work in Windsor and Detroit, where they became known as Paul London And The Capers (later Kapers, after another band called The Capers appeared). For some time, they bounced back and forth across the border, playing gigs with the likes of Bill Haley and Johnny Cash. "We played a couple of months before the border patrol told us to go home," Hudson says. "They told us we had to get permanent work visas, which at the time they mostly gave to hockey players and wrestlers. We told the [musician's] union in Windsor about this — they liked us and wanted to help us out — and they sent a letter to the Detroit union saying that if we weren't allowed to play, then they wouldn't allow any American acts to come into Canada."

Kudlats concurs that the immigration process at the time greatly hampered most Canadian bands' chances south of the border. "We could get an American band to come here and get them immigration papers in a half an hour, but it would take weeks and weeks to get the reverse," he says. "I used to go through so much red tape that sometimes it wasn't worth the effort. We had to send all the write-ups about the band and all the publicity just to prove that they were star quality. There might be more Canadian stars today if we would have had more opportunities to go to the States, because there certainly was a lot of talent."

Although Chuck Berry's pianist, Johnnie Johnson, was Hudson's seminal influence, he spent more time playing saxophone in The Capers. That is, until one night in Detroit when he saw a band with a guy who played an organ unlike any he'd ever heard before. The organ was a Lowery, as opposed to the more common Hammond, and Hudson determined that it would be his sound, too, once he could afford it. Part of this plan hinged on putting out a record, and in 1960 (with their name spelled with a "C") the group recorded "Rosie Lee" b/w "Real Gone Lover" for a small Toronto label called Fascination. The following year (now with a "K"), they were in Chicago's Chess studio recording "Sugar Baby" b/w "Big Bad Twist" for Detroit label Checkmate. That single generated some interest in the U.S., but not enough to get the band out of Canada. The Kapers were playing in London in the summer of 1961 when Helm and Robertson caught them during a rare night away from Hawkins. The pair approached Hudson afterward, and said there would be a place for him in the Hawks, but Hudson politely declined. It wasn't until the end of 1961, when Hudson realized the financial benefits of playing with Hawkins, that he consented to join. He had two conditions, however: first, Hawkins had to get him a Lowery organ, and second, he needed to be paid an extra ten dollars a week for "music lessons," in order to placate his parents' concerns over his throwing away a classical education in favour of rock and roll.

The Hawks lineup of Helm, Robertson, Manuel, Danko, and Hudson (along with saxophonist Jerry Penfound) made its recording debut in New York on February 2, 1962, laying down "Mojo Man" and "Arkansas" with famed young producers and songwriters Jerry Leiber and Mike Stoller. Yet, for unknown reasons, Roulette chose not to release these tracks as a single immediately. The band continued to grind it out on their now well-established circuit between Ontario and Texas, while in the midst of this Hawkins broke one of the most stringent rules he himself imposed on his band: he got married, to a Toronto girl named Wanda Nagurski. Helm followed in short order, marrying Connie Orr, largely so he could become a landed Canadian immigrant and avoid doing military service back home. The lifestyle change was immediately palpable in Hawkins' attitude; there would be no more recording sessions that year, and often, for extended residencies, he would only show up on weekends, forcing the band to do several nights on their own. At these times, Helm handled the rockers and Manuel sang the soul ballads. As a result, the new band, whose members were all roughly the same age and shared similar backgrounds, quickly gelled, just as Hawkins hoped they would. The problem was, after only a year, he could no longer control them.

Roulette still had Hawkins under contract until 1964, and was determined to squeeze whatever it could out of him. Sensing a resurging interest in R & B, someone at the label suggested that Hawkins take another crack at Bo Diddley, whose songs were still the backbone of the Hawks' set. In January 1963, with Henry Glover producing, the band recorded "Bo Diddley" and "Who Do You Love," a Diddley hit from 1956. This sum total of five minutes of music laid the foundation for immortality. Every barrier that had defined popular music to that point, in terms of race, age, and nationality, was made shockingly irrelevant by the sheer force the band used to rip through the songs. It was Hawkins who had to hang on for dear life in the face of Robertson's paint-peeling solos. And, to his credit, Hawkins picked up the gauntlet that his band threw down, delivering a snarling performance that few white rockers could match, before or since. When the dust settled, they weren't sure it would be a hit, but they knew they had recorded something of significance.

"Bo Diddley" b/w "Who Do You Love" was released in March 1963, but aside from a handful of Great Lakes border towns like Ann Arbor, Michigan, where it was heard by a young James Osterberg (later Iggy Pop), no one took much notice. The single didn't even crack *Billboard*'s Top 100. Roulette still clamoured for more album material, though, so on May 7 the band made one last trip to New York to record three songs: "Bossman," "High Blood Pressure," and "There's a Screw Loose," with Hudson's organ playing the dominant musical role this time. Despite the last song being a tailor-made frat house anthem, there seemed to be a sense of finality at this session, and both Hawkins and the others felt it. During the trip, Hawkins even hired another Roulette artist, Bruce Bruno, to front the Hawks so that Hawkins only had to do the closing set each night. The chasm between the band and its employer was widening by the day. More and more, Hawkins' fines over girlfriends, gambling, and smoking pot came off as petty and insulting. As 1963 came to a close, the decision to leave stared them in the face when Danko was nearly fired for bringing a girlfriend to a Toronto gig. With no contracts binding them, Helm told Hawkins that they were prepared to stick together and go out on their own. It would take several years for either side to show any signs of remorse.

"Geez, was he crude. It was almost embarrassing to me," Robertson later said of Hawkins, adding that the split was "a very emotional thing, because he was like a father figure, and we were all still kids. It was painful to him, and to us, but we had grown musically, to a point where the stuff that we produced was much more fun to do, and more satisfying. Doing his songs became more like a novelty. We just surpassed that musically, and his evolution just stopped. Unfortunately, Ronnie felt everyone was better than him."

As their first act of independence, at the start of 1964, the group approached Harold Kudlats to represent them. Having recently been fired by Hawkins, Kudlats was more than happy to comply, and went about booking a full year's itinerary, taking in the circuit the band was now accustomed to: southern Ontario, Quebec, New York, New Jersey, Oklahoma, Arkansas, and Texas. "One morning I came into my office at about nine o'clock, and there was Hawkins's group waiting for me," Kudlats says. "They told me that they'd decided to leave Ronnie, and asked if I would book them. At that time, I would say that Hawkins was about the highest paid lounge act in Canada, so when they asked me to book them I said, 'Geez, I can't get that kind of money without a front man.' Then they told me what they were making with Hawkins, and I said, well, we can take care of that very easily."

Initially billed as The Levon Helm Sextet, retaining Bruce Bruno on vocals, they became Levon & The Hawks following Bruno's departure in May. Although their show had not been radically altered, they revelled in the freedom to play predominantly blues-based material without the fear of being chastised by Hawkins. Additionally, Manuel never failed to choke patrons up with his renditions of songs like, "You Don't Know Me," the Cindy Walker classic that Ray Charles had included on his landmark 1962 album, *Modern Sounds in Country and Western Music.* The British Invasion had arrived, but The Hawks were impervious, as their own exploration of America's complex musical back roads was just beginning. "We had to fight for our musical taste," Robertson reflected much later. "We were combining all of the flavours that we had gathered over the course of our musical journey. We believed we were doing a good duty by turning people on to certain music, because that always seemed to be an exciting thing if someone did it for you."

Those who shared this philosophy naturally gravitated toward them. John Hammond Jr., the blues-singing son of esteemed Columbia Records A & R man John Hammond Sr., befriended them during one of his frequent visits to Toronto to play folk clubs like the Purple Onion. When The Hawks hit their usual New York stop, the Peppermint Lounge, birthplace of "The Twist," in June, Hammond had his sights set on making his first album with a band, and wrangled Helm, Robertson, and Hudson into the studio while he had the chance. Guitarist Mike Bloomfield, of the Paul Butterfield Blues Band, who had also recently met The Hawks in Chicago, was booked for the session, but upon seeing Robertson there, quietly packed up his Telecaster and planted himself at the piano. Released the following year, *So Many Roads* suffered, in part, from not having the full Hawks lineup on board (Hammond's take on "Who Do You Love" could not hold a candle to Hawkins'), but both Robertson and Hudson made a genuine effort to break out of the standard urban blues clichés, something that Hammond himself never could achieve.

With this experience under their belts, The Hawks returned to Canada for gigs throughout the summer, with an eye to making their own record. An opportunity came that fall in the person of Toronto DJ Duff Roman, whose first recording venture with singer David Clayton-Thomas (later of Blood, Sweat

& Tears) scored a surprise hit with a cover of John Lee Hooker's "Boom Boom." He offered to do the same for The Hawks, and got them into Toronto's Hallmark Studios, where they cut James Brown's "Please Please Please," an equally simple R & B number called "Bacon Fat," credited to Robertson/Hudson, and Robertson's long-time guitar showpiece, "Robbie's Blues," which also featured one of Jerry Penfound's last appearances with the group, on flute, of all things. However, the tapes wound up in a box in Roman's house, since The Hawks' hectic schedule would not allow them to negotiate a release.

There were no such problems when they found out that Henry Glover had just started his own label, Ware Records, and offered to cut a single with the provision that The Hawks arrive with material that was not so heavily blues-based. Robertson accepted the challenge, writing "Uh Uh Uh" and "Leave Me Alone" just prior to the March 1965 session in New York. Both songs possessed a swagger more akin to The Rolling Stones, although far more tough-minded. In fact, "Leave Me Alone" was all menace, with Helm and Manuel trading threats over the course of two and a half thrilling minutes. To mark their fresh start with Glover, they promptly became The Canadian Squires, a name that lasted only as long as it took them to realize that U.S. radio wasn't interested in anything that proclaimed an allegiance to Canada.

In April, The Hawks were back in the South, playing a high school prom in Helena, Arkansas. They heard that Sonny Boy Williamson was in town, and decided it would not be inappropriate to offer their services to one of their idols. Williamson had, in fact, just recently returned from a protracted stay in England, where, on December 8 and 9, 1963, he had recorded a live album at London's Crawdaddy Club, backed by house band The Yardbirds. Although Eric Clapton was the band's lead guitarist, Williamson had little tolerance for the white English kids, who nevertheless worshipped him. Still, when Helm humbly approached Williamson, who was easily spotted in his British-tailored suit and bowler hat, he conceded to spend the day jamming with The Hawks at their motel over a bottle of whisky.

Perhaps Williamson instinctively knew that these boys were different from the British kids; the music was flowing, and by late afternoon they made plans to do it for real in the coming months. First, though, The Hawks had to head up to New Jersey for a two-month run at Tony Mart's, in Somers Point. Halfway through, on May 25, they got word that Williamson had died, taking with him their best shot at true blues authenticity.

Things didn't get much better on their way back to Toronto in July, even though they remained the kings of Yonge Street, with Robertson, especially, inspiring legions of young would-be Toronto guitar heroes in much the same way Clapton was doing in Britain. As Helm sped to the airport, where one of their additional vehicles was parked, the police pulled him over and subsequently charged members of the band with marijuana possession.

In the ancient British folk song "Gallis Pole," or "Gallows Pole," as it became commonly known in the twentieth century, a condemned man attempts to bribe his executioner in every way he can conceive of in order to save himself. He finally succeeds after offering the charms of his beloved. Unbeknownst to The Hawks, a young folk singer named Bob Dylan had produced his own variant of the song, called "Seven Curses," in which a girl spends the night with a judge in order to save her father from prison. If this meant that there was some kind of unspoken precedent for such actions, The Hawks were willing to try it if it meant freedom to pursue their livelihood south of the border.

Given The Hawks' status in Toronto, there was no shortage of girls there who eagerly followed their movements. One particularly zealous fan was Cathy Evelyn Smith. Born on April 25, 1947, and adopted by a family from Burlington, Ontario, Smith was lured into rock and roll's underbelly after sneaking into a Hamilton bar called the Grange one night to see the band shortly after it had split from Hawkins. An infatuation with Helm made her a constant presence after that, in spite of the fact that he never failed to pointedly dedicate their version of Larry Williams's "Short Fat Fannie" to her whenever he spotted her in the audience. As the band's trial loomed, Smith — who was by then pregnant with Helm's child — was persuaded to rendezvous with the arresting officer at Toronto's Westpoint Motel. "Then she told him she was fourteen years old," Danko later confessed. "He was the chief witness against us, but this was some *weird shit* for him, and he disappeared, we never saw him again. In the end everyone else got off, and I received a year's suspended sentence on probation."

Kudlats recalls the story a bit differently. "Jack Fisher, who owned the Beverly Hills Hotel and the Concord Tavern, and myself put up $25,000 bail for them. They were booked so solid that we couldn't afford to have them sitting in jail. Jack and all his connections were able to keep getting postponements, and in the end the case was dropped."

As an interesting aside, Kudlats adds, "Years before, sometime around 1956, I started working with a guy named Saul Holiff, from London, Ontario. So a few months after The Hawks were arrested for marijuana, I get a call from Laredo, Texas, and it's Saul Holiff asking me how I got the band off that charge. I said, 'What the hell are you calling me from Texas asking about that for?' He said, 'I'm now managing Johnny Cash and he just got busted at the border, and I want to know if there's any way we can get him out.'"*

With their criminal records cleared, The Hawks found much-needed refuge back at Tony Mart's, on the Jersey Shore, in August. The surroundings also motivated Robertson to start writing more. The song of the moment was Bob Dylan's "Like a Rolling Stone," which began its rapid climb up the charts the day before his controversial "electric" debut at the Newport Folk Festival on July 25, backed by Mike Bloomfield on guitar, as well as other members of the Butterfield band. It was the first pop song that Robertson had heard in a long time that moved him, albeit in a way he didn't understand, and as a result his ideas almost immediately became more narrative. "(I Want to Be) The Rainmaker" was a clumsy first attempt, but he managed to finish

---

*Cash ultimately received a thirty-day suspended sentence and a one-thousand-dollar fine for attempting to smuggle pills from Juarez, Mexico.

"The Stones I Throw (Will Free All Men)," a pseudo-gospel melody unlike anything else the band performed. However, with an offer on the table from New York R & B mogul Eddie Heller to finance a session, "The Stones I Throw" seemed as good an option as any for a single, considering the rising popularity of folk-rock. But during the second week of August, as those plans were being put into motion, Helm received an unexpected call.

Dylan had not been happy with the musicians he had played with at Newport. The Butterfield rhythm section, in particular, could not grasp the swing that Dylan had worked so hard to achieve in the studio. Instead, they turned "Like a Rolling Stone" into "Twist and Shout." With two more important concerts coming up, on August 28, 1965, at New York's Forest Hills tennis stadium, and September 3, at the Hollywood Bowl, Dylan could not afford to have his new sound fall flat again, especially now that media attention was mounting. Making matters worse, the catalyst for that new sound, Mike Bloomfield, turned down the shows. Finding a new guitarist became the top priority, and Dylan turned to his friend John Hammond Jr., who reminded him of the guy he got to play on *So Many Roads*.

A crucial factor was also Mary Martin, a Toronto native who had been drawn to Greenwich Village in 1963. "I had a friend living in New York named Joan Wilson, who was John Court's secretary," she explains. "John Court was an associate of [Dylan's manager] Albert Grossman, who managed Ian & Sylvia to begin with. Joan suggested that I interview for the receptionist job, so I did. I ended up answering the phone — 'Plaza-28715.' After I did my initial stint, I went back to Toronto because John Court said I'd never amount to anything unless I learned secretarial skills. So I enrolled at Shaw's business school and learned how to type. After classes, I ended up spending a lot of time at the Friar's [Tavern] with a girlfriend, hanging out with The Hawks. We talked a lot about Bob Dylan, and they finally did a cover song during one of their sets — their many sets — that they said was a 'Bob *Die*-lan' song.

"When I went back to New York, I became Albert's assistant secretary, and by that time I firmly believed The Hawks were about as good as it got. I started yammering about this band from Toronto and how good they were, so one day I was hauled into a meeting when Bob was there, during which I basically told him to go to Toronto to hear them for himself. I had heard them play one of his songs, so I knew the combination could work. But he also had heard about them through John Hammond Jr., who himself spent a fair amount of time in Toronto. Dylan probably checked with John to see what he thought, and that is important to me because I've often been given the credit for putting The Hawks and Dylan together, but I really feel, in retrospect, that John Hammond was truly integral to all of that. Dylan will always say it was me, but I was just the chick."

After the phone call to Helm in New Jersey, Grossman scout Danny Wiener was dispatched to Tony Mart's, and within days Robertson was summoned to New York to rehearse with the assortment of musicians Dylan had assembled. "I went up there cold turkey and met with him," Robertson says. "He was a jittery little devil, smoking cigarettes with each hand and going on about stuff, and I wasn't sure why I was there. Then we went somewhere where there were a couple of guitars and all the talking stopped. At first he didn't play his songs, but some older songs that I didn't know, and something started to happen. It became so natural. Then he sang a couple of his songs, and we actually did those even better. So he said to me, 'That's terrific, let's do this thing,' and I said, 'What thing?' Then he explained that he wanted to go out and play his songs 'electric,' whatever that meant, and I just said, 'Okay, sure.'"

Trusted organist Al Kooper was confirmed for the lineup, along with top session bassist Harvey Brooks. Who would occupy the drum chair was still to be decided, and when Robertson got a moment alone with Dylan, he lobbied hard on Helm's behalf. With no further time to waste, Dylan agreed, and, for the next week and a half, the quintet ran endlessly over an eight-song set that opened with "Tombstone Blues" and closed with "Like a Rolling Stone."

By all accounts, the less-thoroughly documented Forest Hills show was even more of a circus than Newport. Dylan opened with a solo acoustic set before bringing the band on — a pattern that would be fixed for the next nine months — at which point the divided crowd of folkies and young rockers rose up. As at Newport, boos and insults filled the air after each song, and some even threw fruit. Kids stormed the stage, and one knocked Kooper off his seat. "Just keep playing, no matter how weird it gets," Dylan reassured the musicians. When they got to "Like a Rolling Stone," the kids were singing along, much to the band's relief and dismay, and they were able to escape unscathed. The band fared much better in L.A., where a more sophisticated crowd greeted them. With a demanding schedule coming on the heels of *Highway 61 Revisited*, released the week in between the concerts, the Hollywood Bowl at least proved to Dylan that it was possible to pull off his new sound live.

Before heading back to Toronto to assess their situation, The Hawks made a quick stop in New York to record "The Stones I Throw" with Eddie Heller, along with two other songs, the Motown-ish "He Don't Love You (And He'll Break Your Heart)" featuring a great, gutsy vocal from Manuel, and the ragged "Go Go Liza Jane," a variation on the bluegrass standard "Little Liza Jane." Heller made a deal with Atlantic Records to release "The Stones I Throw" b/w "He Don't Love You" on its Atco subsidiary, but once again The Hawks were too occupied to do much about it by the time the record came out later in the fall.

Dylan was set to take Robertson and Helm on tour, but while in New York, Helm laid down the law with Albert Grossman. In order to get them, Dylan would have to agree to take the whole band. Dylan heard The Hawks for the first time the following week, on September 15, in Toronto at the Friar's Tavern (now a Hard Rock Café), and, upon being convinced, rehearsed with them at the club after hours for the next several nights, a routine the band had already been accustomed to with Hawkins. "While this was going on, Bob had his mother come up to visit him. I thought that was a nice thing," Danko said. "Mrs. Zimmerman wanted to know where we had our suits tailored, and eventually we took Bob over to see Lou Myles, who made him that brown houndstooth suit with the pegged waist that was photographed a lot."

On September 23, The Hawks were flown to Austin, Texas, in the Lockheed Lodestar that had been rented for the tour. There was little trouble with the audience that first night, and the next night in Dallas was equally uneventful, despite the paranoia that still lingered in the city even two years after the Kennedy assassination. Then it was a warm homecoming back in New York, at Carnegie Hall on October 1, where the fans from Forest Hills knew what to expect. After two more shows, an extended break prompted Dylan to get the band into the studio on October 5, primarily to re-record "Can You Please Crawl out Your Window," a song that had been left off of *Highway 61 Revisited*, which he now wanted to release as a single. To say that this take captured their initial joy at discovering each other would be an understatement. That accomplished, there was time to mess around with more typical Hawks-esque rock, and on "I Wanna Be Your Lover," along with the sketchier "I Don't Want to Be Your Partner," Dylan sounded literally swept away by the groove. A further instrumental, arbitrarily entitled "Number One," was essentially a blueprint for the sonic heights they would reach by the end of the tour. "At the start, we didn't think any of it sounded very good," Robertson says. "It seemed very easy to satisfy Bob, but the rest of us were a little confused by that. Eventually, we just agreed that this would be a good experiment in terror, so let's just see where it goes."

The tour resumed in Worcester, Massachusetts, on October 22, followed by a show in Detroit, then back to New England for shows in Hartford and Boston to round out the month. By then, the booing was back. What at first seemed amusing was now beginning to agitate the musicians, who were used to a party every night. After another break, they played Cleveland on November 12, before the highly anticipated two-night stand at Toronto's Massey Hall on November 14–15. But the celebration was killed after the *Toronto Star* delivered the lowest possible blow, chastising Dylan for playing with a "third-rate Yonge Street band." In between shows, however, Dylan gave the paper one of his most straightforward interviews of the era regarding his new sound. "It's easy for people to classify it as rock and roll, to put it down," he said. "Rock and roll is a straight twelve-bar blues progression. My new songs aren't. I used to play rock and roll a long time ago, before I even started playing old-fashioned folk, ten years ago, when I was a kid, for God's sake. Nowadays, the music industry is totally different. You know who the rock and roll singers were ten years ago — Fabian, Ricky Nelson, Bobby Rydell? Rock and roll singers now are a different kind of people; they make the old people look sick."

When asked what he made of the booing, Dylan responded, "If they like it or don't like it, that's their business. You can't tell people what to do at a concert. Anyway, paying out four dollars for a ticket to come and boo — is anyone groovy gonna do that, anyway? Four years ago, I used to sing in Village coffee houses, fifty people and they were packed, fire inspectors all over the place, you know? Then I *knew* my real fans. Now, these concerts, I don't know them, I don't know why they're there. I don't know what they think about when they go away."

The tour struggled on to Columbus, Ohio, then to a half-capacity show in Syracuse, where the local musicians' union caused a stir when it demanded a minimum of fifteen players on stage. The next day, November 22, Dylan secretly married Sara Lowndes, a friend of Albert Grossman's wife Sally, in a judge's chamber on Long Island. The couple got to spend a few days together before shows at Chicago's Arie Crown Theatre on November 26 and 27. The last show of the east coast leg was in Washington, D.C., on November 28, and upon making it back to their New York hotel, Helm told Robertson he'd had enough. Not wishing to belabour the point, he set off for Arkansas the next morning without any further goodbyes. "Levon just didn't feel comfortable not being the leader anymore," was the succinct view of road manager Bill Avis.

The west coast leg of the tour was due to begin on December 3, in Berkeley, California, and there was a recording session booked at Sunset Sound in L.A. on November 30. Dylan was forced to call his frequent studio drummer, Bobby Gregg, to replace Helm, and the others had no choice but to adjust. The song Dylan wanted to record was "Seems Like a Freeze-Out," a surreal epic that had obvious potential to be the centrepiece of his next album. However, the two takes captured on tape, although vastly different from each other, were both plodding and sombre, as Gregg's metronomic meter did little to inspire the other players. It wouldn't be until March, when Dylan took another stab at the song in Nashville, that it would be reborn as "Visions of Johanna."

Despite this minor failure, the Berkeley shows went well, thanks to the Bay Area artistic scene's support. It was a scene that Robertson was easily drawn into, given his proximity to Dylan. He even participated in a photo shoot outside City Lights bookstore in San Francisco with poets Allen Ginsberg and Michael McClure that Dylan briefly considered for his next album cover. Without Helm around, Robertson naturally assumed a leadership role within the band, and became generally less inhibited as the tour meandered up and down the California coast. All the while, he marvelled at the media frenzy Dylan attracted, and the apathetic attitude he used to fend it off. They all wanted a piece of him, yet Dylan proved a master at keeping everyone and everything at bay, simply by speaking the truth as he saw it. By default, that mystique was rubbing off on Robertson more than it was on the other band members.

After a break for the holidays, the band regrouped in New York on January 21 for a session at Columbia Studios, partially to break in a new drummer, Buffalo native Sandy Konikoff — whose recommendation came as a result of his recent stint with Hawkins — but also to work out "She's Your Lover Now." The song was another rambling diatribe in the spirit of "Like a Rolling Stone." But after trying it solo on piano, and at least one attempt with the band that nearly caught fire, Dylan lost the thread and abandoned it. More successful was the rollicking, but lyrically impenetrable "Tell Me Mama," which Dylan earmarked as the electric set's new opening number, a spot it would hold until the end of the tour. Up until then, there would be few opportunities to slow down.★

They were back on the road on February 5, driving up to White Plains, New York, then over to Rochester and down to Pittsburgh. Next they flew south, taking in Memphis, Richmond, and Norfolk, before shifting their home base to Nashville. There in the studio, beginning on February 14, Dylan was finally able to conjure the thin, wild mercury sound of *Blonde on Blonde* out of an amalgamation of country and rock musicians. Of the latter, Robertson made some of the most significant contributions, most audibly on "Leopard-Skin Pill-Box Hat" and "Obviously Five Believers," the album's two hardest rocking tracks. On February 19, the troupe played the Ottawa Auditorium, and kept their winter coats on the entire time. The next night in Montreal was a little warmer, but the heater on the Lockheed broke down, causing them to freeze on their way back to Nashville. There were shows in Philadelphia on February 24–25, then West Hampstead, Long Island, before a jaunt to Miami on March 3 brought some much-needed sun.

Blonde on Blonde was finished a week later, but there were still three more shows to go, in St. Louis, Lincoln, and Denver, before they could catch their breath. On March 14, Robertson and the rest of Dylan's inner circle went to L.A., while the band took a holiday in Taos, New Mexico. Danko spent most of the week off taking peyote, having been introduced to hallucinogens shortly after meeting Dylan. Manuel had tried them, too, but mainly consumed alcohol to excess, as he had since his early teenage years.

Konikoff's stint ended following the last trio of shows in Seattle, Tacoma, and Vancouver, on March 25, and he was thankful to escape the dark, carnival-like atmosphere. Anticipating this departure, Dylan had picked up Mickey Jones, a gregarious

★That month, The Hawks were also called to play on The Barbarians' "Moulty," the inspirational story of their hook-handed drummer, Victor Moulton, who sang the track, which later became a perennial garage rock favourite. Moulton confirmed the long-rumoured session in a 1998 interview with *Discoveries* magazine, although there's nothing distinctively Hawk-ish about the music, apart from the song's "Rolling Stone"-esque chorus.

Texan who was then drumming for Johnny Rivers at the Whisky A Go Go on L.A.'s Sunset Strip. Later, he'd join Kenny Rogers' band, First Edition, before embarking on a successful career as a bit-part actor. Jones's fresh attitude was welcome, as was his hard-driving style. "[Bob] paid me for two years, so that was kinda cool," Jones says. "I found out later on that I got a better deal than everybody else, because he was paying all my expenses — hotels, everything. And I think my meals, too. All the other guys were paying for their own hotels."

Jones made his debut at the April 9 gig in Honolulu, a warm-up for the seven-date Australian tour to come. The group's arrival in Sydney, on April 12, prompted more confusion than controversy, as the national media that was there to greet them seemed more clueless than their U.S. counterparts when it came to Dylan's recent transformation. Perhaps deliberately, the April 13 Sydney Stadium concert ended not with "Rolling Stone," but with the even more scathing "Positively 4th Street."

Over the next two weeks, they bounced around the continent by plane, with Dylan playing his typical cat-and-mouse games with the press. Question: "What do you think of the Vietnam War?" Answer: "Nothing. It's Australia's war." Question: "How much money have you made out of your songs?" Answer: "Seventy-five billion dollars."

A three-day break followed the final Australian concert, on April 23 at Perth's Capitol Theatre, before the long flight to Stockholm, where they were booked to play on April 29. The group arrived singed around the edges due to a steady diet of uppers and downers, all except Hudson, who, due to his mild narcolepsy, was the only one to get any sleep during the flight. When Jones later questioned Hudson about why he slept so often, Hudson replied in his deadpan manner: "Don't you know about dreams?"

In Scandinavia, the touring party expanded with the arrival of filmmaker D.A. Pennebaker, who had documented Dylan's 1965 solo tour of Britain in *Don't Look Back*. His intent was to use the same technique, although Dylan ended up taking control of the footage for use in a television special that had been commissioned by ABC. Still, the camera's constant presence added a new dimension to the insanity, and Dylan encouraged the band to participate whenever possible. During the next stop, in Copenhagen on May 1, Manuel accompanied Dylan on a visit to Kronborg Castle, and afterward (with the camera rolling) they confronted a young couple on a park bench. Dylan urged his companion to proposition the surprised Dane's girlfriend, and, after sheepishly rummaging through his pockets, all Manuel could say was, "Would you take Australian money?"

From there, they made the long-awaited trip to London, checking into the Mayfair Hotel on May 2, where Paul McCartney, Keith Richards, and Brian Jones, among many more fans, were waiting. The next day brought a press conference at the hotel, and later Robertson accompanied Dylan to hear John Lee Hooker play at Blaises. "They had to carry [Dylan] in," Keith Richards described. "I went over to him, and I was pretty frightened." After a day of recovery, the first gig took place May 5, in Dublin, where the crowd erupted in hostility during the electric set. The scene was repeated the next night in Belfast, by which point Dylan's response was to make the band focus its energy on him. "It's true, sometimes Bob would hardly face the audience in the electric set," Jones said. "The audience was only there so we could get paid to do what we loved to do. We were all in a zone."

After the Bristol concert on May 10, they played Cardiff, where Johnny Cash also happened to be. Pennebaker caught Dylan and Cash backstage, caterwauling their way through Hank Williams' "I'm So Lonesome I Could Cry." The scene was a powerful portrait of American song, but also a near-tragic one, given how strung out each of them was. Yet somehow both Dylan and the band were just beginning to hit their stride on the tour, as would become evident at the next show, in Birmingham. Each of the eight electric songs had taken on an almost ritualistic aura, shown in how "I Don't Believe You" was always introduced as, "It used to go like that, now it goes like this," and how Danko always leaned into Dylan's microphone to harmonize at the end of every verse of "One Too Many

Mornings." But mostly, that aura was built upon Dylan spitting out his words in the face of unyielding derision, while simultaneously pushing the others onward like a gale-force wind. A prime example was the consistently chilling bridge of "Ballad of a Thin Man," when Dylan — temporarily taking Manuel's place at the piano — harangued, "Nobody has any respect!" and received a temporary catharsis in return.

A near-perfect recording of "Just Like Tom Thumb's Blues," in Liverpool on May 14 was immediately chosen as the B-side for the next single from *Blonde on Blonde*, "I Want You," providing the first clear glimpse of the myth that was unfolding with each concert. That myth would reach its apex three nights later, in Manchester, where the famous cry of "Judas" came as Robertson calmly strummed the opening chords of "Rolling Stone." That one word caused something to snap inside Dylan, possibly the only time it had happened the entire tour, and what it wrought was, for many, the definitive version of the song; a moment of clarity even more devastating than the original, simply because the assembled audience chose to ignore it.

Their bus headed north to Scotland the next day for shows in Glasgow and Edinburgh, but not before the band sparked more hostility unrelated to the music. "Mickey was a big collector of Nazi memorabilia," said Hudson, who most often roomed with the drummer. "We were on the bus outside the hotel in Manchester, ready to leave, when we saw Mickey come out of a shop down the street holding a huge Nazi flag. He was so happy to have found it that he unfurled it right there to show us. Of course, people started accosting him right away, and he had to run for it. We almost lost him that day."

While such antics went on among the other guys, Robertson's relationship with Dylan continued to strengthen, to the point where he was bestowed the nickname "Barnacle Man." Their musical bond was undeniable. At the hotel in Glasgow, the pair spent an afternoon working through new ideas, among them a gorgeous sketch, later given the title, "Does She Need Me," that clearly pointed toward the country-soul balladry in which both would soon immerse themselves. Following the Newcastle show on May 21, capped off with a rendition of "Rolling Stone" that was even more apocalyptic than Manchester's, the group crossed the English Channel for the Paris show on May 24, Dylan's twenty-fifth birthday. The press conference at the George V Hotel that preceded the concert was another exercise in journalistic futility, although this time the French reporters' blatant anti-Americanism touched a nerve within Dylan. When the curtain parted at L'Olympia for the electric set, a massive American flag, purportedly borrowed from the U.S. embassy, was draped behind the band, driving the crowd into a near frenzy. Pennebaker's camera captured a shaken and barely coherent Dylan back in London the next day, taking a cab ride with John Lennon. The footage abruptly stopped just as Dylan leaned forward to vomit.

The final concerts, at London's Royal Albert Hall on May 26 and 27, proved an anti-climax, with Dylan's cynicism and belligerence no longer under any constraints. To the familiar taunts, he responded, "Why don't you come up here and say that?" and, "Aw, it's the same stuff as always. Can't you hear?" Yet, for the last song of the last night, he gave in slightly, if only to pay tribute to the band that, over the course of a few short months, irrevocably changed the course of music history:

I've never done this before, but I want you to meet Robbie Robertson here, and, uh, Garth Hudson, Mickey Jones, Rick Danko, and, uh [applause swells], *and Richard!* [mumbling mixed with random chord strumming] [Dylan continues smugly] *You promised me you were gonna leave* [more strumming] — *It doesn't mean a thing, you know . . . but they, they're all poets, you understand?* [a single audience member claps] *Ah, if it comes out that way, it comes out that way, but . . .* [now drowsily] *ah, they're all poets. . . .* [rallying his strength] *This song here is dedicated to the Taj Mahal* [nervous laughter]. *And we're gonna leave after this song, and I wanna say goodbye to all of you people. You've been very warm, great people, ah, you know, I, ah —* *you've been very nice people* [genuine applause]. *I mean, here you are sitting in this great, huge place. . . .* [acidly] *And believe me, we've enjoyed every minute of being here!* [Several groans arise from those in the audience who get the joke, as the tour's most punctuated version of "Rolling Stone" commences].

CHAPTER THREE

MORNING DEW

As A TWENTY-TWO-YEAR-OLD, Robbie Robertson was willingly indoctrinated into the hipster elite through his relationship with Bob Dylan. Meanwhile, an education of a different sort was being thrust upon him over the course of the 1965–66 world tour. The presence of Dylan's manager was never far away, and, in some ways, Robertson knew he already owed Albert Grossman just as much as he owed Dylan. That fact was driven home in the way Grossman kept to himself whatever views he might have harboured about the growing chorus of boos that greeted the band in each city. It was a situation that would have led any normal manager to order Dylan to ditch The Hawks for his own good. But Grossman was not a normal manager; he was devoted to his main client's vision, and understood that the music Dylan and The Hawks were developing on a nightly basis was merely the opening salvo of the revolution that was about to change the entire American music industry.

Robertson immediately noticed other unique qualities about Grossman. Unlike other "suits" in the business, he enjoyed taking drugs as much as the musicians did. But above all, he was dogged in protecting his artists from outside forces; Grossman's greatest instinct was his ability to recognize that Dylan and his acolytes had captured the imagination of a generation bent on social change, and the more Grossman could position himself as a buffer against the Establishment, which was equally eager to profit from this phenomenon, the more power he, in turn, would have. "My strongest memories of Albert are how he liked to change the rules of the music business," Robertson says. "He was a man who prided himself on good taste. I learned a lot of worldly things from him. He was unique."

Albert Grossman was born on May 21, 1926, in Chicago, the son of Russian Jewish immigrants. After earning a degree in economics from a small local college, he took an ultimately unfulfilling job as a public housing administrator. By the mid-fifties, his favourite drinking establishment, the Off Beat Room, was booking folk singers, and Grossman grew enamoured of many of the unorthodox performers. Within two years, he and a partner opened their own folk club, the Gate of Horn, in the basement of the Rice Hotel. Realizing that many of the acts he booked did not have management, Grossman stepped into the fray with his first client, Bob Gibson, one of the young modern folk innovators. Gibson urged him to book other singers, such as Joan Baez and Judy Collins, which made the Gate of Horn the crucial hub at the centre of the nascent folk touring circuit. "There was absolutely nothing like it at the time," Gibson recalled. "One unique thing about the Gate of Horn was the fact that if the audience wasn't attentive, if they really didn't *listen* to the act, then they were asked to leave. This was unheard of." He added, "There was a phenomenal grapevine in those days, a vital folk scene that stretched from Manhattan through Chicago all the way to the west coast, where I was. Somehow, Albert heard of me when I was still in San Francisco, and wrote asking me to play the Gate of Horn. One sensed that Albert was brilliant, a man of impeccable artistic taste."

Grossman found Gibson his first record deal in 1958, about the same time he also began managing Odetta, the black female folk singer. Bringing them both to New York for shows led to Grossman forming a relationship with promoter George Wein, who saw Grossman as a key to organizing what Wein envisioned would be the folk equivalent of the popular Newport Jazz Festival, staged every summer in Rhode Island. The first

Newport Folk Festival was indeed a huge success in 1959, and Grossman was soon a permanent fixture in New York, where he quickly established a reputation as an unforgiving negotiator in a world where money was not often the top priority for artists.

On the other hand, Grossman's arrival in Manhattan, at the cusp of the sixties, couldn't have been better timed to capitalize on the full flowering of folk music in Greenwich Village. Although long a hotbed for jazz, the neighbourhood, roughly stretching from Bleecker Street northward to Washington Square Park, had also been welcoming to folk musicians since the Second World War. The Village Vanguard was home to Pete Seeger and The Weavers, and also helped launch Harry Belafonte's career. Later, clubs like the Bitter End, the Cafe Wha?, the Gaslight, and Gerde's Folk City became key destinations for any aspiring, newly arrived folk singer.

Grossman, in his inimitable way, saw unlimited potential in the odd mix of performers scuffling around the Village, and he was not shy about imposing his own musical ideas. His first breakthrough in this regard was instigating the creation of Peter, Paul & Mary — a vocal group concept he had brought with him from Chicago — and turning them into overnight stars through a deal with Warner Brothers Records, which at that time could only count the Everly Brothers as a marquee act. The ensuing pop crossover success of Peter, Paul & Mary's first three singles — "Lemon Tree," "If I Had A Hammer," and "Puff The Magic Dragon" — was nearly all the proof anyone needed that Grossman's influence could reach beyond the expectations of what a folk music manager could do, although by then he had learned how to easily circumvent the limited, anti-capitalist attitudes of most folk revivalists. "[Albert] was concerned first and foremost with *authenticity*," says Peter, Paul & Mary's Peter Yarrow. "Did the music have real substance, value, and honesty? But he was also concerned with having an impact and influence in the larger world, the heartland. It was a very rare combination. Everybody was ready for the change, but how could you reach them? How could you tap the public's ability to take in and incorporate our taste? Albert realized that it wasn't enough to just write and perform songs, that there was a multitude of ways to be successful and to *happen*, to become important, to be wanted by that public. It was necessary to couple artistic success with enormous economic success in order for that to take place."

In Mary Martin's view, Grossman "was a towering man who was kind of remote. He seemed to be wise, or aware that he walked with a real purpose. I think Albert was probably so far ahead of his time that [negotiating] basically came down to, 'if you want me, you have to give me this.' But everybody in the office really loved the people they worked with and for. What was more important to me, and to some of the girls who worked there, was that you were working with the people who made the music you really loved. Whatever the task was, that affection for the music was never very far away."

North American audiences had surely been poised for a popular folk "revival," given rock and roll's fading impact by the end of the fifties. But in Canada, with its absence of such a diverse marketplace, folk remained a commercial nonentity. Rather, it continued to exist as a common musical language inherent to the large segments of Canada's widespread population who still retained ties to their rural European origins. Folk's impassive existence in Canada also stemmed from the fact that it was not being widely stigmatized in the public eye, as it had been in the U.S. during the backlash against socialism in the thirties and forties. Canada could not boast an equivalent to Woody Guthrie; instead, Canadian labour solidarity was championed through more readily available musical sources. In fact, it was an American union organizer, the iconic Joe Hill, who wrote perhaps the first song directly based on a Canadian labour struggle. Using the melody of the Irish ballad "Where the River Shannon Flows," he wrote "Where the Fraser River Flows" in support of a 1912 strike by railroad workers building a line between Hope, B.C., and Kamloops. Later, in 1919, "Onward Christian Soldiers" became the basis for "Onward One Big Union," a theme for the Winnipeg General Strike, which resulted in landmark labour law reforms.

Furthermore, the lack of means to record such songs in

Canada, much less broadcast them, drastically limited folk's influence outside of specific regional boundaries, or beyond a handful of well-connected song collectors. In 1947, Ed McCurdy was the first folk singer to land his own program on English CBC. *Ed McCurdy Sings* was broadcast from Vancouver for two years before he moved to Toronto to host *Singing in the Wilderness*. Born on January 11, 1919, in Willow Hill, Pennsylvania, Edward Potts McCurdy developed his trademark baritone while he was a student in Oklahoma, first by singing gospel on local radio, then during stints in vaudeville and burlesque. A confirmed pacifist, McCurdy turned up in Vancouver at the end of the Second World War, where he immersed himself in whatever songs of his new home he could find, while at the same time writing his own. One of his first originals was "Last Night I Had the Strangest Dream," a song that became an early standard of the Cold War protest era once it was picked up by Pete Seeger, and, later, Simon and Garfunkel.

The song's innocent message of peace also caught on in public schools, and, in 1952, McCurdy switched to performing on radio for children. But within two years, the desire to make records finally lured him to New York City. His first LP was 1955's *Folk Songs of the Canadian Maritimes and Newfoundland*, released on Whitehall Records. Over the next few years he became extremely productive, recording for other folk labels such as Riverside and Tradition, as well as Jac Holzman's newly established Elektra. Specifically, his 1955 Elektra release, *Sin Songs (Pro/Con)*, is notable not only for being an unusual collection of British numbers that equally celebrated vice and virtue, but for a tantalizing self-observation in the liner notes: "I have led a varied and active life — and for various reasons consider myself well qualified to sing about sin." Bawdy material would become something of a specialty for McCurdy, helping to make him a leading attraction in Greenwich Village. And so it was that on January 26, 1960, he appeared on the bill for the opening night of the Fifth Peg, the first club in the village to be completely devoted to folk music, and the precursor to Gerde's Folk City. Fellow singer Phyllis Lynd said of McCurdy, "When

[he] was in his prime, he was very dynamic, warm, giving, and helpful. He was a very sweet man. He did a lot of bawdy songs, but, coming from him, they sounded very beautiful."

Throughout this period, McCurdy continued to entertain Canadian children, both on radio and television, before ultimately returning north for good when his brand of buttoned-down folk fell out of fashion in the early sixties. But he remained a staunch folk purist, and settled into life on the Canadian coffee house and festival circuit. It was a reminder of a simpler time, even though he admitted to battling alcohol and drug addiction. "I have had the good luck and courage to give the abuses up," he said. "Music would have stayed more honest and less hysterical, and rock wouldn't have happened in the way it did, if it weren't for drugs." In 1986 McCurdy became a Canadian citizen, and on March 23, 2000, his heart gave out at his home in Halifax, quite possibly while he was in the middle of a strange dream.

As McCurdy was introducing modern folk styles to radio listeners on the west coast, personal crusades aimed at popularizing folk music were occurring simultaneously in Canada's other major cities. Perhaps no one else did more to give Canadian folk a sense of identity than Edith Fowke. Born Edith Margaret Fulton on April 30, 1913, in Lumsden, Saskatchewan, she married Frank Fowke in 1938, around the time she became actively involved with the socialist Co-operative Commonwealth Federation party (CCF), the forerunner of the New Democratic Party (NDP). The couple moved to Toronto during the war, where Edith wrote and edited for several magazines. A piece on folk music for *The Canadian Forum* in 1949 was one of the first to address the issue of Canadian song collecting, and effectively marked her own entry into the field. That same year, she persuaded CBC Toronto to air its first folk program, *Folk Song Time*, for which Fowke provided most of the recordings, as well as the scripts. Her groundbreaking research into the origins of the Canadian material she aired subsequently led to the 1954 publication of *Folk Songs of Canada*, the first collection of easy-to-read sheet music. It contained seventy-six songs, accompanied by

Fowke's prose, which explained each song's significance.

While Fowke's work at this time was proving to be a huge cultural step forward, one Montreal folk fan was nurturing his interest in the music in more practical ways. As an eighteen-year-old commercial artist in 1948, Sam Gesser bought a Lead Belly album, produced by Folkways Records, during a trip to Chicago. The label had recently been started in New York by a prominent figure of the Jewish left, Moses "Moe" Asch, in order to release the work of blacklisted artists like Pete Seeger and Woody Guthrie. When hearing of this, Gesser made Asch one of his role models and, in 1950, he arranged with Asch to become Folkways' Canadian distributor. Youthful exuberance prompted Gesser to go a step further by making his own recordings of Canadian folk songs for the label to release. Asch reluctantly agreed to a deal that bound Gesser to purchase a minimum of one hundred albums for every tape he submitted. Many of these recordings featured Montreal singer Alan Mills, whose repertoire of songs, both in English and in French, as well as Yiddish, had brought him national acclaim. Still, Gesser soon realized he needed to do much more in order to recoup his investment. "I noticed that I could sell more records if I could get [the artists] to perform, so I started booking acts," he said. "I got a radio program on CFCF about folk music. I would play a record and the audience had to identify which country it was from. The first week we had twenty-three letters. I was sure it was a failure. The program director said it was an amazing success." Gesser went on to produce over eighty albums for Folkways between 1950 and 1964 before moving beyond the record business into concert booking and theatre production. He was the talent coordinator for Expo 67, and a mentor to nearly every Montreal-based music impresario who came after him. Still, the down-to-earth ethics of folk music never seemed to leave him as his work expanded into other areas of popular culture. "Once, you felt that by bringing an artist here you were doing something for the community. That's gone by the board," he said. "Once, the question was, 'Is a person good?' Now it's, 'If you're good, how fast can you make a buck?'"

I wanna tell you a story here . . . I went to see a movie called Hootenanny Hoot. . . . *Don't tell anybody . . . I don't want any of you to go see it. The story is about some kind of hootenanny television show* [audience hisses]*, and the storyline of the movie is some big television producer gets fired in New York City and he's driving out to Hollywood. He's crossing the middle of the country, when all of a sudden he comes upon a hootenanny with 10,000 people. And he says, aha, here's my chance, this thing is really selling. People are really hootenannying it up at this place. He calls back to New York and says, 'You've got to get out here because this is the newest, biggest thing. Hootenanny!' And the guy on the other end says, 'Ah, what's this business? Will it sell soap?' 'It will sell soap, it will sell soap! Come on!' So the guy goes out there to some little town in Kansas with a college where they have a hootenanny tour with a hootenanny dance, and hootenanny songs, everything is hootenanny! He goes out there, and they both sit down and listen to a hootenannier. The hootenannier sings — well, she pantomimes to a song. And this certain hootenannier, I don't remember her by name, but she was singing in a swimming suit, and she was singing about someone who just died — in hootenanny style. All of a sudden drums came in from out of nowhere . . . and the one guy turns to the other guy and says, 'My God, this is great. It is great enough to sell soap!' This is what the hootenanny was trying to do, sell soap. I have to admit I stayed to see the whole movie. In fact, I was so shocked I stayed to watch the other movie that was on with it. They came back and sold soap and everybody was happy. But there's some people that aren't selling soap. Some of us, sometimes, we don't really get mad, we just have to shake our heads. . . . We're selling something different besides soap. We don't even buy soap."*
— Bob Dylan, Carnegie Hall, October 26, 1963

As seeds of the new folk awareness blossomed across Canada, they still faced stiff competition with the arrival of rock and roll. However, in some parts of the country, those roots ran too deep to be choked off completely. George Tyson had come to Alberta from Liverpool, England, in 1906, lured by the same spirit of adventure that would bring Wilf Carter there. But the gruelling work of the open range was more than he bargained for. He continued west until he could go no further — to Victoria, B.C.

— where he settled on a small farm with his wife Margaret. There, he took up the more sedate and prosperous life of an insurance salesman. On September 25, 1933, came their second child, Ian Dawson Tyson. Nearly from the moment he could walk, Tyson was riding the horses his father kept out his love for polo, a sport Tyson grew passionate about, as well, when he began attending private school. But by fifteen, he was ready to push things further. He joined the rodeo circuit, though this dream would be cut short four years later, when a fall during a competition in Alberta required doctors to insert three metal pins into his ankle in order to save his foot.

During his convalescence in a Calgary hospital, Tyson had plenty of time to ponder his future, and it was literally handed to him one day when a fellow patient passed him a guitar. In 1953, Tyson enrolled at the Vancouver School of Art, with the goal of becoming a commercial designer, although his new-found passion for the guitar took up almost as much time as his studies. In learning mainly by ear, Tyson gravitated to the simple, traditional American folk songs of the Carter Family and others who were popular, even in the northwest. "When I was a boy in Vancouver my father took me to see the original Sons of the Pioneers with Tex Ritter as a guest along with his horse White Flash; that left quite an impression on me," Tyson said. But by 1956, Tyson naturally saw rock and roll as the most viable option for gaining the fame and fortune he could no longer hope to achieve through the rodeo. He joined a band called The Sensational Stripes as a rhythm guitarist, although the group's only real shining moment came when it rounded out an October 23, 1957, show at Vancouver's Georgia Auditorium that featured Buddy Holly, Eddie Cochran, the Everly Brothers, and Paul Anka. "They had big touring package shows back then," Tyson recalled. "There was no reason for a local band to be on the show other than, I think, it was a local union stipulation. You had to have a band from the musicians' local on that show. We did rockabilly knock-off stuff, Gene Vincent style. It wasn't a huge thing. It was a beginning, I was very young. I eventually got fired because the girls liked me better than the front guy. I guess I was a good-looking kid."

Having both graduated and fallen out with his bandmates within a matter of months, Tyson put off searching for a full-time job. Instead, he started turning up at folk music nights around Vancouver as a solo act with a mixed bag of songs that included everything from spirituals to current Johnny Cash hits. His style gained some focus after he befriended Roy Guest, a visiting British folk singer who invited Tyson to share the stage when he played Vancouver's Heidelburg Café.* This connection made Tyson aware of the British folk song tradition, something he soon discovered Canadian audiences more often preferred instead of his watered-down versions of southern work songs. But after another fruitless year in Vancouver, Tyson caught a ride to Toronto in 1958, if not to find more gigs, to at least land a job as a commercial artist.

The former proved easier, as many of the city's popular hangouts, concentrated in the Yorkville neighbourhood, near the intersection of Bloor and Yonge streets, were making the transition from jazz to folk, much like the process that was already underway in Greenwich Village. Tyson found a regular gig at one of these former jazz hotbeds, the First Floor Club, and, through his appearances there, came to know Edith Fowke, who occasionally invited him to perform on her CBC program. But the most important event for Tyson of 1958 came when he met a dark-haired country girl who had come to Toronto with musical goals that were similar to his. Sylvia Fricker was seven years younger than Tyson, born on September 19, 1940, in Chatham, Ontario, located halfway between London and Windsor in the heart of the tobacco belt. Fricker learned music at an early age from her mother, a church organist and choir mistress, but turned to folk during her teens, when she picked up the guitar and the autoharp. Without access to records, Fricker learned songs through books such as Fowke's. Upon completing high school, her desire to perform folk music

*A few years later, Guest would have a similar impact back home, providing a launching pad for influential guitarist Bert Jansch through his club, The Howff.

brought her to Toronto, and, ultimately into Tyson's arms. From then on they would virtually only be known as Ian & Sylvia.

The image of a young, attractive couple, in love and in harmony, struck a deep chord with audiences, and almost perfectly encapsulated the folk revival's notion of generational rebirth. It later became firmly embedded in the minds of many through the cover of Bob Dylan's second album, *The Freewheelin' Bob Dylan*, released in late May 1963, which showed him arm in arm with girlfriend Suze Rotolo. The image was conveyed even more powerfully through Dylan's close relationship with Joan Baez, which began soon after. Yet, in Canada, Ian & Sylvia were already proffering that dream, becoming the first instant sensation on the Canadian folk scene, and performing in every major city by 1961, even though they had yet to make a recording. This last glaring fact once again underscored the woefully primitive nature of the Canadian recording industry, and made it an inevitability that the duo would head to the centre of the folk revival, Greenwich Village, not long after Dylan made his initial pilgrimage from Minnesota. "I just think it was natural for people to gravitate to that big city," Fricker says. "There was certainly some activity in the Ottawa area, as well, but it was a smaller scene. And there was an English folk scene in Montreal, as well, but again, smaller. The main problem with it was, you played all of the clubs in Toronto, and in Vancouver, and then Montreal, and then Ottawa, and that was about it, you know? There were maybe ten university concerts you could do in a year. So although there was a lot of music coming out of the Toronto area, there weren't a lot of places for us to perform it."

Ian & Sylvia's farewell to Canada coincided with the event that legitimized the homegrown folk movement, the inaugural Mariposa Folk Festival. The concept paid tribute to humorist Stephen Leacock's popular book *Sunshine Sketches of a Little Town*, with the fictional setting of Mariposa substituting for his actual hometown of Orillia, Ontario, northeast of Toronto. Orillia was thus chosen as the setting for the festival, which was spearheaded by two local folk fans, psychiatrist Dr. Casey Jones and his wife Ruth. There was no question that the program needed to draw heavily from the Toronto scene, and Ian & Sylvia were among the headliners on Friday, August 18, 1961, when the festival kicked off. The influx of beer-drinking college students caused some concern among the town's residents, but the positive response to the all-Canadian lineup was unprecedented. Others who appeared included Alan Mills, the Travellers (Canada's answer to the Weavers), and Toronto's York County Boys, the country's first bluegrass band.

The only other performer to match Ian & Sylvia's freshness that day was Bonnie Dobson. In front of her largest Canadian audience to that point, she took the opportunity to debut a song she had just written, the first, in fact, called "Morning Dew." "I think it must have been 1959 or 1960 when I saw a film called *On the Beach*, and it made a tremendous impression on me," Dobson says. "Particularly at that time, because everybody was very worried about the bomb and whether we were going to get through the next ten years. It was during my second or third engagement at the Ash Grove, in Los Angeles, in 1961 — I'd always stay with a friend there — and one night there was a gathering at her apartment, when, toward the end of the evening, a discussion ensued about the possible outcomes of a nuclear war. It was all very depressing and upsetting. After everyone went to bed, I sat up and suddenly I just started writing this song. I had never written anything in my life. I'd written some poetry as a kid, but I'd never written songs. This song just came out, and really it was a kind of re-enactment of that film in a way where, at the end, there is nobody left, and it was a conversation between these two people trying to explain what's happening. It was really the apocalypse, that was what it was about."

Needless to say, the effect of "Morning Dew" at Mariposa was galvanizing, and provided an overdue acceptance of Dobson in her home country.

Bonnie Dobson was born on November 13, 1940, in Toronto, the second daughter in a family that was heavily involved in trade unionism and the music that grew out of it. It was Dobson's older sister who first inspired her to learn to play guitar and sing, and she welcomed her younger sibling into a circle of friends that included future members of The Travellers, the group that would achieve national prominence in the late fifties for Canadianizing Woody Guthrie's "This Land Is Your Land." In addition, Dobson's teenage years were shaped by summers at a camp near Toronto, where Pete Seeger and other notables entertained on weekends. By then, she had realized that her interest in folk set her apart from most people she knew. Her disillusionment grew during her first year at the University of Toronto, and, just as she was debating whether or not to return for a second year, a friend introduced her to a visiting concert promoter from Detroit who immediately offered Dobson work after hearing her play a few songs. She thought it would be a nice way to spend the summer.

"I did my first tour in May 1960," she says. "I went down to Denver, Colorado, and sang at the Exodus with Sonny Terry and Brownie McGee. They had been my idols, and suddenly I was playing with them. Then I went off to Los Angeles. There was a festival up in Idyllwild, and the University of California had this arts festival every summer where I ended up teaching Canadian folk songs. I never got back to university [in Toronto]. I just kept going, and eventually I hit New York, where I recorded my first album for Prestige." Dobson made two records of traditional material, *She's Like a Swallow and Other Folk Songs* and *Dear Companion*, before "Morning Dew" forever changed her life.

After Mariposa, the song became the focal point of Dobson's sets back in New York, and was first captured on tape in February 1962 for her next album, *Bonnie Dobson At Folk City*. In that intimate live setting, she introduced the song timidly: "This is a song about morning dew, and I hope it never falls on us." But from there, her bell-clear soprano confidently and unhurriedly navigated the ravaged landscape, pointing out each detail with unsentimental clarity. It was truly a song befitting the end of the world.

The first reference to the atom bomb in American music, not surprisingly, came only months after the destruction of Hiroshima and Nagasaki. Jazz singer Slim Gaillard's "Atomic Cocktail" was a virtual toast to the new weapon, which effectively ended the

Second World War, and the song set the tone for a string of others that celebrated U.S. dominance in the new arms race. In 1946, Muddy Waters made one of his first recorded appearances, playing guitar behind Homer Harris on his "Atom Bomb Blues," a soldier's letter telling his girlfriend that he would be returning safely from the Pacific thanks to "all the good work that was done." It wasn't until the policy of regular nuclear weapons testing on U.S. soil began at the start of the fifties that musicians began to look at the issue with a more critical eye. Most commonly, they saw the hand of God at work, as in "Jesus Hits Like an Atom Bomb," recorded as a country song by Lowell Blanchard and the Valley Trio, and as a gospel song by the Pilgrim Travelers. Perhaps the most terrifyingly beautiful example of the bomb as divine retribution was "Great Atomic Power," written and recorded by bluegrass duo the Louvin Brothers in 1952. By asking, "Will you shout or will you cry when the fire rains on high," the song made nuclear holocaust seem all but inevitable.

"Morning Dew" was an answer to the question the Louvins posed, although one that contained no logical explanation, or, more importantly, no hint at a specific location where Armageddon had occurred. This, in the end, made the song the first to make the case that the very thought of a nuclear war was completely nihilistic. It was a position that nearly every performer at the time agreed with, even Dylan, who wrote one of his first songs, "Let Me Die in My Footsteps," in response to the suburban bomb shelter craze. But, like most fledgling songwriters at the height of the folk revival, Dobson had little concept of how to protect her own work. Even after one public performance, songs would become fair game for other singers in the spirit of the "oral folk tradition."

Nowhere was this more apparent than when Dylan wrote "Blowin' in the Wind," on Monday, April 16, 1962. A singer named Gil Turner was present the moment it was completed, and played the song for the first time in public that night, at Folk City's weekly open stage. The immediate impact of "Blowin' in the Wind" in uniting the various anti-war/civil rights/free speech movements set Dylan even further apart from his non-writing peers, and its power did not go unnoticed by those looking to make a buck, either. Dylan had been on Albert Grossman's radar screen since John Hammond Sr. had signed him to Columbia Records in the fall of 1961. Although Peter, Paul & Mary was a massive success for Grossman, Dylan's rapidly developing writing skills suddenly presented a new, rarely explored avenue in the folk world: song publishing. This was the biggest carrot that Grossman dangled when he wooed Dylan in the early summer of 1962, as Dylan's debut album was largely being ignored. After some legal maneuvering to release Dylan from the initial standard publishing deal he had signed — much to Hammond's chagrin — Grossman negotiated a new publishing deal through his associate, Artie Mogull at M. Witmark & Sons. On July 13, Dylan signed a three-year contract that provided a thousand-dollar advance. From that point, Mogull brought Dylan's songs to artists in virtually every genre, not to mention all of Grossman's clients, creating one of most lucrative catalogues since Roy Acuff and Fred Rose gained control of Hank Williams's output. In those first three years, Dylan copyrighted 237 songs. These formed the foundation of the empire that Grossman would build through his large share of the royalties. Peter, Paul & Mary's version of "Blowin' in the Wind," released as a single on June 18, 1963, sold 320,000 copies in its first week, catapulting it to number two on the national pop chart, and that was only the beginning.

For artists like Bonnie Dobson, who lacked such muscle, capitalizing on their work was a much different story. "I would meet people, and they would say, 'I learned 'Morning Dew' travelling on a train from St. Louis to Chicago.' It had sort of travelled like a proper folk song. Then one day Jac Holzman rang me in New York and said, 'You wrote 'Morning Dew' didn't you?' and I said, 'Yes.' He said, 'Have you published it?' I hadn't because I didn't know you had to do that in those days. He said, 'Well, Fred Neil wants to record it, so we would like to publish it.' So I signed a publishing deal with [Holzman], and that was okay. Fred Neil was the first person to, well, rock it, really, because the way I sang it was actually quite lyrical, and he rocked it. He actually changed the lyrics, as well." Neil was a mentor to most of the first-generation Village folkies, and a notable songwriter in his own right. His biggest success before he signed with Elektra was "Candy Man," for Roy Orbison. Later, he achieved national prominence through oft-covered songs such as "The Other Side of This Life," "The Dolphins," and "Everybody's Talkin'." But his decision to rearrange "Morning Dew" for his 1964 Elektra album *Tear Down the Walls* (done with his then-musical partner Vince Martin) marked the next phase of the song's long, strange trip.

Two years later, Tim Rose, a one-time member of The Big Three, along with Cass Elliott (later of the Mamas and the Papas), sought to record the song for his debut album on Columbia, but based his version on Neil's arrangement. Sensing a chance to copyright these changes, much like he would attempt to do when his arrangement of Billy Roberts's "Hey Joe" was used by Jimi Hendrix as a template, Rose put his publisher to work. Dobson says, "I had a call from Manny Greenhill saying that Tim Rose was going to record my song, but he wanted to make a few changes. Greenhill asked, 'Can you write a new lyric?' I remember, I was on a plane flying from Toronto to Vancouver to do a television show, sitting there writing this and thinking, 'What am I doing this for?' I think what happened was there was no way we could not cut him in on the lyric, because I had performed it and [then] published it. I hadn't done it the way you're supposed to do things, so the song was somewhat in the public domain. I never met Tim Rose, but he was subsequently written into the contract. If we're going to be really honest about this, if anyone should be credited as co-writer or co-lyricist, it should be Fred Neil, because all Tim Rose did was take Fred's changes."

"Morning Dew," now credited to "Dobson-Rose," would be recorded dozens of times in the ensuing years by pop artists such as Lulu and rock bands such as The Grateful Dead, The Jeff Beck Group, and Duane and Gregg Allman's Hour Glass. Devo retooled it for the Reagan era, and Robert Plant used it to pay tribute to his hippie roots in 2002. Dobson herself was persuaded to record the song again in Toronto in 1969 for her self-titled album, produced by Jack Richardson and released on his Nimbus 9 label. Soon after that session, she permanently relocated to England. Two more records of mostly traditional material later, Dobson began pursuing a career in academia, which culminated in the late nineties, when she was named head of the philosophy department at the University of London's Berwick College. By then, the sting of not being fully credited for writing "that song" had partially faded, but not totally. "The worst part was when I came to England in 1969 and I gave my debut concert at Queen Elizabeth Hall," Dobson says. "Everybody had thought that Tim Rose had written 'Morning Dew,' because he had never mentioned me, at any time, having anything to do with that song. I've written songs with other people, and I have never claimed them as my own. I just think it was really a dreadfully dishonest thing to do. I still get my royalty check, but I still consider it quite a grievous injury. I remember when Lulu brought it out in 1967, and they took out a full-page ad in *Billboard* saying it was Tim Rose's great hit. I nearly went crazy, but there was nothing we could do."

Such flagrant injustices were never a concern when it came to Albert Grossman's clients. Most artists in the Village admired his business savvy, and those who didn't feared him, but all respected his instincts. Grossman had spotted Ian & Sylvia not long after their arrival in the Village. The novelty of a performing couple perfectly melded with his contemporary vision, exemplified by the heavily image-conscious Peter, Paul & Mary. And after a few months of playing clubs like Folk City, they had their act well honed. According to scene fixture Dave Van Ronk, whose arrangement of "House of the Rising Sun" was lifted by Dylan, and, subsequently, The Animals, "If you were new and hot, the audience would be quiet and attentive, like when Ian & Sylvia were on for the first time. You always got one free ride. From then on, you were just another one of the bums who get in the way of the conversation."

Ian & Sylvia became Grossman clients early in 1962, at which point he urged them to follow Peter, Paul & Mary's example and sign with Warner Brothers. However, the couple, compelled to stay true to their origins, instructed Grossman to get them a deal with Vanguard Records, the most recognizable label in modern folk. Founded in New York in 1953 by brothers Seymour and Maynard Solomon, at the dawn of the LP era, Vanguard initially focused on classical and jazz markets. A few years later, the label gambled on folk, and it paid off with *The Weavers At Carnegie Hall* in 1957. The album marked the group's comeback after being blacklisted by parts of the industry during the McCarthy era for their socialist-themed material, and was a perennial seller thereafter. When Joan Baez became the talk of the folk world after her appearance at the inaugural 1959 Newport Folk Festival, Grossman negotiated her contract with Vanguard, bringing both Baez and the label an international profile. Vanguard would go on to document subsequent Newport festivals until the mid-sixties, capturing many truly legendary performances in the process.

Being on Vanguard made sense for Ian & Sylvia, since their repertoire was still a wide-ranging amalgamation of traditional British and Canadian songs, along with many pseudo-gospel and blues numbers. It all went into the couple's self-titled debut album, released in September 1962. The emphasis on dark, southern material was striking, and, although not as rough-edged as Dylan's first album, the results were similarly incompatible with commercial standards. However, the effortless blending of their voices, underscored by the bass playing of Bill Lee (father of film director Spike Lee), created a sound perfectly suited to a white college audience that was still easing its way toward some kind of understanding of black culture, just as the artists themselves admittedly were. According to Sylvia, "I did most of the research on the traditional stuff. It's amazing material. I sort of think of it as distilled music. You know, it's been through so many hands that all of the fat is cut off, because having gone through so many hands in the oral tradition, people just forgot the boring bits and kept the good stuff."

Conversely, via Edith Fowke's research the duo learned two other songs, both surely suggested by Sylvia: "Un Canadien

Errant" and "Mary Anne." The former, sung in French, was already a standard in that language, and had been written in 1842 by Antoine Gerin-Lajoie in response to the Lower Canada rebellion, which had taken place five years earlier. The rebellion had resulted in the forced exile of many francophones, until an amnesty was declared in 1849. The latter, an aching love ballad said to be the first song the pair ever sang together, is attributed to an unknown trapper, and originally documented by the pioneering Québecois folklorist Dr. Marius Barbeau. But while the notion of displacement is inherent to each, the pair best summed up their feelings of being strangers in a foreign land with their take of "When First Unto This Country," a popular British ballad that told the tale of a newcomer imprisoned for a robbery that had been intended to win the hand of his lover. In Ian & Sylvia's interpretation, strong emphasis is placed on the protagonist's mistreatment, suggesting any number of possible scenarios relevant to the couple's own experiences resulting from their relocation. These three songs, along with the rest of *Ian & Sylvia*, contained merely the raw ingredients for what was to come. The separation from his native land, combined with his proximity to the initial opening of Dylan's creative floodgates, finally inspired Ian to pen his first song. His thoughts drifted back to his student days in Vancouver, when his first serious girlfriend, "the Greek girl," as he later confessed, abruptly left him for a new life in California. From this time-honoured sense of heartbreak came "Four Strong Winds," although its intangible qualities made it unlike any song anyone from Canada had written before. Centred around a seasonal farm worker who must constantly travel from one part of the country to another to make his living, the lyrics partially echoed the great, sweeping cowboy ballads of Tyson's youth (particularly those written by Bob Nolan), although the song's overall solemnity made it almost hymnal. As with the protest anthems heard everywhere in 1963, it was impossible not to get caught up in the soaring chorus of "Four Strong Winds." But the existential heart of the song clearly resided in a place somehow left untouched by the events of the day, making it a thoroughly timeless Canadian story, and, by extension, a more appropriate expression of national identity than "God Save the Queen" or "The Maple Leaf Forever" could have ever been.

"['Four Strong Winds'] meant a lot to me," Neil Young told his biographer, Jimmy McDonough. "I remember playing it down at Falcon Lake [near Winnipeg], listening to it over and over. Just the song, the melody, the whole thing. It had a message, too — leaving things behind. The feeling that something's not gonna work. There's a feeling in that song that I related to."

The obvious appeal of "Four Strong Winds" made it the logical choice to be the title of Ian & Sylvia's second album, released in April 1964. It was the only original composition, but other selections showed that their range was expanding. Most notable was Dylan's "Tomorrow Is a Long Time," a song the author himself would not officially release until 1971. Such a choice was natural, given the mutual respect the pair shared with him, which was based, in part, on Dylan's admiration of their resistance to writing "topical" material, something he himself was struggling to distance himself from at the time. "In a sense, we actually signed with Albert Grossman before Bobby had," Sylvia says. "And we were at least partially responsible for him signing Bobby, not because we said, 'sign him,' but because we said, 'hey, this guy's really great.' We always liked to do other writers' material, even once we started to write. We felt that every writer, after they do stuff for a certain length of time, it starts to sound the same. It gave us a bit more variety in what we were doing. Plus, we really liked the songs, too."

What Dylan and others picked up on in "Four Strong Winds" was how it ardently steered clear of the political discourse that had firmly gripped the Village — and the rest of America — following the Kennedy assassination and the subsequent escalation of U.S. troop deployment to Vietnam. Of course, Ian & Sylvia could not be faulted for being on the outside. The seemingly unshakeable stability inherent in their sound came to reflect Canada's growing international image, and made unprecedented sales of Four Strong Winds at home hardly a surprise. That bond with their Canadian audience was sealed, along with Ian and Sylvia's marriage vows, in Toronto on June 26, 1964, in the midst of a hectic summer touring schedule and the completion of their next album, slated for the fall.★

If that covenant epitomized the blissful dream of folk's ultimate potential, it was a dream that was not totally shared by one artist of Canadian origin. Buffy Sainte-Marie had been a mass of contradictions long before she arrived in Greenwich Village. Born February 20, 1941, on the Piapot Reserve near Craven, Saskatchewan, to Cree parents, she was abandoned only a few months later. Known then only by her given name, Beverly, she was put up for adoption and taken in by a couple of Mi'kmaq descent, Albert and Winifred Sainte-Marie, of Wakefield, Massachusetts. There, she acquired the nickname Buffy and suffered through childhood as a misfit, both at home and within her community. Although she brought herself some solace by teaching herself piano and guitar during her mid-teens, she found acceptance after enrolling at the University of Massachusetts, where she concentrated on studying languages, predominantly French and Hindi. She also reconnected with her own heritage, writing songs with strong Native American themes through the urging of a confidante, the poet Theresa de Kerpely. As her education neared its completion in 1962, Sainte-Marie foresaw a future as a teacher back on her reserve; that is, until her positive experiences within the Boston coffee house scene — the same circuit where Joan Baez had first appeared — prompted a move to New York.

If Ian & Sylvia's arrival there introduced a new twist on the traditional folk performance dynamic, Buffy Sainte-Marie suggested that an entire reassessment was needed. With a cache of original songs that covered topics ranging from Native rights to drug addiction and incest, all sung in a strident tone even more

★On August 24, 1963, Joan Baez's younger sister Mimi married singer-songwriter Richard Farina, and the duo was subsequently groomed by Albert Grossman to be something of an American counterpart to Ian & Sylvia. They would produce two innovative, but low-selling, albums for Vanguard before Richard was killed in a motorcycle accident on April 30, 1966, the day his first novel, *Been Down So Long It Looks Like Up to Me*, was published.

exaggerated than that of other female folk voices, she got everyone's attention in a hurry. "Buffy came down from Boston and
did a three-song set at a [Gerde's Folk City] hoot, and the crowd
went wild," said her soon-to-be manager, Herb Gart. "I worked
with her for seven or eight years. Buffy lived in my office for a
while. I had it set up so that every piece of furniture could be
converted into something to sleep on. Half the Village came up
every night to sleep. But Buffy was really something special.
One thing that would really destroy the audience from early on
was that she used to come out on stage wearing a very tight,
bright red dress made of snakeskin."

With the endorsement of influential *New York Times* folk
critic Robert Shelton, Sainte-Marie signed with Vanguard, and
her first album, *It's My Way!*, appeared almost simultaneously
with *Four Strong Winds* in April 1964. She acknowledged a debt
for several of the album's more militant moments to Native
singer-songwriter Peter LaFarge, author of "The Ballad of Ira
Hayes," the tale of the mistreated Native soldier who was among
the famous group to raise the American flag at Iwo Jima, but
Sainte-Marie's approach was as singular as the album's title proclaimed. In highly personal terms, she presented a world that
was quick to forget the exploited and the marginalized.
Nowhere was this better displayed than in "Co'dine," a harrowing exploration of addiction from the user's perspective. At a
time when drug experimentation was still in its infancy outside
of some artistic circles, the song's brutality was a slap in the face
to most who heard it. Guitarist Danny Kalb, who went on to
form the Blues Project with Al Kooper, said, "When I saw Buffy
Sainte-Marie singing about codeine, I knew it would be several
more years before I had enough experience underneath my belt
to sing the way she did. She was raw and great."

Songs extolling the use of drugs and other substances had
been somewhat of a tradition in the blues, at least since
Mississippi guitarist Tommy Johnson sang of his love of drinking Sterno, a cooking fuel, in "Canned Heat Blues," recorded at
the height of Prohibition in 1928. From then on, few others
shied away from alluding to their addictions, either, although

such references owed a partial debt to the ancient mountain ballads "Moonshiner" and "Darling Cory," each a possible source for the verse that essentially became the epitaph for all demon-driven blues and country singers: "Give me corn bread when I'm hungry, corn whiskey when I'm dry; pretty women standing around me, sweet heaven when I die." Although "Co'dine" was essentially an addict's warning to stay away from the drug altogether, and a decidedly non-traditional absence of hope for redemption was its hallmark, Sainte-Marie caught a bit of the ancient, defiant voice in the song's final verse: "My one satisfaction, it comes when I think/That I'm living my life without bending to break."

"Co'dine" would re-emerge in several new guises through other artists in the coming years, as the debate over the effects of recreational drug use intensified. But it was another song on *It's My Way!*, "The Universal Soldier," that showed Sainte-Marie was also ahead of the curve when it came to the era's other great moral dilemma, the Vietnam War. Written before a performance at Toronto coffee house the Purple Onion, the song took a clear and bold stand against those who would participate in, or support, a war that they believed had no justifiable basis. Dylan's "Masters of War," perhaps his most effective "protest" song, had laid all the blame on the ruling class, but "The Universal Soldier" took direct aim at the rest of the population, arguing that they were the ones who held the power to change policy if they had the will to do so. This was previously unthinkable subject matter for a popular song, and that popularity only increased the following year, when British folk singer Donovan scored a hit with it. Sainte-Marie says, "I was at the San Francisco airport on my way to Toronto in the middle of the night, and I saw soldiers carrying their buddies in on stretchers, all bandaged up. I started talking to some of these soldiers, and as we were talking I started thinking, 'Who is responsible for war, anyway? Is it these guys?' So the song is really about taking individual responsibility for most everything. In a working democracy, we are all ultimately responsible for what happens. You can't just blame the generals."

Such notions apparently proved far more threatening than anyone could have imagined. In the late nineties, Sainte-Marie alleged that the Johnson administration had authorized the covert seizure of her recordings, while at the same time pressuring radio stations not to play "The Universal Soldier." She went on to claim that she was an easy target for censorship due to her growing involvement in Native American causes. The cumulative effect was virtually non-existent U.S. album sales, but *It's My Way!* found a large audience in Canada, especially after Sainte-Marie's rapturously received appearance at the 1964 Mariposa Folk Festival.

Whatever the reason for her barriers in the U.S., Sainte-Marie remained resilient through it all, recording several more albums for Vanguard, as well as adding the haunting sound of the Native American mouth bow on Jack Nitzsche's brilliant soundtrack to the controversial 1970 film *Performance*, starring Mick Jagger. Although her image as an activist was something she could not, and would not, shed throughout the seventies, Sainte-Marie did achieve massive pop success when Elvis Presley, Neil Diamond, Cher, and many others covered "Until It's Time for You to Go," a song from her second album, 1965's *Many A Mile*. Sainte-Marie's close relationship with the volatile Nitzsche also flourished by the end of the sixties, resulting in several collaborations on 1971's *She Used to Wanna Be a Ballerina*, including her version of Neil Young's "Helpless," backed by Crazy Horse (whose lineup included Nitzsche). Nitzsche and Sainte-Marie eventually married — albeit only briefly — in March 1981, and soon after collaborated on the Oscar-winning "Up Where We Belong," sung by Joe Cocker and Jennifer Warnes for the film *An Officer and a Gentleman*.

But it was the blunt poetry of *It's My Way!* that survived to be heard just under the surface of the next generation of outspoken female singer-songwriters, up to Sinead O'Connor, Tori Amos, Ani DiFranco, and beyond. Even when one listens to the album today, it is impossible not to believe that the bridge toward honest, female expression in song did not start there.

In spite of such social awakenings, spurred on by Sainte-Marie and others, folk's golden era was already on its last legs. The beginning of the end came in February 1964, when The Beatles came to America for the first time, playing to millions of kids on *The Ed Sullivan Show*. It was the moment that brought electric rock and roll back into prominence, and folkies started trading in their acoustic guitars in droves. Ian & Sylvia remained holdouts, and Albert Grossman abided the decision, as the unifying effect that "Four Strong Winds" generated within the folk community was bringing the couple more attention than they had ever imagined. Their national profile peaked through appearances on ABC's *Hootenanny* program, a manifestation of the folk craze that hit the air in April 1963 as a showcase for the most commercial end of the folk spectrum. "Four Strong Winds" became a particular favourite for other artists to cover on the show, as well, but *Hootenanny* did not live to see the start of the 1964 fall television season. Despite the exposure, Ian retains few pleasant memories of the show. "It was dumb, it was incredibly dumb," he says. "It was phony, it was forced, it was imitation. It was very uncomfortable for everybody, and technically very inferior. It was just at that period of time where sound technology was finally starting to improve. The rock groups had blown out all the terrible systems, but *Hootenanny* was a dreadful show. Appalling."

The album that Ian & Sylvia had been working on during that summer of 1964, *Northern Journey*, came out just as *Hootenanny* vanished, but with Grossman's continuing support, it managed to ride the momentum that *Four Strong Winds* had initiated. As the title suggested, the bulk of the material was drawn from obscure Canadian folk sources: "Four Rode By" was the tale of the little-known Wild McLeans, a gang of outlaws who terrorized the B.C. fur trade in 1879; "Brave Wolfe" was a tribute to one of the heroes of the Plains of Abraham; and "Nova Scotia Farewell," was a popular sea shanty. The real breakthrough was Sylvia's emergence as a songwriter, as her first composition, "You Were on My Mind," kicked off the album in energetic style. But the song's undeniable drive and rousing chorus was a sign that the duo was not impervious to the British Invasion. In fact, it sounded tailor-made for the folk-rock revolution that was soon to come, and was ultimately given that treatment by a San Francisco group called We Five, whose version climbed to number three on the *Billboard* pop chart in early August 1965. It was the first hit for A & M Records that had not been made by label co-founder Herb Alpert. "That was quite a surprise," Sylvia says. "It was actually a hit before I knew about it. We were on the road in California. We were driving down Highway 101, turned on the radio, and there it was. I wasn't that thrilled with how they changed the lyrics, but I certainly knew the limitations of pop radio in those days, and that the lyrics, 'I got drunk and I got sick' probably wouldn't pass muster. I definitely had a gospel-influenced song in mind when I wrote it."

"You Were on My Mind" would go on to be covered several more times, but the duo's apparent unawareness of its popularity illustrated the widening gap between traditional folk artists and the swing toward commercial folk-rock. Those who had not found the success that Greenwich Village had promised saw new opportunities playing the same music in a rock band format. That door was kicked open once The Byrds — a group comprised of former folkies Jim McGuinn, Gene Clark, David Crosby, and Chris Hillman — effectively "Beatle-ized" Dylan's "Mr. Tambourine Man" in early 1965. At the same time, Dylan himself was making the transition to electric rock and roll. Almost overnight, a slew of others caught the wave, among them Zal Yanovsky and Denny Doherty, who, in 1961, were just another pair of destitute Canadians scrounging around the Village.

Yanovsky had come from Toronto; he was born on December 19, 1944, the son of Avrom Yanovsky, the official cartoonist of the Communist Party of Canada. He dropped out of Downsview Collegiate at sixteen, and was already determined to live as an itinerant folk singer and escape his constant clashes with his father. Yanovsky's journey first took him an hour west, where he briefly worked at a coffee house in Kitchener, before he headed to an Israeli kibbutz. He was told to leave after accidentally levelling a building that was under construction with a front-end loader, and resurfaced as a street busker in Tel Aviv. Unable to make ends meet, Yanovsky returned to Toronto penniless and spent the next year drifting from house to house, often sleeping in laundromats and stealing milk bottles for the deposit money.

One night he shared a stage with a folk trio from the Maritimes called The Colonials, fronted by Denny Doherty, a Halifax native. The two gregarious personalities immediately clicked, and Doherty was so impressed with Yanovsky's guitar technique that he offered him a job after The Colonials became The Halifax Three and signed a short-lived deal with Epic Reconds in 1963. The result was one album, *San Francisco Bay Blues.* "Zal had been into rhythm and blues and folk music," Doherty said. "Our gig paid him a couple hundred bucks a week, and we toured a lot, so through that he met other musicians and started hanging around New York."

The ultimate demise of The Halifax Three left the pair at loose ends until scene cohort Cass Elliott brought them to the attention of her manager. Together, they formed a new contingent called The Mugwumps. Although that band remained more of a secret until its scant recordings were posthumously released by Warner Brothers in 1967, it kept Yanovsky and Doherty active until new possibilities arose, and, separately, both struck gold in short order. Doherty filled a spot in The New Journeymen, a traditional group led by John Phillips, which lasted until early 1965, when Phillips sensed the winds of change and sought to form a new folk-rock outfit with Doherty and his waifish young wife Michelle. To achieve gender balance, Doherty suggested they add Elliott, and they became The Mamas and the Papas just prior to signing with ABC-Dunhill that September. A string of ten *Billboard* Top 10 hits followed over the next three years.

Through his Mugwumps connections, Yanovsky also discovered an ideal partner in the form of homegrown Village folkie John Sebastian. Together with bassist Steve Boone and drummer Joe Butler, they formed The Lovin' Spoonful — the name inspired by a Mississippi John Hurt song — and offered their version of "good time music," which stood in stark contrast to the increasingly aggressive and abstract songwriting that was becoming the norm in rock and roll. Their sound was perfectly suited to the band's image, especially the innocence Yanovsky projected, which made even The Beatles' initial public antics seem contrived. Yet, for all of Yanovsky's clownishness, his clever, subtle lead guitar was the perfect complement to Sebastian's odes to puppy love and endless summer days. The Lovin' Spoonful would go on to rival The Mamas and the Papas in terms of hits, inextricably linking them as America's most successful pop response to the British Invasion, although both bands would not survive much beyond it.

Doherty's affair with Michelle Phillips, which began early in The Mamas and the Papas' reign on the charts, made the group's 1968 split inevitable. Yanovsky, for his part, never adjusted to life as a pop star, and left The Lovin' Spoonful in 1967, after a marijuana bust in San Francisco. While each continued on their individual musical paths, the ensuing, and in many ways unforgiving, changes in rock and roll would drive them both back to Canada, where they each attempted to build normal lives around the legacy they would forever share. Yanovsky became a reclusive restaurateur, and Doherty a very public raconteur, who, inevitably, got the last word. "He did not follow any book," Doherty commented upon receiving news of Yanovsky's death, on December 13, 2002, in Kingston, Ontario. Doherty followed him on January 19, 2007, from his home in Mississauga, Ontario.

The idyllic days of mid-sixties folk-rock were indeed ancient history by then, falling prey to the excesses of the psychedelic movement before finally being clouded over by the drug culture's aftermath. Nevertheless, it all remained a world far removed from the one in which Ian & Sylvia existed at the time. The Tysons recorded their follow-up to *Northern Journey* at the onset of the folk-rock movement, yet there was no sign of drums or electric guitars. Instead, there was another varied selection of traditional material, but also some songs by an unknown Canadian songwriter Ian had just discovered. Ian further acknowledged the young man's talent by making one of the songs, "Early Morning Rain," the album's title track. That songwriter was Gordon Lightfoot, and with songs as good as his, there was no need for embellishment. Albert Grossman understood this, too, and it wouldn't take long for him to add Lightfoot to his increasingly profitable stable of artists.

PART TWO

I TOLD YOU WHEN I CAME
I WAS A STRANGER

CHAPTER FOUR

THE WAY I FEEL

THE SONG LINGERED LIKE A BAD OMEN throughout the autumn, a dirge-like sea shanty that left everything else on the radio cowering in its wake. When the voice came, it sang with a clarity and a purpose that challenged all who heard it to grasp their innermost fears — fears that had been present since childhood, but were now placed in a stark new reality that transcended a mere report of a shipwreck that had claimed twenty-nine lives.

After seven verses in six and a half minutes — an immeasurable amount of time on the radio — the nightmare was over. The DJ never failed to announce the song in an unusually sombre tone, as if he felt, like his audience, that he had personally witnessed the deaths of these men. The shared unease was compounded by a vague sense of complicity that came with being a voyeur, and, with that, the inevitable sense of being utterly alone in an indifferent universe.

The fact that "The Wreck of the Edmund Fitzgerald" became a Top 5 *Billboard* single — Rod Stewart's "Tonight's the Night" kept it out of the number-one spot for two straight weeks in November 1976 — was another example of Gordon Lightfoot's inexplicable imperviousness to trends. It had been ten years since the release of Lightfoot's debut album, and even then he seemed impossibly out of step, a well-groomed folk-pop troubadour at the dawning of psychedelia. Even in the year before that first album was released, when a slew of international artists had massive hits with songs he had written, it was easy to believe that the enigma known as Lightfoot came from the same unfamiliar land that Ian Tyson had introduced to the wider world through "Four Strong Winds."

The pair had a unique advantage in that they approached their songwriting as if it were a blank canvas. Tyson's creative spark lay in his knowledge of folk music's history — a history that viewed the music as an essential aspect of daily survival — while Lightfoot knew only the craft. But Gordon Lightfoot understood musical structure better than nearly all of his contemporaries, and once he was allowed to ply his trade, the few pop guidelines he was, at first, compelled to follow were quickly shed. What Lightfoot undeniably shared with Tyson was a voice that ignored the call for mass rebellion, which was heard everywhere in the early sixties folk boom. He acknowledged the inner turmoil of the many who felt ambivalent, whose small-town upbringings caused them to resist the pressure to choose sides, or even dare to look at life in black-and-white terms, since nature alone was the great equalizer. Tyson captured this idea like lightning in a bottle with "Four Strong Winds," and could not preserve it. But it would be the starting point for nearly everything Lightfoot would write.

It was an idea that went straight to the heart of the Canadian psyche, and Lightfoot's unmatched output over the last half of the sixties was driven by the Canadian audience's desire to vicariously experience the place his songs embodied. It was a place they knew had existed all along, but could not locate within their increasingly urbanized lives. Canada's version of the folk revival, essentially embodied by Ian & Sylvia, had drawn a partial map using only wide, sprawling vistas; Lightfoot's songs were the first step in connecting these sometimes immeasurable distances, where the real destination was often the trip itself.

It was inevitable, then, that Tyson and Lightfoot would cross paths. Lightfoot was, in fact, an ardent admirer of Ian & Sylvia from as far back as their 1961 Mariposa appearance. He took every opportunity to see them play when he moved to Toronto shortly afterward, in order to get his folk singing career officially underway. As part of a small artistic fraternity, Lightfoot and Tyson became acquaintances, although during those initial years Lightfoot clearly saw himself as a kind of apprentice, noting all of the aspects of the Tysons' repertoire in great detail. His ability to make progress with his own work at that time spoke volumes about Lightfoot's determination. By the summer of 1964, he had been a regular face on mainstream television musical variety shows, both in Canada and Britain, had split up his moderately successful duo with a singing partner he'd worked with since high school, and had married an exotic Swedish visitor to Toronto who was three years his elder.

Listening to Bob Dylan seemed to be the only thing that kept Lightfoot grounded in the midst of all of this activity. The vivid imagery on *Freewheelin'* and *The Times They Are A-Changin'* spoke directly to Lightfoot; whoever this kid was, he understood what it meant to grow up in a small, northern town. The longer Lightfoot listened to Dylan, the more he realized that there was something wrong with the music he himself had been creating. In order to make the breakthrough he sought, Lightfoot needed to reconnect with the upbringing he had all but turned his back on. One afternoon that summer, Lightfoot sat in his downtown Toronto basement apartment, as his wife tended to their newborn son, and made his first attempt at a new way of writing. He wanted it to be a song that reflected the transient turn his life had unexpectedly taken, beginning with the day he landed in Los Angeles to attend college, while conversely avoiding the traps of traditional folk lyrics. This latter trait was the most strikingly unique aspect of Dylan's work. What emerged was "Early Morning Rain," a song that brought the familiar figure of the lonesome traveller into the jet age. Like many who had come before him, the song's protagonist stands in the rain, destitute, having gotten all he could out of the town he had just passed through, and wanting only to move on to the next. But the scene does not take place outside of a train depot or on the side of a highway; the traveller is at the airport, watching the jets take off to places that are home to pleasures and spoils he can barely imagine. This was Canada's post-war sentiment expressed in the broadest terms — a newfound knowledge that the world was bigger than anyone had previously imagined, and that the old ways were no longer sufficient.

Lightfoot used "Early Morning Rain" as a cornerstone for a revamped repertoire, one he determined would consist entirely of original material and be recorded before the end of that year. From there, the songs came in a torrent, some quickly revised from past ideas, but all of them consistent with his new, expressionistic approach: "I'm Not Sayin'," "Ribbon of Darkness," "The Way I Feel," and "For Lovin' Me." These were the songs Lightfoot was performing at Steele's Tavern, on the Yonge Street strip, when the Tysons dropped in one night from their recently purchased home in the upscale Rosedale neighbourhood. From the moment he heard these new songs, Ian Tyson saw Lightfoot for the first time as the kindred spirit he was. More importantly, Tyson recognized an untapped source of contemporary material on par with Dylan's. Upon his return to New York for the release of *Northern Journey*, Tyson told Albert Grossman about Lightfoot's undiscovered cache of songs, and his desire to record some of them. Suitably intrigued, the manager sent his chief associate, John Court, to Toronto to check out Lightfoot at Steele's, and within weeks of Court's enthusiastic report back to his boss, Lightfoot was in Grossman's office discussing his immediate future. With Dylan about to alienate his folk audience with a move toward rock and roll, Lightfoot was the perfect remedy to keep the publishing royalties flowing in.

Gordon Meredith Lightfoot was born on November 17, 1938, in Orillia, Ontario, the second child and only son of Gordon Sr. and Jessica (née Trill) Lightfoot. At the time of Lightfoot's birth, his father was still coping with the latest in a series of setbacks in his life. These began with the death of his mother while he was still an infant. His decision to marry had cost him his job as a banker — the bank believed poor young newlyweds were more prone to embezzling — so to support his family he took the first decent job he could find. It was backbreaking, menial work running a small dry-cleaning firm, yet it would be the only job he would hold for the rest of his life. His frustrations often boiled over when he came home, and young Gordon was most frequently on the receiving end of his father's fury. In one of his few acts of rebellion, Lightfoot left school early one day at age twelve and buried the belt his father used to beat him with in the backyard. However, by then the beatings had taken an irrevocable toll on his personality. "You know what? I'm too humble," Lightfoot later surmised. "I'm humble to the point of feeling inferior most of the time. And I've had this treated, because I suffer from depression. I came face to face with my mortality at age ten. With some people, it happens a little bit later in their lives. You realize you're gonna die. It hits everybody between the eyes like a big stone around preadolescence. It hit me when I was ten, and I've been depressed ever since."

At the same time, Orillia's pastoral setting offered an ideal childhood, especially during the war years. This helped nurture Lightfoot's interest in singing, which, as a boy, he did nearly every night as he fell asleep. His mother was, not surprisingly, enraptured by her son's emerging talent, and encouraged him to sing in their church choir, at weddings, and at school. Lightfoot says, "I think the first significant tune I ever sang was 'Tura Lura Lural (That's an Irish Lullaby)' in grade four. I recorded it at school [with his sister Beverly on piano] for a parents' day event to be broadcast over the public address system, and it came out quite well. So after that I started getting involved in singing competitions and all that stuff. I wish I could sing as well now as I did when I was ten. I was really an excellent boy soprano." It was at that age that he began studying voice and piano with his choirmaster, Ray Williams, who was so moved by Lightfoot's treatment of "The Lord's Prayer" that he helped produce a 78 RPM recording of it. At age twelve, Lightfoot moved on to competing in the Kiwanis Music Festival, held annually in Toronto, and in 1952 he won first place in the "soprano unchanged voices" class. Significantly, this was also his first appearance at Massey Hall, the venue that would post his name on its marquee more than any other.

Although Lightfoot took great pride in his accomplishments, the onset of puberty clearly presented a challenge to the development of his musical career. Undeterred, he formed a barbershop quartet called The Collegiate Four, just before he entered high school in 1953. A year later, they entered a CBC television talent competition called *Pick the Stars* and won first prize. Once in high school, Lightfoot's rugged good looks and curly blonde hair made him a natural for the stage, and he tried a few musical roles. But adding acting to the mix proved more difficult than he expected, and in 1954 Lightfoot turned his attention to getting another vocal group together. Non-threatening white American groups like The Four Freshmen and their Canadian counterparts The Four Lads were still in vogue in the days just prior to rock and roll's arrival, and Lightfoot found his equivalent with The Teen Timers, a quartet that shared its name with a popular New York–based youth clothing manufacturer. This group became a local success, placing high in several 1955 competitions. As they discovered more opportunities for work, Lightfoot and one of The Teen Timers, Terry Whelan, each learned how to play cheap, four-string guitars in the summer of 1956 and began appearing as The Two-Timers. It turned out to be one of the few concessions Lightfoot ever made to rock and roll, as several current Everly Brothers hits were easy choices for the pair to play.

Lightfoot's graduation from high school in 1957 also meant the end of The Teen Timers. Lightfoot envisioned refashioning himself as a songwriter, and his first effort was a well-reasoned, topical ditty called "The Hula Hoop Song." In a bold move, he pitched it directly to Harold Moon, who was American music publishing organization BMI's Toronto representative. Although Moon recognized right away that the song came from an untrained adolescent his encouragement thereby furthered Lightfoot's musical obsession. Briefly putting songwriting aside, Lightfoot contemplated taking up drums and entering the jazz field, if only to prove to his parents that a career in music was a viable option. Lightfoot began charting his course after seeing an ad in the jazz journal *Downbeat* for Westlake College of

Modern Music in Los Angeles, which was the first accredited American music school. Using all the money he and his parents could scrape together, Lightfoot enrolled in the fall of 1957. However, like many kids leaving home for the first time, Lightfoot had trouble adjusting to his new surroundings, as well as to the demands of learning theory and arrangement. His dwindling finances compounded the problem, prompting him to scour Hollywood for any work in the commercial production field. Broke and dejected over disappointing his parents, Lightfoot came back to Orillia at the end of the academic term in 1958, just long enough to inform them that he was moving to Toronto to make his own way.

Ironically, his father's old banking connections helped Lightfoot get a job as a teller while he searched for after-hours work as an arranger and backup vocalist. It was all still a far cry from the performing regimen he had become accustomed to in high school, but he caught a break when he landed a spot in a song-and-dance group called The Swinging Singing Eight, which most often appeared on the CBC television program *Country Hoedown*. The half-hour variety show aired Friday nights, and served as a showcase for the country's up-and-coming country music talent. Some, like Lightfoot, had first received attention through *Pick the Stars*, but his appearances over the next two seasons on *Country Hoedown* were limited to The Swinging Singing Eight's square dance numbers. "They could have been called Rancho Vegas, or something like that," he said years later. "I was paid to scale, and I worked for peanuts." In 1959, Lightfoot was only beginning to appreciate folk music, and took his first stabs at playing guitar.* What got him motivated was hearing The Weavers' Carnegie Hall album, as well as the work of Bob Gibson, whose duets with sometime partner Hamilton Camp gave Lightfoot the idea of reviving a partnership with Terry Whelan. Whelan was game, and upon his

---

*In fact, Lightfoot had not yet given up his dream of being a jazz drummer. Even as late as 1960, he took the opportunity to get behind the kit of a Toronto revue called Up Tempo, though under the pseudonym Charles Sullivan.

arrival in Toronto the pair picked up where they left off, this time as The Two Tones, and turned up on the Toronto coffee house circuit with a none-too-spectacular mix of popular folk material and primitive Lightfoot originals. It was a show that was even rejected by the organizers of the inaugural Mariposa Folk Festival, who turned the hometown boys down on the grounds that they sounded too commercial.

Lightfoot's television connections eventually gave The Two Tones a leg up. Over the course of his stint on *Country Hoedown*, he had purposely gotten to know the show's musical director, Art Snider, after learning that Snider also ran his own record label, called Chateau. Started in 1956, chiefly as a vehicle to promote his wife Jackie's group, The Allen Sisters, Chateau had a catalogue of nearly one hundred singles and LPs by 1961, making it one of the few successful Canadian independent pop labels. With their far-from-radical approach, The Two Tones were an ideal match for Snider's view of folk music, and their potential to appeal to the youth market led him to sign on as their manager. As a first step toward reaching this market, Snider undertook a live recording of a Two Tones show on Saturday, January 20, 1962, at a tiny Toronto coffee house called the Village Corner. The atmosphere of this stormy evening was captured remarkably well, supposedly by Lightfoot and Whelan themselves, in the liner notes to the eventual Two Tones album, *Live At the Village Corner*, released domestically a few months later.

They wrote, "Toronto was in the process of recovering from one of its famous ice storms. There was still ice on the telephone lines, with the gusty wind shaking bits of ice from the trees onto the heads of the unsuspecting souls below. Despite the conditions, the after-midnight crowd was there waiting for us. Whoever thought up the name 'Village Corner' wasn't far wrong. It is what used to be a house, about the size of a shoebox. Everyone was jammed in like matchwood, waiting for us to begin. It was so dark you could hardly see. The air was hot and sticky, the air conditioner wouldn't work, but the coffee machine was working overtime. The smoke hung over everything like fog.

"We went down the narrow stairwell, which led to the club. We wormed our way through the smoke and crowded tables to the tiny stage at the end of the room. The mikes were all set up when we got to the stage, and we opened with 'We Come Here To Sing.' The rest of the session speaks for itself herein. The driving bass of Howie Morris was there at all times in the up-tempo stuff, and he played imaginatively throughout. Everyone was clapping and singing and having a ball. By the time we finished the last chorus of 'Lord I'm So Weary' we really meant it, which is the way it should be. They wanted more, and we were glad, but we left them wanting."

Even for the time, parts of the album were painfully corny, mostly the between-song banter from Lightfoot and Whelan, which owed much to the role that bad jokes had played on *Country Hoedown*. Much of this can be blamed on Lightfoot's choice to approach the show's host, Gordie Tapp, for advice on stage patter. Tapp would later become a regular comedian on the U.S. variety show *Hee Haw*. Still, the harmonizing throughout *Live At the Village Corner* was impeccable, and several moments served as a glimpse into Lightfoot's immediate future. Most impressive was Lightfoot's solo take on Merle Travis's "Dark As a Dungeon," the Appalachian miner's lament he first heard through Ian Tyson, which contained strong elements of the frank, bittersweet story-telling style he would soon adopt. It was clear that Lightfoot sounded more comfortable with that song than with others on the album that were derived from Irish, Afro-American, and even Caribbean sources, although the pressure to remain "entertaining," unfortunately, took precedence.

The live album was received well at home, but there would only be one other Two Tones release, the single "Lesson in Love" b/w "Sweet Polly," before Snider urged Lightfoot to go out on his own with the songs he had been writing. They were primitive attempts, to be sure, as Lightfoot was still learning how to play the standard six-string guitar. Nevertheless, Snider was savvy enough to know that the best quality recordings could only be made in the U.S., and Lightfoot was sent down to Nashville for his first serious sessions. Lightfoot recalled, "Art Snider got some

Toronto artists together in '62 — I was one of them — and we went down to Nashville and got some real ace musicians. Got some real good sides, but I came out sounding like a cross between Jim Reeves and Pat Boone." Lightfoot's Nashville sessions began popping up on Chateau singles later that year. With a dearth of Canadian talent on the national radio charts, "Daisy Doo" b/w "Remember Me (I'm the One)" — both original compositions — easily cracked the domestic Top 10. Snider even managed to license this single to ABC Records in the U.S., and Decca Records in London, where it established an important presence for Lightfoot in England. There, a large audience still beckoned for this brand of quaint, provincial folk-pop. Lightfoot's profile had risen so much that he and Whelan were invited to play the second Mariposa Folk Festival that July, redeeming their failure of a year before. But it was Lightfoot's star that continued to rise during the rest of the year, with two more country crooning singles, "It's Too Late He Wins" b/w "Negotiations," and "Adios Adios" b/w "Is My Baby Blue Tonight." By now, Whelan had been replaced by a new companion, a fellow tenant in Lightfoot's Toronto boarding house, Brita Olaisson.

Olaisson and Lightfoot married in Stockholm on April 6, 1963, and, after a honeymoon, Lightfoot flew to London, where Snider had arranged for him to host an eight-episode BBC summer fill-in television series called *The Country and Western Show* broadcast Sunday nights just before *Perry Mason*. The show's content barely lived up to its name, as evidenced by guests like British vocal group the Kaye Sisters, who at that moment happened to have a hit with Cecil Null's Nashville standard "I Forgot More Than You'll Ever Know." The show's narrow focus hardly mattered though, since the entire island would soon be firmly in the grip of Beatlemania. There was no way that Lightfoot himself could not have sensed the shift in youth culture that was occurring around him, but whatever effect it may have had did not dissuade him from his chosen folk path after he returned to Toronto. By then, he had almost no other option; Snider had shut down Chateau in favour of new music-related projects, and Lightfoot could not bring himself to return to the artificial musical environment of *Country Hoedown*. On the other hand, embracing rock and roll was also out of the question since he had never had any interest in it before. He tried his hand, clumsily, at joining the growing ranks of protest singers, coming up with "Echoes of Heroes," a song he would never record, and would perform only briefly. Still, the lyrics hinted at an emerging ability to tackle complex subject matter in a simultaneously objective and poetic manner.

It also led to Lightfoot's realization that audiences in Toronto were paying attention to what he was saying. If they had even known of the "square" route he had taken to get to where he was, it was largely irrelevant. In 1964, the craving for literate folk music had reached its peak through Dylan's unrivalled creative standards, and whether he knew it or not, Lightfoot stood at the cusp of taking what was essentially his last stab at getting a piece of the action. He thought about how to do it all through that summer. And then one hot afternoon he wrote "Early Morning Rain." "It was so basic in its nature," Lightfoot said of that initial spark. "I think both Ian Tyson and I agreed at that time that, if [Dylan] could do it, at least we could sit down and write one! It was like an inspiration toward the work ethic, I suppose; get your tail down and get busy."

When Gordon Lightfoot first came to New York in the fall of 1964 to record, there weren't many indications that he was going to be the next Dylan. Grossman had convinced Warner Brothers to finance some demos, and most of what Lightfoot presented was middle-of-the-road country fare such as "A Love That's True" and "Betty Mae's A Good Time Gal," which seemed tailored to other artists. Not surprisingly, the label rejected him. Nevertheless, Grossman soon got him signed up with M. Witmark & Sons, a timely publishing deal given that the standard of Lightfoot's writing was about to be raised dramatically. In late 1964, he set up in Columbia's Studio D, with John Court producing. Although the emphasis was naturally placed upon Lightfoot's own strongest material, three significant covers were also recorded — the British folk standard "The First

Time Ever I Saw Your Face," "Changes," by American protest singer Phil Ochs, a regular visitor to Toronto who wrote the song during a residency there, and "Pride of Man," by one of Lightfoot's initial inspirations, Hamilton Camp. But, true to his word, Lightfoot's shows from that point on, with few exceptions, would consist entirely of original material.

On January 23, 1965, Peter, Paul & Mary released their version of "For Lovin' Me" as a single, which scraped into the *Billboard* Top 30 a month later. While it was an impressive debut for an unproven songwriter, the real breakthrough came when Marty Robbins' version of "Ribbon of Darkness" was released on March 22. It would hit number one on *Billboard*'s country and western chart on April 17, and remain on the chart for the next six months, earning Lightfoot an American Society of Composers, Authors and Publishers (ASCAP) award for writing. Ian & Sylvia's *Early Morning Rain* followed in July. The album contained both the title track and their take on "For Lovin' Me," but by then Lightfoot's earthy, straightforward style was reaching even further. A prime example was the German actress/model Nico, whom Albert Grossman had met in London during Dylan's British tour that spring, choosing a Lightfoot song for the A-side of her first single, "I'm Not Sayin'" b/w "The Last Mile," produced by twenty-one-year-old guitar prodigy Jimmy Page, and released on August 26. The following year, Nico was in New York, recruited by Andy Warhol to front his venture into the music industry, The Velvet Underground.

Lightfoot said, "I was very fortunate that Ian & Sylvia helped me out in the beginning, because I don't think without them anything would have ever happened — I just sometimes think that way. I would have been able to make a living, but it was through them that I was able to get involved with the American management. And believe me, I was tentative, too — because I'm such a conservative person by nature, and kinda shy — about getting involved in some of the deals when things would come to me. I used to find it hard to sign things. Like signing a contract with management for seven years would cause me to stop and wonder. But in the aftermath of that decision, I found that I got quite a few cover recordings because their publishing connections were really good."

The spate of chart placements led to Lightfoot's American television debut on *The Tonight Show*, shortly before he appeared — along with virtually all of Grossman's clients — at the Newport Folk Festival on July 25. In fact, Lightfoot took the stage in the afternoon prior to Dylan's brief, tumultuous electric set that night. It was the sound that essentially drove a stake through the heart of the Greenwich Village scene, but it could not discourage the growing interest in Lightfoot's songs. Wherever he performed that year — the Oddessey in Boston, the Second Fret in Philadelphia, the Living End in Detroit, the Gaslight South in Miami, Le Cave in Cleveland — audiences eagerly anticipated the hits, which others had already made famous. In many ways, it was part of Grossman's often brilliantly successful technique of building a mystique around an artist before fully offering them to the general public. In Lightfoot's case, the tactic was even more appropriate, since his songs proved popular with pop and country audiences alike. This was an unintended benefit of his never having had any association with rock and roll, or with the more radical side of folk.

Mary Martin says, "It was only a natural follow-through that Ian & Sylvia and Gordon were enabled to reach a broader audience [because of] Albert. Yes, I think that they had a different perspective on culture, and they were obviously writing from an entirely northern point of view that touched a lot of people's hearts. I mean, what could be better than 'Four Strong Winds?' But I always believed that the purity in the well-constructed songs of Gordon Lightfoot and Ian & Sylvia could not be denied."

Although Dylan was decisively pushing pop songwriting into a more sophisticated, mature realm that would eventually seamlessly blend folk, country, and rock, Lightfoot, in much more subtle ways, was already there, partially due to the values that were ingrained in him. "The thing is to try and make it on your own terms," he said in 1966. "I could write rock and roll tunes . . . you know, 'Death After The Senior Prom.' But I'm looking for my own sound, my own kind of music. It's not that I don't like rock and roll. It's just that I don't want to follow any beaten paths. I want to make it with a sound that's completely me."

Speaking forty years later, he betrayed no further hints of sentimentality. "The folk thing was already past [in 1964], because The Beatles had come along, and the folk revival was gone. For all intents and purposes, it only lasted for about three years. I just sort of carried on along that tangent throughout the rest of my career, adding a lot of material and getting more into the up side of the material, you know? The more positive aspect of it. Getting into family life, having children coming along, and working at the music. There was never, actually, any deviation from that particular objective."

Lightfoot earned impressive royalties even before his first album had been released, and appeared settled. He and Brita, who would soon bear their second child, bought a house in Toronto as the offers to perform kept pouring in. Around the time of Lightfoot's twenty-seventh birthday, Grossman arranged his New York coming-out party at Town Hall, where he was backed by the newly recruited duo of guitarist Laurice "Red" Shea, another veteran of *Country Hoedown*, and bassist John Stockfish. The drummer-less electric combo was another example of Lightfoot's ambiguous place within the wider musical sphere, but it was a format he would stick with, again with only minor variations, over the coming decades. The performance earned praise from Robert Shelton of *The New York Times*, although he pointedly added, "With a little more attention to stage personality, [Lightfoot] should become quite popular."

This viewpoint was, of course, still based on a single performance, since Lightfoot had gone the entire year without the benefit of having an album in stores. Grossman eventually found Lightfoot a deal with United Artists, a label with a reputation as amorphous as Lightfoot's own, mostly because the bulk of its product consisted of soundtracks to films that had been made by its parent company. *Lightfoot!* (his decidedly straight Anglo given name seemed purposely left off) was finally released in January

1966, and although the sound was a year behind the times, the songs themselves proved to be much more than mere blueprints for the cover versions. What stood out most was Lightfoot's Zen-like sensitivity to nature on the previously unheard "Long River" and "Sixteen Miles," a sharp contrast to the moralizing that characterized the more "contemporary" material, especially the cover songs. Lightfoot did not totally realize it yet, but his voice was most effective when it was immersed in the moment, not commenting after the fact. For all of the songwriting lessons he might have learned from Dylan and others, Lightfoot's expressions of emotion for nature itself, rather than as metaphors for human relationships, were still relatively unexplored territory in American popular song. Brian Wilson had almost single-handedly created the mythological California through his simple odes to beaches and surf culture. Now, with his first album, Lightfoot had taken the first unwitting step in creating a mythological Canada.

It was a situation that hit him head-on in February 1966, when he played to 3,500 people at Toronto's Varsity Arena before embarking on a nine-city British tour with the Tysons. In May, he was back in Toronto for an extended run at the Riverboat, in the heart of Yorkville. Although the venue was tiny, the crowds that packed it beyond capacity night after night were the manifestation of Lightfoot's common touch, and statements like the following, made to *The Globe and Mail*, solidified that down-to-earth image: "To write a song like ['Early Morning Rain'] you have to like earth movers, big ships, jet planes, and locomotives. You've got to get a charge out of seeing a big machine work. I guess it's really an appreciation of the power of big machines. It also manages to capture the romantic values, which I suppose makes it a good song. Everything I've written has come from something that's happened to me, something I've seen, something that's impressed me. Take a song like [the unreleased] 'Talkin' High Steel.' I spent some time with the high riggers [window washers] at the Toronto Dominion Centre. They were on about the forty-eighth floor at that time. Anyway, I got to know them, I got to understand what they're all about, how they think, so I could write about them."

His desire to remain in Toronto was a major point in Lightfoot's favour as well, when it came to building an audience at home. He had not applied for permanent status to live and work in the U.S., and never would. This was in spite of Grossman's insistence that Lightfoot needed to drastically curtail his appearances in Canada by the fall of 1966. By this time, his schedule was also contributing to the first cracks in his marriage. However, all of that did not prevent Lightfoot from accepting an unusual commission from the CBC to write a song in honour of Canada's centennial, and, more specifically, the construction of the continental railway line. The mere idea of a popular recording artist doing anything on behalf of a government institution seemed unconscionable in the mid-sixties. But the seeds of Canada's emergence from under the shadow of American political and economic dominance were taking root under the Liberal government of Lester B. Pearson, and would grow to full fruition in 1967, with the ascension of his successor, Pierre Trudeau. In this sense, Lightfoot's role during this crucial moment of national awakening, through his vision of Canada's landscape and history, was just as important.

Lightfoot premiered the six-minute "Canadian Railroad Trilogy" on a New Year's Day, 1967, CBC television special, setting the tone for an ensuing twelve months of ongoing collective epiphanies centred around Expo 67 in Montreal. Of course, it instantly became his most popular song at home, a fact that, perhaps, first shed light on the general limitations of being defined as a "Canadian" artist.★ Conversely, songs from the first album had continued to hit the U.S. country charts throughout 1966, in versions by RCA artists Waylon Jennings and George Hamilton IV, raising expectations for a new crop of Lightfoot material. As part of his creation of RCA's "Nashville Sound," Chet Atkins introduced a folk element, using almost entirely

---

★Ironically, Lightfoot's inspiration for the structure of "Trilogy" was Bob Gibson's "Civil War Trilogy." Lightfoot also wrote "Crossroads" at the behest of the CBC.

Canadian-penned material, to many of his artists. The North Carolina–born Hamilton became its biggest Nashville champion after he discovered Lightfoot's "Steel Rail Blues." Over the next few years, he would go on to record songs by the Tysons, Joni Mitchell, and Leonard Cohen, along with a healthy dose of Lightfoot, which led to Hamilton's own CBC television show and an honorary Juno award.

But it was the precedent set by Dylan's *Blonde on Blonde* that ultimately brought Lightfoot, Shea, and Stockfish to Nashville for recording sessions after a January 1967 run at the Riverboat. The ensuing results, on *The Way I Feel*, again produced by John Court, were, in their way, just as inscrutable as Dylan's work had been. Utilizing two of the key *Blonde on Blonde* players, drummer Kenny Buttrey and multi-instrumentalist Charlie McCoy, certainly brought Lightfoot closer to a contemporary folk-rock sound than ever before. This was most obviously heard in the revamped version of the title track, which had already appeared on *Lightfoot!* Although he later admitted to a preference for the New York version, and chose to include it in the 1999 retrospective *Songbook*, the swirling intensity that the Nashville ensemble achieved perfectly matched the depths in which the song's protagonist was placed and his need to escape by means of transfiguration.

While this revision of "The Way I Feel" would forever hold a unique place within Lightfoot's canon, the album as a whole appeared to make pop concessions that he would never again feel comfortable making. However, the rich storytelling of "Go-Go Round" and "Home From the Forest" foreshadowed the encroachment of urban realities on country/folk–based songwriting that would soon divide the Nashville establishment, leading to the rise of a new, contemporary blue-collar expressionism. None of this was generally noticed in Canada, where Lightfoot's position in the vanguard of the nation's cultural renaissance was already secure. *The Way I Feel* was released in late February 1967, coinciding with his first Massey Hall concert on March 31. Accolades poured in throughout the summer, including a "Gordon Lightfoot Day" in Orillia on August 5.

Still, Lightfoot's overall American record sales remained

disappointing, not exceeding 20,000 copies for either album. With "Go-Go Round" generating the first substantial airplay he'd ever had on his own, the urgency for Lightfoot to break into the U.S. before the folk-rock boom was completely overwhelmed by the burgeoning psychedelic scene became imperative. Lightfoot was thus introduced to John Simon, a twenty-six-year-old staff producer at Columbia Records, whose first major credit, "Red Rubber Ball," by The Cyrkle, was an early psych-pop hit in 1966. Simon had drifted into the Grossman clique, which was now essentially based in and around the manager's isolated Woodstock, New York, retreat, shortly thereafter when Peter, Paul & Mary's Peter Yarrow asked for Simon's help with the soundtrack to an experimental film he was producing called *You Are What You Eat*. By the summer of 1967, Grossman had signed Big Brother & The Holding Company, fronted by Janis Joplin, and landed them a deal with Columbia on the strength of their lauded performance at the Monterey Pop Festival that June. Simon was tapped to produce their first album for the label, *Cheap Thrills*, along with the debut album for another Grossman act, Al Kooper's innovative jazz-rock ensemble Blood, Sweat & Tears.

Simon met Lightfoot during an engagement at Philadelphia's Second Fret that fall, which led to more serious discussions later back in Toronto. As expected, Lightfoot had a wealth of material compiled, the most intriguing song being "Black Day in July," inspired by the race riots that had occurred in Detroit that summer. It was Lightfoot's boldest attempt yet at writing an overt "protest" song, although he would later admit that the decision to record it was more of a test to see if a market for such songs still existed. The plan ultimately backfired when many U.S. radio stations boycotted the song (along with stations in Windsor, Ontario), citing its potential to incite further violence, and this remained a contentious issue with Lightfoot many years later. "That particular song was a song I wrote for an album, and it looked like the record company wanted to release it as a single," he said. "And it was released as a single. I really didn't have anything to do with that. There were also two or three other really good songs that were written right at that time, too, about the Detroit riot in 1967, and a couple of those made it up high on the charts. They were good rock tunes, and they were very well handled. Mine was a little bit too direct. I was really happy that it got banned. I didn't want it to be on the radio, anyway."

That aside, the New York sessions with Simon in December 1967 essentially saw the birth of Lightfoot's trademark sound, when the producer introduced strings after initial tracks were laid down. Lightfoot's own liner notes to *Did She Mention My Name*, released in January 1968, expressed surprise that the combination could work, yet Simon's subtle orchestration perfectly complemented the haunting timbre of Lightfoot's voice. The opening track, "Wherefor & Why," even seemed to be an attempt by Lightfoot to address the mysterious source of his creativity. While there could be no definitive answer, the song cast a defiant stance in the face of increasing pressure to mould his image. In fact, *Did She Mention My Name*, for all its musical innovation, marked the beginning of the end of Lightfoot's relationship with Grossman. With still little radio play, the manager kept pushing for more prestigious gigs in the U.S., and throughout 1968 Grossman facilitated Lightfoot's debuts in San Francisco and Washington, D.C., as well as at the Bitter End in New York, the Troubadour in L.A., and the Hollywood Bowl, the last as an opener for Peter, Paul & Mary. In between, Lightfoot briefly escaped to England in order to write a batch of new songs he hoped would speed up his release from United Artists. His frustrations with the label's ineffective promotion were compounded by the realities of his now-irreparable marriage. Lightfoot's longing for a simple family life had already reared its head at several points on *Did She Mention My Name*, but as he worked in his London hotel room, the longing completely spilled out in songs like "Bitter Green," "Cold Hands From New York," "Don't Beat Me Down," "Unsettled Ways," and "The Gypsy." Back on the road that summer, he wrote the dramatic "Affair on 8th Avenue" in Denver, which set the stage for sessions in September with producer Elliot Mazer, a leading member of the young Nashville establishment who had just worked with the Tysons on their first tentative stabs at a country crossover, *Nashville* and *Full Circle*.

Given Lightfoot's state of mind, it was no surprise that *Back Here on Earth* was his most sombre recording yet. If anyone needed advance warning, they only had to read the lengthy poem on the back cover, which amounted to a desperate cry for stability: "I see the poet as a word prophet/A dealer in songs and phrases/Of whistful melodies and subtle warnings/Passing his nights in loneliness/Tormented by blank pages/Which cry out with dying breath/To be filled with the/Secrets of his heart." Lightfoot found a modicum of that stability, as always, in Canada. For his third straight year of headlining at Massey Hall, he determined to record his four March 1969 shows, both for posterity and to close the book on his United Artists contract. The resulting album, *Sunday Concert*, revealed much more diversity than might have been expected. Lightfoot made a point of including several older, previously unrecorded songs. The most significant of these was "Ballad of the Yarmouth Castle," written in the immediate aftermath of the November 13, 1965, fiery sinking of that ship off the coast of Miami. Lightfoot's choice to debut this epic piece now, over three years later (George Hamilton IV had recorded it in 1967), was a sharp statement against those who may have doubted his instincts. Although the song did not achieve as much notoriety as others would in the future, the sheer effortlessness of its storytelling remained a benchmark that Lightfoot would not forget.

The spring of 1969 was to be a season of renewal for Lightfoot in nearly all respects. Free from United Artists, he set Grossman to work on finding a new record deal. It would be the manager's last major task on behalf of his client, as Lightfoot would soon set up his own Toronto-based company, Early Morning Productions, to handle all aspects of his career. He would no longer go out of his way to cater to the American marketplace; it would have to come to him. He also reconciled himself with the fact that his marriage was over, although freeing himself from that guilt would take much longer.

As the seventies dawned, a large segment of American music fans seemed ready to accept Gordon Lightfoot on his own terms. In part, this was because Bob Dylan had popularized the stripped-down country-folk sound of Lightfoot and the Tysons in rock circles with his "post-accident" albums *John Wesley Harding* (1968) and *Nashville Skyline* (1969). Dylan even conceded, in a 1969 interview, the impact Lightfoot was having with his own quest to break down genre barriers: "I'd heard the sound that Gordon Lightfoot was getting with Charlie McCoy and Kenneth Buttrey. I'd used Charlie and Kenny before, and I figured if he could get that sound, I could. But we couldn't get it. It was an attempt to get it, but it didn't come off. We got a different sound, a muffled sound."

That original sound also reflected the sensibilities of Lenny Waronker, the young head of A & R at Warner Brothers, which now boasted many of the best singer-songwriters outside of Nashville, including Randy Newman, James Taylor, and Van Morrison. The never-ending arguments over country versus pop, or folk versus rock, did not appear to affect any of the label's decisions, making a respected artist like Lightfoot a natural fit, despite what other labels would have considered his disappointing sales history. Waronker's L.A. office was truly a unique, artist-friendly environment. As staff producer Russ Titelman described, "It was people who knew about music and had a lot of fun making it. The signings were incredibly hip. Lenny turned Arlo Guthrie into a pop act, which wasn't easy, and he made hit records with Gordon Lightfoot. It created a certain vibe and a certain perception. In a way — a good way — it was all things to all people."

During the initial sessions in L.A. for *Sit Down Young Stranger*, co-produced by Waronker and Joe Wissert, Lightfoot was adamant about staying true to his usual guitar/bass backing, but Waronker was equally adamant about incorporating some of Warner's immense talent pool, suggesting Randy Newman to do string arrangements, and fellow label mainstays Ry Cooder and Van Dyke Parks for added texture. Lightfoot could hardly complain about such attention to detail, and selected his material in accordance with this fresh approach to the U.S. market. Surprisingly, he pinned his hopes on someone else's song. Lightfoot had first heard Kris Kristofferson during a stop in Nashville in the summer of 1969 to appear on *The Johnny Cash Show*. A one-time Rhodes scholar, U.S. army officer, and Texas oil field chopper pilot, Kristofferson had been pushing his songs around Nashville for several years. Although he shared many stylistic similarities with Lightfoot, he had not made any headway until he convinced Johnny Cash to record the gut-wrenching "Sunday Morning Coming Down" by (as the legend goes) personally delivering a demo to Cash by helicopter. The tape that Lightfoot heard contained the song "Me and Bobby McGee," and he could immediately hear himself putting his own spin on its simple, lilting cadence. Lightfoot displayed even more foresight in understanding how the song — with the quintessentially American notion of freedom at its core — could help him finally break onto the U.S. pop charts. Conversely, when Kristofferson heard of Lightfoot's plans to record it, he urged that "Me and Bobby McGee" not be released as a single, since he knew Roger Miller's soon-to-be released version was sure to be a hit on the country charts. Before the year was out, Janis Joplin's posthumous version would also be released.

Initial sales of *Sit Down Young Stranger* were therefore handicapped upon its release in May 1970, although Lightfoot's loyal fan base embraced the album as the fresh start it effectively was. One of those fans was a Seattle DJ who started regularly playing the poignant track "If You Could Read My Mind." Its inherent melancholy was perfectly suited to the damp Pacific Northwest, and led to a flood of listener requests. After several other stations in the area added the song, Warner Brothers made the unorthodox move, in the autumn of 1970, of not only rushing it out as a single, but recalling all copies of the album and renaming it *If You Could Read My Mind*. In February 1971, the single hit number five, and the album hit number twelve on the *Billboard* charts, giving Lightfoot his first U.S. gold records.

Yet, for all the financial and artistic security Lightfoot enjoyed both at Warner Brothers and through the tight-knit

Toronto coterie that now managed his career, his personal life remained a minefield of potential disasters. Chief among them was his relationship with Cathy Evelyn Smith, whom Lightfoot had met in 1966 when she was a waitress at the Riverboat. Smith, who was still grappling with being shunned by Levon Helm, found in Lightfoot a more grounded, yet still glamorous, partner, and he, in turn, did not resist engaging their initial affair in the midst of his marital strife. By 1971 they were living together in Toronto, with Smith acting as part nursemaid and part muse, leaving Lightfoot plenty of space to churn out an astounding amount of material. The result was three more successful albums over the next two years: *Summer Side of Life*, *Don Quixote*, and *Old Dan's Records*.

However, Lightfoot's creative outpouring was largely motivated by his fear that his career was about to end. Lightfoot had to stop one of his 1972 Massey Hall concerts when his face suddenly went numb, preventing him from singing. He was diagnosed with Bell's palsy, and immediately started a strict regimen of drugs and therapy to combat the disease. It also increased his alcohol intake, making his mood swings violent and unpredictable.

While Smith relished her domestic role during Lightfoot's recovery, her undiminished desire for excitement, along with Lightfoot's mental state and inborn suspicion, were a dangerous combination. The situation was not helped by Lightfoot's frequent attempts to reconcile with Brita, which caused Smith to counter with her own threats to see other men. Smith finally followed through on these by having an affair with Brian Good, a member of Lightfoot's frequent opening act, The Good Brothers. Also comprised of Brian's twin brother Bruce, younger brother Larry, and friend James Ackroyd, the band's star was rising in the country-rock world, having signed to Columbia in 1970, and recorded its first album in San Francisco, with help from members of The Grateful Dead and Jefferson Airplane. Throughout that entire period, Lightfoot had managed to keep his personal pain separate from his music, and instead stayed within the safe territory of songs such as "Alberta

Bound" and "Cotton Jenny." But he perceived Smith's affair
with Good as such a calculated blow to his ego that he was
forced to respond.

Released at the start of 1974, "Sundown" possessed an under-
stated air of dread, and subtle hints of violence: "You'd better
take care, if I find you've been creepin' 'round my back stair."
This set the tone for a year that would cap off Lightfoot's string
of miseries, all of which came at the height of his success, as
both the album *Sundown* and the title track hit number one in
America at the end of June. In March, his father died of cancer.
This had been preceded by the finalization of his divorce from
Brita, which awarded her custody of their two children, along
with the largest cash settlement of any previous Canadian
divorce. By year's end, his relationship with Smith had also dis-
solved in a haze of alcohol-fuelled physical abuse. He naturally
insulated himself even further, but a major 1975 American magazine profile caught him in a moment of reflection, despite his
vehement denials of being an alcoholic.

Lightfoot said, "The effect of my music on my personal life
is devastating. One thing I know, when you're greedy to out-
grow that period in your life when you want to go out with
different people, you make a decision. If you're going to make
a commitment to a permanent relationship, and there's going
to be children involved, you should at least be willing to make
a commitment to fidelity. It seems that people can't sustain a
romantic figure nowadays. They feel that when the romance has
died they're actually deceiving themselves. There must be
something between a man and woman besides being just lovey-
dovey. The sexual part of it definitely runs up to a peak and
then levels off. Everybody knows it. When you're away from
the woman, continually confronted by other women, you suddenly find yourself in a weak moment. Then you've gone and
stepped over the traces and you gotta go home and confront
your old lady. It's a two-way street. You're going to have to offer
her the same deal. You can't ask the woman to be faithful if
you're not going to be faithful to her. That's where it's broken
down for me twice."

Everywhere, participants in the sexual revolution seemed to be receiving their comeuppance by 1975. In this respect, Bob Dylan showed that he still had his finger on society's pulse with his universally lauded "comeback," *Blood on the Tracks*. While that album would be endlessly scrutinized, few acknowledged the obvious debt it owed to Lightfoot's work of that period. Sonically, it shared the simple, acoustic-based arrangements and intimate performances that were Lightfoot's stock-in-trade, but lyrically Dylan's maturation as a poet echoed Lightfoot's long-held belief in complex, character-driven material rather than the earnest, confessional stance taken by most other singer-songwriters of the period. Many of these were unfortunately tagged "the new Dylans." In 1985, Dylan himself put it simply: "Gordon Lightfoot, every time I hear a song of his, it's like I wish it would last forever."

Dylan's personal wish was the almost unavoidable effect generated when "The Wreck of the Edmund Fitzgerald" was first heard. That the song became a hit at all remains one of pop music's great mysteries. As with "Ballad of the Yarmouth Castle," Lightfoot was inspired after reading a news report about the November 10, 1975, sinking of the Great Lakes freighter on Lake Superior. However, the relatively low death toll, coming on the heels of America's ignominious withdrawal from Vietnam, was a story that a majority of the country passed by, or had simply forgotten, by the time the song was released, along with the album *Summertime Dream*, in May 1976. But in those seven verses, Lightfoot produced an account that was as insightful (despite a few factual inaccuracies) as anything a journalist could have written.

In some ways, the rise of "Edmund Fitzgerald" up the charts was spurred on by every song about maritime, mining, or railroad disasters that had come before it. What made this song unique, though, was that men were not supposed to die as anonymously as Lightfoot portrayed it. Indeed, "all that remains is the faces and names," but Lightfoot chose to reveal no more. The myth created by the song was therefore not of the men themselves, as a traditional balladeer might have written it, but of their unwilling sacrifice, a notion that narrowed the song down to its essential unanswerable question: "Does anyone know where the love of God goes/When the waves turn the minutes to hours?"

Within a year, the task of posing such questions of faith and sacrifice within the realm of pop music would be taken up by a new generation, as America's post-Vietnam/post-Watergate political culture inevitably descended into a media-driven, good-versus-evil world view. As a result, events similar to the *Edmund Fitzgerald* sinking would achieve instant heroic status, just as any artist hoping to generate discourse about the actual merits of such an honour would be instantly marginalized. While there was no indication that Lightfoot was striving for anything beyond objectivity in the song, from that point on even objectivity would come at a premium in pop music. To that extent, "The Wreck of the Edmund Fitzgerald" marked the end of the brief twenty-year lifespan of folk balladry as a main-stream art form, and Lightfoot would never again reach such commercial heights.

Nonetheless, he would persevere in the coming decades, set-tling into family life once again while never failing to please his loyal audience with new records and regular tours. But his refusal to drastically alter his aesthetic somehow made it seem more antiquated as the years went on. Moreover, the simple act of playing a few chords on an acoustic guitar and adding some poetry was no longer enough to escape the massive burden that Lightfoot's first decade as a recording artist placed upon his image. As always, it hardly mattered; those who weren't interested could leave him alone. And while this attitude ensured that his iconic status would be preserved in Canada, the songwriters who did dare to change would create a necessary challenge to Lightfoot's vision of the country, one that would ultimately encompass a complex view of the rest of the world, as well.

CHAPTER FIVE

LAST YEAR'S MAN

"THE SONG WAS BEGUN, and the chord pattern was developed, before a woman's name entered the song. And I knew it was a song about Montreal, it seemed to come out of that landscape that I loved very much in Montreal, which was the harbour, and the waterfront, and the sailors' church there, called Notre-Dame-de-Bon-Secours, which stood out over the river. And I knew that there were ships going by, I knew that there was a harbour, I knew that there was Our Lady of the Harbour, which was the Virgin on the church which stretched out her arms toward the seamen, and you can climb up to the tower and look out over the river, so the song came from that vision, from that view of the river.

"At a certain point, I bumped into Suzanne Vaillancourt, who was the wife of a friend of mine. They were a stunning couple around Montreal at the time, physically stunning, both of them; a handsome man and woman. Every man was in love with Suzanne Vaillancourt, and every woman was in love with Armand Vaillancourt. But there was no . . . Well, there was thought, but there was no possibility, one would not allow oneself to think of toiling at the seduction of Armand Vaillancourt's wife. First of all, he was a friend, and second of all, as a couple they were inviolate, you just didn't intrude into the kind of shared glory that they manifested.

"I bumped into her one evening, and she invited me down to her place near the river. She had a loft, at a time when lofts were . . . The word wasn't used. She had a space in a warehouse down there, and she invited me down, and I went with her, and she served me Constant Comment tea, which has little bits of oranges in it. And the boats were going by, and I touched her perfect body with my mind, because there was no other opportunity. There was no other way that you could touch her perfect body under those circumstances. So she provided the name in the song."

Leonard Cohen was speaking more than a quarter-century after the fateful encounter that inspired his first great song. His honest, vivid recollection of "Suzanne" still brimmed with the raw passion of self-discovery the song subsequently brought out in each first-time listener, whether through Cohen's own version or any of the dozens of covers. The potential of such a song to have immediate resonance on a broad scale was surely the furthest thing from Cohen's mind after this specific evening with Suzanne Verdal (the name she later reverted to after splitting up with the sculptor Vaillancourt) in her apartment, at 115 De La Commune Ouest — now room 202 in the hotel L'Auberge de la Place Royale. At the time, 1966, Cohen was experiencing his first flash of fame, albeit within the relatively insular community of Canadian literature. In fact, that year an earlier draft of "Suzanne" had made it into a collection of his poetry, called *Parasites of Heaven*. But not enough people read poetry, much less bought it, even as the media began grooming Cohen to be the voice of Canada's enlightened post-war generation. What few knew was that this golden boy of Canadian letters also admired the decidedly less academic storytelling associated with country and folk music.

On February 20, 1966, Cohen was in Montreal's Place Des Arts to hear Bob Dylan and The Hawks. Accompanying him was his mentor, the poet Irving Layton, along with a group of Layton's students. Cohen had first become aware of Dylan after being awed by the biblical reckoning of "A Hard Rain's A-Gonna Fall" in 1963, but lost touch with the folk boom during a self-imposed exile he largely spent writing the novel *Beautiful Losers*. But as Cohen sat mesmerized, like everyone else, for the

solo first half of Dylan's concert, he saw his future. At the inter-
mission, Cohen shared his revelation with Layton, who, in his
typical blustery manner, proclaimed to the students that Cohen
was now a singer-songwriter.

Understandably, there was much laughter.

If Dylan opened Gordon Lightfoot up to the expressive possibilities of his surroundings — essentially making him aware of
his poetic potential — then his effect on Cohen was to release
much deeper and complicated reservoirs of emotion. Dylan had
made a point of trying to write songs unlike any that had been
written before; Cohen's epiphany was that he himself had written songs of this sort, only he had neglected to set them to
music. "I always thought of myself as a singer, and kind of got
sidetracked to literature," he said only two months after the
Dylan concert, when he was supposed to be talking about
Beautiful Losers. The novel's publication that April was the cul-
mination of a two-year struggle due to its experimental
structure and what some deemed obscene sexual depictions.
With many stores refusing to stock the book based on these
latter accusations, initial sales did not exceed 5,000 copies for all
of North America. For Cohen, who had been carefully nurturing his reputation since his first poetry collection was published
in 1956, his original dream of beatnik glory appeared dead.

It was a dream that Dylan had partly shared, as well, although
he had managed to integrate it into his explorations of folk
music's darker corners. Yet, by 1964, he began getting serious
consideration from literary critics after using a series of poems
called "11 Outlined Epitaphs" as the liner notes for *The Times
They Are A-Changin'*; they were followed later that year by
"Some Other Kinds of Songs," included on *Another Side of Bob
Dylan*. In fact, Dylan was churning out a remarkable amount of
prose at the time, not the least of which was the surrealist novel
Tarantula, leading to speculation that he was preparing to abandon music altogether. There was certainly no shortage of new
songwriters with poetic affectations waiting in the wings if this
was indeed the case. Even prior to Cohen's formal appearance

on the scene, hints of existentialism were hitting the pop charts through the work of Paul Simon. More significantly, pop song form was completely erased when Jim Morrison, a UCLA film student also immersed in the work of French symbolists such as Baudelaire and Rimbaud, updated the Oedipal myth on "The End," the riveting twelve-minute playlet that closed The Doors' self-titled debut album. Simultaneously, on the east coast, Syracuse University English major Lou Reed was channelling the brutal visions of Raymond Chandler and Hubert Selby Jr. into the songs on The Velvet Underground's first album, particularly the S & M fantasy "Venus in Furs" and the monumental "Heroin," which owed a huge debt to the Beat writers William S. Burroughs and Allen Ginsberg.

The atmosphere, therefore, couldn't have been more conducive for Cohen's transition to songwriting, whether or not he was fully aware of it. On Monday, May 23, 1966, as Dylan and The Hawks were preparing to stir anti-American ire in Paris, Cohen turned up at the CBC television studios in Toronto, ostensibly for an interview to promote *Beautiful Losers*. Instead, he brought his Spanish guitar along, and took the opportunity to present himself as a singer for the first time before the entire country. He was allowed to play three songs: the now fully realized "Suzanne," the more traditionally structured "So Long, Marianne," and "The Stranger Song," a lengthy, almost impenetrable piece that could have come directly from the novel. Yet, while it was clear that Cohen was in large part following Dylan's blueprint, as "The Stranger Song" demonstrated, there were few changes in his lyrical approach to this new medium. Still present was the religious symbolism, a virtual taboo in the pop world, which he made more provocative by intertwining it with sex. But that aside, with this single performance, it seemed that Cohen had done what no Canadian writer before him had dared to do. Within a year, every other poet in the world would envy his new audience.

"I was always more interested in the exile, somebody who can't claim the entire landscape as his own." And so it would be from the moment Leonard Norman Cohen entered the world on September 21, 1934, the second child of Nathan and Masha Cohen. Unlike many other Jewish families, the Cohens had come to Montreal at the end of the nineteenth century already self-sufficient. Leonard's devout great-grandfather Lazarus ran a dredging company that survived on lucrative government contracts, generating earnings that allowed him the time and resources to aid many Canadian Jewish organizations. It was a mantle passed on to Leonard's grandfather, Lyon Cohen, who made his home in the decidedly non-Jewish Montreal neighbourhood of Westmount, and carved out his own successful niche running a men's clothing factory. This business was passed on to his sons, Nathan and Horace, with the former relegated to overseeing operations on the shop floor due to an injury he had suffered during the First World War. It was a circumstance that left Nathan somewhat at odds with the rest of the family, although he made no objections to meeting Masha Klinitsky-Klein, whose father, a Lithuanian rabbi, had emigrated to Montreal through the aid of Lyon Cohen. Nathan and Masha were married in 1927, and gave birth to a daughter, Esther, shortly thereafter.

From his earliest days, Leonard thrived in the presence of his maternal grandfather, where he listened intently to readings from the Torah and the Old Testament. These visits compensated for the lack of attention Leonard usually received from his father, whose declining health often darkened his mood. He died in 1944, at age fifty-two, three years before Leonard's bar mitzvah. Cohen found solace by continuing his religious studies, which also helped him come to grips with his first awareness of Nazi atrocities as he entered high school. Once there, he became a prominent figure, participating in student council, various athletics, and the drama society. These soon led to more solitary interests, however, namely writing, music, and — surprisingly — hypnotism. The concept of possessing power over others, although not necessarily for the purpose of manipulating them, was a manifestation of Cohen's desire, by his mid-teens, to escape his sheltered upbringing. This was occurring at the same time as he was discovering the opposite sex. During one of his sojourns into downtown Montreal, he happened upon a flamenco guitarist playing to an enraptured group of girls, which prompted him to immediately get his own guitar and persuade the man to give him rudimentary lessons. Simultaneously, Cohen was also immersed in the work of Spanish poet Federico Garcia Lorca, and suddenly an entirely new personal identity presented itself.

It came at the right time, as Masha remarried in 1950, adding to Cohen's growing estrangement from his family. That year, he became a counsellor at the Jewish summer camp he had attended since his father's death, and his nascent guitar-playing abilities were quickly improved as he learned many pro-union, anti-fascist ballads from *The People's Songbook*, which was popular among his fellow counsellors, and one of the most accessible pre-folk revival sources for such material. Learning these songs opened up still more possible worlds for Cohen, but after graduating from high school in the spring of 1951, a lingering sense of duty to his family forced him to enroll at McGill University. Cohen's unspectacular grades in his first year suggest that he regretted the decision, despite the fact that he excelled on the school's debating team and performed many duties on behalf of the Jewish students' organization.

What he ultimately found at McGill was the guidance he had been seeking to focus his burgeoning creativity. For the first time, Cohen's writing was critically assessed, and by some of the most prominent figures in Canadian literature who happened to be teaching at McGill, among them novelist Hugh MacLennan. With this encouragement, Cohen wrote vociferously, further establishing his presence on campus. Off campus, his interest in folk music as an avenue to learn guitar had expanded to country and western. From his Montreal bedroom, Cohen could easily pick up the powerful signal from WWVA in Wheeling, West Virginia, not to mention the *Grand Ole Opry*, where Hank Snow's star was beginning to rise. In these simple, straightforward songs, Cohen heard a drastically different language from the texts he was now spending most of his time deciphering.

However, it was not a comparatively soothing language, especially when a Hank Williams performance would come down the wire; it described a land filled with as many mysteries as Lorca's Spain, but a land much more accessible to the eighteen-year-old Cohen.

Although replicating Williams' sound was beyond his grasp, there surely weren't many more peculiar sights than when Cohen and his two compadres in The Buckskin Boys showed up to play. Cohen had formed the trio in the summer of 1952 to provide music for the square-dancing events that were held at churches and high schools on most weekends. "We lived about four or five houses down from each other on Belmont Avenue, and we'd play commandos together in the park as kids," says Frank Dodman, whose brother Mike played in The Buckskin Boys. "Sometimes we'd go over to Lenny's basement and fool around with his father's German Luger, which he got during the war. My father worked for the Hudson's Bay Company, where he'd gotten this buckskin jacket. My brother took it over, and that inspired the name of the group. They would rehearse in our basement with a friend of theirs named Murray on harmonica. Hank Snow was a big favourite, but they would play other country hits of the day. My brother got interested in square-dance calling, so he started lining up square-dance gigs, which is what I mostly remember them doing. You could tell that Lenny was different from other kids, but at the time it wasn't unusual for him to be playing country music. We were all just kids from the same neighbourhood trying to have some fun. The band stayed together for probably two or three years, until Lenny got more involved in debating and other things at university."

In 1954, Cohen was still contemplating a career in law when his life was forever altered by meeting Irving Layton. In Layton, Cohen acquired not only a literary role model, but also the father figure that had largely been absent through his teenage years. Twenty years Cohen's senior, Layton also came from eastern European Jewish stock, although, being only one generation removed from it, his writing was infused with all the passions that were the by-product of hard-won freedom. Cohen had been aware of Layton since his first ventures into the Montreal underground in the late forties, and forged a deep connection with Layton's first two poetry collections published during those years, work that was marked by a highly sexualized style and attitude that was virtually foreign to Canadian art. When Cohen discovered that Layton was working as a teaching assistant in McGill's political science department, he jumped at the chance to have the older poet read from his latest book at Cohen's fraternity house. Layton reciprocated by evaluating some of Cohen's work, and from that point on they were inseparable. The pair travelled together to Layton's readings in Toronto and elsewhere, and Cohen eagerly played the role of what was, in his estimation, the master's apprentice. He was, likewise with Layton, at the first Canadian Writer's Conference, held at Queen's University in Kingston over the last weekend of July 1955. It was there that the unknown Cohen saw firsthand what he was up against in terms of making the leap into the publishing world, and, with the larger-than-life Layton in his corner, it seemed only a matter of time before he would gain acceptance.

It came shortly after his graduation in 1956, when another of his important teachers, the poet Louis Dudek, offered to publish Cohen's first collection, *Let Us Compare Mythologies*, under a new, McGill-funded imprint. The book, containing forty-four pieces, some written as early as age fifteen, appeared to justify the image Cohen had been cultivating. He even insisted that the first edition be released in hardcover, and personally chipped in three hundred dollars to cover the cost. Poetry's groundswell in popularity, spurred on by Allen Ginsberg's highly publicized October 13, 1955, reading of *Howl* in San Francisco's Six Gallery, was not being overlooked by Sam Gesser, either. As part of the free reign he had to make Canadian recordings for Folkways, Gesser gathered Cohen, Layton, Dudek, and three other writers for the spoken-word album *Six Montreal Poets*. Cohen was given ample focus — seven selections — although, like most of Gesser's recording projects, the album remained a curiosity for some time after its 1957 release.

Yet, aside from the brief excitement surrounding his book's publication, the rest of 1956 found Cohen struggling with his post-graduate future. He spent the summer hanging out with other Montreal artists, smoking marijuana, dropping LSD, and trying to get laid. Being published helped procure all three, but along with these pursuits came the first signs of depression and an increasing pressure to face the reality of his troubled family life. Instead, Cohen chose to escape, enrolling at Columbia University, just as Lorca had done. But, like his time at McGill, classes were far from his top priority. Turned loose in New York City, Cohen suddenly found himself absorbed in his Beat fantasies. He heard poets reading overtop of jazz combos for the first time, and one night even talked his way into a party at Ginsberg's apartment, where he encountered Jack Kerouac half comatose under the dining room table. Cohen returned to Montreal in the summer of 1957 burning with new ideas. He attempted to start a poetry magazine, which lasted one issue, and completed a novella based on his grandfather's descent into senility. Unable to sell it, Cohen reattached himself to Layton, as well as to the family business, as a means of support, and by the spring of 1958 he was making every attempt to recreate what he had experienced in Greenwich Village in Montreal cafés.

For the next year and a half, Cohen honed his work and was rewarded with, first, interest from McClelland & Stewart to publish his next poetry collection, and, second, a substantial Canada Council grant for a proposed novel. The influx of cash quickly set in motion a plan to do his writing at various locales outside Canada, and he first set his sights on London in December 1959. Cohen worked diligently there through the winter, protected from the elements by a blue raincoat he'd purchased upon arrival. By spring, he was restless, and a suggestion to move to an artists' colony on the Greek island of Hydra fully germinated. The island turned out to be a bustling getaway destination, not only for many prominent English-speaking artists, but for film stars and politicians as well. Cohen found accommodation with husband-and-wife Australian journalists before purchasing his own home in the fall for $1,500. By then, Cohen had taken up with Marianne Ihlen, a Norwegian model who, along with her young son, had been abandoned on the island by her companion. The relationship sustained Cohen emotionally, but by the end of the year, a need for money forced him to briefly return to Montreal.

Coming home produced an immediate culture shock, and aside from catching up with Layton and finalizing the details for the publication of his next book, Cohen found no reason to linger any longer than absolutely necessary. His next destination of choice was Cuba, again based on its association with deceased literary heroes. However, this time Cohen's timing couldn't have been worse, as tensions between Castro and the U.S. were reaching a fever pitch. Cohen mingled well within Havana's artistic circles, but his presence at a time of extreme national paranoia led to his brief detainment as a suspected American spy. An urgent letter from Layton told Cohen that a U.S. invasion was imminent, and two days later the Bay of Pigs fiasco had most citizens with the means to leave scrambling for the airport. If the situation had shaken Cohen, he didn't show it in his correspondence, written in the heat of the military action. The raids and gunfire had instead charged him, providing what he surmised to be the perfect fodder for his image as a contemporary poet with a global perspective. But a narrow escape to Miami showed him the danger of getting too close to the action, and ultimately Cohen's Cuban excursion resulted in only a handful of poems published over the next few years.

There was more than enough attention awaiting his return to Canada at the start of May 1961. He was part of a major gathering of Canadian writers at Toronto's O'Keefe Centre, reading alongside Layton, MacLennan, Mordecai Richler, Northrop Frye, and others, followed shortly thereafter by the release of the love poetry collection *The Spice-Box of Earth*. The book received rave reviews and sold out its first printing. At twenty-six, Cohen was a public figure in his homeland, with as much youthful appeal as any musician. However, such status was no longer what he wanted; by the fall he was back on Hydra, back to Marianne, the drugs, and the freedom to push his vision to its limit.

When Leonard Cohen's publisher, Jack McClelland, organized the 1964 campus poetry tour, which also included Layton, Earle Birney, and Phyllis Gotleib, he saw an opportunity to take full advantage of each writer's relatively high public profile. Nothing like it had been attempted before in Canada, and the strictly timed itinerary resembled how rock tours would soon be managed, complete with limousines, radio interviews, and autograph sessions. A review of the University of Waterloo stop on Monday, October 26, in the campus paper said that the poets had no trouble keeping the crowd entertained, although the reporter saved her verdict on Cohen until the end. Noting that he "showed forcefully his dislike for totalitarianism," she added, rather awkwardly, "He felt that every action of man was a trap with a bait endeavouring to tempt someone. He had a good, clear voice, seemed very calm, and a little superior."

Also along to document the proceedings was a National Film Board (NFB) crew, headed by esteemed director Donald Brittain. Although the intention was to give each poet equal focus, Cohen's charm and distinctive relationship with his audiences quickly made the idea of a film solely about him irresistible. Following the final tour stop, at McGill on October 30, the film crew stayed in Montreal to get footage of Cohen's daily routine, along with one-on-one interviews. The camera captured his habit of staying in cheap downtown hotels while in his hometown — "a kind of temple of refuge, a sanctuary," he explained. The underlying suggestion was that he was still rebelling against his Westmount roots. This notion was reinforced with scenes showing Cohen being treated like a regular at Ben's, one of Montreal's famous working-class restaurants, known for its smoked-meat sandwiches. There were also tantalizing glimpses of his nascent musical ability, when a scene filmed at a gathering of old friends broke into a singalong that probably wasn't dissimilar from Cohen's days as a camp counsellor.

But most crucially, *Ladies and Gentlemen . . . Mr. Leonard Cohen*, as the film was called, revealed an artist fully in control of his talent, and somewhat bemused at how everyone around him was responding to it. The world got a similar view of Bob Dylan a few years later through D.A. Pennebaker's *Don't Look Back*. The only major difference was the swarms of media that followed Dylan's every move. The absence of this instead allowed Cohen to delve into his philosophies at length, along with indulging his ego. Of his Cuban trip he said, "I was very interested in what it meant for men to carry arms and to kill other men." He paused before adding, "The real truth is that I wanted to kill, or be killed." He further observed that he had no objections to being photographed (a relief for the filmmakers), saying that, "Such material will some day be of value." And on the subject of sex, he said, "Although one man may be receiving the favours of a woman, all men in her presence are warm. That's the great generosity of women, and the great generosity of the Creator, who worked it out that way." The film, released in 1965, became the only worthwhile end result of the reading tour, which, after expenses, netted no money for any of the participants.

By the start of 1965, Cohen was back on Hydra, working on *Beautiful Losers*, fuelled by a steady diet of amphetamines and hashish that left him a physical wreck by the time he submitted the manuscript in the spring. Both his Canadian and U.S. publishers were mystified by the surreal storyline, which involved the love triangle of three contemporary characters tied together by the narrator's work documenting the life of Catherine Tekakwitha, the Iroquois virgin. On top of that, McClelland faced threats of censorship over the graphic sexual language. The advanced controversy led to hot critical debate about the book, with Cohen even drawing comparisons in the U.S. to Joyce, Burroughs, and Henry Miller. But it was not enough to attract readers. As he entered his thirties, Cohen had written two novels and four collections of poetry, and was nearly spent. He seriously contemplated an offer to become a television journalist for the CBC, but the thought of taking a full-time job was more abhorrent now than it was when he was forced to work in his father's factory. There could be only one course, and as he watched Dylan on stage, even as reaction to *Beautiful Losers* poured in, Cohen knew it to be true.

During the long days of writing on Hydra, when his system could no longer handle the drugs, Cohen most often found relief in the country music broadcasts from the U.S. Armed Forces Radio. It was an unbreakable connection to his life half a world away, with country and western remaining the only English music Cohen knew of that contained an emotional quality remotely close to his own writing style. With his decision to devote himself to music in early 1966, the notion of Cohen fronting a rock band as Dylan did was ludicrous. However, presenting himself as a lone balladeer was entirely conceivable. "In hindsight, it seems like a very foolish strategy," Cohen admitted, "but I said to myself, 'I *am* a country musician, and I *will* go down to Nashville, and I'll get work down there, either as a player or a singer,' or, 'I have songs, and this is the way I'm going to address the economic crisis.' It seems mad. So, I borrowed some money from my friend Robert Hershorn. On my way to Nashville, I stopped off in New York, and I sort of got ambushed. First of all, I went to the Penn Terminal Hotel on 34th Street. Then I moved to the Hudson Hotel on 57th Street, and they had a great swimming pool, one of the reasons I liked it there. And then I found out about the Chelsea Hotel. I don't know how that emerged. Once I hit the Chelsea Hotel, there was no turning back. I was on speed, I weighed about 116 pounds. It was a very crazy time. That's when I found out about everything that was going on in New York."

The building, erected at 361 East 23rd Street, promised a new concept in urban living in 1884, one that allowed tenants to purchase their apartments and share maintenance expenses with stores on the ground floor. In essence, it was New York's first co-op. Furthermore, the Chelsea — named after the original estate built on the site in the mid-eighteenth century by Captain Thomas Clarke — also became the city's tallest structure (albeit briefly), and centrepiece of a revived vaudeville district. Yet, as the old century passed, the massive changes in store for New York did not include the Chelsea. Theatre found its permanent home on Broadway, and frequent economic panics led to the co-op experiment being scrapped. By 1905, new owners could only make the building profitable by turning it into a hotel. However, most of its unique designs — built to the original apartment owners' specifications — were kept, quickly making the Chelsea the destination of choice among visiting creative minds, who stayed for both brief and extended periods. Mark Twain, O. Henry, Edgar Lee Masters, and Thomas Wolfe were among the first, followed later by Dylan Thomas, Arthur C. Clarke, and William Burroughs. By the sixties, the Chelsea's laissez-faire ambience was also favoured by the new school of abstract expressionists and pop artists, including Andy Warhol and his associates.

Cohen's arrival at the Chelsea in the summer of 1966 was, therefore, hardly out of the ordinary. He took one of the smaller single rooms on the fifth floor, and immediately got close to his neighbours, among them Joan Baez and the legendary folklorist and filmmaker Harry Smith. Cohen asked Marianne to come to New York with her son so they could all be together again, but within days of their arrival he realized it would be impossible to rekindle the simple life they had on Hydra. The manic pulse of the city had Cohen in its grip, and he could see that vestiges of the folk revival remained in Greenwich Village that he could utilize, even though the innocence had long since disappeared. However, for both artistic and personal purposes, this fact played directly to Cohen's strengths. He consolidated his repertoire of songs, all of which were now tinged with the wasted grandeur he saw all around him.

That summer his old university friend Robert Hershorn introduced Cohen to Mary Martin, who at that point was seeking to leave Albert Grossman's office and enter the management field on her own. She had initially pinned her hopes on a Toronto folk-rock group called The Stormy Clovers. Fronted by the hauntingly beautiful vocalist Susan Jains, the band was one of the first in Canada to give a full electric treatment to folk-based material, bringing a touch of the emerging San Francisco scene to the clubs in Yorkville. "Susan was absolutely dedicated to becoming successful," Martin said. "At the beginning of it all, she lived in Montreal with Gordon Sheppard, who was a filmmaker for the National Film Board, and I believe he introduced her to Leonard Cohen."

Not surprisingly, Cohen became smitten with Jains, and gladly encouraged The Stormy Clovers to adapt "Suzanne" and "The Stranger Song" to their sound, making them the first performers anywhere to cover Cohen's material. For Martin, the addition of Cohen to the scenario was in many ways a dream come true. "As a young Canadian, *The Spice-Box of Earth* and his other volumes of poetry were very dear to me and my pals who just really loved Leonard's romantic side — it was important to be able to quote some of those," she said. "Somewhere along the line Leonard did meet with Albert, probably through Judy Collins, but that obviously didn't work out, so Hershorn introduced me to Leonard. At the time, Dylan was on hiatus, so it made me think that they needed a new singer-songwriter at Columbia."

Martin's decision to refocus her energy on Cohen inevitably came at the expense of The Stormy Clovers. The only glimpse most people would have of them playing Cohen songs — including "Hey, That's No Way to Say Goodbye," penned during his initial stay at the Chelsea — was in a twenty-minute documentary Sheppard made of the group, as well as a handful of CBC television appearances. Nevertheless, the ease with which Jains sang the songs instigated a pattern of Cohen's music being seemingly more suited to female performers.

It was as if he alone had been able to tap into some previously off-limits aspect of the female psyche, while other writers — Dylan among them — could only manage bittersweet observations such as "Just Like a Woman." That fact was borne out when Cohen's formal introduction to the U.S. came through Judy Collins. Shortly after Peter, Paul & Mary, Collins similarly managed to cross over to the pop charts, and had come to rely on the new generation of songwriters in order to remain there. Cohen recalled meeting Collins for the first time in her New York apartment in the summer of 1966, where he presented several songs to her. However, it wasn't until Martin contacted Collins that she began showing any serious interest in Cohen's work. "I really didn't know what I was doing," Martin described, "but I knew that one had to have some kind of tape in order to make some kind of decent presentation to the various record companies. So I made

Leonard come to my apartment on Bleecker Street and I made him sing his songs in the bathtub into my little tape recorder. Then I called Garth Hudson and asked him if he would be able to make lead sheets from these tapes in order to copyright the songs, so Garth did that and they were masterpieces of calligraphy. Leonard's songs were not what you might call short, but Garth was ever so diligent and I have no idea where those beautiful pieces of artwork are now. I knew that Leonard and Judy Collins were friends, and I knew Judy, so I gave her these tapes and off she went with 'Suzanne,' and that was the wonderful beginning."

Along with "Suzanne," Collins adapted "Dress Rehearsal Rag" and recorded both songs for her *In My Life* album, released in November 1966 on Elektra. It would eventually crack the Top 50 on *Billboard's* album chart. As Collins prepared to lay down the tracks, Martin approached John Hammond Sr. at Columbia, a shrewd move considering the venerable A & R man was still stung over losing his stake in Dylan to Albert Grossman. Hammond was intrigued after his initial meeting with Martin, who further urged him to go to the National Film Board's New York office and view *Ladies and Gentlemen . . . Mr. Leonard Cohen*. From there, Hammond met with Cohen alone. "He took me to lunch at this restaurant on 23rd Street that is no longer there," Cohen recalled. "Then we went back to my room at the Chelsea and I played him these songs, and he said, 'You've got it,' and he signed me." Although the deal was indeed a coup for the thirty-two-year-old unproven performer, Cohen was not yet prepared to leave poetry behind. As Collins' version of "Suzanne" was drawing attention, the book *Parasites of Heaven* was published, providing early drafts of what Cohen planned to offer on record, with pieces such as "Teachers," "I Believe You Heard Your Master Sing," and "I Fell Into an Avalanche" soon to become familiar in new forms.

But, from the outset of 1967, Cohen appeared determined to present himself as a legitimate singer, albeit in his own unorthodox way. In Canada, at least, his already burgeoning female fan base took it in stride, as one breathless admirer's account of his February concert at York University in Toronto recounted in a

Saturday Night article two years later, showed: "What he did, he mesmerized the five hundred people in the hall. He walked on to the stage and lit some incense and looked out into the audience and said, very quietly, 'The person here in the most pain is me.' Then he went into a soft chant and got everybody in a nice trance. After that, he talked and read and sang for three hours and every single person worshipped him. It turned into a Leonard Cohen love-in night."

At the show's conclusion, he promptly left the hall, leaving behind his books and guitar, even the money he'd made that night. "He's always doing that, disappearing and deserting his people and his possessions," the fan's assessment continued. "He's always alone, and he does almost all of his living inside his own head. He never really lives anywhere physically, and I always wonder where he changes his clothes and what he does with his underwear. He actually does see himself as a constant wanderer, as a kind of travelling body of pain. You can hear all of that in the words to his songs, and I think the image of Leonard in pain, in danger, attracts a lot of girls. I mean, it isn't a big sex thing with most of them. They want to mother Leonard and protect him. I worry about Leonard — like, is he going to be alive next year?"

If it was all an elaborate ruse, Cohen wasn't about to let on, as he told an interviewer around that time: "I've always felt very different from other poets I've met. I've always felt that somehow they've made a decision against life. I don't want to put any poets down, but most of them have closed a lot of doors. I always felt more at home with musicians. I like to write songs and sing and that kind of stuff."

After another solo appearance, at Buffalo State University on April 6, Cohen was given his first major spotlight in New York as a guest of Judy Collins during her Town Hall concert on April 30. Collins recalled that Cohen was so nervous he could only get through the first verse of "Suzanne" until sustained applause persuaded him to finish the song. "I didn't really know much about singing in public, and it was generally a frightening experience," Cohen said in 1993. "I didn't really know what was at stake, either. I didn't really realize that careers were being made at this point, and alliances with companies were being forged. I had a rather naive, self-concerned approach to the whole thing." In spite of that, Cohen consented to appear on May 22 in front of 4,500 people, along with Buffy Sainte-Marie and several rock bands, at a "love-in" in front of Toronto's provincial legislature before heading to Montreal to share the stage with The Stormy Clovers at Expo 67. If that summer-long event was the watershed moment for the country, Cohen's appearance there was a personal turning point. After playing his music on such a grand scale in his hometown, Cohen, as well as his critics, could not deny that his choice to become a singer-songwriter was entirely justified.

Other showcases followed that summer, some with Collins, along with important solo debuts at the Newport and Mariposa festivals. Yet, there's a picture from Newport that, poignantly, illustrates Cohen's inner conflicts as he faced the crossroads of his career. A group stands at the side of the stage watching an unseen performer. Among them are Joni Mitchell and Joan Baez, juxtaposed in almost yin-yang fashion. Behind them, and framed in nearly perfect isolation stands Cohen, next to a garbage can, hands in the pockets of his latter-day Beat uniform — cheap suit and open-necked work shirt — with his guitar slung across his back in true troubadour style. He studies the performer more intently than anyone else in the picture, perhaps knowing that he's on next, and the worry is palpable.

Anticipation for his first recording was stoked even further when, in September, the CBS cultural affairs program *Camera Three* ran an in-depth profile, borrowing footage from the NFB film, but also including a new interview, clips of poetry, and an improvised song based on a section of *Beautiful Losers*, "God Is Alive, Magic Is Afoot." The segment turned out to be far from the customary Sunday morning television fare, and drew an overwhelmingly negative response from viewers.

As autumn arrived, Hammond Sr. and Cohen got to work on the album at Columbia's New York studios. Never one to make things complicated, Hammond essentially wanted Cohen's guitar and voice to stand on their own. However,

Cohen still had to overcome a lack of confidence in front of microphones. To compensate, he requested that a full-length mirror be brought into the studio, Cohen's reason being that he had always felt more comfortable watching himself play guitar. When this didn't have the desired effect, Hammond brought in musicians on short notice to craft some ad hoc arrangements. For Cohen, the initial results were disappointing, and the entire project seemed doomed when Hammond unexpectedly bailed out. "I don't recall him absenting himself from the project on an aesthetic basis," Cohen says. "That I certainly have no recollection of. It was something in his personal life. Either he or his wife got sick and he just couldn't do it."

Cohen later elaborated, "I remember I always had that sense of, 'If I can just finish the damn thing!' And you keep notching your standards down, degree by degree — not 'Is it going to be beautiful, is it going to be perfect, is it going to be immortal?' 'Can I finish' became the urgent question. When John Hammond [left] it kind of threw me for a loop. I felt I'd lost contact with the songs. I actually went to a hypnotist in New York — I wanted her to return me to the original impulse of the songs. It was a desperate measure, and it didn't work. I couldn't go under. The whole episode had a comic quality I could not escape."

Hammond asked for John Simon to take over, and while his more sensitive approach was in line with Cohen's original objectives, it was still not easy to deliver the record in time for its December 26 release date. Simon was also slated to work with Gordon Lightfoot on *Did She Mention My Name* that month. Cohen recalled, "John Simon and I had words about the arrangements, and he said, 'Look, Leonard, this is as far as I'm going to work on the record. I'm going on Christmas vacation, you finish it.'" While Cohen did come to admire most of Simon's contributions, such as the female choir on "Sisters of Mercy," they fought continuously over the direction of "Suzanne" and "So Long, Marianne." Coincidentally, the former was in the *Billboard* Top 100 at that moment, in the form of a syrupy version by Noel Harrison (son of actor Rex Harrison) who would score an even bigger hit in 1968 with "Windmills of Your Mind." This fact certainly didn't help settle the arguments over the final arrangement of "Suzanne," but Simon was adamant about exploiting the potential of "So Long, Marianne" to make the charts, particularly since it was the only song on the album that had a chorus. Taking a cue from fellow producer Tom Wilson's electrified treatment of Simon and Garfunkel's "The Sound of Silence," Simon added a band and female singers to Cohen's original track, turning it into the best approximation of a pop song that he could. Cohen was not impressed. In fact, the entire process had nearly destroyed him, as he wearily confessed to *The Village Voice* at the time of *Songs of Leonard Cohen*'s release: "I think my album is going to be spotty and undistinguished. I blame this on my total unfamiliarity with the recording studio. They tried to make my songs into music. I got put down all the time. It was a continual struggle — continual — they wanted to put me in bags. I thought I was going to crack up." He added, ominously, "When you get wiped out — and it does happen in one's life — that's the moment, the *real* moment. Around thirty or thirty-five is the traditional age that poets commit suicide of the poet, did you know? That's the age when you finally understand that the universe does not succumb to your command."

Cohen's pessimism appeared to have some merit, as *Songs of Leonard Cohen* received mixed reviews in both the U.S. and Canada. *The New York Times* and Canada's newsweekly, *Maclean's*, were lukewarm, while pre-eminent rock critic Robert Christgau was more sympathetic, conceding that although "Cohen's voice has been called monotonous, it is also the most miraculous vehicle for intimacy the new pop has produced." After several months, *Songs* had barely entered *Billboard*'s Top 100 albums chart, even as Judy Collins' latest album, *Wildflowers*, which contained three Cohen-penned tracks, "Sisters of Mercy," "Priests," and "Hey, That's No Way to Say Goodbye," reached the Top 5 and would remain her best-selling work. He found far more acceptance in England, where the album reached number thirteen, and, on January 27, Cohen was invited to perform on folk singer Julie Felix's popular BBC television variety show.

But Cohen was still hesitant to tour, and often returned to the safety of poetry readings during the spring of 1968. Indeed, the audience for his prose remained undiminished, as *Selected Poems 1956–1968*, published in June, would go on to sell 20,000 copies over the summer. Such a personal triumph was surely welcomed, as Cohen had decided to finally split with Marianne while he was in the throes of a spiritual identity crisis that led him to Zen Buddhism. Before that, though, during a flirtation with Scientology, he met Suzanne Elrod, a Miami Jew he immediately fell in love with. Thankfully, she felt the same, and brought some stability back to Cohen's life, even though he continued to bounce between New York and Montreal on his own. While in Los Angeles earlier in the spring — where he had partaken in dinner and drinks with Jim Morrison at the Troubadour — Joni Mitchell had introduced Cohen to David Crosby, producer of her debut album. Ever an opportunist, the recent ex-Byrd offered his services for Cohen's next record, and in May they laid down some preliminary tracks together.

However, after a chance meeting with Columbia producer Bob Johnston back in New York, Cohen's dream of working in Nashville was rekindled, and, moreover, easily fulfilled, given Johnston's close ties to the city. The affable Texan agreed to produce Cohen's next album, and even found him a quiet residence in which to work on the songs. "I liked [Johnston] immensely," Cohen said. "I had no place to live at the time and he said, 'There's a cabin to rent for seventy dollars a month on a farm with 1,500 acres outside of Franklin.' So I moved there and stayed for a couple of years. It was a lovely little place beside a stream. I had a horse. I thought I could ride — we used to ride at summer camp — but this horse changed my idea. It was sold to me by a rodeo champion, Kit Marley. I guess he saw a city slicker, and it was a kind of practical joke. I also had a rifle and, during winter, when icicles formed on this slate cliff a few hundred yards from my cabin, I'd stand in the doorway and shoot them. I got quite good. I was living alone, but Suzanne came down from time to time."

Thus, isolation eventually became the foundation for Cohen's sessions with Johnston throughout the fall and winter of 1968. Cohen envisioned a much starker sound, and was not about to compromise, as he had on his debut. Johnston, having produced Dylan's austere *John Wesley Harding* the previous year, fully grasped the intention, and stuck with Cohen's rigid no-drums policy. As they toiled in the studio, fans got another preview of Cohen's new material, again through Judy Collins, when she included "Bird on the Wire" and "Story of Isaac" on her *Who Knows Where the Time Goes* album, released in November. But Cohen seemed to be moving further and further away from the insulated folk world that Collins still inhabited, a fact made abundantly clear when his own versions of these songs were heard on *Songs From a Room*, released on March 17, 1969.

The album pulsated with slow-burning violence. Death, or the shadow of death, was present in nearly every song. A military theme suggested the spectre of the Vietnam War, although it was never directly referenced. Still, sacrifice for an ideal became the common thread connecting "Story of Isaac," "A Bunch of Lonesome Heroes," and "The Partisan," the last a piece Cohen took from *The People's Songbook*. Self-sacrifice emerged elsewhere, from the suicide at the core of "Seems So Long Ago, Nancy," and the heroin imagery of "The Butcher." The only glimmer of hope that most saw on the album was in "Bird on the Wire," whose brutal imagery skirted what was essentially a maudlin plea for redemption. By year's end, it would be familiar to rock audiences through Joe Cocker's version, from his second album, as well as a favourite of the emerging British folk-rock movement, led by bands such as Fairport Convention.

But, as Cohen later recounted, the despair at the heart of the song was all too real at the time. "[Depression] was a component of my life, the background — although not usually the content — of the work, and it was the engine of most of my investigation into the various things I looked into: wine, women, song, religion. Just trying to beat the Devil. Just trying to get on top of it. I never knew what it was, because I had nothing to complain about, but still there was this background of anguish that seemed to prevail." Of "Bird on the Wire" itself, Cohen commented, "I don't feel I've ever finished that song. I feel it's a really great song that I didn't nail, I didn't finish, and it's the one that bugs me." Nevertheless, he was surely buoyed by the fact that *Songs From a Room* fared a little better on the U.S. charts than the previous album, while making it to number two in the U.K.

Based on this, Cohen accepted Johnston's offer to put a band together for him so he could finally go on tour. The lineup, christened The Army after a line from "A Bunch of Lonesome Heroes," consisted of many of the top Nashville session stars who had played on the album, including Charlie Daniels and guitarist Ron Cornelius, along with two female backup singers. Following a few warm-up dates, the tour began in Europe at the start of May 1970, and played large halls in Amsterdam, Hamburg, Frankfurt, Munich, London, Paris, and elsewhere. After a short break, they turned up at several large festivals in North America, the most memorable being the July 25 show at a rainy Forest Hills tennis stadium in New York, which Dylan attended. Many of those present for the post-show meeting between the two artists recalled a tense atmosphere, presumably owing to the fact that Cohen had scooped Dylan's producer and several trusted backing musicians at a time when he — Dylan — was ready to make a new album. "It was like two cats with their hair up," Cornelius told Dylan biographer Howard Sounes. When pressed about the encounter, Cohen doubted that there were any negative repercussions, and his relationship with Dylan remained one of deep mutual respect throughout the ensuing years.

However, the most significant appearance was before 300,000 people at the Isle of Wight Festival early on the morning of August 31. Just as the year before, when it was essentially remembered as "Europe's Woodstock," the bill featured many top rock acts, The Who and Jimi Hendrix among them, which made Cohen's performance incongruous in some critics' estimation. The unenviable circumstances under which he had to play didn't help matters either. Slated to follow an indifferent Hendrix — who would die in London only three weeks later — Cohen, undressed and unshaven, first had to be awakened. Any lingering drowsiness didn't prevent him and the band from carrying out their pre-show ritual of taking Mandrax (European Quaaludes), leading to even more time spent tuning up. As they launched into "Bird on the Wire," the crowd was equally stultified, and the next ninety minutes passed in a blur, until Cohen fearlessly wrapped things up with an epic gospel-infused recitation, "Please Don't Pass Me By (A Disgrace)." While some in the British press felt let down, the tour continued on through the fall in North America, ending in December with well-received concerts in Toronto, Ottawa, and Montreal.

It was proof that his Canadian fans still worshipped him, even though he had raised eyebrows by declining a Governor General's Award in 1969 for *Selected Poems*, citing how it might affect his image among Quebec separatists. Although he was not a public supporter of the movement, he was keenly aware of his support among francophones, specifically those who identified with the radical politics espoused by the character F. in *Beautiful Losers*.

As a new year began, Cohen's decision to leave the relatively safe world of literature did indeed appear to be coming back to haunt him. While he had won the respect of many of his peers in the music world, the frequent critical jabs at his voice and his soporific style began to wear down his confidence. The growing self-doubt extended to his relationship with Elrod, whom he perceived to be a major factor in furthering it, prompting Cohen to respond by falling back on the most convenient remedy available: drugs. "I tried all that stuff, all the anti-depressants right up to Prozac," Cohen said. "Most of it made me feel worse than when I started. Nothing worked — and it lasted most of my life." Still, with another album to deliver, Cohen went back into the studio with Johnston during the winter of 1971. This time, though, he had little time to write new songs, so several earlier pieces were resurrected to combat a general morose theme that emerged as a reflection of his state of mind during and immediately after the tour.

As *Songs of Love and Hate* took shape, it became evident that while the older lyrics hearkened back to the romanticism of the first album, Cohen's hard-won experience as a performer over the two previous years was pushing the songs into daring new territory. His distance from some of the material also added to the regret inherent in songs like "Famous Blue Raincoat" and "Last Year's Man," but most especially in the terrifyingly raw take of the suicide drama "Dress Rehearsal Rag." Elsewhere, the chaotic atmosphere of the live show came out in the ragged, over-the-top "Sing Another Song, Boys" and "Diamonds in the Mine." Yet Cohen brought many familiar themes of his writing together for the album's *coup de grâce*, "Joan of Arc," a song he had begun at the Chelsea, but had not been able to finish until these sessions. Again, religion, sex, and sacrifice converged within the space of six minutes, bringing a satisfying, if unintended, conclusion to the trilogy of albums, the first of which featured a painting of Joan of Arc on its back cover. But without a clear-cut fragment of hope for listeners to cling to, such as "Bird on the Wire," *Songs of Love and Hate* languished at the bottom of the *Billboard* chart following its March 17, 1971, release. As expected, it fared far better in England, reaching the Top 5, but by this time Cohen seemed eager to take a break from the music business.

What made that decision easier was a message from director Robert Altman, which came during the sessions. According to Cohen, it was an incredible coincidence. "That afternoon, I had seen [Altman's current film] *Brewster McCloud* — twice. It had been raining in Nashville, and I had just ducked into a theatre and sat through one and a half versions of it. I thought it was an incredibly wonderful picture, and he phoned me that evening. He said he'd like to use the music, that he'd been writing a script while listening to my songs. I said, 'Is there anything I might know that you've done?' He said, 'I did *M*A*S*H*.' I said, 'I heard it was a great success, I didn't see it. Is there anything else?' He said, 'Well, there's a picture you probably wouldn't have seen called *Brewster McCloud*.' I said, 'I just sat through it twice. Use anything you want.'" The new film was *McCabe & Mrs. Miller*, Altman's existential western, starring Warren Beatty and Julie Christie. Cohen was persuaded to record some incidental guitar passages, but mostly the soundtrack was built around already existing recordings that perfectly matched the cold, harsh conditions depicted onscreen. Although the film initially received mixed reviews, the inclusion of Cohen's songs temporarily reignited interest in his work, allowing him to spend the remainder of 1971 pursuing other interests, mainly crafting a new poetry collection and getting deeper into Buddhism. Most importantly, he became a father when Elrod bore his son Adam, the first of two children they would have together.

The songs would continue to come at a much slower pace from then on, leading to even more diminished sales figures. But what Cohen had fashioned with his first three records would somehow withstand the changes on the pop landscape that followed, and, in some instances, directly inspire them long after the fact. The so-called rock-poets he was most commonly lumped in with always seemed to require that prefix, the inference being that their words could not stand on their own without the music. With Cohen, the notion of his lyrics ever having anything to do with rock and roll tradition was laughable. Yet his unique skill at plumbing the depths of the human soul would eventually find new exponents as the seventies wore on; first through a handful of poetically based artists in New York, such as Patti Smith and Television, and then, after the subsequent punk-rock insurgence in England, through the emotional rawness of bands such as Joy Division, and, later, the unrestrained outpourings of The Smiths' lead singer Morrissey. Cohen seemed to put out a new album just in time for it to become a touchstone for each generation, which, in turn, was thankful to know that, in Leonard Cohen, there would always be at least one person who understood the root causes of society's ills, and could still somehow display complete dignity while coping with it all.

The news shocked everyone, even his non-fans: "Leonard Cohen is broke," proclaimed *Maclean's* in August 2005. The stories of bad investments, unpaid taxes, and a crooked manager were sadly not uncommon in rock and roll, but surely, most believed, these could not apply to a cultural icon like Cohen. Yet, at age 70, the fruits of his labour — five million dollars in a retirement fund, along with all of his publishing rights — were gone. Having never made much of that fortune through record sales, Cohen had to face up to the reality that his future, once again, depended on putting himself on public display, with the real possibility that he would not fulfill expectations.

"That was a sad thing to me, that my childhood hero was reduced to that state," Rob Hallett of international concert production company AEG Live told music journalist Johnny Black. "I said, 'When you think you've got a band, and you feel ready to go out again, I'll put it together. Then we'll do a deal on the back end, recoup our costs and you'll get the rest.'" Cohen was hesitant, but nonetheless could not turn down such a generous offer. It was only the first of many that would result in one of the greatest career revivals in popular music history.

In late 2007, the announcement came that Cohen was to be inducted into the Rock and Roll Hall of Fame, an honour he did not feel worthy of receiving, even as he made his acceptance speech in January 2008. "This is a very unlikely occasion for me. It is not a distinction that I coveted or even dared dream about," he said. Yet, even by then his name — and more importantly his music — was beginning to be heard again with increasing regularity. The song "Hallelujah" had usurped "Suzanne" as Cohen's signature piece from the moment it was heard on his 1984 album *Various Positions*, and since then there seemed no end to the line of vocalists hoping to crack its seemingly impenetrable core. Around the time of the Hall of Fame induction ceremony, millions of viewers heard an *American Idol* contestant, Jason Castro, valiantly make his attempt. Only days later, the unrivalled version by the late Jeff Buckley became the most downloaded track on iTunes. "All of that was serendipity," Hallett said. "I planned none of it, but all those things made Leonard more aware of his own worth."

On May 11, 2008, Cohen performed his first concert in fourteen years at the seven-hundred-seat Playhouse Theatre in Fredericton, New Brunswick, as innocuous a starting point as any in order to test his stamina with forty-eight dates yet to come. But after a twenty-song set that included four encores, the audience still wanted more. It was a heart-wrenching scene that was repeated at every venue, and the numbers of those wanting to experience it grew exponentially. In Dublin, 36,000 tickets sold out for three shows, and Cohen's headlining appearance at England's Glastonbury Festival was witnessed by over 175,000 people. Demand proved unlimited, and dates continued to be added throughout Europe.

If all that seemed improbable, the year ended with not one, but two versions of "Hallelujah" topping the British singles charts during Christmas Week, with an over-the-top version by the winner of the U.K.'s equivalent of *Idol* beating out a dogged downloading campaign by Buckley fans. Cohen's own version came a distant third. All the furor even prompted Britain's most recognizable art critic, Simon Schama, to weigh in. He wrote in *The Guardian*, "If there's just a touch too much of happy self-regard about some of those early ballads, from the mid-seventies on, the onset of years Cohen saw in his musical mirror encouraged him to use imagery as building blocks in beautifully constructed, authentically poetic narratives. So perhaps it's not surprising that 'Hallelujah,' the song in which music making and love making wrestle with each other, is the one most covered by other singers, and without draining the power of the piece into empty rhapsody. But to get the heartache you want from Cohen — and you know you do — you need to hear the old(ish) baffled, battle-scarred Cohen himself sing 'The minor fall, the major lift,' his voice falling for the forbidden Bathsheba bathing naked on the roof, where 'Her beauty and the moonlight overthrew you.' But nothing works out as planned. The overthrow happens as the music soars, the omnipotent sovereign-psalmist is bound and shorn, and it's from that moment, when the composing-lover is pierced to the quick, that music gets born. Hallelujah."

Cohen, perhaps allowing himself a brief smile at seeing justice served, did not comment on the chain of events that had brought him to that point. His tour was still set to continue into the spring of 2009.

CHAPTER SIX

URGE FOR GOING

A DARKNESS HUNG OVER THE SUMMERS in those days. No one talked about it directly, but the fear was obvious in parents' faces when they let their children out to play in the fields of tall, yellow grass in the morning. The boys would organize primitive baseball games, while the girls skipped rope. And when they all came home at night for supper, their every movement would be keenly scrutinized for traces of fever or twinges of pain. If anything was detected, the mothers would calmly put the children to bed, and then stay up all night silently praying that when dawn came they would hear the familiar din of small feet on the wood-plank floors, and voices expressing eagerness to spend another day outside with their friends.

Mothers who were not so lucky would awake to silence, or worse, to the screams of a child suddenly unable to move. Polio was a curse that by the early fifties could not be tolerated much longer. In Canada, as in most countries around the world, the disease was in the process of scarring its third generation, and the only treatment was painful therapy or confinement in an iron lung. Yet, for the children who survived the physical and psychological trauma of the disease, it was a rite of passage that no one else could begin to understand. For them, something fundamental had changed; those old enough to comprehend their mortality discovered new paths that were not contingent on physical abilities, while those too young to know how close they had come to dying eventually noticed that people looked at them differently. They were somehow stronger, they were survivors, and were duly shown respect.

In 1951, a five-year-old boy caught the disease on the eve of his return to school in the tiny village of Omemee, Ontario, an hour's drive northwest of Toronto. The proximity to the big city saved his life, although he would require several months of rehabilitation to learn how to walk again. Two years later, a nine-year-old girl from the town of North Battleford, Saskatchewan, caught it, and was similarly spared any major damage after being brought to the closest modern hospital, in Saskatoon. When they met for the first time, in Winnipeg in 1965 — the boy was visiting for Christmas and the girl was passing through, performing her folk songs — something deeply familiar struck each of them. It was partially the music she played, music unlike anything the rock and roll–crazed boy had heard before, but mostly it was something he felt within himself: the mark that the pain had imprinted on her fearless personality. She picked up on his internal marks right away, too, and, after finding an opportunity to talk, they spoke to each other in a way only they could fully understand. The mark left them with a belief that a part of them was indestructible, and merely knowing that there were other people in the world who possessed such a quality allowed them to share something greater than mere romance (she was already married, anyway). They had seen up close what lay ahead for everyone — what must eventually consume us all — and they had learned from it that there was much to be accomplished before they ultimately landed back in some anonymous hospital bed, alone, in spite of everything. They had been given their second chances long before others had realized that life had so much more to offer. The young man thought of this as he listened to her angelic voice and pictured her in the same leg braces he had been forced to wear. Her voice told him it was now time to put everything else that had ever bound him behind him for good.

Roberta Joan Anderson was born on November 7, 1943, in Fort MacLeod, Alberta, the only child of a Royal Canadian Air Force lieutenant, Bill Anderson, and Myrtle McKee, a Regina native he had met and married in a whirlwind while on leave the previous year. Fort MacLeod had the nearest hospital to his base, and the family remained there after Joan's birth until the end of the war, when they settled in Maidstone, Saskatchewan, where Bill got a job managing the town grocery store. By the time Joan began school, her father had been transferred to his store chain's outlet in North Battleford, and she assumed the image of a tomboy. Simultaneously, she exhibited a talent for drawing, along with an interest in several of her friends' musical pursuits. Following her recovery from polio, Joan fully embraced her artistic side, something that was of great benefit when she entered high school in Saskatoon, her father's next destination. A self-described bad student, she wrote poetry and a column for the school paper, and painted backdrops for school drama productions to compensate for her grades.

She also utilized her artistic talent to paint portraits of her teachers, and as a gift for one of these, Joni — the new spelling inspired by an art teacher, Henry Bonli — received, in return, a selection of Miles Davis albums. An interest in jazz replaced her natural teenage infatuation with rock and roll from then on, and it would remain her primary musical love even after the folk revival swept her friends away as their high school days wound down. There was no avoiding folk music in 1962, though, and during summer excursions with friends to remote northern lakes that year, Joni's natural desire to join in led her to pick up a guitar and chime in with a few simple chords, or simply sing along with the choruses. "I had a lot of attention as a youngster," she said. "I was popular, a dancer in high school. I didn't have anything to prove. At the heart of me, I'm really a good-time Charley."

The search for fun carried on through her final school year, as most kids had by then discovered the Louis Riel, Saskatoon's own bona fide beatnik coffee house. It was there, on Halloween, that Joni made her first public performance as a singer, earning a few dollars in the process, and enough positive reaction to come back and sing a few more songs the following week. Yet, for all the misgivings she may have still harboured about the folk movement, the following summer she was faced with the need to earn enough money to cover her enrolment at the Alberta College of Art and took a job waitressing at the Louis Riel, while supplementing her income with work as a model for several Saskatoon dress shops.

As she endured serving coffee against the backdrop of a steady stream of touring folk performers, Joni eventually could not resist getting on stage again herself. After purchasing a cheap baritone ukulele, she regularly participated in the café's weekly hootenanny, and was soon caught up in the ideas of the folk revival, ideas she realized were more applicable to her circumstances than the more distant, urban world of jazz. She showed up everywhere with her ukulele that summer, and took every opportunity to play her expanding repertoire of popular standards. At one of these informal gatherings, Joni captivated some employees of a television station in the northern Saskatchewan city of Prince Albert. Afterward, they asked if she could do a one-off half-hour program in place of the station's normal Saturday night show dedicated to moose hunting (the season for which didn't start until the fall). Joni immediately agreed, and the August 1963 broadcast brought her first taste of fame, just before she set out for Calgary and her post-secondary education.

The task of studying art came easily, although Joni was unable to completely adjust to the college environment. As she explained, "I found out that I was an honour student at art school for the same reason that I was a bad student [in general] — because I had developed a lot of technical ability. As a result, in the free classes, where I was really uninspired, my marks remained the same, whereas people who were great in free class, who were original and loose [but] didn't have the chops in a technical class, would receive a mark that was pretty similar to their technical ability. The first year was like a time to decide whether you wanted to be a commercial artist or a fine artist, so I became pretty disillusioned with art college, even though I enjoyed being near the head of my class for the first time in my life."

Part of her disillusionment stemmed from the fact that soon after arriving in Calgary she heard of a new coffee house about to open called the Depression, allowing her a chance to build on her Louis Riel experience. Upon meeting Joni, one of the owners, Peter Elbling, was sufficiently charmed by her looks and personality that he insisted she appear at the club's opening night on September 13. Joni continued to regularly perform three nightly sets at the Depression until the end of 1963, which led to gigs at Edmonton's coffee house, the Yardbird Suite, and at various ski lodges in northern Alberta. The following February 14, Joni hit the airwaves again as part of a University of Alberta–sponsored hootenanny broadcast by a local television station, and, on April 16, she was on the bill for a major hootenanny staged at Calgary's prestigious Jubilee Auditorium. This was followed in short order with a long trip to Winnipeg to play the Fourth Dimension club, a performance that was cut short because of a thunderstorm.

At Joni's side for all of these events was a fellow art student, Brad MacMath. Their relationship had blossomed faster than any she had experienced up to then, and even before the end of the school year they were making plans to travel east in search of better gigs for Joni, and also to attend the Mariposa Folk Festival that August. Yet, by the time they boarded the train, shortly after Joni performed two shows as part of a Calgary Stampede hootenanny on July 9, 1964, she knew something was physically wrong with her. Joni was pregnant, and, aside from MacMath, no one could know. Bearing a child out of wedlock in the early sixties, as Joni would later describe, "was like you killed somebody."

The couple did manage to make it to Mariposa, although Joni's excitement about witnessing Buffy Sainte-Marie's debut was dampened by last-minute scheduling chaos that forced the festival to take place in Toronto at the behest of an Orillia town council that was besieged by protests from angry residents. Joni and Brad did not return to Calgary for the fall term; the pregnancy was too much to bear for both of them, with MacMath's response being to leave his girlfriend to cope as well as she could on her own.

Joni's situation grew even more dire when she discovered that the coffee house scene in Toronto was much more difficult to break into than those in the west. The majority of Yorkville clubs required performers to be members of the musicians' union, and Joni could not scrape up the $160 needed to join. She took a job as a sales clerk in the women's fashion department of the Simpson-Sears department store, but her minimum-wage salary was barely enough to pay for lodging at the hippie flophouse she had found at 504 Huron Street. As her desperation grew, Joni managed to land some non-union gigs that autumn, mostly in YMCA clubs, and, specifically, a "scab club," the Half Beat on Avenue Road, where she appeared consistently throughout October and November. Now playing a standard acoustic guitar and writing her own songs — she came up with the first, "Day After Day," on the train to Toronto — Joni realized that her own voice was emerging. "I began as a [traditional] folk singer," she said. "Once I began to write, my vocal style changed. My Baez/Judy Collins influence disappeared." Still, the stress of the pregnancy increased in the first two months of 1965, as Joni came to term. Single and unable to work, she moved in with Vicky Taylor, a fellow singer she had befriended, who had a small apartment near Yorkville. Joni gave birth on February 19, to a daughter she named Kelly Dale Anderson.

Caring for the child completely drained their already limited resources a month later, so Taylor came up with the idea for them to perform as a duo called Day & Night, a highly appropriate name given that Taylor's long, straight black hair contrasted sharply with Joni's. "Vicky was the only one on the folk scene who was nice to me," Joni said. "Every time she went to an audition, Vicky would insist on dragging me along." The pair made the rounds of the usual Yorkville open stages, until Joni was able to land her own gig at the Penny Farthing, a new venue started by the Half Beat's founders, John and Marilyn McHugh, which reserved its downstairs room for unproven local acts. After a respectable opening, Joni appeared there on an almost nightly basis throughout most of April. During one of these nights, a visiting folk singer from Detroit named Chuck Mitchell, who was playing upstairs, caught some of Joni's set and was instantly smitten. Her emotional vulnerability left her with little defense against Mitchell's advances, but over the course of the next few days he professed his true love for her, newborn baby and all. Mitchell lived up to his words by proposing to Joni as he was about to return to Detroit, and she, undoubtedly seeing no better options, accepted. The wedding took place on June 19, in Mitchell's hometown of Rochester, Michigan. At the reception afterward, the newlyweds marked the occasion by singing a few songs together. Three days later, they were on stage together at the Folk Cellar in Port Huron, and on July 20 they began an engagement at Chuck's regular haunt, the Chess Mate in Detroit.

Their shared musical ambition soon took precedence over family life, and it became evident that Chuck was not about to live up to his commitment to raise the baby. Joni had already considered giving her daughter up for adoption before she met Chuck, but, as more travelling loomed on the horizon, she came to the painful conclusion that the child would be better off in a more traditional family.* As Joni recovered from the trauma of giving up her child, Estelle Klein, head of the Toronto Folk Guild, offered her a last-minute invitation to play the 1965 Mariposa Folk Festival. Now relocated to the Innis Lake campground, in the rural community of Caledon, northwest of Toronto, she was billed as Joni Anderson, and performed to her largest audience yet, alongside Gordon Lightfoot, Ian & Sylvia, Buffy Sainte-Marie, Phil Ochs, and blues legend Son House. In some ways, the weekend was Joni's first real test to see if she belonged in the same league as the established artists. And, at least in Klein's view, she failed. Afterward, Klein told Joni in plain terms that she was timid and unoriginal. On top of that, playing the guitar was still a challenge for Joni, due to the lingering effects of polio in her hands, yet she took up Klein's

---

*Kelly Anderson was adopted by a Toronto couple and renamed Kilauren Gibb. She would not learn her mother's identity until 1997, after initial inquiries about a "folk singer from Saskatchewan who has moved to the United States" eventually led to a much-publicized reunion.

challenge immediately after the festival by channelling all of the strain of the previous two years into "Urge for Going." The song, which she later described simply as a "protest" against the brutal Saskatoon winters, nevertheless perfectly encapsulated an overwhelming desire to escape the corner she had been painted into, while at the same time accepting her fate, just as all Canadians must accept the change of seasons.

Joni added "Urge for Going" to her repertoire during an early October return trip to the Fourth Dimension in Winnipeg, where she also appeared on a locally broadcast folk music television program. From there, she and Chuck made a brief jaunt to Florida for a few gigs on his established circuit before returning to Detroit for another run at the Chess Mate in November. They were back in Winnipeg a month later, when her fateful first encounter with Neil Young took place. "We were there over Christmas," she explained. "I remember putting up this Christmas tree in our hotel room. Neil came out to the club and we liked him immediately. He was the same way he is now — this offhanded, dry wit. He was this rock and roller who was coming around to folk music through Bob Dylan." Young worked up the courage to play a song he had written the previous November to mark his nineteenth birthday. The bittersweet innocence of "Sugar Mountain" touched Joni so deeply that soon after she composed "The Circle Game," a similar coming-of-age ode, made even more heart-wrenching by thoughts of her daughter growing up in another family. "None of us had any grandiose ideas about the kind of success we received," she continued. "In those days, it was really a long shot, especially for a Canadian."

For this reason, the Mitchells kept an open-door policy for touring folk singers at their cheap, three-bedroom apartment near Detroit's Wayne State University, where they had settled right after their wedding. Chuck often went a step further by getting their guests gigs at the Chess Mate. Thereby, the Mitchells' place became a refuge for many Canadian artists, in particular Gordon Lightfoot, during his periods of marital strife. In turn, the Mitchells began performing some of his songs as duets. Several prominent names from within the Greenwich Village scene passed through the apartment, as well, and this often allowed Joni to open for them. Tom Rush, a Boston native who had recently signed with Elektra, was so bowled over by "Urge for Going" when they shared a bill together that, after the show, he asked Joni to make a tape of it. She obliged, also including an embryonic arrangement of "The Circle Game." Rush immediately incorporated both songs into his repertoire, and belatedly released his versions on his 1968 album, *The Circle Game*, the best-selling record of his career. Interest from other artists prompted both Joni and Chuck to set up their own publishing companies in order to retain ownership of the songs. It was a shrewd decision, since word of Rush's songwriting discovery quickly made the rounds. George Hamilton IV happened to hear Rush play "Urge for Going" on a Boston radio station, and, through Lightfoot, got Joni to send him a demo. His version would spend twenty-one weeks on *Billboard's* country chart, peaking at number seven on January 21, 1967. Both Ian & Sylvia and Buffy Sainte-Marie would release versions of "The Circle Game" during the first half of the year, as well.

The Mitchells' optimism was reflected in a *Detroit News* profile published on February 6, 1966, that described their unusual take on domestic bliss. According to Chuck, "Joni and I have developed our act. We are not just folksingers now. We do comedy, sing some ragtime, and do folk-rock. We're ready for the big clubs now." They got their chance that June with their New York debut at the Gaslight. Afterward, Joni was thrilled to meet Joan Baez for the first time; that is, until being told by one of her early influences that she sounded a lot like Sainte-Marie. "I always thought the women of song don't get along, and I don't know why that is," she reflected many years later. "Joan Baez would have broken my leg if she could have, or at least that's the way it felt as a person coming out. I never felt that same sense of competition from men."

Disheartened by their reception in New York, the couple spent the rest of the summer in Canada, playing extended runs at the Fourth Dimension clubs in Winnipeg and Regina, and culminating the trip with a much more positively received return set by Joni at the Mariposa Folk Festival. She remained in Toronto on her own throughout the fall, playing around Yorkville at the 7 Of Clubs and the Riverboat, where she had been turned away the previous year. It was proof that, by the start of 1967, the couple's increasingly hectic schedule was starting to show results. But for Joni, a desire to develop her own writing voice was taking precedence over the day-to-day grind of being a touring folk-singing duo. Sensing this growing rift, she produced "Both Sides, Now," borrowing the crucial imagery of clouds from Saul Bellow's novel *Henderson the Rain King*. However, the song's core was a sharp response to those people, including Chuck, who underestimated Joni's ability. "'Both Sides, Now' is like an old person reflecting back on their life," she said. "My life had been very hard, and I think at twenty-one I was quite old. I'd gone through a lot of disease and personal pain. I was not unaware of my mortality, but, somehow, I was still very young for my age, in spite of my experience."

The song also marked the beginning of Joni's experimentation with alternative guitar tunings, which made up for her technical limitations, and, as she would discover, allowed her to manipulate melodies much like a painter mixes colours. "I found the tunings were a godsend," she said. "Not only that, but they made the guitar an unstable thing. Whenever you used a new tuning, you had to rediscover the neck and search out the chordal movement. You'd find five or six chords, and then have to chain them together in a creative manner. It was very exciting to discover my music."

Joni debuted "Both Sides, Now" during a March 1967 run at the Second Fret in Philadelphia, a venue that had become one of her regular stops after she became close friends with the manager, Joy Schreiber. Many more people heard the song when Joni played it during a guest spot on a popular Philly folk-radio show, during which she also gave a rare performance of "Sugar Mountain." Her excitement for "Both Sides, Now" was contagious, and in many ways signalled Joni's imminent split with Chuck — they performed together for the last time at

Wilf Carter in the early 1930s, at the onset of his fame as Canada's first internationally known recording artist.

An early portrait of Hank Snow, prior to shedding his singing cowboy image and becoming one of the most successful country music artists of all time.

Opposite: Hank Snow with Elvis Presley (right). Not pictured, Col. Tom Parker, the man who came between them.

Ronnie Hawkins (with beard) and The Hawks, shortly before they left the nest for good. Left to right: Richard Manuel, Rick Danko, Levon Helm, Robbie Robertson, Garth Hudson.

Bob Dylan, 1963.

Ian & Sylvia, mid-1960s, when "Four Strong Winds" and "You Were on My Mind" were being heard everywhere.

Opposite, top: Bonnie Dobson, 1963, composer of the endlessly interpreted "Morning Dew."

Opposite, bottom: Gordon Lightfoot, late 1960s.

The last gasp of the folk revival: Bob Dylan's Rolling Thunder Revue, 1975. Left to right, foreground: Joni Mitchell, Joan Baez, Dylan.

Opposite: Leonard Cohen, early 1970s.

Opposite: Anne Murray, 1969.

Great Speckled Bird, one of the pioneering groups to combine country and rock in the late 1960s. Left to right: Ken Kalmusky, Buddy
Cage, N.D. Smart II, Sylvia Tyson, Ian Tyson, Amos Garrett.

Bruce Cockburn at the outset of his long and prolific career.

Opposite: David Wiffen, at the time of 1973's Juno-winning *Coast to Coast Fever*.

Murray McLauchlan, in full troubadour mode.

Opposite, top: Kate and Anna McGarrigle, late 1970s.

Opposite, bottom: The iconic image from The Band's *Music From Big Pink*, 1968. Left to right: Rick Danko, Levon Helm, Richard Manuel, Garth Hudson, Robbie Robertson.

Neil Young, 1974, beginning to emerge from under the dark cloud of *Tonight's the Night* and *On the Beach*.

Boston's Club 47 on April 29. It was there, conceivably, that Tom Rush heard the song for the first time, and, according to his label mate, Judy Collins, pitched it to her shortly thereafter. Collins released her much-loved version that November, along with Mitchell's "Michael From Mountains," on *Wildflowers*. Rush told Mitchell biographer Karen O'Brien, however, "The first I knew of the tune was when I heard [Judy singing] it on the radio. I remember being a bit miffed that Joni hadn't sent it to me first." Whatever the case, Collins was sufficiently won over to ask Joni to participate in a songwriter's workshop at that year's Newport Folk Festival, where she was also introduced to Leonard Cohen.

She and Cohen bonded over a sense of being Canadians on the outside of a scene that, nonetheless, was fawning over them both, and for Mitchell the new friendship couldn't have come at a better time. After abruptly leaving Chuck, she went south, performing a couple of shows at armed forces bases in the Carolinas ("My father was in the air force, and I guess I was still romantic about being a comfort to the boys coming and going from the war, like Bob Hope.") Then it was north to Ottawa for her first three-week stint at that city's leading folk venue, Le Hibou, and on to Montreal for Expo 67 festivities. But, from her first moments in Cohen's presence, Mitchell could feel her poetic sensibilities changing. After Newport, she accompanied Cohen back to the Chelsea, and settled into the idea of making New York her new home. As with Cohen, the atmosphere of the hotel was an inspiration, and the sense of rebirth Mitchell felt while she was there was captured in "Chelsea Morning," a song filled with as much innocence as "Both Sides, Now" was filled with experience. "A long time ago I purchased some stained glass windows that were about to be demolished because the house for unwed mothers that they were in was being wrecked," she explained while introducing "Chelsea Morning" in October 1967, with the song's creation still clearly fresh in her mind. "I rescued them for five dollars each and set them up in a very peaceful place, and every morning when the sun came up the rainbows came in. Then one day I moved to New York City, which is a very different place — very different circumstances for writing under because it's noisy all the time. So I put my stained glass windows up where there was just a postage-stamp piece of sky, and I wrote a very different kind of love song, as noisy as New York City."

The affair between Mitchell and Cohen would be short-lived, but the artistic impression they left on one another would be permanent. Mitchell's stint in New York didn't fail to turn other heads, either, as Cohen explained: "I was walking up 23rd Street, the street the Chelsea Hotel was on, with Joni, a very beautiful woman, and a big limousine pulled up — Jimi Hendrix was in the back seat, and he was chatting up Joni from inside the limo."

Mitchell's appearance at Newport also caught the attention of Joe Boyd, a Boston native who had set up Elektra's London office in 1965, but later struck out on his own, becoming a catalyst for the British folk-rock boom through managing Fairport Convention, and Nick Drake. After noting Mitchell's lack of management, Boyd offered to bring her over to England, although the handful of dates, several of them as an opener for one of his other groups, the Incredible String Band, did not create much of a stir outside of folk circles. Once again, it would be Mitchell's songs that did the bulk of the work on her behalf. Boyd generously passed around demos to his clients, and the Fairports, in particular, took to them right away. The group's original lineup, fronted by vocalists Judy Dyble and Ian Matthews, recorded "Chelsea Morning" and "I Don't Know Where I Stand" on its self-titled debut album, released in early 1968. Later that year — with Sandy Denny having replaced Dyble — they included another Mitchell song, "Eastern Rain," in sessions for the follow-up, *What We Did on Our Holidays*.

The fact was, by the autumn of 1967, Mitchell was overflowing with musical ideas, although she did not feel ready to sign a record deal. Surprisingly, Albert Grossman showed little interest in working with her, and an offer from Vanguard was rejected outright due to Mitchell's lack of representation. Mitchell later admitted that she had observed how frequently the label demanded albums from Sainte-Marie and did not want to get caught on a similar treadmill. Instead, she continued to chip away at a niche within the Greenwich Village scene in order to merely make a living. "The last thing I wanted to be was famous," she said. "I even wrote a poem in school about Sandra Dee and Bobby Darin when I was fifteen or sixteen. It was about how awful if must be to be teen idols and having everyone look at them. I called it 'The Fish Bowl.' I remember people around me, Tom Rush, for instance, thinking that I was ambitious. I apparently said to him that I'm going to be a star, but I don't think he understood the context. It was bewilderment and dread."

Nonetheless, Mitchell's break arrived on October 26, 1967, in the unlikely form of Elliot Roberts. Born Elliot Rabinowitz, the native New Yorker had started his career in the entertainment business the same way as his future partner, David Geffen, had — through the mailroom of the William Morris Agency's New York office. After Geffen got a toehold in music management with his discovery of Laura Nyro, the idiosyncratic New York singer-songwriter who ultimately failed to the reach the potential that others ultimately had with her songs, Roberts decided to follow the same path. Still, according to Mitchell, he had come to the Cafe Au Go Go that night to catch a set by a prospective client, comedian Howard Hesseman (later known for playing DJ Dr. Johnny Fever on the sitcom *WKRP In Cincinnati*), who was sandwiched between her and headliners Ian & Sylvia. Being the first act of the night meant that Mitchell faced an ambivalent crowd, but, in the midst of the chatter, Roberts was transfixed, and immediately approached her with a management offer. Mitchell was scheduled to play in Michigan for the next several evenings, and told Roberts that if he was serious, he needed to come along.

They forged an instant rapport, mainly through Roberts's humour, and, although he needed no further convincing of her talent, the shows drew some of the most appreciative audiences Mitchell had seen to that point. Roberts enthusiastically headed back to New York armed with demos intended for the major label heads, while Mitchell continued on to Florida for dates at the Gaslight South in Miami. There, by coincidence, was David Crosby, ousted from The Byrds earlier that October during sessions for *The Notorious Byrd Brothers*. His fate had essentially been sealed as far back as June when, at the Monterey Pop Festival, he launched into a rambling diatribe about the Kennedy assassination during the band's set, and later popped up on stage with rivals Buffalo Springfield, in place of an absent Neil Young. The final straw came when his fellow Byrds opted to include Carole King and Gerry Goffin's "Goin' Back" on the album at the expense of Crosby's ménage à trois celebration "Triad," prompting the founding member to leave L.A. to lick his wounds. He planned to do some sailing around the Caribbean, but a chance to get back in the game stared him straight in the face when he showed up to see Mitchell.

"I was extremely fascinated with the quality of the music and the quality of the girl," Crosby recalled of his first impression. "She was such an unusual, passionate, and powerful woman. I was fascinated by her tunings, because I had started working in tunings, and I was writing things like 'Guinnevere.' So things like that made me very attracted to her." Indeed, Mitchell was taken aback by Crosby's adulation, but put up little resistance to both his creative and romantic overtures.

"I had just come back from London," Mitchell said. "That was during the Twiggy era, and I remember I wore a lot of makeup. I think I even had false eyelashes on at the time, so one of the first projects in our relationship was to encourage me to let go of all of this elaborate war paint. It was a great liberation, to get up in the morning and wash your face, and not have to do anything else."

Within days, she phoned Roberts to say that Crosby would produce her first album. The manager's suspicions over this turn of events were heightened when the couple eventually turned up at his New York office looking in all respects like the prototypical hippies they were. Still, Roberts could make few arguments given that his initial efforts to find Mitchell a record deal had been fruitless. Both Columbia and RCA had no interest, and even Elektra rejected Mitchell's demos on the ironic grounds that she sounded too much like Judy Collins.

"Everything about Joni was unique and original, but we couldn't get a deal," Roberts said. "The folk period had died, so she was totally against the grain. Everyone wanted a copy of the tape for, like, their wives, but no one would sign her." With winter approaching, Roberts eventually caved in to Crosby's suggestion that they all go to California, where Crosby was confident he could make something happen. In early December, following a short detour to Toronto, where Mitchell taped several segments for the CBC television show *The Way It Is*, she and Roberts flew to L.A., where influential DJ B. Mitchel Reed put them up in his home near the Sunset Strip. For the next several weeks, Mitchell adjusted to her new surroundings, in the midst of being hustled around town by Crosby and Roberts.

Crosby explained, "My favourite trick at the time was to invite everyone over, roll a joint that was stronger than they could possibly smoke, and get her to play. They would walk out stupefied. They'd never heard anything like her, and it was a lot of fun." For a record deal, Crosby instructed Roberts to see Andy Wickham, the British "house hippie" A & R man at Reprise Records. Once a mere vanity label bestowed upon Frank Sinatra by its parent company, Warner Brothers, Reprise's profile in the rock world had increased dramatically in 1967 when Wickham helped secure the North American rights for Jimi Hendrix on the heels of his definitive performance at Monterey, leading to the release of *Are You Experienced?* soon after. To Roberts' pleasant surprise, Wickham's true musical love was folk, and he duly persuaded his boss, label head Mo Ostin, to sign Mitchell to a demo deal with Crosby as producer.

The recording sessions for what would become *Joni Mitchell* (also known as *Song to a Seagull*) took place in February 1968 at Sunset Sound. In a bold move, Mitchell chose to avoid recording songs that others had already made hits, and instead divided each side into distinct themes, while Crosby kept arrangements to a bare minimum, occasionally allowing his friend Stephen Stills to contribute bass in between sessions for Buffalo Springfield's final album, *Last Time Around*, which were taking place in an adjoining studio. Yet, from the outset, the artist and producer butted heads. "It stopped being fun when I started producing her first record," Crosby says. "Joni is not a person that you stay in a relationship with. It always goes awry, no matter who you are." However, he admitted that his inexperience as a producer was at the heart of most of the conflict, and derailed his original intention to present the music in the purest form possible. "I didn't know enough to know what I was doing, but we did get the actual songs done without a bunch of other crud on it, and that made me happy."

Technical shortcomings aside, the album's opposing tracks perfectly captured Mitchell at this crucial turning point in her life. Side one, subtitled "I Came to the City," opened with "I Had a King," an unflinching account of the breakdown of her marriage, but in the end a powerful declaration of independence ("You know my thoughts don't fit the man/They never can they never can"). The next four songs brimmed with the electricity of her time in Yorkville and Greenwich Village, and her impressions of Toronto were captured with particular clarity in "Night in the City." She described the song at the time by saying, "The people in Toronto are very funny about their 'Village' (Yorkville), because although it's one of their main tourist attractions and quite a lovely place to go — except on weekends when you can't walk down the street — people tend to criticize it a lot. But Torontonians, when they get away from Toronto, are very proud of their 'Village,' and being an ex-Torontonian, I decided to go back and look at it as much through tourist eyes as I possibly could. So I spent a night walking up and down the street and sampling the music as it came spilling out of the doorways of the clubs. Then I went back to the place where I was staying, took out my yellow pad of paper and my black felt pen and wrote that song."

The second side, "Out of the City and Down to the Seaside," built upon that freedom with a song cycle clearly inspired by her time in Miami with Crosby. "Cactus Tree" closed the album as a natural bookend for "I Had a King," with Mitchell meditating on a series of lovers vying for her affections, something the song says she is not prepared to do again if it means reverting to the domestic role that her ex-husband ultimately wanted her to play. Few female voices had expressed such wisdom on record before; Mitchell refused to paint herself as a muse for others — as Nico and many female artists of the time did — instead allowing the men in her life to play that role for her. It was a voice that the male-dominated industry was not prepared for. In advance of the album's release, Reprise came up with a print advertising campaign that declared "Joni Mitchell Is 90% Virgin," a cheap joke that undercut the creative control she had fought for in her contract, control that even extended to the album's cover art, which consisted of one of her own paintings.

By the album's completion, Mitchell was also through with Crosby as a lover. In March, she returned to Canada for extended runs at the Riverboat and Le Hibou. On March 19, Hendrix was also in Ottawa, and, following his show at the Capitol Theatre, came to the club to catch Mitchell. With her album still a few months away from being released, the guitarist recorded the show for his own enjoyment, and the pair shared an intimate conversation afterward. "Jimi was a sweet guy," Mitchell said. "He became very uncomfortable with the image he had presented. He felt it humiliating after a while, and degrading because he had presented an image that was shocking, a violent act, and people assumed he was dangerous."

But it was another visiting musician who would ultimately emerge as a successful suitor, and subsequently use Mitchell as the springboard to the next stage of his career. Graham Nash was ready to leave The Hollies, the band he had started with his boyhood friend Alan Clarke, and had scored a few hits with during the tail end of the British Invasion. As a friend of Crosby's, Nash had likewise been urged to come to California, already a place that had lured many other British musicians away from the dismal climate of their homeland.

Mitchell turned up at a party at the Château Laurier following The Hollies' Ottawa concert on March 17, and Nash spotted her in a corner of the room. Having heard of her through Crosby, he introduced himself, and the pair spent the rest of the night keeping other partygoers at bay. Nash said many years later that it was love at first sight, but he had to leave the next day to finish his tour. When Mitchell returned to L.A. in May, Nash was there with The Hollies, although he was laid up at Crosby's house, recovering from an illness. Adopting a Florence Nightingale role, as she later put it, Mitchell brought Nash to her new home in Laurel Canyon, which she had purchased with her advance from Reprise. There he would remain, effectively ending his time with The Hollies.

By then, *Joni Mitchell* had crawled into the lower reaches of the *Billboard* album chart, where it peaked at number 189. However, in L.A. she was the talk of the town. Mitchell made her live debut in the city at the Troubadour, playing twelve straight nights starting on June 4, each one a sellout. After only two days off, she flew to New York for a further seventeen shows at the Bitter End. The familiarity of the venues made her performances even more mesmerizing, prompting Robert Shelton to declare in *The New York Times* that a folk renaissance was truly underway. Indeed, the sudden dissolution in 1968 of many beloved bands, such as Buffalo Springfield, Cream, and The Byrds (who would reconfigure themselves that year as a country band with the addition of Gram Parsons), combined with the hype surrounding *Music From Big Pink*, was certainly indicative of a sea change. Neil Young had met Elliot Roberts for the first time during his reunion with Mitchell at Sunset Sound back in February, and, within days of Buffalo Springfield's farewell concert on May 5, sought out Roberts to manage him as a solo artist.

Meanwhile, Crosby and Nash were hatching their own scheme. At a party at Cass Elliott's house on July 3, Stephen Stills started playing a new song, "You Don't Have to Cry," and, as he hit the second verse, Crosby and Nash chimed in with harmony parts that sent the three of them, as well as the rest of the room, into ecstasy. Combined with Mitchell's first album and Neil Young's solo debut, which was completed later in the year, the creation of Crosby, Stills & Nash marked the start of a new era for the L.A. scene. It focused around Warner Brothers Records, and the offices of Elliot Roberts and David Geffen, a nexus that would soon come to dominate the music business as a whole.

Although hard rock had an equally important role, the "California Sound," as it came to be known, was characterized by introspective singer-songwriters in the Mitchell/Young mold.

Springtime in Tennessee can be life-affirming, and the grounds around Johnny Cash's estate in Hendersonville smelled particularly sweet in early 1969. The master of the house was fully recovered from a debilitating addiction to pills, and was back on the charts in a most unexpected way: with an album recorded live at a California prison. This had led to his own television variety show on ABC, and for its first episode, on May 1, Cash wanted to send the message that he was in total control. As an artist who fully understood the nature of songwriting, he only wanted the best in the field, despite what his mainstream country and western audience might have thought of young, longhaired folks. He wanted to send the same message of artistic freedom to his guests, as well, if only to give them a small sense of comfort before they arrived in a part of the country that was as foreign to some of them as Canada was to Cash in his younger days. To this end, he did what came naturally, and brought them all to his house for some simple southern hospitality.

After they had been fed, Cash broke the ice with a song. One by one, the guests followed suit; Bob Dylan sang "Lay Lady Lay" in a sweet crooning voice none of them had heard him employ before, Mitchell sang "Both Sides, Now," a song they had heard sung by others, but rarely by its author, and her companion, Graham Nash, sang "Marrakesh Express," a song his new group was about to release on its first album. Not to be outdone, Cash's Nashville cronies chimed in; Shel Silverstein, the great humourist and children's author/illustrator, offered a song he had written for Cash knowing that he was the only singer with enough confidence to pull it off. Cash would subsequently play "A Boy Named Sue," for the first time in front of inmates at San Quentin prison. Then Kris Kristofferson sang "Me and Bobby McGee," containing a chorus — "Freedom's just another word for nothing left to lose" — that would soon become the mantra for the latest lost generation. Yet no one could have believed those sentiments to be true that night being in the presence of such a significant cross-section of post-war popular songwriting. When they were put in front of the cameras at the hallowed Ryman Auditorium, it was a different story; Dylan, in a conservative brown suit and patchy peasant beard, looked clearly ill at ease as he attempted to find middle ground with the heartland masses. Mitchell, in a dress that covered everything from her neck to her feet, was almost childlike in the presence of the host, making Cash appear even more nervous: "So I hear that you're from Saskatchewan. What do they call people from there?" "Um, Saskatchewanians. What do they call people from Tennessee?" But as they began a duet of "Long Black Veil," with her voice soaring with strength during the choruses, the song was suddenly stripped of its past as a contemporary murder ballad, and became something that folk music had always aspired to be, something almost holy.

Mitchell's appearance on *The Johnny Cash Show* coincided with the release of her second album, *Clouds*, recorded in between concerts at Carnegie Hall on February 1, 1969, and an emotional return to Saskatoon on March 13 and 14. In many ways, the album was a reconciliation with her past, as well. Dispensing with a producer, Mitchell constructed the record around simple takes of some of her most time-tested material, including "Both Sides, Now," "Chelsea Morning," "I Don't Know Where I Stand," and a concession to the anti-war movement, "The Fiddle and the Drum." Also bearing a self-portrait and a dedication to her maternal grandmother, *Clouds* was essentially the album Mitchell's fans expected her to make. Its chart performance bore this notion out, as it peaked at number thirty-one in the U.S. and number twenty-two in Canada by mid-July. But an ever-expanding fan base was not necessarily what Mitchell wanted now that she had found some semblance of stability as a musician, and the audiences she played to that summer were not the ones who came to see her in clubs, or at Newport and Mariposa, both of which she appeared at in July. With Crosby, Stills & Nash (now with Neil Young in tow) generating huge demand for their debut live performances, Roberts and Geffen naturally wanted Mitchell to share in the expected windfall. They persuaded her to open the group's first show in Chicago on Saturday, August 16, although everyone was consumed by what was happening that weekend in upstate New York, a gathering that had become bigger than anyone could have imagined.

Both Mitchell and Crosby, Stills, Nash & Young were scheduled to play at Woodstock on Sunday, but reports of closed highways and heavy storms drenching a crowd approaching half a million got them spooked. As their chartered planes landed in New York, Geffen, in particular, had decided not to subject Mitchell to the stress that the festival was sure to put on her, especially when she was slated to be back in the city on Monday for what Geffen assumed would be a more worthwhile appearance on *The Dick Cavett Show*. She acquiesced, and stood by as the boys boarded helicopters bound for the site. Later, in Geffen's apartment, while keeping apprised of the festival through television news reports, Mitchell had an epiphany. "The deprivation of not being able to go provided me with an intense angle on Woodstock," she said. "I was a little 'God-mad' at the time, for lack of a better term, and I had been saying to myself, 'Where are the modern miracles?' Woodstock, for some reason, impressed me as being a modern miracle. So I wrote the song 'Woodstock' out of these feelings, and the first three times I performed it in public I burst into tears because it brought back the intensity of the experience and was so moving."

Crosby, Stills, Nash & Young played their set in the wee hours of Monday morning, before Hendrix closed out proceedings after sunrise before a scant 60,000 diehards. By then, the quartet was back in New York for the Cavett show, where Mitchell was eager to play them her new song. The first creative response to the festival, "Woodstock" was also its most stirring by-product, next to Hendrix's interpretation of "The Star Spangled Banner." In a similar way, the song, intentionally or not, managed to capture the creeping paranoia that was pervasive throughout 1969 in its juxtaposition of Mitchell's optimistic message over a moody, dirge-like piano melody. It was immediately proposed that Crosby, Stills, Nash & Young work up a rock arrangement of the song, but their escalating infighting made it highly dubious that they could sing about peace and brotherhood with any conviction. Compounding matters was the death of Crosby's girlfriend, Christine Hinton, in a car accident on September 30, two weeks after the band, along with Mitchell, played the Big Sur Folk Festival. The news sent Crosby straight to the needle, and cast a pall over the recording sessions for their new album, *Deja Vu*, completed under much duress in November. It was the season of Charles Manson and Altamont, a season of reckoning that even indelibly stained Mitchell's ode to the modern miracle she had witnessed, one that could not be masked by Nash's "Teach Your Children," a blatant attempt to write his own version of "The Circle Game," or his sentimental tribute to his and Mitchell's domestic bliss, "Our House."

Little did Nash know that by the start of 1970, Mitchell was already breaking free of him, as she was with other aspects of her career, specifically performing live. On January 17, she declared that her performance that night at London's Royal Festival Hall would be her last for the immediate future. "I had a bad attitude about [performing]," she admitted two years later. "I felt like what I was writing was too personal to be applauded for. I even thought that maybe the thing to do was to present the songs in some different way — like a play or a classical performance where you play everything and then run off stage and let [the audience] do whatever they want, applaud or walk out." Yet, when it came to making her next album, *Ladies of the Canyon*, Mitchell was still not ready to let go of her past. She finally laid down "The Circle Game" for posterity, along with the Detroit/Chelsea-era "Morning Morgantown" and "Conversation." But if the choice to record these songs revealed an artistic contradiction within Mitchell, it was manifested more directly in the new songs "For Free," a statement on her recent financial success, "Big Yellow Taxi," a more playful comment on the business world that would quickly become the anthem of the nascent environmental movement, and "Willy," her love letter to Nash.

By summer, those close to the couple were calling the song

an unapologetic kiss-off, as word spread of an affair between Mitchell and Stills just prior to Crosby, Stills, Nash & Young's much-hyped U.S. tour. With *Ladies of the Canyon* selling even more copies than *Clouds* despite her self-imposed ban on touring (it cracked the Top 30 in America, Top 20 in Canada, and Top 10 in England), Mitchell could afford to extricate herself from her romantic entanglements. However, for the next year the soap opera of the L.A. scene would be played out on other records, notably Crosby's "Cowboy Movie," from his 1971 guest-filled solo album *If I Could Only Remember My Name*.

As Crosby, Stills, Nash & Young collapsed under the weight of its collective ego, Mitchell and a female companion from Ottawa were on the Greek island of Crete, following Leonard Cohen's example. She purposely travelled light, perhaps recalling his tales of living on Hydra, and left her guitar behind in favour of the more portable dulcimer. This ancient stringed instrument was still utilized at the time by contemporary Appalachian folk artists such as Jean Ritchie, with whom Mitchell would have surely crossed paths on the early festival circuit. She revelled in her temporary anonymity, spending the bulk of her time with a group of young dropouts living a communal existence in a tiny coastal village. Although the scene was idyllic, over the course of her five weeks there the pull of songwriting returned, as did the need to face crowds again. There were the usual calls to play the large festivals, many more of which had sprung up in the wake of Woodstock, and partly for this reason she was coaxed back to the stage for a few selective appearances. One of these displayed her loyalty to Mariposa, now held on Toronto's Centre Island over the last weekend of July 1970. Amid the accolades that came with this tentative, albeit triumphant, return was another fateful encounter. Also at the festival was James Taylor, the troubled singer-songwriter who also happened to be one of Warner Brothers' highly touted signings, as shown by the success of his latest album, *Sweet Baby James*. Finding themselves outside the glare of L.A. brought the pair into each other's arms that weekend, and in Taylor Mitchell found someone more in tune with her own creative disposition (apart from Cohen) than any of her previous partners, in spite of Taylor's well-known heroin habit.

The couple settled into a relationship back on the west coast for the next month, until Mitchell flew to England to fulfill her only other commitment that summer, at the Isle of Wight Festival. It was to be her personal reparation for missing Woodstock, but nothing could prepare her for what awaited. Even though Mitchell was slated partway through the second day, prior to headlining sets by The Doors and The Who, the 600,000 in attendance were by then already on the verge of revolt. Some threw bottles and cans at the stage soon after she began with "The Gallery," and two songs later she was in tears, pleading for respect. Her emotional outburst did get the crowd to calm down enough for her to finish, and even attempt two brand new songs she had written at the height of her homesickness on Crete, "California" and "A Case of You," but, overall, the appearance only reinforced how fragile her music was in the face of such masses of humanity. However, Mitchell couldn't make a quick escape from England. She was booked to shoot an episode of the BBC's *In Concert* television series two days later, and this environment ultimately provided enough space for the songs to breathe. Mitchell turned in a brief but remarkable performance, including the new numbers again, and in the process managed to salvage some dignity out of what could have been a completely futile exercise.

Back in the U.S. Taylor had, surprisingly, been tapped for a lead role, along with Beach Boy Dennis Wilson, in Monte Hellman's film *Two-Lane Blacktop*, an existentialist road picture in the spirit of *Easy Rider*. Mitchell was a frequent visitor to the set, and entertained the crew with new songs in between takes. After shooting wrapped in late October, she and Taylor set out for a short stint of touring, including two warmly received shows by Mitchell at London's Royal Festival Hall on November 20 and 21. But as they grew closer as a couple, Mitchell could not avoid becoming wrapped up in Taylor's addiction, and the toll it took on her psyche cast looming clouds over the final song selection she needed to make for her next album.

When she entered Sunset Sound in January 1971 to record

Blue, only engineer Henry Lewy was permitted to witness what would be the catharsis to which Mitchell's life had been building. "That album is probably the purest emotional record that I will ever make in my life," she said. "To survive in the world you've got to have defenses, and at that time in my life, mine just went. Actually, it was a great spiritual opportunity, but nobody around me knew what was happening. All I knew was that everything became kind of transparent. I could see through myself so clearly, and I saw others so clearly that I couldn't be around people."

She continued, "In order to make that album, we had to lock the doors of the studio. When the guy from the union came to the studio to take his dues, I couldn't look at him. I'd burst into tears. I was so thin-skinned, just all nerve endings. As a result, there was no capability to fake. I'll never be that way again, and I'll never make an album like that again."

Stories about the tortured creation of *Blue* immediately became part of rock and roll lore, along with Brian Wilson's sandbox and Phil Spector's penchant for firearms, but few had gone to such extremes to bare their soul in the studio before. Mitchell began, as with her previous two albums, by dipping into her unreleased back catalogue for anything that could serve as a foundation for the new material. She chose "Urge for Going" and "Little Green," the song she had written in the wake of her daughter's birth, along with the rarely performed "Hunter (The Good Samaritan)." The album's core themes of desire and abandonment were thus set in motion, split between the "Greek" songs: "Carey," "California," and "A Case of You," and those more evidently sparked by her draining relationship with Taylor: "Blue," "This Flight Tonight," and "My Old Man." The album's centrepiece was "River," a song that, for the first time, plainly displayed Mitchell's longing for the homeland she had left behind. The simple piano melody and stark imagery painted an unforgettable picture of the innocence Mitchell once possessed, juxtaposed with her life in L.A., which was in many ways its antithesis. Still, she realized she could not go back; late in the sessions, Mitchell shelved "Urge for Going" and

"Hunter" in favour of two new songs that saw a partial rejuvenation of her self-confidence, "All I Want," and "The Last Time I Saw Richard." The last-minute addition of these tracks as bookends for the album was a daring, but necessary, move. The former exuded a loving vulnerability, while the latter showed the other side of that coin; the coldness required to firmly end a relationship. Given the song's reference to "Detroit '68," most assumed it was Mitchell's final word on her ex-husband, but, in essence, it was a comment on all of her previous relationships, as well as the ray of hope she had glimpsed at the end of them all — when her time in dark cafés became "Only a dark cocoon before I get my gorgeous wings/And fly away."

Blue was released in June, after overdubs were added to several songs by a few familiar faces, Taylor among them. This time, Mitchell adamantly declined to give any live performances, but the album nevertheless surpassed its predecessors, hitting number fifteen in the U.S. and making the Top 10 in both Canada and the U.K. However, her catharsis was not complete until she left her Laurel Canyon house that summer and trekked north to British Columbia, finding an isolated spot at Half Moon Bay, on the Sunshine Coast, where she built a makeshift cottage. The solitude she sought would not last long. David Geffen had been making rumblings all summer that his long-held dream to start his own record label was about to come true. Much of it hinged on the fact that Mitchell's contract with Reprise was about to expire, and Geffen wanted her as his flagship artist. For Mitchell, it seemed like a natural move, considering that Geffen and Roberts were now her co-managers, having officially incorporated their partnership to oversee the careers of most of L.A.'s singer-songwriter community. This gave Geffen the luxury of hand-picking from his own established clientele for his label, ambitiously (or ironically) dubbed Asylum Records. Yet, after she accepted Geffen's proposal and moved back to L.A., rumours abounded that Mitchell felt threatened by the presence of other women on the label, particularly Geffen's newest discovery, Judee Sill, whose self-titled debut album would be Asylum's first release in late 1971. Sill, in fact, shared a lot of traits with Mitchell, mostly an angelic voice and a classically inspired gift for melody. However, like many others in L.A., she was a junkie with a troubled past, and would make only one more emotionally charged record before falling off Geffen's radar and into a long, painful descent that ended with her death in 1979.

Geffen eventually realized that in order to keep Mitchell, and, more importantly, get another outstanding record out of her, she needed to be his primary focus. He offered her his house in Bel Air, and in the fall of 1971 she moved in and began working on *For the Roses*. Throughout her stay, Geffen continuously nudged Mitchell to write a hit single, something she had never had, and she responded in a typically insouciant way with "You Turn Me On (I'm a Radio)." He also convinced her to go back on the road, and proceeded to set up a fifteen-date North American theatre tour beginning on February 16, 1972. The prospect of facing audiences again was made easier by having her latest flame, Jackson Browne, as the opening act. Browne, another favourite of Geffen's, had just released his debut album on Asylum after shopping his songs for years to the likes of The Byrds and Nico, with whom he was also romantically linked. Although barely into his twenties, Browne's relationship with Mitchell fell into her familiar pattern, and subsequently fuelled her performances.

However, the new songs largely reflected her lingering feelings toward Taylor, especially "Cold Blue Steel and Sweet Fire," which illustrated many unflinching details about life with a junkie. Mitchell's affair with Browne ended acrimoniously by the summer, after they had completed a European jaunt. The split sent her into depression once again, but, as she told Penny Valentine of *Sounds* during the tour, she already had a clear plan for the new album. "I'm going to start looking for [musicians] who are untried, who have a different kind of enthusiasm that comes from wanting to support the artist. The music is already a growth, a progression from *Blue*, the approach is stronger and melodically it's stronger. I think that will be noticeable whether I make a sparse record, as I did with *Blue*, or not. I feel I want to go in all directions right now. But rushing ahead of ideas is bad.

An idea must grow at its own pace. If you push it and it's not ready, it'll just fall apart."

Indeed, the sound of *For the Roses* was merely a tentative step toward the full-band arrangements that had already brought many of Mitchell's contemporaries into the mainstream by that point. And despite what she may have thought about "You Turn Me On (I'm a Radio)," it did fulfill Geffen's wish by becoming a Top 30 single, and helped to push the album higher than *Blue* had gone. Mitchell marked its release that November with a four-night stand at the Troubadour, but the year ended on a sour note when *Rolling Stone* dubbed her "Old Lady of the Year," with an accompanying list of her high-profile affairs, some of which were inaccurate. It was a clear double standard, although some within the scene defended the title, given the sheer amount of heartache that had spilled onto vinyl as a result. Mitchell was naturally offended, at first, by the magazine's attack on her character, but eventually shrugged it off. There were still very few women in music with as much creative control as Mitchell had, so she wisely refused to rise to the bait. In any case, she had taken up with singer-songwriter J.D. Souther, effectively breaking up his relationship with Linda Ronstadt. As Mitchell said in a late-1973 interview that was later published in *Maclean's*, "The rock and roll industry is very incestuous; we have all interacted and have all been the source of many songs for one another, and I think that a lot of beautiful music came from it."

Such a succinct statement showed Mitchell's growing maturity that year. It was greatly helped by having her property in B.C. to escape to whenever necessary, but she also found pleasure through her platonic relationship with Geffen, whose consolidation of power within the industry continued unabated. He now had his sights set on signing Bob Dylan, whose contract with Columbia was up for renewal in 1973. Making him the brightest jewel in his crown became an obsession, and Geffen pursued every avenue to try to make it happen. Geffen made his boldest move by befriending one of Dylan's most trusted confidantes, Robbie Robertson, who had moved close to Dylan in Malibu shortly after completing The Band's *Moondog Matinee*.

Geffen suggested that Robertson and his wife Dominique accompany him and Mitchell on a vacation to Paris, and while he put on a facade of relaxation, Geffen remained intent on persuading Robertson not only to get Dylan to sign to Asylum, but also to get Dylan and The Band back together.

Mitchell was able to take in all this with great amusement, and managed to capture Geffen's mood immediately after the trip in a new song, "Free Man in Paris." Its observations on the "star maker machinery" that now ran the L.A. music scene set the tone for recording sessions she undertook in the fall of 1973, backed by many of the city's top jazz players. The reasons behind this decision were simple, she explained: "No section had been able to play my music. It was too intricate harmonically and rhythmically. I tried for four projects to find a band, but it always squashed the music. Finally, it was recommended to me that I look for jazz musicians. And I found the L.A. Express, and that worked well."

Mitchell's more sophisticated musical turn mirrored many aspects of her social life. In L.A., there was no room for the side of her that could tough it out in the wilds of British Columbia. Through Geffen, she had access to the most powerful figures in the industry, and her fascination with this, in many respects, amoral lifestyle emerged in songs such as "People's Parties," "The Same Situation," and "Trouble Child." However, the change in lyrical perspective hardly mattered. When *Court and Spark* was released in January 1974, its high gloss was embraced by critics and radio stations alike, resulting in a previously unimaginable three hit singles. It added up to giving Mitchell confidence to go on the road with a band for the first time, and the bulk of 1974 was taken up by touring, including guests spots in Crosby, Stills, Nash & Young's huge shows on Long Island, and at Wembley Stadium in August.

But for all the acclaim *Court and Spark* rightly received in the midst of mid-seventies musical excesses, Mitchell's inevitable experimentation with jazz idioms ran counter not only to the few remaining folk purists, but to a new generation that was out to tear down the new rock establishment as represented by Geffen and his perceived money-grubbing clients. The convergence of these two forces was something Mitchell was unable to overcome with 1975's *The Hissing of Summer Lawns*, roundly dismissed in rock circles as a middle-of-the-road mess, when, in fact, most of its lyrics took direct aim at California's lassitude. Further albums generated even more controversy with critics, and apathy from record buyers, even though she now counted among her collaborators jazz heavyweights Charles Mingus, Herbie Hancock, Wayne Shorter, Pat Matheny, and Jaco Pastorius.

"I entered the game as a folk singer, but it took me six records to find a band that could play my music," Mitchell said. "That was a jazz band, and lots of my fans threw up their hands. In truth, *Mingus* was the only jazz album I did. Everything else, while it may have sounded jazzy at times, is outside the laws of jazz. With *The Hissing of Summer Lawns* I cut my players some slack, and they imposed some jazz chords on my music. People said it was kind of weird at the time, and I can see that now. At the same time, some of those experiments were necessary for me to move forward. They probably cost me a lot of popularity, but I wouldn't change anything."

Being out of step with popular tastes was something Mitchell had always accepted, but had never faced head-on before. A complicated message was not what her fans wanted, but after years of wearing her heart on her sleeve, Mitchell no longer had to pay that price for artistic fulfillment. By continuously challenging both herself and her audience in the coming years, she would earn a newfound respect, to the point where, two decades later, *The Hissing of Summer Lawns* would be widely lauded as a masterpiece by the likes of Elvis Costello and Prince. But without the benefit of her unparalleled musical gifts, most of her contemporaries had to reach similar creative advancement by other means during the collective mid-seventies malaise that *The Hissing of Summer Lawns* so subtly undermined.

PART THREE

DESERTER'S
SONGS

CHAPTER SEVEN

LOST MY DRIVING WHEEL

AFTER CONCLUDING THE EUROPEAN CAMPAIGN, Albert Grossman granted Bob Dylan and The Hawks two months' rest before another North American tour was due to begin in August 1966. It was to be far more gruelling than the last one: sixty-four dates, including one at New York's Shea Stadium, and even a proposed trip to Moscow, all partially intended to boost sales of *Blonde on Blonde*, rock and roll's first double album. In the interim, Dylan attempted to follow through on what now seemed an ill-conceived decision to personally edit D.A. Pennebaker's footage from Europe for the ABC television special, as well as finish his long-delayed novel, *Tarantula*. His contract with Columbia was also up for renewal, and Grossman was using all the leverage he had acquired over the past four years to squeeze out every possible cent during the negotiations.

There was also a new and growing family for Dylan to consider (on top of what was rumoured to be a growing heroin habit), adding no end to the mounting strain on his mental and physical well-being. On Friday, July 29, a week before the tour was scheduled to resume at the Yale Bowl in New Haven, Dylan and his wife Sara stopped by Grossman's Woodstock-area home so Dylan could pick up a motorcycle and take it to be repaired. Only minutes after departing, both of them returned to the house in Sara's car. Dylan staggered to the porch, and was met again by Sally Grossman, who was on the phone with her husband in Manhattan. Sara explained that Dylan had fallen off the bike, but that no police or ambulance needed to be called. Dylan was instead taken to his doctor's home, some fifty miles away in Middletown, and he remained there for the next six weeks, safely isolated from the press, his manager, his record company, and everyone else who wanted a piece of him. Whether it was a well-planned strategy or not, in hindsight the accident proved absolutely necessary for Dylan to re-emerge as the person he needed to be in order to get his life back.

By the autumn of 1966, most American listeners had already accepted that electric groups had marginalized folk singers. Dylan's unexpected disappearance from the public eye was the symbolic act that made it real, just as the collective teenage let-down that accompanied news of Elvis Presley's army induction had crippled the first wave of rock and roll. The previous March, Ian & Sylvia had released *Play One More*, which contained a noticeable twang with covers of Porter Wagoner's signature hit "A Satisfied Mind" and the bluegrass standard "Molly and Tenbrooks." The album was also their first to have fleshed-out arrangements, courtesy of a young New York electric bassist named Felix Pappalardi, who had been knocking around the Village picking up gigs with the likes of Fred Neil while trying to learn production at Atlantic Records under the aegis of its famed house producer, Tom Dowd. Along with his contributions to *Play One More*, Pappalardi went on the road with the Tysons. "Felix had more of a rock sensibility, although he had a fairly extensive classical background," Sylvia said. "I don't know if his heart was ever really into folk music. An interesting story about Felix, actually, is the first time he saw Cream was when he was playing with us in Boston. And it might have been their first North American appearance." After meeting Cream during the spring of 1967, and learning that their North American rights were held by the Atlantic subsidiary Atco, Pappalardi persuaded label head Ahmet Ertegun to get him involved in the group's next album, which they planned to record in New York on the final weekend before their work visas expired. Pappalardi subsequently earned a production credit on *Disraeli Gears*, the album that launched an incalculable host of sludgy imitators, among them Pappalardi's own successful power trio, Mountain, which allowed him to leave the folk world behind forever.

But for Ian & Sylvia, that spring of 1967 held few other options apart from either continuing in a folk-pop direction or going deeper into what now seemed their more natural place, country and western. They opted to try the former first on *So Much for Dreaming*, released in February. It contained their version of "The Circle Game," but, more significantly, was their first album to be recorded with a full band. It was also the Tysons' last album before their Vanguard contract expired, and Grossman quickly landed them at MGM, the label that at the time appeared to be Dylan's most likely destination as well. From the outset of this new deal, it was clear that the label had an unwavering intention to expand on *So Much for Dreaming*'s approach, leading to the much-maligned *Lovin' Sound*, produced by John Court and released in June. Sylvia recalls, "I think that with the *Lovin' Sound* album, there was a little pressure from the record company to do something that might be aimed a little more toward pop music. We were fortunate in that we didn't have a lot of that kind of pressure, but I think that that album was, in fact, a result of the record company wanting something that might go a little more toward the pop mainstream. And, although I think there are some good songs on that album, there are some flaws in the arrangements, which show that we really were not pop artists."

The album's harsh reception led to an easy decision to make the next record a full-fledged Nashville effort. In fact, Vanguard was demanding one more original album to fulfill its contract, and the pair gladly obliged, using their first trip to Tennessee in February 1968 to knock out *Nashville* with some of the city's top pickers. The recording sessions coincided with those for The Byrds' *Sweetheart of the Rodeo*, and, likewise, included some of the first airings of "basement tapes," songs that Dylan had written the previous summer. Indeed, *Nashville* was a worthy candidate to be called the first country-rock album, a title that

Sweetheart ultimately claimed largely due to Vanguard's fading presence within the industry. Undeterred, and now comfortable in their new southern setting, the Tysons returned to Nashville for their next MGM sessions, this time with producer Elliot Mazer. Utilizing the same band as before, anchored by drummer Kenny Buttrey and bassist Norbert Putnam, *Full Circle* followed closely on the heels of *Nashville* in the fall of 1968, making the records almost inseparable companion pieces, which, taken together, effectively consummated the union between contemporary folk and country.

That fall was also the season of *Music From Big Pink*, and few musicians in any genre could avoid the sweeping stylistic changes that The Band's debut album ushered in. Of course, no one was more pleased about this turn of events than Albert Grossman. Upon brokering a new four-year contract for Dylan with Columbia on July 1, 1967, Grossman was finally able to attend to the latest additions to his stable. By the summer of 1969, having The Band, Janis Joplin, and Dylan as his three marquee artists had put Grossman in a most enviable position. He realized he could now circumvent the labels he privately despised by putting records out himself. He began by constructing a state-of-the-art recording studio near his home in Bearsville, New York. In the process, he struck a deal with the Ampex Company, makers of recording equipment and tape, to press the records and serve as the label's other main stakeholder, while simultaneously bringing his long-time partner Warner Brothers on board as the distributor. All Grossman needed now was some music, and it walked into his office one day in the form of a young, tall, skinny rock and roller from Philadelphia carrying a handful of demos.

Todd Rundgren explains, "I had planned to become a producer when I left [my band] The Nazz — that was what I wanted to do, because I was really into the recording process as opposed to performing. What happened was that one of the guys who had been co-managing The Nazz had left doing that, and went to work for Albert Grossman. I went up to see this guy, who introduced me to Albert, who was starting a new label at the time, and I brought them this band from Philadelphia [The American Dream], and when they decided to sign the band, I got to produce them, kind of like a package. The whole situation was so embryonic that I could take advantage of its disorganized nature. If it had been more of a complete structure, I might not have been able to do it, but since I was in on the seminal level, I got the opportunity to produce the band, and, through that, I got other opportunities."

Rundgren's third project for Grossman's label, initially called Ampex Records, but later changed to the more appropriate Bearsville, was Ian & Sylvia's new band, Great Speckled Bird. Following the release of *Full Circle*, the couple concluded that they needed a band to play their latest material live, so they started making calls to see who was available. "We felt really isolated," Sylvia explains. "We were on the road almost all the time. And when we did the two albums in Nashville, we took almost a year off after those albums were put out. We realized that part of what we were feeling was that we did not want to go out on the road with just a guitar player anymore, that if we could not reproduce the material that was on those records, then we didn't want to be performing. And that's when we put the first version of Great Speckled Bird together." What made the band unique from the start was that it avoided established Nashville players, Ian & Sylvia had used in the studio, in favour of young and largely unknown musicians who merely had a passion for country music.

Among the recruits were guitarist Amos Garrett, known to the Tysons from his work with the eclectic, but highly popular Yorkville band The Dirty Shames. He immediately became the new band's secret weapon, able to play virtually any style, although his fresh take on country music was only surpassed by such L.A. session stars as Clarence White and James Burton. Ken Kalmusky, formerly of The Rockin' Revols with Richard Manuel, heard about the group and joined on bass, while the Tysons discovered pedal-steel guitarist Buddy Cage in Nashville, even though he had been playing honky-tonks in Toronto since his teens. Rounding out the lineup was drummer

N.D. Smart II, an Ohio native who had recently been ousted from Mountain following the release of the band's first album and its appearance at the Woodstock festival.★ Everything about Great Speckled Bird presented the Tysons in a new and intriguing way. The band's name came from the title of Roy Acuff's first hit in 1937, a song that could be traced further back, to an Assembly of God hymn, with the speckled bird representing, according to some, a bloodied hen that had been set upon by hawks.

But it was the group's musical chemistry that became the key to making Great Speckled Bird's eponymous album stand out amid rock's growing infatuation with country. This trend emerged in the wake of Dylan's *Nashville Skyline* and The Flying Burrito Brothers' *The Gilded Palace of Sin*, both released in the spring of 1969. What *Great Speckled Bird* offered, as opposed to *Music From Big Pink*'s complete transmogrification of accepted American musical forms, was a view that Canadian attitudes were also easily adaptable to the new "longhaired" country aesthetic. Much of the credit for this rested, simply, in Ian & Sylvia's choice to share equal billing with the band and allow them to craft a funky sound that invariably became the couple's own back-door introduction to rock and roll audiences. At times they sounded overwhelmed as vocalists in this new environment, but, simply as an experiment, *Great Speckled Bird* proved to Canadian artists that, in the post-folk revival world, they did not have to abandon their identities in order for their music to be relevant.

That point was also made emphatically, although not immediately, in the fall of 1969 with the release of Anne Murray's second album, *This Way Is My Way*, containing her signature song, Gene MacLellan's "Snowbird." Born Morna Anne Murray on June 20, 1945, in Springhill, Nova Scotia, the erstwhile physical education teacher initially charmed much of Canada with her genuinely wholesome performances on such CBC television shows as *Singalong Jubilee*, *Let's Go*, and *Sounds '68*. Shortly after-

---

★Smart was replaced in Mountain by Montreal-born Corky Laing.

ward, she was persuaded to make her first record with fellow Nova Scotian Brian Ahern, who had backed Murray up on many of her TV appearances.

Ahern recalls, "I used to be a fan of this show that was on every Saturday night in Halifax, and I noticed one night the guitar player was missing. So the very next Monday I walked to the station, which was all the way on the other side of the city from where I lived, with my cardboard case holding my guitar, and auditioned for them and got the job. That led to me becoming the musical director on *Singalong Jubilee*, which was where I met Anne when she showed up for a few guest appearances. I was really impressed, because when I'd coax and prompt things out of her, she always seemed to respond."

Although Ahern was making a decent living playing in as many as three bands on top of his television work, he had already decided that recording was his real passion. "I'd been listening to radio all my life, and I'd noticed that there were minds and hands behind the music, something that was stimulating it and creating it and shaping it. Even though I liked being a musician and getting the accolades for being on stage, my curiosity was drawn more to the hands and minds behind the music rather than the bands that played it.

"After the success of *Singalong Jubilee,* the powers at CBC decided to do a pop music show called *Music Hop* from each of the main cities in Canada. It dawned on me that to be the best of all the *Music Hops* — I think we were on Friday nights — our best shot would be to record the music, and then have the artist do their thing live over that pre-recorded music, so we would sound the best. The offshoot of that was that I got to listen to hits from the radio and reproduce them. We would bounce from one machine to another like Les Paul — we didn't have any big multi-track machines. I had to study the records and actually duplicate what the other producers had done. That's how I got into being a record producer, and I decided I liked doing that."

Both Ahern and Murray had taken part in a *Singalong Jubilee* cast album, released through Toronto-based Arc Records in

1966, and shortly thereafter Ahern moved to Toronto to try to persuade the label to allow him to record Murray as a solo artist. "Arc was, what they called at the time, an impulse-purchase label," he says. "What they would do was reproduce The Monkees' hits and put them in drug stores, sort of propped up on a rack so there would be an impulse to buy it, if someone happened to like the Monkees. I eventually convinced them to let me make a record with Anne Murray, because she was on television, and because of that they could sell a few in the drug stores. She was at that time still at the University of New Brunswick, I believe, and I wrote her a long chain of registered and certified letters, and eventually she gave in and came to Toronto. On top of that, I had to ask her for money to get my guitars out of hock."

For Murray's first album, *What About Me*, her voice, as beguiling as Gordon Lightfoot's with its effortless tone, which somehow suggested sorrow and cold detachment all at once, was showcased through popular material such as "Both Sides, Now," Tom Paxton's "The Last Thing on My Mind," and Dallas Frazier's "There Goes My Everything." But the standout track came courtesy of a relatively unknown Canadian songwriter named David Wiffen, appropriately entitled "David's Song." The combination of Wiffen's bound-for-moving-on lyrics, Ahern's pseudo-psychedelic arrangement, and Murray's breezy vocals defied the safety of the rest of the album. Such experimentation would not sit well with Murray in the future, yet her professional relationships with emerging writers like Wiffen would reap huge dividends once her record sales started to reach unprecedented heights for a Canadian artist. Ahern insists that taking chances on material by emerging Canadian artists was part of his plan for Murray from the start.

"That definitely was a concept I had," he says. "At the time, Canada was gaining its autonomy, and there seemed to be a hunger for things Canadian to reinforce this whole idea. It wasn't anti-American or anti-anything, just pro-Canadian. It was a very healthy and positive thing. I thought that if I could find a recording artist that sounded different from things coming out of England and different from American music, and could be identified as something Canadian, then it would do well. I saw that in Anne Murray, and also in the songs of a lot of Canadian writers. So I tried to wrap her in a sound that was different from American ‚or English records. An example is 'Snowbird,' which, to me, didn't sound like anything else. Before Anne's first album, I actually had a big record with a song called 'Canada' by The Sugar Shoppe [a Toronto vocal group featuring actor Victor Garber] when I was just starting to tap into that thing. I don't think Anne knew what I was up to. I think she just knew that I did a good job on *Singalong Jubilee*, and I was probably okay. I'd paid her back for the pawn ticket."

David Wiffen was born on March 11, 1942, in Surrey, England (the same suburban area where Eric Clapton would be born three years later), and, like most others of his generation, his introduction to music came through skiffle, that uniquely British melding of folk and the early rock and roll impulse. At sixteen, he came to Toronto with his family, and within four years he was a part of the nascent Yorkville scene, playing clubs like the Village Corner, where he befriended Ian Tyson and the recently arrived Denny Doherty. But there was an entire country waiting to be discovered, and Wiffen hitchhiked west in the summer of 1964, landing first in Edmonton and then settling in Calgary, where he eventually assumed management of the Depression coffee house. Among those he met there were Vancouver folk singer Brent Titcomb, with whom Wiffen forged an instant bond. The pair played a few times as a duo before Titcomb headed home, leaving an open invitation for Wiffen to come to the coast. Wiffen took him up on the offer late in the year, and, upon arrival, landed an appearance at Vancouver club the Bunkhouse as part of a planned hootenanny live recording. However, due to a lack of participants, Wiffen played a full set, ranging from "Four Strong Winds" to his own first songwriting efforts, and the tape somehow made it to a small New York label, International Records, which released it as *David Wiffen Live at the Bunkhouse* in early 1965.

When that album quickly vanished into obscurity, Wiffen

accepted an offer to join a Vancouver rock band called The Pacers, which had its sights set on a recording deal in Montreal. The agreement turned out to be merely a ruse to get the band onto the local club circuit, and, after a few weeks of gruelling five-hour sets per night, The Pacers, demoralized, returned west. Wiffen, however, still had folk music to fall back on, and chose to stay in the east, moving to Ottawa and its thriving scene, the epicentre of which was Le Hibou coffee house. By the time Wiffen came to town, the club had relocated to a large room at 521 Sussex Drive — just down the road from the Prime Minister's official residence — and had become a venue not only for music, but for actors and comedians, as well. Wiffen was warmly accepted into this circle, and for the next year he thrived, generating enough attention to land a slot at the 1966 Mariposa Folk Festival.

In due course, he was asked to join locally popular Ottawa folk-rockers The Children, replenishing a line-up that also included a twenty-one-year-old guitar prodigy named Bruce Cockburn. Cockburn was a hometown boy, born on May 27, 1945, although he had spent three months busking in Europe before attending three semesters at the Berklee College of Music in Boston. Joining The Children in late 1965 gave Cockburn some creative freedom, although both his and Wiffen's stints with the band would not last much beyond 1966.

By then, Wiffen's friend Brent Titcomb had found good fortune with 3's a Crowd, a paisley-tinged folk-rock group that had become the darling of Yorkville through its first single, "Bound to Fly" b/w Gordon Lightfoot's "Steel Rail Blues," recorded in New York and released throughout North America on Epic. In the wake of this success, Titcomb and the other principal members, Donna Warner and Trevor Veitch, opted to expand the band at the start of 1967. Wiffen was offered a spot, along with bassist Ken Koblun, who had been a member of The Squires, Neil Young's Winnipeg group. The new lineup allowed 3's a Crowd more prestigious gigs, and they were among the host of home-grown talent showcased at Expo 67 pavilions that summer. It was after one of these performances that Cass Elliott approached them. She was searching out new opportunities following The Mamas and the Papas' recent split, and immediately saw the potential of 3's a Crowd to step into the role her band had just vacated. Elliott helped the group land a new deal with her label, ABC-Dunhill, which resulted in what amounted to 3's a Crowd's only album, *Christopher's Movie Matinee*, recorded in Los Angeles.

Although hopes for the album were high, the band members' interest had drastically waned by the time it was released in February 1968. They had escaped a close call when, during a run of shows at a club called the Ice House in Glendale, California, Neil Young left an invitation for the band to attend a party at Stephen Stills' ranch in Topanga Canyon on March 20. Also present was Eric Clapton, who was in town for shows with Cream. When an ensuing jam session got out of hand, the police arrived, which led to a mad scramble to dispose of all the drugs within reach. By the time the members of 3's a Crowd arrived, everyone who was there — with the exception of Stills, who made a dash and managed to call his lawyer — had been arrested. It was a soul-destroying scene that inevitably marked the end of Buffalo Springfield, and, subsequently, 3's a Crowd's original lineup, by May.

However, the impact of *Christopher's Movie Matinee* would continue to resonate throughout the year, as it became a calling card for several promising Canadian songwriters. Wiffen had gotten his chance to shine with "I Don't Wanna Drive You Away" (later coupled with Dino Valente's ubiquitous flower-power anthem "Get Together" as the album's second single), but it was Wiffen's insistence to cover several songs by Bruce Cockburn that played the biggest role in the album's final design. Cockburn ended up with four credits on the album: "The Way She Smiles," "Gnostic Serenade," "View From Pompous Head," and the A-side of the first single, "Bird Without Wings." The B-side was "Coat of Colours," written by another largely unknown Canadian folkie, Murray McLauchlan.

Born on June 30, 1948, in Glasgow, Scotland, McLauchlan came to Canada by boat at age five, and his family settled in Toronto. By his teens, he had fallen under Bob Dylan's sway, and assumed the image of a drifting troubadour, even going so far as hopping freight cars and hitchhiking around the country following a stint in art school. By 1967, McLauchlan had built a reputation in Yorkville, helped by an appearance on Oscar Brand's CBC television show *Let's Sing Out* alongside Joni Mitchell, which led to his debut at the Mariposa Folk Festival that summer. It was there that he met 3's a Crowd, and eagerly played them his handful of original songs. They were drawn to one called "More Than a While," but suggested renaming it "Coat of Colours," after the song's repeated refrain. The single's minor success on radio was enough to legitimize McLauchlan's status among his peers, and he set about pushing his songs elsewhere, just as they had. McLauchlan found a companion in this pursuit in Cockburn, when they met for the first time upon sharing a bill at Le Hibou in 1968, and played together again at that summer's Mariposa Folk Festival.

Cockburn had yet to fully establish himself as a solo artist, having spent the latter part of 1967 and early 1968 as a member of The Flying Circus, a psychedelic band later known as Olivus. That band enjoyed several high-profile gigs during its short lifespan, including the opening slot for Jimi Hendrix's March 1968 Ottawa concert, as well as for Cream's appearance there the following month. However, Cockburn left the group soon afterward to follow his desire to play acoustic music. It turned out to be a daunting enough challenge that, by autumn, he readily accepted an offer to join a revamped 3's a Crowd, which still included David Wiffen, ex-drummer for The Children Richard Patterson, and Cockburn's frequent songwriting partner, poet William Hawkins. The group's main raison d'être was to tape a series of performances for a proposed television musical variety show called *One More Time*, produced by one of their principal investors. But when the group's unusual treatments of the Broadway-style songs they were given to play didn't live up to expectations, the band embarked on a final, disheartening U.S. tour in the spring of 1969 before calling it quits. Cockburn and his wife Kitty decided to seek greener pastures in Toronto, and were soon sharing an apartment on Queen Street with

McLauchlan and his wife Patty. The arrangement proved suitable in most respects, although Cockburn and McLauchlan's artistic temperaments were markedly different, with the former far more introverted and seemingly driven by spiritual forces. Cockburn and his wife would ultimately leave Toronto that summer, moving their belongings into a camper so they could drift around the country. McLauchlan, sensing a similar need for inspiration, took an opposite tack, and moved to New York City at the end of 1969.

With her debut album not selling much outside of the Maritimes, Anne Murray had spent most of 1969 adjusting to the realities of touring in order to promote her music. This was still in addition to her television work, although Brian Ahern's efforts to sign her to a major label paid off by the summer. "I took that first record over to Capitol Records in Toronto, and a fine gentleman named Arnold Gosewich [Capitol's president] heard the promise of it, even though, I have to say, we'd done it pretty cheaply. But he thought I could do the job, and gave us a contract and a budget. At that time she had no manager, we did it all ourselves."

With more money to work with, Ahern pulled out all the stops to make a commercial recording, but *This Way Is My Way* received little attention in the face of other late-1969 releases like The Beatles' *Abbey Road*, The Rolling Stones' *Let It Bleed*, and *Led Zeppelin II*. Murray could only bide her time, to paraphrase the album's first single, for which "Snowbird" was the B-side. "In February 1970, Capitol wanted me to come to Toronto for a press conference," Murray said. "Apparently, somebody at CFRB in Toronto had discovered the album — four months after it had been released. Nobody had touched it before because of the miserable, rotten cover." Getting some notice in Toronto was certainly a major step for Murray, but it was just a prelude to what was about to come. "The first thing I heard was that 'Snowbird' was bubbling under the U.S. charts. I didn't even know what 'bubbling under' meant. Capitol sent me out on a promotional trip to Cleveland, Pittsburgh, Detroit, and New York. The record started to take off from Cleveland and Pittsburgh.

"It didn't really hit me until July, when I was on vacation. Capitol called up and said that 'Snowbird' was number forty-five in the U.S. I suddenly realized that it was almost in that legendary Top 40, and I really started to get excited. It passed the million mark [in sales] by November. I thought 'Snowbird' was hot from the moment I first heard it. Later on, I found out that Gene had written the song the year before with my voice in mind. At that time, we hadn't even met. But there was no way I thought it could be a hit. I'm a Maritimer and a Canadian; things like that just didn't happen here." Murray would have another big hit with a Gene MacLellan song, "Put Your Hand in the Hand," from her next album, *Honey Wheat & Laughter.* But with "Snowbird" starting to be covered by others — Elvis Presley recorded his version in September 1970 — Capitol went to the extreme measure of repackaging the best tracks from the two records on a single album for the U.S. market, entitled *Snowbird.* "They allowed Brian and I to program it and pick the cover, which was fine," Murray says. "But when we handed them an album with seven of the songs by Canadian composers, they were a little taken aback. Before they played the tape, they complained about the lack of recognizable songs, but when they heard the stuff, they completely forgot their hasty judgment."

Along with the songs by MacLellan and Wiffen, Murray also recorded Bruce Cockburn's "Musical Friends," a track that reflected the seemingly carefree gypsy life he was then experiencing. Cockburn's newfound rustic image was attracting notice from filmmakers, as well. Director Don Shebib wanted a soundtrack for *Goin' Down the Road* that captured the sense of desperation at the core of the film's story of two hard-luck Maritimers who migrate to Toronto in search of work. He originally wanted Ian Tyson to work the same magic he had with "Four Strong Winds," but when Tyson insisted on recording with Great Speckled Bird, a mutual friend told Shebib to hire Cockburn. Drawing upon his own rootless existence, Cockburn's intricate acoustic score played a huge part in the film being hailed as Canada's first unique success in the world of commercial cinema.

The dawn of a new decade was inspiring other nationalistic entrepreneurs, too. Bernie Finkelstein had been following the progress of Albert Grossman's label, and sensed the time was finally right for a wholly independent Canadian record label based on a similar model. Grossman had been Finkelstein's mentor and benefactor, having purchased the rights to Toronto rock band The Paupers — the first successful band Finkelstein had managed — for $20,000 in March 1967. Finkelstein parlayed that money into his next act, Toronto psychedelic folk-rockers Kensington Market, and landed them a two-album deal with Warner Brothers. Both of these, *Avenue Road* and *Aardvark*, were produced by Felix Pappalardi. But when that band ultimately crashed and burned following a disastrous San Francisco debut in September 1969, the relative stability of running his own label became too tempting for Finkelstein to put off any longer. Following Grossman's example, Finkelstein called upon his trusted musical contacts to find artists, and, through Gene Martynec, a principal member of Kensington Market, he was introduced to Cockburn. "I'd been out on my own for about a year when I bumped into Gene in Toronto," Cockburn explained. "We had a couple of coffees, and got to rapping on our ideas of what an album should consist of — him from the production side, me from the musical side. We found that our ideas were pretty much the same. Gene knew Bernie personally, and also knew he was the only person with enough money to make an album. Bernie also wanted to start True North Records, so it seemed a good opportunity to fulfill all aspirations."

Cockburn recorded his self-titled debut album with Martynec at Toronto's Eastern Sound in December 1969, using minimal instrumental embellishment. Along with "Musical Friends," songs like "Going to the Country," "The Bicycle Trip," and "Spring Song" reinforced Cockburn's clear pastoral tendencies. That vision, coupled with his unparalleled guitar-playing skills, put Cockburn in rarefied company. His only real peer was probably British singer-songwriter Nick Drake, whose own debut album, *Five Leaves Left*, had appeared earlier that year. Still, Cockburn's sound was a risky proposition on which to found a record label, but with Finkelstein persuading Columbia to take on distribution duties, *Bruce Cockburn* sold enough to put True North on solid footing.

In a way, Finkelstein knew he couldn't lose, since long-time lobbying efforts by the Canadian recording industry to get the federal government to enact laws that forced radio stations to broadcast a minimum one-third Canadian-produced material were coming to fruition. On May 22, 1970, the Canadian Radio-Television and Telecommunications Commission announced that the Canadian content law would take effect on January 18, 1971, much to the chagrin of broadcasters, who staunchly maintained that there was not enough music available to fill such a quota.

Yet, apart from helping Canadian artists to actually sell records at home, the new regulations made little difference in the distinction between Canadian and American songwriters. Those who were already established continued to have their songs covered, and the growing popularity of country-rock provided plenty of opportunities for musicians on both sides of the border to build closer ties. If an event was required to consummate this relationship, it came in the summer of 1970 with the Festival Express tour. The brainchild of Toronto promoter Ken Walker — who the previous summer had pulled off the massive Toronto Rock 'N' Roll Revival show that had John Lennon's first official performance as a solo artist as its main attraction — and his partner Thor Eaton, an heir to the Eaton's department store chain, the audacious plan was to stage four stadium shows across the country and transport the dozen or so equally split Canadian and American acts by train. "It was one of the greatest jam sessions ever," Rick Danko recalled shortly before his death. "It was one hell of a party. It was sex, drugs, and rock and roll at its best." Once again, The Band's communal philosophy set the tone for the rest of the acts, which included co-headliners Janis Joplin and The Grateful Dead. However, Danko was the only member of The Band who chose to ride on the train; the others headed back to Woodstock after each show to complete work on their third album, *Stage Fright*. It turned out to be a fateful decision. Following the June 27 and 28 shows at Toronto's Exhibition Stadium, which spawned a riot over ticket prices,★ the ensuing week-long rail journey, first to the Winnipeg concert on July 1, then ending with two shows at Calgary's McMahon Stadium on July 4 and 5, provided undeniable proof that debauchery was a common trait among all North Americans.

For Ian & Sylvia, who were bringing Great Speckled Bird to audiences for the first time, the chaos that came with rock festivals was a new and unsettling experience, especially in their home country. Speaking of the violence in Toronto, Sylvia said, "It made life hell for the promoters. It was mainly young kids who wanted to get in free, and were using a political stance to create a problem. I thought it was pretty dumb." It was also a new experience for Sylvia to be around Joplin, whose personality kept the few other women on the train at a distance. "She was never one of the girls. Ever. It wasn't her thing. She preferred to be with the guys. She was very upfront about that." The ever-present excesses kept the relatively straightlaced Sylvia excluded, as well. "It was Delaney Bramlett's birthday, and The Grateful Dead had made him this enormous cake. I remember this young woman going around with it and saying, 'Which side of the cake do you want?' I laughingly said, 'One side makes you smaller and the other makes you larger, right?' And she said, 'Yes.'" But it was the endless stream of booze on the train that made the biggest impact in close quarters, she admitted. "Somebody you knew who smoked a lot of grass was very different when they started drinking a lot. It got a little testy at times. The drinking thing tends to be a little more aggressive."

On stage, however, there wasn't any animosity, as the final Calgary show concluded with many of the artists, the Dead and

★The planned tour kickoff in Montreal was cancelled over fears it would conflict with rowdy celebrations of St. Jean Baptiste Day.

Great Speckled Bird among them, taking part in a lengthy jam on "Will the Circle Be Unbroken." But this was one of only a few positive memories that remained at the tour's end, especially for Ken Walker, who was confronted by an irate Calgary mayor, Rod Sykes, just after the train pulled into town. "He asked me to 'let the children of Calgary in free,'" Walker recalled. "I refused, and he called me eastern scum and a capitalist rip-off son of a bitch. I still have his teeth marks in my fist. After that tour, I decided to quit [the music business]. I felt the audiences weren't worth the effort. They didn't turn out, and they were protesting. We were giving them too much."

The good vibes were also spoiled for the Tysons immediately after the final show. As they drove out of the stadium, along with bandmates N.D. Smart and Buddy Cage, they were followed by a group of young protestors who hurled insults at them all way to their hotel. A melee subsequently broke out on the street, with Ian Tyson landing a punch that injured his left hand. The timing couldn't have been worse, since the Tysons were about to start production on a new television series called *Nashville North*, to be taped in Toronto for the CTV network. Similar to *The Johnny Cash Show*, it featured Great Speckled Bird as the house band, with a wide variety of musical guests. When the first episode aired on September 14, it was unusual to see Tyson without a guitar due to his broken hand, and also unusual to see that Sylvia was not given equal billing. The show's producer, Gerry Rochon, addressed this issue: "Sylvia was dropped from the initial concept because if you have a co-host you get hamstrung with giving her song time and spots to introduce guests; this way, Ian is the host and Sylvia does about half the shows as a guest."

Despite this rocky start, *Nashville North* was an instant hit, attracting top country artists such as Willie Nelson, Waylon Jennings, Kris Kristofferson, and Loretta Lynn, along with Linda Ronstadt, The Eagles, and many others. The new CanCon laws also made Gordon Lightfoot, Buffy Sainte-Marie, and Anne Murray regular guests. It was an easy gig for the Tysons, but it kept them from doing any further touring with Great Speckled Bird. As a result, changes in the band became common, with

David Wilcox replacing Amos Garrett, and Ben Keith replacing Buddy Cage early in the first season. By the second season, the show was syndicated in thirty-two U.S. markets, and also renamed *The Ian Tyson Show*, leading to further speculation that a split with Sylvia was either imminent or had already taken place. The couple managed to keep up appearances with the 1971 album *Ian & Sylvia*, released on Columbia, followed the next year by *You Were on My Mind*, produced by Keith and featuring a new Great Speckled Bird version of Sylvia's title tune, along with the darkly portending "The Beginning of the End." Although the band did briefly go on the road again following these releases, the shared spirit that had originally made Great Speckled Bird such a unique experiment had been lost somewhere in the grind of the television show. Still, the show would ultimately outlast the Tysons' marriage; they opted to separate in 1974, unbeknownst to fans of the program, who continued to watch it for another two years until Ian finally pulled the plug. While Sylvia retained a passion for making her own music, Ian's disgust with the business brought him back to the life he had always wanted, but had exchanged for a guitar. In 1977, he bought a horse ranch near Calgary and assumed the image of a working cowboy. In the process, he took a new teenaged bride who bore him a daughter. Eventually, he start writing songs again, albeit strictly based on his new lifestyle, as the cowboys he had left behind continued to roam the streets of L.A., Nashville, and Toronto looking for that elusive big break.

Murray McLauchlan assumed he had received his when he cut a deal with Albert Grossman's management company that gave it sole ownership of his entire song catalogue to that point. Although the price was only $1,400, McLauchlan saw it as the way into the U.S. he had been seeking. He and his wife promptly adjusted to life in the Village and sought out gigs, a prospect that was much different than it had been a decade before. McLauchlan befriended a few respected names within the scene, like Tom Rush and David Bromberg, both of whom adapted one of his more accessible tunes, "Child's Song," but, after six months in the city, the money was quickly running out.

When he heard about Bernie Finkelstein's move to start True North, McLauchlan returned to Toronto in the summer of 1970 simply for the opportunity to make a record. Much to his surprise, stories of his time in New York had been greatly exaggerated, and he was suddenly given treatment at home that was normally reserved for artists like Gordon Lightfoot. That suited Finkelstein fine, as he had no qualms about signing McLauchlan to True North, and his first album, *Song From the Street*, did indeed get a warm reception in Canada upon its release in the summer of 1971, not only from critics, but from new FM stations in desperate need of homegrown music. "Both myself and Bruce [Cockburn] came along exactly at the time when FM radio was in its infancy," McLauchlan says. "So all these big broadcasting companies had bought these FM licenses and they didn't know what to do with them; they just bought them because they were there. The money was in AM radio and the Top 40, so they hired all these dope-smoking hippies to be DJs and babysit these tiny FM stations all night. These guys didn't see any difference between the new Jethro Tull album and the new Murray McLauchlan album, so they'd play an entire side of the record all night. The fans didn't see the difference, either, when it was presented in the same light. They adhered to us just as easily as they adhered to Cream."

The success of the album allowed McLauchlan to tour in earnest for the first time, and in early 1972 he found himself opening for the Everly Brothers on the west coast. Although the Everlys' hit-making days were long gone, they still took great pride in their live show, and enlisted many of the best young L.A. session players to back them up. The bandleader was a classically trained pianist and song peddler named Warren Zevon, whose edgy personality offstage was more akin to the New York that McLauchlan had experienced. They became instant drinking and drug buddies, and shared their unrecorded songs as the tour bus wound its way inland through the Rockies. McLauchlan was preparing to record his next album, which Columbia Records had already assigned to its subsidiary Epic, an option that was part of the label's agreement with Finkelstein. It was a major coup in terms of profile, but mainly it provided a much-needed cash infusion for the project called, simply, *Murray McLauchlan*. Production was handled by Ed Freeman in New York, who had helmed Don McLean's then-current smash *American Pie*, and McLauchlan came well-prepared with a cache of more tales based on his fondness for downtrodden characters. Following this pattern, he was adamant about recording a song he had picked up from Zevon about a strung-out L.A. junkie. McLauchlan's version of "Carmelita" would be the first thing most of the world would hear from Zevon, who wouldn't release the song himself until four years later when his solo career finally got off the ground with his self-titled album on Asylum.

"Warren and I would sit up all night and do what musicians do, talk into the wee small hours and trade songs," McLauchlan says. "I played him stuff like 'Honky Red,' and he played me 'Carmelita,' and eventually, when it came time to do the second record in New York with Ed Freeman, I played him this song and he loved it. So we did this beautiful Tex-Mex version and when Warren heard it he really loved it. That was long before Linda Ronstadt did what I'd say is a rather inferior version. Warren and I remained pals, and he was a real character. He was a bit of a hit-and-miss guy as a performer, but sometimes you only need one hit to be remembered, and certainly 'Werewolves of London' was the biggie for him."

The album also contained what effectively became McLauchlan's signature number, "The Farmer's Song." Its simple, heartfelt message received a groundswell of support in Canada, where it sold 70,000 copies as a single, further motivating him to crack the U.S. market. However, McLauchlan would soon realize that the grip Grossman and other east coast figures once had on the music business was inevitably shifting Zevon's way, toward the west coast. David Wiffen had sensed that change when 3's a Crowd broke up. By 1970, he was in California at the invitation of Berkeley-based Fantasy Records, the label built upon the success of hometown heroes Creedence Clearwater Revival. Fantasy had been aware of Wiffen through 3's a Crowd, and offered to produce a solo album if he could find a way to get to the Bay Area. Wiffen eagerly obliged, and was promptly put into the studio with Ed Bogas, later known for providing music for Ralph Bakshi animated films like *Fritz the Cat*. Although Wiffen came with top-notch songs, not the least of which was "Lost My Driving Wheel," an archetypal country-rock anthem, everyone else present for the recording sessions was hardly as prepared. Bogas proved an inept producer, and overdubs later had to be done without Wiffen's approval. As a further insult, the album, *David Wiffen*, was given a belated release in Canada in April 1971, after only a handful of promotional copies had made it into the hands of U.S. and British reviewers the previous year. "Lost My Driving Wheel" would instead be introduced to wider audiences by Tom Rush on his 1970 self-titled album (which also included McLauchlan's "Child's Song" and "Old Man Song"), and then by Roger McGuinn on his first post-Byrds album in 1973. Both Eric Andersen and Jerry Jeff Walker also soon covered "More Often Than Not," another of *David Wiffen*'s standout tracks.

The notoriety Wiffen received from these versions did lead to another record deal with United Artists, and he chose to work closer to home with a more trusted producer, his close friend Bruce Cockburn, along with Brian Ahern on one track, "White Lines," written by Toronto singer-songwriter Willie P. Bennett. The album, *Coast to Coast Fever*, was a critical hit in Canada, and earned Wiffen a Juno nomination following its March 1973 release. It was a solid representation of Wiffen at his creative peak, highlighted by "Skyward Station" and "Smoke Rings," and the gracious inclusion of songs by Cockburn and McLauchlan. Sadly, *Coast to Coast Fever* would also be the last time most people heard Wiffen's rich baritone, as alcoholism and chronic back problems eventually forced him out of music for a large part of the next twenty-five years.

For Brian Ahern, the session with Wiffen was only one of many that came his way due to his successful relationship with Anne Murray, and the daunting task of staying on top of them all inspired his next move. "I wanted to have my own studio, but

I didn't want to be stuck in the same place every day," he says. "That's when I got the idea for the mobile unit, and one night I went up on my garage roof in Rosedale with all the cardboard and plywood I could find in the neighbourhood and started designing what I thought I wanted, which was the first totally self-contained audio recording studio. So I went down to a jetty in New York City where there was this graveyard for semi trailers, and after poking around there for a while we found a suitable one and I bought it for $2,500. We cleaned it up and dragged it back to Toronto and started building the Enactron truck."

He explains further, "I'd always had trouble recording strings in Toronto because I always thought the players were a bunch of irascible Paganini wannabes who would complain if they had to tune to an acoustic guitar. But with the truck, I could go to Massey Hall, their home, where they did not dare to perform less than their best. I pulled up with three albums I was working on, and with three different conductors, and we went from one song to the next, and they performed great. Their attitude was great, because I was in their house. That's just one example of how building that mobile unit paid off."

Having the truck also made it more realistic for Ahern to work in the U.S., where Murray's record sales continued to exceed all expectations. While her mellow sound caused critics like Lester Bangs to chide her as "the ultimate tease, because she gives you nothing but her vibrating *presence*," the slew of albums in the wake of *Snowbird* had tapped into the growing "easy listening" market. Where there was money, there were managers, and Shep Gordon, who also happened to guide the career of Alice Cooper, had taken Murray into his fold. Cooper and Murray did meet on at least one occasion, at a 1973 Thanksgiving party Gordon threw at the Troubadour, which was also attended by John Lennon, then in the midst of his legendary "lost weekend," in response to a temporary separation from Yoko Ono. "It was really all a blur," Murray says of the night. "Shep Gordon kept trying to find a hook to hang me on, a gimmick. He couldn't accept the fact that I was who I was, nothing more. I mean, Alice was just a regular guy. So he decided to throw this big party. I had string players behind me on this stage that looked like a turkey, and the musicians wore tail feathers." On August 3, 1974, Gordon put Murray in the similarly awkward position of following Bruce Springsteen & The E Street Band in New York's Central Park. Midway through Springsteen's set, Gordon realized the mistake he'd made in insisting that Murray headline and attempted to force Springsteen — then in the midst of completing *Born to Run* — off stage before the end of his set. There was no way the crowd would allow it, however, and it turned out to be the last show Springsteen ever played as an opening act.

Not surprisingly, incidents such as these made Murray reluctant ever to leave Toronto, but by 1974 Ahern no longer had the patience to be at her beck and call. That year he was contacted by Mary Martin, now working as an A & R rep for Warner Brothers, to see if he would be interested in working with the label's latest addition, Emmylou Harris. The singer was still dealing with the death of her mentor, Gram Parsons, on September 18, 1973, and playing shows with the remnants of his final band, The Fallen Angels, which had included former Great Speckled Bird drummer N.D. Smart II. Martin bought a plane ticket for Ahern to catch Harris at the Red Fox Inn in Silver Springs, Maryland, near her home in Washington, D.C., and he brought along a portable tape recorder to capture the sets. Martin was thrilled at the quality of the tapes, and with them she convinced her superiors to make what would be Harris's first solo record in L.A.

"I had spent a little time back in Toronto, and I sort of got familiar with [Ahern's] comings and goings," Martin said. "There was a song by Kenny Loggins called 'Danny's Song' that I said he should get Anne Murray to do, and he did. So I got to be kind of friendly with Brian, and when I got my job at Warner, I couldn't think of anyone else to work with Emmy because he was really skilled at choosing songs that musically showed off the singer's talents. But talk around the office became, here's Brian Ahern, so maybe we can also [sign] Anne Murray. I hadn't thought of that, but that was sort of the ploy. That's when I became sort of obstructionist, because it was Emmy, not Anne

Murray, that I cared about — not that Anne Murray is bad. My mission was Emmylou Harris, but I learned a valuable lesson there, that sometimes you have to say other things that may not necessarily be true, but the carrot's there, you know? It actually took a few bits and pieces of lobbying, and, in fact, I believe that Linda Ronstadt made a call to [Warner head] Mo Ostin to talk about Emmy."

Ahern drove the Enactron truck down from Toronto and parked it at 9500 Lania Lane, a large, rundown house in the Beverly Hills canyon rented for the session. "For someone who was sort of a hippie from the sixties, this house was one of the most aesthetically offensive places," Harris said. "It had all the kind of overdone excess of the fifties we hated — the fountain and the pool with swans spouting water. I thought, 'I don't know how I can be soulful and find magic in this place.'" For Ahern, the setting took a back seat to directing the musicians assembled for the project, several of whom, including pianist Glen D. Hardin, guitarist James Burton, and drummer Ronnie Tutt, were veterans of Elvis Presley's Las Vegas band, which had also played on Gram Parsons' solo albums. While this left no doubts about the quality of the music, for the songs themselves Ahern went with an eclectic mix of classic country and pop, not unlike what he developed early on with Anne Murray.

"I don't really know what the ratio was, but my function always seemed to be to pick the 'stretchers' — the songs that were, like, Beatles songs, songs that she wouldn't normally do," he says. "But it was always pretty much fifty-fifty from what I can recall. I didn't know much about her history with Gram, but I'd actually met Gram before I'd met Emmy. He was a song-writer who was pitching me songs for Anne Murray. It was in a small house in the Hollywood Hills, that's all I remember. But even then, before I'd met Emmy, I always thought we were doing country-rock. I never drew any lines there."

And, just as Ahern had employed previously unknown song-writers like David Wiffen and Gene MacLellan, he now insisted on giving a break to a young singer and guitarist from Houston, Texas, named Rodney Crowell, whose songs immediately connected with Harris when Ahern had played them to her in Maryland. "Skip Beckwith, Anne Murray's bassist, came back from the road with a tape of songs that Rodney had given her band for me to hear," Ahern explained. "I ended up buying Rodney's songwriting contract from Jerry Reed's company, Vector Music, and I signed him to a new contract with my company, Tessa Publishing in Toronto. I then flew him into Maryland to meet and write with Emmylou. I knew Emmy wanted to do Gram's songs, and that I would need more material with poetry and depth. Rodney went on to join Emmy's Hot Band. That airline ticket launched his career. I still have the receipt in his old itinerary file."

The album, *Pieces of the Sky*, released on February 7, 1975, was a crossover success, hitting the Top 10 on Billboard's country and western chart and Top 50 on the pop chart, helped in part by the single "If I Could Only Win Your Love," a faithful cover of a Louvin Brothers song. Before the year was out, Bob Dylan tapped Harris to sing harmonies on *Desire*, and she also released her second album, *Elite Hotel*, which would net her a Grammy for best female country vocal performance. The album stuck with the same formula as the debut, although it notably featured Crowell's later oft-covered "'Til I Gain Control Again" and no less than three Parsons songs, an unabashed move by Harris to instill in her new audience an unwavering belief in her guiding spirit's unheralded brilliance. Yet, by January 1977, she had partially managed to let that part of her past go, as her relationship with Ahern led to their marriage that month in Halifax. Over the next five years, they would build a prodigious catalogue in the face of the "urban cowboy" movement that only occasionally tampered with the blueprint they had originally designed — 1980's bluegrass homage *Roses in the Snow* and the Christmas album *Light in the Stable* being the notable exceptions. But, just as they were completing 1983's *White Shoes*, Harris walked out on the marriage, and, in the process, one of the most fruitful partnerships in country music history. "The lowest point in my career was when I had to file for divorce [from Emmylou]," Ahern admits. "It was more than the breakup of a marriage. My identity was caught up in being the producer of this quality body of musical work, which was about to come to an end."

Ahern would eventually bounce back, finding a permanent home in Nashville and steady work with the likes of George Jones, Johnny Cash, Roy Orbison, and even Harris again on her widely praised 2008 album, *All I Intended To Be*. Like Harris, her close friend Linda Ronstadt had made her name as a song interpreter in the wide-open field of early seventies California country-rock. With a powerfully soulful voice and girl-next-door looks, she presented a highly desirable feminine counterpoint to the largely male-dominated scene, something that was further heightened by her grasp of classic country and folk songs. But Ronstadt was still an underground figure up until 1974 when, at the same time Harris and Ahern began recording in Beverly Hills, she and her new producer, Peter Asher (one half of British Invasion duo Peter & Gordon), made *Heart Like a Wheel*. Showing more of an appreciation for rock than *Pieces of the Sky*, the album became Ronstadt's long-expected breakthrough into the mainstream, selling two million copies and spawning the smash pop/country and western crossover single "You're No Good" b/w Hank Williams's "I Can't Help It If I'm Still in Love With You," followed up by "When Will I Be Loved," which topped both charts on its own.

Earning its place as the album's title track was a song by one half of a little-known Canadian sister act who seemed among the most unlikely artists to be lured by the California dream. It was a sound rooted in Kate and Anna McGarrigle's distinct French Canadian–Irish upbringing that ended up giving all who heard them a fresh perspective on what folk-based songwriting could still achieve in the mid-seventies. Born in Montreal barely a year apart (Anna on December 4, 1944, and Kate on February 6, 1946), they were surrounded by music at an early age. Their father, Frank, had grown up playing piano in his father's silent movie house in New Brunswick, while their mother, Gaby, had played violin in Montreal's Bell Telephone Orchestra. Following the francophone tradition of their mother's family, the sisters were sent to parochial school in Saint

Saveur, north of the Montreal in the Laurentian Mountains. There, they took piano lessons from the nuns, but also absorbed the wide variety of music heard at their house. This ranged from the songs their father would play to their older sister Jane's interest in folk and blues. It wasn't long before they pestered their father to buy them a guitar and banjo, as well. "We were children of the middle class," Kate said. "My dad played funny ditties and drinking songs from the thirties. We didn't really have an Irish folk tradition, even though we were half Irish. There was no Irish folk tradition because they [the Irish] were subsumed under the prevailing English-Canadian culture. The French, on the other hand, were quite the opposite. As an oppressed people, it was quite important for them to remember their language, history, and music. No conqueror would take that away from them."

By the time they entered high school in Montreal, the McGarrigles were staunch folk fanatics, and found a suitable hangout at the Finjan Club. Run by Shimon Ash and his wife Niema, it hosted many American performers such as Sonny Terry & Brownie McGee, John Lee Hooker, and Josh White, cultivating a loyal clientele that eagerly anticipated each weekly show. Among this crowd was Jack Nissenson, who, on July 2, 1962, had his tape recorder rolling at the Finjan as Bob Dylan gave one of his first performances outside New York City. Dylan collectors subsequently treasured the recording for its quality and intimacy. Nissenson also had his own group, The Pharisees, which played traditional material, but after he got to know the McGarrigles as regulars at the club, he offered to form a new group with them, along with fellow Pharisee Peter Weldon, called The Mountain City Four. "We entered into the folk scene through the records of Joan Baez and Bob Dylan," Kate said. "But when we met Nissenson and Weldon, they introduced us to music at the sources and said, 'Forget about Joan Baez! Go to the sources at all times. Don't copy styles, just learn the original music.' I think that's why we have an original sound. We didn't try to imitate anyone, with the possible exception of Dylan, who everyone tried to imitate at one time or another."

The Mountain City Four remained a semi-serious pursuit for the McGarrigles as Kate earned an engineering degree at McGill and Anna studied painting at L'Ecole Beaux Arts. However, the group continued to appear regularly at Montreal's other coffee houses, the Seven Steps and the Café André. A loose contingent of like-minded artists formed within this scene, including Galt McDermott, future composer of the songs for the musical *Hair*, into its circle, along with Anna's future husband, Dane Lanken, and singer/guitarist Roma Baran, who teamed up with Kate when Anna decided to stop performing in 1968 in favour of a career in social services. Taking a cue from their heroes, Kate and Baran headed for Greenwich Village. At first they believed that they had to play the expected folk standards in order to get work, but Kate saw that the clubs were dominated by folk singers doing pale imitations of other performers' original material. She called her sister, brimming with confidence that they could easily survive in such an environment. "I said, 'God, people are doing stuff, and a lot of them aren't very good,'" Kate recalled. "Anna said, 'Isn't that funny? I just wrote a song.' I said, 'Make a tape and send it to us!' It was 'Heart Like a Wheel.' It was Anna's first song." From then on Kate became a familiar face in Village and one night at the Gaslight, she was compelled to approach that evening's performer, Loudon Wainwright III, and compliment him on his set.

"She was very attractive," he says. "I think every guy in the Village, they were all interested in Kate. When you heard her sing and play, you were knocked out. She was a wild and crazy swingin' folk chick." Wainwright was not the typical anti-establishment folk singer. Born into a storied New York family — his father was an editor at *Life* magazine and his bloodline included one of the founders of Manhattan, Peter Stuyvesant — Wainwright did not take up songwriting until the late sixties, during a stint working at a Rhode Island harbour. He appeared in clubs clean-cut and wearing a suit and tie, an image that fit his unusually urbane and witty, but often bitingly cold lyrics. He and Kate grew into a couple throughout 1970, as Wainwright landed a deal with Atlantic, while Kate and Baran started to gain some attention at folk festivals. The duo's usual closer was "Heart Like a Wheel," but Kate was also beginning to write her own songs. The sisters were urged to make demos, and, through Kate's relationship with Wainwright, there was immediate interest. In fact, Linda Ronstadt heard "Heart Like a Wheel" during this time, although the first to record it were latter-day folk-rockers McKendree Spring on their 1972 album *3*. The following year, Kate's "The Work Song" turned up on Maria Muldaur's self-titled album alongside the number-one hit "Midnight at the Oasis," with its famous Amos Garrett guitar solo.

It was all cold comfort for Kate, who had stopped performing in late 1970 when she married Wainwright upon learning she was pregnant. Intense arguments between them soon became the norm. These were compounded when Kate suffered a miscarriage during an extended stay in London. Still, Wainwright's career continued on an upswing. His third album, in 1973, contained the novelty hit "Dead Skunk," and he landed a brief reoccurring role on the TV series *M*A*S*H*. These breakthroughs brought some stability to the marriage, enough for Kate to finally bear their first child, Rufus, on July 22, 1973. However, there was little time to try to settle into a family routine. Before the year was out, Muldaur had chosen another McGarrigle song, "Cool River," for her next album, *Waitress in a Donut Shop*, and asked Kate to play piano on it. When Kate informed her that it was actually one of Anna's songs, producer Joe Boyd thought it would be a good idea for the sisters to record on their own, and, in May 1974, they were together in an L.A. studio for the first time, making a demo for Warner Brothers.

Upon inking a deal, the McGarrigles were put up at the Chateau Marmont, and the label spared no expense for the sessions. While "Heart Like a Wheel" was a clear centrepiece, along with Kate's crushingly romantic "(Talk to Me of) Mendocino," they largely bucked all expectations by sticking to a clear vision of a homespun folk record that in many ways lived up to the musical example their parents had laid out. Several Montreal cohorts, including Peter Weldon, were invited to contribute, alongside top-level hired guns Lowell George, Steve Gadd, and

Tony Levin. Anna even had the nerve to suggest recording "Complainte Pour Ste-Catherine," which she had written with an old university friend, francophone poet Philippe Tatatcheff. Almost everyone else involved with the album had trouble making sense of it all. "They saw us as soulful piano player chicks," Kate recalled. "When we first got into the studio, there were fights between [co-producer] Greg Prestopino, who wanted to have a pop sound with no folk instrumentation, and Joe Boyd, who wanted an eclectic folk-pop sound. When we got to recording 'Complainte Pour Ste-Catherine,' for example, we heard it as Cajun, Greg heard it as pop, and Joe heard it as reggae."

The sisters continued battling Warner right up until the scheduled release date of *Kate & Anna McGarrigle* in late 1975. The label planned to launch the record with a string of shows in Boston featuring a hired backing band. After three weeks of frustrating rehearsals, the sisters squelched the entire tour. With Kate pregnant again, going on the road was a frightening prospect, anyway, but when the album was released in Britain in February 1976, it received so much rapturous notice that they had no choice but to embrace their new audience. "[Warner] wanted to kill us," Kate says. "In America they did nothing. But there was this buzz in England. So we come to England. We bring our own band, Anna and I. We picked three people in Montreal who weren't necessarily great musicians, but we said, 'It doesn't matter, let's go with our own people.' So we hit the stage and we felt so comfortable. *The London Times* said it was the best show of the year." Not long after, on May 8, Kate gave birth to Martha, although the tempestuous pregnancy deepened what ultimately was an insurmountable rift in her marriage — opened up when Wainwright began seeing Suzzy Roche, coincidentally a member of a similar folk sister act, The Roches. McGarrigle and Wainwright permanently split that fall, and the family drama would continue playing out in song for the next thirty years, as both Rufus and Martha Wainwright developed into highly original songwriters in their own right. Still, Rufus concedes that none of it would have happened without that one song. "On several levels, 'Heart Like a Wheel' is responsible for Kate's and

Anna's careers in music, as well as mine and Martha's. My mother and aunt hadn't planned on being professional songwriters, but when Ronstadt picked up the song, it altered their paths and accidentally led us all into a life in show business."

In the end, a picture of romance and family life in the most innocent stages is what *Kate & Anna McGarrigle* came to represent for its many admirers around the world. The sisters would sporadically record again after that, but nothing they released ever won as many hearts as that first album did.

If it took a pair of unproven sisters from Quebec to momentarily drag California's musical community out of its descent into mediocrity, another Canadian would accomplish the same feat, albeit in a way that took much longer for most to comprehend.

CHAPTER EIGHT

AMBULANCE BLUES

"WE BELIEVED THAT THOSE WHO OPPOSED the war in Vietnam would be satisfied with our withdrawal, and those who favoured an honourable ending would be satisfied if the United States would not destroy an ally."

National Security Advisor Henry Kissinger made this statement following the signing of the Paris Peace Accord on January 27, 1973, marking an end to America's official involvement in the Vietnam War. When the talks between the U.S. and North Vietnam formally began on January 8, Neil Young stood on stage at Cobo Hall in Detroit. It was the fourth concert of the largest tour he had ever undertaken as a solo artist — sixty-four shows over three months — the result of unexpectedly large sales of the album *Harvest* and Young's first chart-topping single "Heart of Gold." From the outside, the tour's expansiveness seemed a well-deserved acknowledgement of Young's artistic stature apart from his association with Crosby, Stills & Nash. Privately, though, Young had already determined to use the tour as a means to face the reality of his own personal conflicts. Like the resolution of the Vietnam War, the eventual outcome would be dragged out over the next two-and-a-half years.

The fact that Young and his music had become so identified with Vietnam was unusual considering his Canadian upbringing. The reasons stemmed directly from the dichotomies at the core of his work; the bipolar swings between ethereal folk and unhinged hard rock were merely what showed on the surface. He had surrendered his innocence as far back as "Sugar Mountain," and from there a general confusion over what to believe, which side to take, and, most importantly, the cost of those choices, came to dominate his writing, just as it would the thoughts of anyone in the position of being sent to southeast Asia. Young had been accused of being preachy when it came to other matters, but when he wrote about Vietnam it was as if he knew it intimately, or at least desired to. In Detroit that night, he presented his own welcome-home gift to GIs in the form of a brand new song, one whose point was missed by the overwhelming chorus of voices ordering Young to play familiar numbers. Young pulled no punches in "Lookout Joe," painting a picture of an urban America that most soldiers wouldn't have sacrificed themselves to defend. It was a world populated by hustlers, transvestites, and dope fiends, albeit far from the twisted glamour of Lou Reed's New York. The song's caustic refrain, "old times were good times" only reinforced how irrevocably the country had changed in its ever-evolving pursuit of happiness.

But for all of the grotesque impressions of "Lookout Joe," it also reflected a destructive cycle from which Neil Young himself could not escape, despite his increased public profile. His only defense was that he had been preparing himself for this moment ever since he realized the bargain he had made in order to be a musician. Of course, at Cobo Hall, he played the songs from *Harvest* that people wanted to hear, but these were only a prelude to the show's main focus: a litany of other new songs in the same unapologetic vein as "Lookout Joe," which stripped away the artifice the *Harvest* songs now seemed to possess. It had actually been over a year since *Harvest* was completed, an eternity for the ever-prolific Young, so simply giving audiences what they expected was out of the question, anyway. But by the time the tour dates came around, the stage was the only place where he could be free.

I've always felt that for The Band, and maybe Robbie Robertson in particular, that they saw the United States as a foreign country, and that's what allowed them to dramatize it so effectively. It was strange to them, and they always had somewhere else they could go back to that was home in a way that the United States would not be. Certainly, Robbie and Garth and Rick Danko have all said to me at different times that one of the reasons they settled in Woodstock [New York] was that it reminded them of places where they grew up in Canada. Not only because it looked the same, but because it was distant, it was cut off, it was not culturally integrated into the mainstream in a similar way that Ontario in the 1950s was distant. I've always thought that that had a lot to do with why they were able to get so deeply into America as a construct or an accent or something that didn't have to be the way it is. Whereas with Neil Young, I don't think any of that at all, none of it. Neil Young, who I know slightly, but certainly I know his music, seems as much of a Californian as I am, and he ain't. But he seems like he is.

— Greil Marcus, 1997

When "Heart of Gold" shuffled onto the radio like a world-weary hobo in 1972, what the rest of North America heard confirmed its suspicions that the California dream wasn't all it was cracked up to be. Canadians, especially, rallied around the song as a means of reclaiming Young, taking it as a sign that his instilled values had not been totally corrupted. It was, to that point, the most succinct statement on how Young had come to be defined as the eternal outsider locked into a kind of modern-day vision quest.

It was simply the sound of "Heart of Gold" and the bulk of *Harvest* that touched most nerves. The austere acoustic arrangements and rigid rhythms combined with Young's pervasive self-doubt to create what amounted to an elegy for the entire folk revival. "Heart of Gold" may have been the entry point to exploring this notion, but Young summed it up best in the opening of "A Man Needs a Maid," a verse he had added long after he began performing the song live, and one that remains a lasting testament to his poetic ability: "My life is changing in so many ways, I don't know who to trust anymore/There's a shadow running through my days, like a beggar going from door to door." That shadow, which could have represented any number of setbacks on the way to Young's epiphany, had been palpable in California for some time, but few others aside from Young had the strength to resist it, much less subsume their fears within a package as attractive as that of *Harvest*. In this context, he couldn't have picked a better album title. His generation was beginning to reap what it had sown, and new seeds had to be planted.

Of course, Young was no stranger to personal upheavals. The longing for an uncomplicated existence that first manifested itself in "Sugar Mountain" had its roots in a traumatic childhood and early adolescence. It didn't start out that way. He was born Neil Percival Young on November 12, 1945, in Toronto, the second son of established journalist (and later acclaimed author) Scott Young and his wife Edna (née Ragland), known affectionately as Rassy. After living in several locations in and around the city following Neil's birth, the family settled in the tiny town of Omemee, an hour's drive northeast into the hinterland, just prior to Neil starting school. Then, less than a year later came the bout with polio. He got dangerously thin and nearly lost the use of his left side, but he survived. The illness and the subsequent long, painful recovery were equally stressful on his parents' relationship. Adding to it all was Scott's struggle to publish his fiction. When he finally succeeded in 1956, a last-ditch effort to keep his family together saw them move to a new home, closer to Toronto in the town of Pickering. It was there that Neil put the nightmare of polio behind him as he discovered the joy of earning his own living as a small-scale egg farmer. He also discovered the joy of listening to wildly primitive rock and roll and country music on his transistor radio.

Sadly, this most stable period of Young's early life was brief. By 1959, Rassy had accepted that her husband was having affairs, and, late that year, shortly after Scott returned from a writing assignment that consisted of more than work, she threw him out of the house. Neil had just started high school at Toronto's Lawrence Park Collegiate, and turned to music to help him cope with the split, while at the same time using it to establish his own identity. The act of spinning a constant string of 45s and 78s with friends did provide a natural escape from the ever-increasing tension between his parents, but nothing could prepare Young for what ultimately resulted from their divorce the following year: a choice between remaining with his father in Toronto or moving with his mother to her family's home a thousand miles west in Winnipeg. He chose what he believed to be the easiest solution, staying with his mother, and stoically packed in preparation for the two-day drive through the wilds of northern Ontario.

Young's most trusted companion was a guitar, which he had progressed to playing after starting several years earlier on the ukulele. It became his way into a Winnipeg rock and roll scene that was already thriving thanks to bands like Chad Allan & the Expressions, soon to become The Guess Who. That band's formidable advantage was guitarist Randy Bachman, who seemed to be adept at playing any style, but was most partial to the melodic, reverb-laden instrumentals of Duane Eddy, Link Wray, and little-known British groups like The Shadows. Getting to see Bachman play regularly at weekend dances galvanized Young's determination to acquire an electric guitar and gain enough skill to form his own band. There were many false starts during 1962, after Young and his mother moved into a more reputable neighbourhood and he transferred to Kelvin High.★

By the start of 1963, Young had solidified a quartet he dubbed The Squires, with his closest friend, Ken Koblun, on bass. Their entire repertoire was instrumental, although Young's original ideas comprised nearly half of it, the result of a self-imposed regimen of practicing and writing. After six months of steady local gigs, The Squires attracted the attention of Winnipeg DJ Bob Bradburn, who invited them to his station,

★Morley Walker, *Winnipeg Free Press*, November 10, 2008: "It's not every day that you drive home from grocery shopping to find Bob Dylan rubbernecking in front of your house. But that's what happened to city employees John Kiernan and Patti Regan, whose Grosvenor Avenue home was the early-1960s domicile of music icon Neil Young. They showed him Young's old bedroom, now painted bright pink and occupied by Kiernan's sixteen-year-old daughter. 'So this is where Neil would have listened to his music,' Dylan mused.

CKRC, to record. On July 23, they laid down two of Young's numbers, "The Sultan" — complete with gong — and "Aurora," which were pressed as a single and distributed locally by Winnipeg label V Records several weeks later. The record did little to change The Squires' fortunes, though it did persuade Young to trade in his golf clubs for a new Gretsch hollow-body guitar similar to the one Bachman played.★

The arrival of the British Invasion in early 1964 changed everything in the Winnipeg scene virtually overnight. For The Squires, it necessitated the addition of a singer, something Young was not prepared to do, largely to avoid the expense of having another member in the group. As leader, he took it upon himself to fill the role, and promptly worked up a clutch of Beatles covers. At the same time, Young tried writing his own lyrics, and had several new songs ready for the band's next recording date at CKRC on April 2. Needless to say, no one was happy with Young's singing, meaning The Squires' next release had to be put on hold. The realization that he had a long way to go to become the performer he wanted to be struck a nerve with Young, and led to little activity with The Squires that summer. Instead, he spent much of it hanging out with friends and mulling over his future in the popular resort town of Falcon Lake, near the Manitoba–Ontario border. It was the summer of "Four Strong Winds," but also the summer that Young discovered Bob Dylan. Hearing such an obviously untrained voice sing impossibly moving songs gave Young a renewed confidence in his own writing. Still, with interest in folk music waning, having a band provided a distinct edge in finding work.

Now finished with school, Young was even more committed to becoming a professional musician, meaning The Squires had to expand their scope beyond Winnipeg. He set his sights on the closest suitable city, Fort William, just over the Ontario border on

---

★Golf remained Young's pastime of choice. His older brother Bob made golf a career, and Young has admitted that if he had not succeeded in music, he probably would have followed the same path.

Lake Superior, and a U.S. entry point.★ The Squires headed east by train on October 12, 1964, and got a warm reception at the first bar they entered, the Flamingo Club, where they played for the next five nights. They went over well enough to maintain a regular residency for the next month, supplementing their income with shows at Fort William's Fourth Dimension club. It was the longest stretch Young had ever spent away from his family, and as he sat in his hotel room on November 12, his nineteenth birthday, the flood of emotions from those thoughts spilled out in "Sugar Mountain," a song that somehow managed to encapsulate the entire gamut of teenage angst, from a yearning for a carefree childhood to inevitable independence — wanted or not. The song shared a thematic resemblance with "Big Rock Candy Mountain," the folk standard first recorded by cowboy singer Harry "Mac" McClintock for RCA in 1928, and although Young's utopian vision was far more personal than McClintock's humourous paradise of "cigarette trees and lemonade springs," at each song's core was an inherent sorrow over an unattainable dream. Whether Young had McClintock's dream in mind when he wrote "Sugar Mountain" hardly matters; it was a major achievement, and Young knew enough not to hand it over to the band and try to turn it into a pop song.

The Squires had several other Young originals to draw upon when they next recorded, on November 23 at Fort William station CJLX, under the supervision of DJ Ray Dee. They cut two songs, "I'll Love You Forever" and "I Wonder," which Dee immediately sent to a Capitol Records sales rep he knew in Winnipeg. Both were rejected, and The Squires came home for Christmas virtually back at square one.

A final recording session in Winnipeg in early 1965 could not improve upon the previous ones, and in April The Squires — now a trio consisting of Young, Koblun, and drummer Bob Clark

★In 1970, Fort William amalgamated with Port Arthur and was renamed Thunder Bay. Its most famous son remains bandleader Paul Shaffer (born on November 28, 1949), who played organ with local rock group The Fugitives in the late sixties before attending the University of Toronto.

— drove back to Fort William for an open-ended stay. Before long, however, Young was plotting his escape. That month saw a surprising wealth of folk-rock talent from the U.S. pass through town, and Young made a point of absorbing it all, from Tim Rose's trio The Thorns to blues duo Sonny Terry & Brownie McGee. But he found an instant connection with a guitar player from Texas named Stephen Stills who was a member of a modern folk group called The Company. When they had time to swap songs and drink a few beers together, Stills' tales of his strict southern upbringing and subsequent time in Greenwich Village enraptured Young. It was all he needed to hear in order to make his next move. Knowing that his mother was not in a position to help financially, Young waited for any excuse to go to Toronto and hit up his father for money. That excuse came with a request to drive a friend south to a gig in Sudbury, Ontario, but Young's car, a hearse he had named Mort, would only make it to the small town of Ironbridge. When he was told that Mort needed a new transmission, Young went the rest of the way on the back of a motorcycle, and showed up at his father's door like a prodigal son. Feeling his own sense of remorse, Young's father didn't hesitate to let his son move in, and didn't argue when Neil insisted that the other Squires make the trip, too. His father went further by loaning Neil money for a new car and a rehearsal space, while Neil contacted Martin Onrot and convinced him to manage the band. Onrot had become the best-known promoter in Toronto after booking The Beatles' 1964 Maple Leaf Gardens concert. From the outset, Onrot imposed his own ideas on The Squires, starting by renaming them Four To Go, and the group suffered through endless attempts to shape their sound and image for the remainder of the summer. Making little progress, and feeling pressure from his father to pay back the loans, Young moved into a cheap apartment on Isabella Street and found a job as a bookstore stock boy.

Mired in isolation, and starting to experiment with drugs, Young began writing in earnest — surreal, folk-based songs like "Nowadays Clancy Can't Even Sing," about an outcast high-school acquaintance from Winnipeg. When Onrot called in late October and said he'd booked the band for an extended run at a Vermont ski resort, Young quit his job without hesitation, but rounded up the other band members with some reluctance. Four To Go was fired after the first night's show, and Young didn't put up much of a fight. He was finally in America, and, more importantly, close to New York. Stills had mentioned a former bandmate, Richie Furay, who was then still playing around the Village, and Young made it his mission to find him. Dragging Koblun along, the pair ultimately located Furay, and the affable Ohio native was more than happy to let the Canadians hang around for a few days. Young played some of his latest songs, and Furay immediately locked onto "Clancy," adding a distinctive harmony part. Soon he was playing the song himself, and it managed to catch the ear of someone at Elektra who tracked down Young back in Toronto and offered him an audition. It came at the right time, as Young was now resolved to his fate as a solo artist, but the return to New York in November turned out to be a hard lesson. Set up in Elektra's office with only a simple tape recorder, and playing a cheap guitar through a malfunctioning amplifier, Young nervously ran through seven songs, including "Sugar Mountain" and "Clancy," which were hastily rejected.★ He returned to Toronto again, this time demoralized and nearly destitute. There were some gigs to be had in Yorkville, but he was at the bottom of the food chain there. After the Christmas visit to Winnipeg, where he met Joni Mitchell for the first time, Young survived the onset of winter back in Toronto by playing hootenannies and crashing with friends, Mitchell's former roommate Vicky Taylor among them.★★ When opportunities

---

★Young himself kept developing at least two other ideas, "Don't Pity Me Babe," which became "Don't Cry No Tears," and "The Rent Is Always Due," which became "I Am a Child."

★★Another female singer Young befriended in Yorkville was Elyse Weinberg. He would play lead guitar on the track "Houses" from her now-rare 1968 debut album, *Elyse*. The song was covered by San Francisco folk-rockers Vetiver on their 2008 album *Thing Of The Past,* with a faithful recreation of Young's solo.

arose to play in distant places like North Bay and Ann Arbor, Michigan, he most often hitchhiked there.

Young must have cast a desperate figure, tramping the frozen streets of Yorkville with his guitar and amplifier, at least desperate enough to have been spotted by Bruce Palmer, the bassist for that most rare of species, an authentic Canadian R & B group, called The Mynah Birds, one day in January 1966. Much of the band's credibility rested on the shoulders of its singer, Ricky James Matthews III (actually James Ambrose Johnson, born on February 1, 1948, in Buffalo, New York), a would-be soul star who had fled to Canada in July 1964, just as he was due to start training in the U.S. Navy Reserve. Matthews was welcomed into the Toronto scene and joined his first band — the aptly named Sailorboys — the following month. The band would become known as The Mynah Birds at the insistence of its first manager, who also owned a Yorkville pet store. With their colourful image and Matthews's authentic R & B chops front and centre, the band landed a deal with Columbia, although it would only record one single, the novelty song "Mynah Bird Hop," which disappeared shortly after its release in January 1965. The band persevered, however, nabbing Palmer from The Sparrows (later to become Steppenwolf) and finding a benefactor in John Craig Eaton, who was as determined as his brother Thor to use their family's fortune as a way into the music business. Eaton named his friend Morley Shelman the band's new manager, and within months Matthews persuaded his uncle, Melvin Franklin of The Temptations, to do the unthinkable by helping to get The Mynah Birds — essentially a white Canadian group — signed to the biggest black-owned label in America, Motown Records.

However, guitarist Tom Morgan sensed right away that the label was only interested in Matthews. This prompted him to quit as the deal was being finalized, leaving the band in urgent need of a replacement. The mere fact that Young owned a guitar and an amp seemed enough to fit the bill, and he immediately moved into Matthews's apartment and learned the ins and outs of being a Mynah Bird. Not being in charge was a new situation for Young, but he could hardly complain about being given brand new gear and an imminent recording date with a top-notch label. The band only had a few weeks to sharpen up, and did so with gigs in Toronto before driving to Detroit for the late-February sessions. Over the course of a week with producer Mickey Stephenson, they cut as many as sixteen songs, with most partially credited to Motown staff writer R. Dean Taylor, who was partnered with the group mainly because he was white and originally from Toronto.* Word of a debut single, "I've Got You in My Soul," was leaked to *Billboard* by the first week of March, but the songs ultimately chosen were "It's My Time" and "Go On and Cry." The former, co-written by R. Dean Taylor, was closer to folk-rock than typical Motown fare, mostly because of Young's prominent twelve-string lead guitar. Unfortunately, it would take four decades for anyone to hear it. The single was pulled on the day of its release after Motown president Berry Gordy Jr. learned that Matthews was AWOL from the navy and immediately turned him over to the authorities.**

With the rug so violently pulled out from under them, Young and Bruce Palmer came to the conclusion that their only viable option was to pack up and move to where the real action was, Los Angeles. Part of the impetus was undoubtedly revenge, as the pair aimed to finance the trip by selling all of The Mynah Birds' equipment, which Eaton had paid for. Young took part of the money and bought another used hearse, and, on March 22, he, Palmer, and four other friends with money to contribute left Toronto. By all accounts, it was a nightmarish drive. On top of Young's fear of the hearse breaking down, dodging state troopers kept the stress level high. The car, in fact, did need to be

---

*Taylor would have a massive hit in 1970 with "Indiana Wants Me."

**Matthews would serve a short sentence and return to Motown as a staff songwriter. After joining a further series of unsuccessful bands throughout the early seventies, he would finally find fame in the disco era as Rick James. Most close to the story acknowledge that manager Shelman informed on Matthews after Shelman was fired, upon which he absconded with the group's $25,000 advance and was never seen again.

repaired by the time they reached Albuquerque, at which point Young also broke down in their motel room. This marked the first sign of the epileptic fits that would plague Young for the next several years. Part of the remedy was to leave two of their female travelling companions behind, and on April 1, the hearse completed its journey.

Within days, the harsh reality set in: Young and Palmer had no real plan, and they prepared to head north to San Francisco. Unbeknownst to them, Richie Furay had also recently arrived in town at the request of Stephen Stills, who was bent on forming a band after losing a spot in The Monkees to Peter Tork. Stills' partner in this endeavour was his neighbour Barry Friedman, in charge of publicity for the Troubadour. "Stephen and I started talking about putting a band together [for him]," says Friedman, who later changed his name to Frazier Mohawk and now runs a recording studio located, ironically, near Toronto. "I told him to wish up a band and we started contacting the people and bringing them into town. Richie Furay came out and Stephen kept talking about this guy Neil Young he had met up in Canada.

"One day we were driving along Sunset Boulevard in my Bentley. I was in the left-hand lane driving down the street and I looked over to the right and there was this hearse pulling up next to us. I had never met Neil Young, but I'd heard about the hearse and I turned to Stephen and said, 'This is your friend here, Neil Young!' and it was. It was really telepathic and quite bizarre. Actually, it was Neil and Bruce Palmer.

"As far as the eventual name for the group, Buffalo Springfield, we pulled up in front of the house one day when they were repaving Fountain Avenue. There was a steamroller there, and on the back it said, 'Buffalo Springfield.' I said, 'Hey, that's the name!' I pried the sign off, took it into the house, and nailed it on the wall."

The only remaining problem, finding a drummer, was solved less than a week after that miraculous encounter, when Stills got a call from Dewey Martin, who had recently been ousted from popular L.A. bluegrass group The Dillards. By coincidence,

Martin was also Canadian, born Walter Dwayne Midkiff on September 30, 1940, in Chesterville, Ontario, a dot on the map between Ottawa and Cornwall. He had left Canada by the age of twenty, as well, and headed to Nashville, where he found work as a touring drummer for the likes of Patsy Cline and Roy Orbison. This experience proved essential for the new band as they made their debut on April 11 at the Troubadour. This was in preparation for a string of opening gigs around California with The Byrds that Friedman had hastily arranged through his friendship with David Crosby. By the start of May, Buffalo Springfield was installed at L.A.'s Whisky A Go Go for a six-week stretch. With a formidable front line of Young, Stills, and Furay, and each member donning various styles of frontier clothing, this period was in many ways their most exciting and cohesive. "The Whisky was as good as we ever were, because we were working every day," Furay described. "That's where we worked everything out. We were tight, we were good, and we felt we were good."

Stills put it more bluntly: "The first week at the Whisky was absolutely incredible. That's when we peaked, and after then it was downhill. Neil flipped out in the Whisky A Go Go, and so did I, and so did Bruce, because immediately there were all these chicks hanging out and feeding us more and better dope." Virtually every record company rep in town was there to check them out, too, which put tremendous pressure on Friedman to play his cards right. His strong connections with Elektra made Buffalo Springfield a natural fit there. With the band suddenly such a hot commodity, however, Friedman was unceremoniously forced out of the picture by two of the more persistent suitors, Charlie Greene and Brian Stone, the management team behind Sonny & Cher. The pair already had a reputation for creating bidding wars among the labels, and in the case of Buffalo Springfield they didn't need to make much of an effort. At first, the most tantalizing offer came from Warner Brothers; Lenny Waronker loved the band and convinced Jack Nitzsche to produce them. Nitzsche thought Young, in particular, had the most potential, but he wouldn't get to explore it right away after the band went with a more lucrative offer from Atlantic's Ahmet Ertegun.

By late June, the band was set up in Gold Star Studios — site of Phil Spector's greatest triumphs — with Greene and Stone at the controls. It turned out to be a trial by fire for everyone. "At the first session we played a six-and-a-half minute song," Stills recalls. "The engineer said, 'It's too long, could you play it faster?' Neil and I looked at each other and said, 'Oh boy, I think we'd better learn how to do this.'" On July 10, Young was driving to a session in his newly purchased Corvette when he spotted a friend of the band in an argument with the police over a traffic violation. Both wound up in jail.

"We were in the cell and they were calling us names," Young says. "This one cop with a brush cut and horn-rimmed glasses called me an animal, so I called him a grasshopper. He got some other cops to come in, and they knocked my tooth out and banged us around. It happened really fast. I didn't put up much of a fight, obviously. But that was the ambience. If you were freaks in a pretty cool car like us, you could end up in jail for who knows what."

On July 25, Buffalo Springfield opened for The Rolling Stones at the Hollywood Bowl. At the same time, their first single, "Clancy" (with Furay singing lead), was being rushed out, and it became an immediate local hit. Even though Young acquiesced to having more polished vocals on the track, the fact that his song beat out Stills' "Go and Say Goodbye" for the A-side was the first clear indication of the conflicts that had started to develop within the band over the previous two whirlwind months. Perversely, their managers often fuelled the rivalry between Stills and Young, but the strain manifested itself in a more dramatic form when Young began to experience epileptic seizures on stage, normally at the height of a frantic guitar solo. One of the earliest of these incidents came on September 3 at Anaheim's Melodyland Theatre when Young had to be carried off on a stretcher.

In spite of it all, the album *Buffalo Springfield* was finished by October and plans were set for a January 1967 release. Young could not be completely barred from singing, and his other main contributions to the record — "Burned," "Out of My Mind," and "Flying on the Ground Is Wrong" — were stand-outs, even though Stills ended up getting the last laugh. The highly publicized clashes between teens and police over curfews imposed on the Sunset Strip during the autumn of 1966 inspired him to write "For What It's Worth," a prescient comment on the often heavy-handed tactics of the authorities. Noting its timeliness, the band wanted to record it right away, and within days of the December 6 session, several L.A. radio stations were playing acetates. The song hit the *Billboard* singles chart on January 28, and peaked at number seven in March, giving Atlantic little choice but to re-press *Buffalo Springfield* with "For What It's Worth." The album was re-released on May 1, and sales picked up considerably.

Yet, even before this breakthrough, the band was already falling into disarray. They flew to New York just after Christmas for a two-week east-coast debut at Ondine's (a bill that also included Otis Redding), while squeezing in sessions for the next album at Atlantic's studio. The major accomplishment was laying down the foundation for Young's charging rocker "Mr. Soul," which took lyrical swipes at the L.A. groupie scene while at the same time rationalizing his doubts about fame and his fear of seizures. But escalating arguments between Young and Stills over song choices hampered any further work. The tension was exacerbated by Young's illness and growing sideline conflicts with Greene and Stone. Things came to a complete halt shortly after the "Mr. Soul" session when Bruce Palmer was charged with marijuana possession at their hotel and subsequently deported back to Toronto. On January 20, they were musical guests on the *Hollywood Palace* TV variety show, performing an odd lip-synch medley of "For What It's Worth" and the unfinished "Mr. Soul" acetate, with band confidant Richard Davis lurking off-camera pretending to play bass. The loss of Palmer also meant the loss of Young's closest ally, and he insisted on summoning Ken Koblun to take over on bass for a package tour through California and the southwest. After only two weeks, the group bailed out over a payment dispute, and Koblun headed home, astounded by the battles Young had to fight on a daily basis.

As recording sessions for the album, already tentatively titled *Stampede*, continued into March and April, Young and Stills were more likely to be found working on their own. Young had enlisted Nitzsche's help, and he, in turn, brought in Spector session mainstays Don Randi and Carol Kaye to record the haunting acoustic track "Expecting to Fly." Nitzsche later revealed, "When I made that record, Neil wasn't there. He came back and put his vocal on after it was finished. I had been hanging out with him a long time. Of all the songs he was playing me, that was one of my favourites. I just played it over and over until I had learned it well enough to play and sing it myself. I loved the song, so a lot of ideas came. And they're all there. I put them all in one arrangement."

Young seemed more preoccupied with perfecting the guitar overdubs for "Mr. Soul" in anticipation of it being the band's next single. When Stills strongly objected to this, claiming the song's main riff was too reminiscent of The Rolling Stones' "Satisfaction," it finally pushed Young to leave the group on the eve of a scheduled appearance on *The Tonight Show* at the end of May. Having found in Nitzsche someone who intrinsically grasped his unorthodox musical approach, Young determined that the two of them could go their own way. At first it seemed entirely possible; Nitzsche was intent on starting his own label, The Original Great Western Gramophone Company, with Young as a cornerstone. But that plan was ultimately dismissed when, late in July 1967, Young heard the acetate of "Mr. Soul" on the radio and questioned his reasons for leaving the group.

On August 12, Young was welcomed back at Buffalo Springfield's gig in Huntington Beach, California. He showed honest remorse and turned in a raucous six-and-a-half-minute rendition of "Mr. Soul." With Palmer back in the fold, as well, the original lineup set about completing the new album, now essentially a patchwork of tracks from the past six months. With songs like Stills' "Bluebird" and "Rock & Roll Woman," as well as Furay's "A Child's Claim to Fame" alongside "Mr. Soul" and "Expecting to Fly," it added up to a near-flawless collection. In

September, Young produced a further studio creation, "Broken Arrow," to finish off the record. With its intricate, avant-garde structure, the song required over a hundred takes to get right. But its message, written at the height of Young's admitted identity crisis that summer, went to the heart of the looming divides that would rupture American society the following year. The song's overall vision of past sins wreaking havoc on the present was devastating when coupled with Young's free-form tape experiments. In these three songs alone, Young established himself at home as a singular voice that employed both Dylanesque social commentary and the use of leading-edge technology.

It was, therefore, an unexpected letdown when, upon the release of *Buffalo Springfield Again* in early November, the band spent the entire month opening for the Brian Wilson–less Beach Boys. Old habits on the road soon reared their heads, and on January 26, 1968, Stills and Young came to blows backstage at a benefit show for underprivileged kids held at the University of California's Irvine campus. Later that night, Palmer and an underage girl were stopped for impaired driving, and within days he was deported once again. Needing a quick fill-in for further dates with The Beach Boys, the band called upon their frequent studio engineer, Jim Messina, who was already in the process of assembling tracks for the next album. But becoming a full-fledged band member only put him in the awkward position of trying to steer a sinking ship. Stills and Young were now separate entities, leaving Furay and Messina in charge. They would largely complete the album *Last Time Around* (released in August 1968) together before forming the successful country-rock outfit Poco later that year.

On February 5, Young made his final Buffalo Springfield recording, the bittersweet "I Am a Child," at Sunset Sound. It was also on that day that he learned Joni Mitchell was in an adjoining studio with David Crosby. This led to a long-overdue reunion and an introduction to Elliot Roberts, who, after quickly assessing Buffalo Springfield's situation, became bent on saving the band. Young, not surprisingly, had already made up his mind that it was over and blocked Roberts' every offer to take over management duties. However, two weeks after the band's final show on May 5 at the Long Beach Sports Arena, Young, now faced again with life a solo artist, showed up at Roberts' door seeking assistance. Roberts got Young on the bill the next night, opening for Dave Van Ronk, at the Ice House in Glendale — his first gig on his own since leaving Toronto — and, although terrified, Young rose to the occasion. "Had they booed him, life would've been a hundred per cent different," Roberts says. "It was after that night that Neil's vision became clearer, because he was resolved that he could do his own material better than anyone else — and that there was an audience for it."

While Elliot Roberts may have been convinced there was an audience, Neil Young was still trying to find his place in the L.A. music scene in the summer of 1968. He had been able to escape the trappings of the Sunset Strip once Roberts, with the help of Jack Nitzsche, landed him a deal with Reprise, but his new community, just outside of town in Topanga Canyon, proved even stranger. Young, never one to shy away from shady characters, embraced it. Among the first of such characters he met was David Briggs, a producer of obscure records for comedian Bill Cosby's vanity label, Tetragrammaton, who picked Young up hitchhiking one day. By coincidence, Briggs was now living on Stills' old ranch, the site of the fateful March 20, 1968, marijuana bust. Young was soon back there again on a regular basis for parties that drew many others who shared Briggs's outlaw mentality. Someone who turned up occasionally was a slight, wild-eyed hustler who was trying to sell songs after spending most of his life up until then behind bars for petty crimes. Charles Manson was introduced to Young by Beach Boy Dennis Wilson, and, whether it was the drugs or merely his general state of mind, Young recognized some weird spark of talent in Manson, at least enough for Young to put in a good word for him at Reprise.

There were many other distractions for Young that summer, though, not the least of which was the purchase of his first home, a small but towering structure that overlooked the canyon. He would soon share it with Susan Acevedo, a local restaurant owner with a young daughter. But with Briggs and Nitzsche helping him record his self-titled debut album in August, Young refocused his energy on going on the road as a solo act. The first test was a twelve-night run at the Bitter End in New York starting October 23, which gave him an opportunity to pull out nearly every song he had on hand. On November 9 and 10, there was a quick stop at the Canterbury House in Ann Arbor, and in this relatively low-key setting Young felt confident enough to set up his Sony reel-to-reel in order to gauge his progress. Listening back later to his uncharacteristically chatty performance, Young grew so fond of a version of "Sugar Mountain" from the second night that he would never attempt to record the song again, instead using this tape as the source for all of the song's future releases, mainly as a B-side for several singles.

Back home, Young made preparations to marry Acevedo on December 1, with the new album hitting stores shortly thereafter. However, initial impressions suggested that, from the primitive portrait of Young on the cover to the often-unsettling sheen added to the final mix, it was a misstep after all the promise he had shown with Buffalo Springfield. Although the conflicts with Stills were gone, what *Neil Young* most clearly lacked was any sense of chemistry, which was present whenever Young functioned within a band. He seemed to recognize this, too, even as the album was being pressed.

Young had known of a hardscrabble bar band called The Rockets for about a year, and became even more familiar with it after he discovered its members were among the Topanga misfits. When they jammed together, Young felt something altogether different from the competitiveness of Buffalo Springfield. It was the sense that the band was operating as a single unit, and this allowed him to draw upon the full range of his melodic gifts. Just after the new year, as he lay in bed with a high fever, Young had that unified sound pounding in his head, and it motivated him to write three songs in quick succession: "Cinnamon Girl," "Down by the River," and "Cowgirl in the

Sand." As soon as he recovered, Young told Briggs to book studio time and summoned three members of The Rockets to learn the tunes: guitarist/singer Danny Whitten, bassist Billy Talbot, and drummer Ralph Molina. The quartet recorded them all in single takes mere days later — with the latter two songs clocking in at ten minutes each — providing the basis for what would be Young's true rebirth. The Rockets would also be reborn as Crazy Horse, a name in keeping with the take-no-prisoners sound they drew out of Young. While it would require some time for them to relinquish their autonomy, Young, in typical fashion, had no qualms about asserting his authority by subtitling the eerie, almost ancient-sounding "Running Dry" (which was recorded at the next session) "Requiem for the Rockets."

Before that March 1969 recording, Young returned to Canada for his first official round of solo dates there, encompassing twelve shows split between Le Hibou and the Riverboat between January 28 and February 9. Rather than the triumphant homecoming it might have been, he was billed as "formerly of Buffalo Springfield." The Toronto shows in particular were low-key affairs, according to Brian Ahern, whom Young employed to record them. "People knew who he was, but there certainly weren't lineups around the block," Ahern says.

Making peace with his father seemed to be of equal importance to Young. "The Riverboat that night was the first place I had heard Neil play and sing as a professional," Scott would later write. "I can see it still: a dim little place with a small stage a few inches off the floor, nearby booths holding the offspring of friends who used to visit us twenty years earlier. Some had known Neil since they were babies. Some were a little hostile toward me. The story had gotten around that he and I were at odds because I hadn't rushed to help when he needed to buy an amplifier. [But] after his first set someone came to me and said, 'Neil wants you to come up to his dressing room.' A news photographer took a picture of us [there], Neil's arm around my shoulder, both smiling into the camera, the first photo taken of us together for ten years."

In May, even as fans were still digesting *Neil Young*, came the album with Crazy Horse, *Everybody Knows This Is Nowhere*. Its mix of unvarnished country-rock, extended jams, and hushed acoustic ballads was the soundtrack to Topanga: inherently dangerous and paying no lip service to the Hollywood establishment. The nowhere that Young sang about was the L.A. he sought to leave behind, but what gave the album a lasting resonance for listeners all over the world was how Young's nowhere could be applied to anywhere. The freedom he found with Crazy Horse essentially erased any space or time constraints, and it would remain Young's most natural element.

However, he would not allow himself to be constrained by Crazy Horse, either, at least not after Stills approached him with a financially tempting offer to join his new group, whose eponymous debut album was poised to become one of the year's best-sellers. Adding Young was merely a well-reasoned insurance policy that Crosby, Stills & Nash would become one of the top-grossing live acts, as well. Young's position that he wasn't joining the group because of the money was a necessary stance in terms of public perception, but he surely wasn't going to be discouraged by Roberts, or David Geffen, for that matter, both of whom rightly foresaw a cash cow as long as all the members could keep their egos in check. As they rehearsed at Stills' home in Laurel Canyon through the early summer, it appeared as though it would work. But Young couldn't help revealing a little truth when Canada's leading rock critic, Ritchie Yorke, paid a visit. "I'm not going to say that I don't like the money," Young said. "I do like the money, and it's going to make me a lot of money, and that definitely plays a part in my being here. I think that's the way it is with everybody. If we weren't getting paid, we'd obviously be doing something else."

But as the fawning praise piled up after Woodstock and the group's ensuing dates throughout the autumn, the camaraderie quickly devolved into a miasma of drug-fuelled infighting. The ever-guarded Young found himself reliving the Buffalo Springfield experience of working on his own when the band got down to recording the album *Déjà Vu* in October. His only real contributions became "Country Girl," a pastiche of previously unfinished ideas that ultimately didn't gel, and "Helpless," an ode to his childhood in Omemee. He had already cut the latter with Crazy Horse in August, and Crosby, Stills & Nash decided it was a natural showcase for their harmonies. In much the same way, "Helpless" stood alone within Young's catalogue, turning the homesickness of "Everybody Knows This Is Nowhere" into a deeper exploration of the sense of place he yearned for. Canadians, naturally, immediately fell for the song, making it a cornerstone of a musical identity along with "Four Strong Winds" and, soon after, Joni Mitchell's "River." It was a song that someone like Gordon Lightfoot, whose work was as intrinsic to the landscape as trees or rocks, could never have written. Young, on the other hand, was more akin to the "big birds" that provided one of the lasting images of "Helpless," always in flight but never failing to return home.

Indeed, as the world awaited the privilege of hearing *Déjà Vu* in March 1970, Young was back with Crazy Horse, now with Nitzsche added on keyboards. The plan was to do a short tour and then make a new album that would reflect their more egalitarian country-rock brotherhood, mostly by including songs by Danny Whitten. However, as his "Come on Baby Let's Go Downtown" displayed, a dalliance with heroin threatened to doom the project from the start. The drug also had Crosby, Stills, Nash & Young drummer Dallas Taylor, Crosby himself, and others within the scene in its grip, making it easy for Whitten to conceal his addiction. But as the tour reached its climax with a two-night stand at New York's Fillmore East (with, bizarrely, Miles Davis as the added attraction) on March 6 and 7, Whitten was visibly fading. Young, enraged at seeing the band break down, dismissed any thoughts of making the album. After a few more perfunctory gigs in California at the end of the month, he detached himself from the dark cloud that was descending on Crazy Horse.

With a month before Crosby, Stills, Nash & Young's hugely hyped summer tour was set to kick off, Young reached out for anything that could help him rebound from mounting frustrations. A Topanga neighbour, actor Dean Stockwell, had told

Young of a script he was working on called *After the Goldrush*. While its surrealist ideas proved unfilmable, Young's interest in doing the soundtrack provided the spark he needed for his next album. It was another spontaneous affair, but without Crazy Horse to lean on (two tracks, "I Believe in You" and the cover of Don Gibson's "Oh Lonesome Me," were salvaged from the August 1969 recording sessions), he called whoever was available to his house, where the bulk of recording took place. Among them was an eighteen-year-old guitar prodigy named Nils Lofgren, who had asked Young for advice on getting his band, Grin, a record deal the year before, and wound up playing piano on several songs. Even still, Young's vision for the music was as crystal clear as the sound he and Briggs managed to achieve in the cramped surroundings.

After the Goldrush became a further important step toward Young's arrival at the elusive purity he knew was at the heart of his music, although, unlike *Everybody Knows This Is Nowhere*, this time he found it in the quieter moments. The unprecedented absence of any sonic embellishment made his unschooled piano playing on the title track profoundly moving, and, moreover, gave crucial emotional weight to the song's odd imagery of aliens coming to rescue the human race from its dying planet. More accessible were "Only Love Can Break Your Heart" and "Tell Me Why," which became the template for the growing host of L.A. singer-songwriters who were aiming to follow Young's autonomous example.

With the album in the can, Young was able to go back to Crosby, Stills, Nash & Young with little more to prove. But when reports came of National Guard troops firing on student demonstrators at Kent State University in Akron, Ohio, on May 4, he unleashed his anger in the form of "Ohio." What precipitated the tragedy was President Nixon's televised message the previous week, which said that as many as 30,000 U.S. troops had invaded Cambodia in order to cut off Vietcong supply lines. Furthermore, his announcement that 150,000 more recruits would soon be drafted set off a new flurry of violent protests on campuses across the country. Kent State turned out to be the bloodiest, with four students killed and nine others wounded by gunfire. Young's "Ohio" b/w "Find the Cost of Freedom" was released as a single on June 20, and peaked at number fourteen on *Billboard* only three weeks later. It was a miraculous show of solidarity with the band's audience, and also a heady example of the power wielded by Crosby, Stills, Nash & Young, getting the song released so quickly. It all helped set a foreboding tone for the ensuing tour, but, with *After the Goldrush* being released to rapturous acclaim at the tour's conclusion in August, Young emerged head and shoulders above the others in many fans' estimation.

He could afford to retreat even further, and found a reason to when his marriage collapsed not long after he returned from the tour. Young reacted by dipping into his expanding bank account and purchasing a sprawling ranch near San Francisco, which he rechristened Broken Arrow. The setting and the space provided the closest approximation to the landscape around Omemee without having to completely cut ties with L.A. This allowed him to fully assess all that had taken place since he had left his homeland. From this wide range of musings quickly emerged a new batch of songs that dwelled on age, desire, fear, and identity, songs even more naked than those on *Goldrush*. Living in virtual isolation played the biggest role in the musical sparseness he had tapped into, and it was an easy decision to present the songs to his audience in such a way. Roberts booked Young into many of the continent's most prestigious venues, including a tour de force two-night stand at Carnegie Hall on December 4 and 5. In such a hallowed setting, Young's introspection, mixed with just enough touches of his easy humour, was a mesmerizing combination. Even expansive songs like "Expecting to Fly" and "Cowgirl in the Sand" lost none of their power once their arrangements were stripped to the bone.

All of this boded well for the rest of the tour, slated to continue until the end of February. But as Young was doing work around the ranch during a break for the holidays, he suffered a near-crippling back injury that sent him to L.A. for immediate medical attention. He was comforted by the latest love of his life, actress Carrie Snodgress, whom he had just met after seeing her Oscar-nominated performance in the film *Diary of a Mad Housewife* a few weeks earlier. This combination of unusual circumstances was immediately channelled into a new song, "A Man Needs a Maid" as Snodgress doted on Young when he returned to the ranch fitted in a back brace. The tour was set to resume in Vancouver on January 6, taking in Edmonton, Winnipeg, and Toronto as it plowed east through the dead of winter. Young didn't take this first significant trip across Canada lightly, and composed the piano ballad "Journey Through the Past" to mark the occasion. Like the other song directly inspired by the ranch, "Old Man," it seemed an attempt to reconcile his material success in the context of his humble Canadian upbringing, conveying, as Hank Snow had done before him, not so much a longing for anything specific he had to leave behind, but an entire way of life. Many Canadians had already heard that message in "Helpless," and, unfortunately, "Journey Through the Past" would really only find its place as a sort of theme song for the tour, despite cropping up sporadically during concerts in years to come.

This time, the residents of Young's hometown were prepared to greet him as a returning hero on a much grander scale than his previous visit. The two January 19 concerts at Toronto's Massey Hall were highly emotional affairs, and rank among the greatest performances Young would ever give. Along with his well-known songs, his new material, which had been compiled during his recuperation in December, showed his intense focus on building upon his intimate relationship with audiences, which the tour was revealing to him. As Ritchie Yorke wrote about the concerts: "The applause that followed was unlike anything I had ever witnessed in three years of covering rock concerts at Massey Hall. Never had a Canadian been granted such enthusiastic acclaim by fellow Canadians. Apart from Young's fine solo performance, given under difficult personal conditions, I doubt I'll ever forget the degree to which Canadians had at last shown they could support a Canadian rock artist."

The tour headed back west through the U.S., and the new

songs evolved with each show. A stunning recording of the January 30 concert at UCLA's Royce Hall provided the first glimpses of the tour's riveting atmosphere. Young extracted "The Needle and the Damage Done" and "Love in Mind" from this source for official release. The latter, a fragile piano ballad inspired by late-night telephone conversations from the road, showed Young at his most vulnerable. But it was the former that was instantly recognized as the most fully formed song he had yet crafted. Young already knew it was possible to write unsentimental anti-heroin songs through two of his primary acoustic influences, Bert Jansch's "Needle of Death" from 1965, and Tim Hardin's "Red Balloon" from 1968. But all Young needed to recall were images of a strung-out Danny Whitten from the year before. In its scant two minutes, "The Needle and the Damage Done" would remain a stronger statement against drug abuse than the myriad of advertising campaigns that followed in its wake, providing a rare case of a song having a direct social impact.

Many more would hear it for the first time on February 17 when Young's appearance on *The Johnny Cash Show* was aired. He had gone to Nashville after the final L.A. concert, at the Dorothy Chandler Pavilion on February 1, to tape the show, which also featured a performance of "Journey Through the Past." While there, a chance meeting with producer Elliot Mazer led to an impromptu studio session where "Old Man" and "Heart of Gold" were cut with a hastily assembled group consisting of Ben Keith, Kenny Buttrey, and bassist Tim Drummond, along with fellow Cash show guests Linda Ronstadt and James Taylor. Although a potentially brilliant live album lay in the recordings from Toronto and L.A., this initial Nashville session was a watershed moment in both Young's life and his career. In these players, he discovered an outlet for another of his musical personalities, just as he had with Crazy Horse. Furthermore, in Keith he found his most trusted friend and musical foil. The possibility of putting a new spin on country music was suddenly made real, but it would take a few more months for the impact of the recordings to sink in. At the end of February, Young had to go to England to end the tour officially with a concert at London's Royal Festival Hall that debuted still more new songs. "Out on the Weekend" and "Harvest" seemed tailored to the Nashville aesthetic, while "The Bridge" was another naked piano ballad, albeit based in uncharacteristic hope inspired by Hart Crane's 1930 poetry collection of the same name. A separate show filmed for the BBC's *In Concert* series also consisted of this unheard material, and was no less affecting. Before leaving, Young booked Nitzsche to come over to conduct sessions with the London Symphony Orchestra for "A Man Needs a Maid" and "There's a World," a song that took a wider view of Young's frequent complaints about California's pollution. These seemed an improbable paradox when put up against the Nashville songs, but they revealed how quickly Young's restless nature caused him to grow bored with the solo arrangements. Further recording took place in Nashville and at the ranch throughout the year as Young continued to regain the strength in his back. But in spite of "Heart of Gold" shocking everyone by hitting number one a month after *Harvest's* much-delayed February 25, 1972, release, the album turned out to be disappointingly erratic, displaying Young at both his best and his worst, as on the unnecessarily turgid rock of "Alabama" and "Words," along with the overblown orchestral tracks.

But this could only have been a concern to those who had followed Young's recent movements with a magnifying glass. *Harvest* would nearly double *After the Goldrush's* two-and-a-half million total sales, allowing Young time to rest and await the birth of his first son, Zeke, on September 8, 1972. Shortly after this, Young bowed to pressure to mount the large-scale arena tour that was by then mandatory for all top-selling rock acts, a practice that Crosby, Stills, Nash & Young had played a major role in establishing. Without Crazy Horse to call upon (they recorded an album on their own late in 1970 that included "Come on Baby Let's Go Downtown" as well as Young's unreleased "Dance Dance Dance"), he assembled the Nashville musicians at the ranch and rechristened them The Stray Gators. However, despite the fact that Crazy Horse's album had established the band's own identity, Danny Whitten had gone into heroin free fall since its release, and many close to Young, like Jack Nitzsche, reckoned that making him part of the tour would provide one last chance to straighten him out. Young obliged, and over several weeks of rehearsals he gave Whitten every chance to earn a spot in the band until it became clear that he was neither mentally nor physically up to the task. On the morning of November 18, Young reluctantly handed Whitten a plane ticket back to L.A., and late that night got a phone call that he had been found dead in a friend's apartment after overdosing on a mixture of alcohol and depressants.

The news sent everyone at the ranch into shock. Before getting back to work, Young poured his grief into "Don't Be Denied," a song that told his own life story in the most savage terms, as if in repentance for the guilt he felt over Whitten's death. Moreover, every song they had rehearsed needed to be reassessed in those terms, and suddenly what should have been the *Harvest* tour took on elements of raw psychodrama that quickly grew beyond Young's control once the band stepped into the cold arenas. Each show opened, predictably enough, with a solo set that varied from night to night (but which always pointedly avoided "The Needle and the Damage Done") before a perfunctory trio of *Harvest* hits with the band. After that, though, anything became fair game. Most often, audiences were subjected to Young's psychic wounds in songs drenched in the same bitterness as "Don't Be Denied," such as "Time Fades Away," "Yonder Stands the Sinner," and "Last Dance." It was too much for Buttrey, who was fired mid-tour, about the same time Crosby and Nash were added in order to boost sagging ticket sales once the bad reviews began piling up. This move only ratcheted up the madness, and, at the March 31 show in Oakland, Young's fuse finally ran out when fighting between the audience and the police providing security prompted him to walk off stage as the band trudged through "Southern Man."

It was as ignominious an exit as anyone could have imagined, and reviews of the album *Time Fades Away*, released in October and intended to be a snapshot of Young's schizophrenic state of mind on the tour, backed up that assertion, despite some stunning takes of the most recent songs. The imbalance was not lost on *Rolling Stone's* Bud Scoppa: "If Young appears foolish and arrogant at various points on the album, he seems to be allowing us a glimpse of these flaws, rather than letting them slip through and spoil his big moments without his consent, as happened on *Harvest.*" Yet, by the time this review appeared in January 1974, the Neil Young it described no longer existed.

Neil Young is a mediocre superstar. With this point in mind, his Monday night gig was not too bad. In fact, it could have been worse had he not performed. At $5.25 a ticket, everyone could see the show in relative comfort in small, classroom-sized chairs. After the opening acts vacated the stage, the Neil Young official roadies started to decorate it with silver hubcaps, platform-soled boots, a palm tree, and a red Indian chief (a dummy) holding a guitar — an attempt to create a "Miami Beach" atmosphere. The "MB" atmosphere proved to be stronger than Neil Young's performance, which, in a word, was tolerable. One could say that Young seems to have a fixation on the primitive — the back-to-the-roots syndrome that is currently prevailing in the music world — although it was odd to hear him plead with the audience to get off their seats and to "think of me as James Brown." The crowd readily obeyed orders and a happy time was had by all.
   — John Morris, review of Neil Young at Waterloo Lutheran University. *The Chevron*, November 2, 1973.

Audience member: *"Rock and roll!"*
Neil Young: "I'd love to go see some."
   — Rainbow Theatre, London, England, November 5, 1973

Danny Whitten's death forced Neil Young to realize that no matter how much he tried to preserve the panacea of his youth, through his ranch or by playing sold-out gigs in Canadian theatres, he was still part of a community awash in drugs that could snuff out life at any moment. Having already warned against this with "The Needle and the Damage Done," the summer of 1973 saw Young give in and take a lead role in dealing with the waste that was occurring all around him. The catalyst was the heroin-overdose death of Bruce Berry on June 7. A roadie for Crosby, Stills, Nash & Young, he had been turned on to the drug by Whitten and followed his example by selling guitars to pay for his habit, only in Berry's case the instruments belonged to the artists he worked for. While others in the band, understandably, felt deep remorse, Young saw the death of a kid with unlimited potential as another symptom of the darkness that seemed to have permanently shrouded Los Angeles.

Two months later, he had written enough songs that captured these complicated emotions, and called together the only musicians he knew who had any hope of interpreting them. It was the first time he had played with Billy Talbot and Ralph Molina in over three years, and they brought along Nils Lofgren, who, along with fronting Grin, had become a de facto member of Crazy Horse during Whitten's decline. Rounding things out was the ever-faithful Ben Keith, who set the tone by opening a bottle of tequila and tossing the cap away. Sessions at Studio Instrument Rentals (SIR), the company that Berry helped establish, subsequently turned into a wake–cum–lost weekend. With David Briggs also back and providing a modicum of control over the situation, the band connected on the basest spiritual level during songs like "Tired Eyes," "Mellow My Mind," and the one that attempted to raise Berry and all the rest from the dead, "Tonight's the Night." It was terrifyingly real, and, Elliot Roberts deduced, coming on the heels of the soon-to-be-released *Time Fades Away*, would surely cripple Young's career, if not end it altogether. Yet, mere days after sessions at SIR wrapped, Young and the band, christened the Santa Monica Flyers, fulfilled a commitment to Roberts to help open the Roxy, the club in which Roberts and David Geffen had invested as an upscale alternative to the Troubadour. It was more than a little ironic, then, that Young's four-night stand in front of everyone Geffen, in particular, hoped to impress, including Robbie Robertson and Cher, merely shifted the decadence from SIR to another location. Of course, no one objected to anyone getting fucked up, just as long as it was kept off the stage.

However, Young was heedless of this unspoken rule, which ultimately led Roberts to balk at supporting any further touring.

Murray McLauchlan explains, "The *Tonight's the Night* tour started with shows in Ontario, basically because Bernie Finkelstein and Bernie Fiedler, who managed me, were promoting shows at Massey Hall for Elliot Roberts. So there was some history there. We all knew each other. Neil wanted to perform all these dark songs about Bruce Berry, but he wanted to perform them in more intimate venues, which by then for him was under 10,000 people. And Elliot, being his manager, said, 'Do you want to squander your touring opportunities and not make the kind of money that you should? Well, I'm not interested; go shoot yourself in the foot on your own time.' So Elliot bailed out of the tour, and it was taken over by Neil's producer David Briggs, and it became a very ad hoc kind of thing." With McLauchlan opening along with Grin, the tour began with shows at McMaster University in Hamilton on October 28, and continued over the next two nights at campus venues in Waterloo and Guelph. Audiences did not recognize the Neil Young who showed up. In his place was a bearded and emaciated MC/preacher in a cheap suit, virtually masked by oversized Presley-style sunglasses. Adding even further confusion was an absence of any recognizable songs, although crowds got familiar with "Tonight's the Night" in a hurry during its requisite three airings per show.

The brief Ontario jaunt was a precursor to Young's first extended trip to England, where The Eagles took over warm-up duties from McLauchlan. But for rabid fans in places like Manchester, Newcastle, and Liverpool who had waited years for the occasion, the shows took on aspects of the standoffs Dylan and The Hawks had faced in 1966. Even by the second date, in Bristol on November 4, Young was on the verge of coming unglued by the incessant heckling, launching into a monologue during the third run through of "Tonight's the Night" about Berry stealing guitars and putting them into his arm, as Lofgren wailed a demonic guitar solo behind him. The song, as well as the concert, finally ended with Young unleashing a terrifying primal scream. "Nobody in England understood what we were trying to do," Lofgren says. "In Bristol I remember jumping up on the piano — I used to wear these combat boots and ankle weights to help me feel like I was cemented into these slow grooves. I wound up getting up onto the piano and starting to bang these heavy boots into the piano strings trying to break them, and playing with my teeth, kind of hovering over Neil, kind of trying to answer him while he was doing this crazy rap."

On November 15, they were back in New York City for the start of a week-long trek across the country. McLauchlan was on board for the trip again, as well. He says, "During the Ontario dates, I think that Neil was genuinely surprised because I was just kind of coming up at that point and doing my own concerts at universities, and when I walked out on stage to open the show, people did back flips, I mean they really went crazy. After the first show Neil said, 'Why don't you come on the whole tour?' So I ended up going on between him and Nils Lofgren and Grin, all the way, basically, from Boston Symphony Hall to Berkeley Community Center, and it was an education. That tour was crazier than anyone could ever imagine." While it did provide Young with some form of catharsis, he was still unable to get a handle on the recordings from SIR once he and Briggs turned their attention back to the album in January 1974. After grappling with several ultimately unsatisfying mixes, Young shelved the project and set about recording new material at the ranch in March.

If *Tonight's the Night* had the purpose of explicitly documenting the demise of the once-liberating drug culture, what became *On the Beach* was in some ways even more disturbing in the way it showed Young seemingly trapped inside that culture. In effect, he was. Although the ranch sessions produced the core tracks "Walk On" and "For the Turnstiles," once the scene shifted to Sunset Sound in L.A., Young willingly embraced the degradation of the Sunset Strip.

From that point on, the music no longer resembled traditional songs so much as Young's version of Dostoyevsky's *Notes From the Underground*, as he accused his audience (mostly his critics) of placing unrealistic expectations on his work. It was a subtle retaliation though, best exemplified in the three songs that comprised the original album's second side, almost undeniably Young's best sustained twenty minutes on record. Done in one heavily sedated night, the title track, "Motion Pictures," and "Ambulance Blues" drifted by in a slow-motion blur, a kind of sonic cousin to Robert Frank's suppressed 1972 Rolling Stones tour documentary *Cocksucker Blues*. It was the brief flashes of unexpected dream-like images that gave the songs such a jarring effect: Young alone at the microphone waiting for a radio interview that will never happen, then cut to a decrepit motel room as a film flickers silently on the television. *Though my problems are meaningless, that don't make them go away.* He closes his eyes, falls back on the grubby bed, and thinks of those memorable nights at the old apartment on Isabella Street, after the Riverboat closed. *It's easy to get buried in the past, when you try to make the good thing last.* He awakes at the break of dawn to find his hometown abandoned, with the exception of a farmer who merely scoffs at his predicament. Young ultimately fades into the ether with a warning to the listener not to trust anything they hear.

Young's isolation during the several months it took to make *On the Beach* had caused irreparable damage to his relationship with Carrie Snodgress. By spring, she had left the ranch for good, something that compounded the darkness as Young put the finishing touches on the record. Roberts, sensing another commercial disaster, approached Young to reconsider working with Crosby, Stills & Nash, and, much to everyone's surprise, he agreed to participate in a massive summer stadium tour. From the outset, no one hid the fact that it was awash in excess cash and drugs. Still, Young set his own terms, demanding that several *On the Beach* songs — and even fresher material — be included in the sets, and by travelling separately from the rest in a beat-up motor home. Midway through the tour, on August 8, Richard Nixon announced his resignation. While this would have been cause for communal celebration only a few years prior, it passed with only a cursory mention amid the cocaine and clashing egos.

It would take Young much longer to put Nixon and the other touchstones of his life into perspective this time. As Roberts predicted, *On the Beach* sold little despite being released to coincide with the start of the July Crosby, Stills, Nash & Young tour. The same was true when a revamped *Tonight's the Night* was finally released a year later, almost as an afterthought. Only four months after that, in November 1975, came *Zuma*, the first clear sign of rejuvenation thanks to the backing of a reconstituted Crazy Horse. But it was only one of many concerted efforts Young made at the time to regain his focus, a period that produced several great songs, such as "Like a Hurricane" and "Long May You Run," but little overall cohesion.

It would take until the summer of 1976 for Young to have a moment of clarity, while he was on a bus during an ill-fated tour with Stills. It was the height of America's bicentennial celebrations, and as Young pondered his circumstances within his adopted country, the words began pouring out: "I am a lonely visitor, I came too late to cause a stir, though I campaign all my life toward that goal. . . ." Pausing to collect his thoughts, he gazed out the window and saw the roads stretching out like healthy veins. They were the same roads that had brought him to California, and they still had the capacity to ferry anyone else. It was all a state of mind, where anybody could be whatever they perceived themselves to be; where even Richard Nixon had soul.

A few days later, Young instructed his driver to head back to California, leaving Stills to finish the tour on his own.

CHAPTER NINE

THE WEIGHT

THE FIRST TAKE COMES ON LAZILY, without vocals, just an attempt to show that recording all of the instruments together in the same room isn't as crazy an idea as first thought. As a result, it's the freest take of all. By the second, the band members are already struggling with the song's introduction. On the third, they try adding voices. The pace suddenly becomes sluggish, causing the harmonies to get swamped. The producer calls a halt halfway through, realizing that balancing the host of disparate elements is the key. By take four the group is becoming conscious of this, too, as the organ and piano wrestle each other off the top. "Sloppy! Sloppy!" the producer can't help but exclaim over the intercom. They get it together on take five, but now the song sounds stilted, with the players deliberately trying to stay out of each other's way. Take six features the most stately organ introduction, but is even slower, with every move now telegraphed, and the swing is replaced by the heavy-handed beats they thought they had left behind in those cold British theatres. On take eight, the voices begin to loosen up and live together. Certain lines start taking on special emphasis: "one voice for all," "there's no need to slave," "I'd rather be burned in Canada than freeze here in the south." "It's getting there," the producer is forced to admit. Before take nine, they pause to address some phrasing issues, but the organist is chomping at the bit and unaware of his instrument's increased volume. The moment is on the verge of being lost, but they press on through three more incomplete takes until the swing comes back. On take thirteen they nail it, with each voice breathlessly telling its own version of the same story, and all three of them exude the same sense of relief over its outcome: "We can talk about it now." Whatever "it" is doesn't matter, only that this sound they have harnessed will lead everyone who hears it over the coming months to engage in a dialogue they have never had before, and probably never imagined having.

"We Can Talk" was among the tracks completed at the initial recording session for The Band's *Music From Big Pink*, on January 10, 1968, at A & R Studios in New York. Behind the board was John Simon, fresh from completing Gordon Lightfoot's *Did She Mention My Name* and *Songs of Leonard Cohen*. He had only become aware of the group a few months earlier, while he was working with Howard Alk, Woodstock filmmaker and co-founder of the Second City theatre. "It was Howard's birthday, Halloween, and there was this godawful sound coming from outside," Simon recalled. "There were the guys from The Band — not Levon because he wasn't there on the scene yet — in funny costumes playing instruments that they really couldn't play, serenading Howard for his birthday. Howard had been on the road with the last Bob Dylan tour and they were buddies. So that was how I first met them."

That impromptu performance was indicative of the largely carefree existence that Robbie Robertson, Richard Manuel, Rick Danko, and Garth Hudson had lived since any further touring with Dylan was halted following his motorcycle accident. In the immediate aftermath, they were all kept in relative comfort in New York City on a retainer that Albert Grossman provided, and were attended to by well-known music journalist Al Aronowitz, who, aside from showing them a good time, tried to provide them with a space that was conducive to working on new material. While this proved difficult, it was an especially beneficial period for Robertson personally; he crossed paths once again with Montreal-born Dominique Bourgeois, whom he first met at the May 24, 1966, Paris concert, which she had attended as a freelance journalist. Bourgeois became enamoured with Robertson from that moment on, and they were inseparable once she located him in New York. But after sampling everything Greenwich Village had to offer, the couple eagerly made the trip north to Woodstock that fall on an invitation from a fully recovered Dylan.

"The reason I went to Woodstock was that [Bob] was working on *Eat the Document* and he asked me to help on the film," Robertson said. "I went up and lived at his house and worked on the film for a while, and it seemed like a nice scene. We had been living in New York, and there was nothing really happening outside of it being more of a pain in the ass than anything else, so Woodstock was a nice relief." As winter set in, Dylan continued to be more preoccupied with making the movie than making music. Having free reign within the tiny community made it easy to act on almost any idea, and Dylan soon called the rest of his band to come up and pitch in on some scenes shot over the winter, but which were ultimately scrapped, like the rest of *Eat the Document*. With Robertson and Bourgeois having found their own house just east of Woodstock, in the hamlet of Glasco, Danko and Manuel stayed at a motel for several weeks until they heard of a small pink house for rent at $125 a month, tucked away north of town in West Saugerties. Its isolation provided the ideal working environment, and word was sent to Hudson to bring up his gear and recording equipment, which he duly set up in the dank concrete basement. By the time the snow had cleared and the area's sharply twisting roads were once again passable, the house now known to all as Big Pink became the natural place not only for Robertson to reconnect with his band mates, but for Dylan to find new musical inspiration.

It would come from the most unexpected sources. During their first series of recorded gatherings, in the early summer of 1967, Dylan appeared bent on showing the others his folk and country roots, something he had hardly had a chance to do until then. Much of this was music the group had ignored during their R & B apprenticeship, but in this new setting they suddenly discovered previously unknown nuances to songs like The Impressions' "People Get Ready" and Brendan Behan's Irish prison ballad "The Royal Canal." Furthermore, Dylan's song choices often seemed intended to acquaint the group with fellow Canadian artists. A string of Ian Tyson songs were attempted, including "Four Strong Winds," "The French Girl," and "One Single River," the last of which was also known as "Song for Canada," co-written by journalist Peter Gzowski as a plea for anglophone and francophone unity. As well, several of Hank Snow's best-loved hits, such as "I Don't Hurt Anymore" and "A Fool Such As I" were trotted out, an echo of Dylan's appreciation from his formative years when, still known to all as Bobby Zimmerman, he attempted to write his own version of Snow's "The Drunkard's Son" after hearing it performed on the radio. "We may have reminded Bob of Canada," Robertson says, "but these were just songs that he knew."

The purpose, instead, became not so much an exercise in deconstructing this material, but merely playing it with as much gut instinct as possible. Having learned how to play on a completely visceral level from Ronnie Hawkins, the early basement tapes revealed the group learning from Dylan — just as he was teaching himself — how to play on a level that showed utter sympathy toward what any given song demanded at its core. Of course, as these were initial experiments, not all of them worked, but the looseness of the daily Big Pink meetings spurred Dylan to write. "In the living room at Big Pink, there were always a couple of typewriters," Robertson says. "We noticed how he would often write the words and then set them to music, and I had never heard of anyone doing that before. Certain things started to make sense to me after that, like why Bob's songs were so long, but also his connection to these Beat writers I never knew much about. There suddenly weren't any limits, and eventually we all started writing things. It got to be almost like a newsroom there. But we never thought that anybody would actually hear this stuff."

This outburst of activity naturally drew upon whatever strange mood was in the air on any given day. Consequently, many songs toyed with the notion of an insular rural existence dominated by Old Testament morality, while others showed the flipside of that coin, presenting a cast of odd characters who were thoroughly at home with the surreal situations in which they were placed. At the same time, these were songs too intangible for Dylan to conceive of recording himself, and so the game became envisioning how others might interpret them. With much mystery still lingering about Dylan's physical and mental health, he was aware that even the most insignificant sign of his creative well-being would be eagerly embraced. But when Dylan's new publishing company, Dwarf Music, created upon the expiration of his Witmark contract, began circulating acetates of fourteen basement originals as demos at the end of August, few could have expected the overwhelming reaction that ensued.

The first glimpse of what was going on in the basement came in November when Peter, Paul & Mary released "Too Much of Nothing" as a one-off single. It peaked at number thirty-five at the end of the year. Only a few weeks later, British group Manfred Mann released "Quinn the Eskimo (The Mighty Quinn)," which fared much better, topping the chart in their home country and hitting the Top 10 in America. Over the next several months, artists on both sides of the Atlantic scrambled to get their hands on this material. The Byrds recorded "You Ain't Going Nowhere" and "Nothing Was Delivered" on *Sweetheart of the Rodeo*, while Julie Driscoll (backed by Brian Auger & The Trinity) scored a huge British hit with "This Wheel's On Fire." The origin of these songs became even more puzzling when, at the end of 1967, Dylan officially returned to the marketplace with *John Wesley Harding*, a stunningly sober collection recorded in Nashville that October with no trace of any Hawks influence.

Although improvising with Dylan proved to be an amusing and worthwhile distraction, the quartet had not lost sight of their ultimate goal of making their own music. Perhaps surprisingly, it was Rick Danko who showed the most initiative in this area, pestering Albert Grossman at every opportunity to get them their own record deal. In September, Grossman finally acquiesced, taking the still drummer-less group to New York to record demos under his supervision. The experience turned out to be a wake-up call for Robertson, in particular, in terms of how they would eventually transfer the Big Pink aesthetic to the studio. "It didn't really work at all," he told Band historian Rob Bowman. "We had to do this stuff really quick. We just went in and slammed these things down and Albert just kind of gave the engineer a little bit of input on it. The results, I thought, were very questionable. It just didn't sound good. What I liked about records, I didn't hear any of that on there." Nevertheless, Grossman started shopping the tape around, and after failing to make a deal with either Columbia or Warner Brothers, got an unexpectedly warm reception from Capitol Records, an L.A.-based label, far removed from the New York scene he dominated. The fact that the group did not yet have a name didn't seem to pose a problem, either; for a label to have any association with Dylan, however remote, was enough at the time.

When all parties agreed to the deal in principle in early November, Danko called Levon Helm in Memphis and explained that they could be a full-time unit again. The atmosphere at Big Pink couldn't have been more different than the last time Helm had seen them all; each member now contributed equally to the overall sound, and was open to any musical configuration that suited a particular song. Helm's return solidified this new approach, and enabled him to immediately draw deeply from the folk and country music of his childhood. In the two months that led up to the first *Music From Big Pink* recording session, they ran through a wide range of ideas accumulated that summer, some of them half-formed basement nonsense and some bearing the haunting, almost parable-like qualities of Dylan's more finely crafted basement songs. Into this latter category fell "This Wheel's on Fire," for which Danko contributed the haunting melody to Dylan's equally ominous lyrics, the Dylan–Manuel collaboration "Tears of Rage," and "I Shall Be Released," which Manuel chose to sing in an aching falsetto, adding to the song's inherent desperation. This sense of drama eventually became the template for choosing the remaining songs from among those written by Robertson and Manuel. A common understanding soon emerged that they were in a position to defy whatever expectations may have existed.

The idea of "rebelling against the rebellion" that the members would commonly use to describe that formative period in years to come was, in many ways, merely an attempt to create a sense of stability that each had abandoned in pursuit of their rock and roll dreams. And it was not to be the libertine communal family model that was enticing so many kids to San Francisco and elsewhere with phony promises of free love and unlimited drugs. There had certainly been plenty of that during their time as Hawks, but living in Woodstock allowed them to connect with a way of life they could have had if they had not left southern Ontario, or, in Helm's case, rural Arkansas. What became so intriguing about this philosophy, which was preceded by other naturalist movements in art and literature, was not in how it rang true, but in how no one until then had dared to challenge the basic tenets of pop music in order to express it. Having been raised on the "improper" sounds of rockabilly and rhythm and blues, the members knew full well the implications of choosing that music as the basis for their individual identities. The question became: why should rock and roll still be the cause of social divisions? Was it not true that what they and Dylan had been doing to entertain themselves at Big Pink was no different from what generations of North Americans had been doing for hundreds of years? Once this became clear, ideas of conflict between young and old, and unity based on anything other than shared humanity, seemed utterly incomprehensible. Big Pink became a place that was essentially out of time, but also a very real state of mind for the many who came to perceive it as a musical Eden.

The pull of all of this was enough to distract from the fact that *Music From Big Pink* itself was recorded in a New York City studio. Along with "We Can Talk," the earliest songs cut were "Tears of Rage" (always intended to open the album at a shockingly funereal pace), "This Wheel's on Fire," "Chest Fever" (Garth Hudson's showpiece, and the album's only nod to then–*de rigueur* instrumental flamboyance), and "The Weight," a song that was, among many others, up for debate for inclusion. When Robertson moved to Woodstock, he made a point of catching up on what he felt was a missed education. Part of this was spurred by his companion, Bourgeois (who became Dominique Robertson in the spring of 1968 and gave birth to their first child, Alexandra, that December), who suggested reading material like the novels of Jean Cocteau. However, Robertson found it easier to connect with Cocteau's work as a filmmaker, which led to his interest in other experimental directors, such as Kurosawa and Luis Bunuel. All of this played a role in the conception of "The Weight," in which an unwitting main character gets caught up in a dream-like series of events upon being sent to pass on greetings from the mysterious Fanny, whose unseen presence is the song's dominant force. While it carried some of the enigmatic basement vibe, the symbolism of "The Weight" was beyond anything Robertson had written to that point, and even he wasn't completely sure what it represented.

"We'd tried it a number of different ways, but we weren't that excited about it," Robertson explained. "So our attitude was, 'Well, just in case something else isn't working, we've got this song to fall back on.' So we were in the studio, and just out of trying to not be boring, we said, 'Well, let's give that 'Take a load off Fanny' song a shot.' And very quickly, someone suggested that maybe Garth should play piano and Richard should play organ, because it seemed like there was room for some fills that would sound more natural coming from the piano than the guitar. So they swapped, and we recorded it, and it wasn't until we listened back to it that we realized, 'Holy shit, this song's really got something.'"

Although "The Weight" opened with a seductive Curtis Mayfield–like guitar signature from Robertson, the real thrust of the song came right after, with several cracks of Helm's snare drum, producing quite possibly the most lonesome sound ever recorded. Helm took the lead vocal, as well, the only time he did so on *Big Pink* due to his late arrival. But the choice of featuring his Arkansas twang immediately put the setting into an American context, thereby firmly linking it to an egalitarian song tradition that stretched back through the genre collision of Elvis Presley's Sun career to the earliest country, folk, and blues recordings. What appeared on the surface to be a rather innocuous cultural overlap became another crucial aspect of the new world that *Big Pink* seemed to open up overnight.

As a single, the song couldn't even crack the Top 50 in the fall of 1968, so it would be left to other artists to fully exploit its potential to be a uniting force in the wake of the racial tension that had escalated following the assassination of Martin Luther King. The first cover of "The Weight" was by white pop/soul vocalist Jackie DeShannon, and was released almost simultaneously with the original in July 1968. It would fail to enter the Top 50. However, Robertson was paid what, for him, was the ultimate compliment when The Staple Singers recorded it for their 1968 Stax Records debut album *Soul Folk in Action*. Over the next year, "The Weight" was unavoidable: Aretha Franklin's gutbucket version, featuring a then-unknown slide guitarist named Duane Allman, barged into the Top 20 in April 1969, while The Supremes and The Temptations collaborated on a version that charted in September. But the song truly achieved iconic status when it was included on the soundtrack to the film *Easy Rider*, released in the summer of 1969. Director Dennis Hopper had wanted either The Band or Crosby, Stills, Nash & Young to compose a score for the film, but when the budget wouldn't allow for that, he instead obtained the rights to songs he frequently listened to while editing the endless footage of him and Peter Fonda on the road. "The Weight" became the ideal backdrop for Hopper's skewed Kerouac-ian vision of the two lead characters' discovery of an America that wanted no part of them.* *Easy Rider* would be the first film to transcend

---

*When a soundtrack album was assembled for release on Warner/Reprise in October 1969, Capitol held out on allowing The Band's version of "The Weight" to be used, prompting a hasty cover by pop/soul group Smith, which was then on the charts with a cover of The Shirelles' "Baby It's You."

the hippie exploitation genre, spawning many similar films, such as *Two-Lane Blacktop* and *Vanishing Point*. However, the attitude of *Big Pink* could also be detected in the revisionist westerns of that year, like *Butch Cassidy and the Sundance Kid* and *The Wild Bunch* — stories that told of the need for fraternal loyalty amid changing times.

Even if, by then, audiences knew "The Weight," many listeners still did not know who the group was that performed it. It had taken nearly up to the release of *Music From Big Pink* for the name The Band to be chosen. At the time the group signed the contract with Capitol, Helm had lobbied for them to be called The Crackers, a long-standing term of derision for poor southern whites whose dietary staple was cheap cracked corn. Early country and hillbilly groups used it frequently and without irony, but, like the other name that was briefly considered, The Honkies, it had become tantamount to a racial slur. In the end, they settled on an inside joke based on another insult they heard frequently throughout the 1965–66 tour: "Tell the band to go home." But what ultimately tipped the scales in favour of "The Band" was that it seemed to be the most reasonable compromise in terms of what Robertson later described as "[getting] past the goofiness of wanting to be celebrities."

He continued, "At the time it was: burn the flag, stab your mother and father, wear goofy clothes. All those things were happening, but we loved our mothers and fathers. After the Ronnie Hawkins thing, everybody was listening to a very corny kind of music. It was the Frankie Avalon period, while we were playing obscure music, musical music. We were never interested in trends. Our launching period was that time of fifties discontent. We were all really vulnerable to oppression — that's part of it. And also we didn't like psychedelic things. I wasn't interested in wearing paisley pants. We wore suits and ties. When we played with Bob Dylan, we wore jackets and ties. He hated it. He kept telling us, 'You guys gotta do something with your clothes.'"

However, Dylan himself was sporting a beard and conservative rural attire when he called upon The Crackers — as they were still then known — to back him at the January 20, 1968,

Carnegie Hall tribute to the recently deceased Woody Guthrie. Together, they managed to defy the piety of the rest of the evening with ramshackle versions of Guthrie's "I Ain't Got No Home," "Grand Coulee Dam," and "Dear Mrs. Roosevelt." But this first test of bringing Big Pink to the stage was almost totally eclipsed by the fact that it was Dylan's first public appearance since his motorcycle accident. Little did the band members know that it would take another year for the next chance to come around.

Soon after the Guthrie tribute, Capitol offered to bring the group to L.A. to finish the album in its studio, and over the course of several lazy weeks more often spent in the sun, they cut the remaining tracks with John Simon, along with a handful of unused songs for posterity, at Gold Star Studios. With the album mixed by May, attention turned to the package. The cover featured a primitive painting by Dylan, representing him and the group, with even (it could be argued) Albert Grossman perversely appearing in the form of an elephant. Using it also allowed them to avoid attaching a name to the outside, and only "Music From Big Pink" appeared on the back, with a picture of the real star, the house. The interior sleeve listed the relevant information, alongside a brief liner note by Dominique Robertson, a black-and-white group shot taken in the Catskills that could have been from the previous century, and a large colour portrait taken at the Danko family farm near Simcoe that included everyone's immediate family.

From a marketing standpoint, the album flaunted every preconception, but it became the best illustration of Grossman's tactic of forcing the rest of the world to accept greatness on its own merit. He and the rest of The Band were prepared to be patient, since none of the members were eager to go back on the road. Consequently, *Music From Big Pink* took a month to chart after its July 1968 release, eventually peaking at only number thirty. However, glowing reviews poured in from all corners, and the album's overall emphasis on humility was overpowering to some. Eric Clapton had been handed an acetate of *Big Pink* during the L.A. stop on Cream's spring 1968 tour, and he instantly recognized it for what it was: the complete antithesis of his band's false front as rock's premier virtuosos. Cream's next tour that October would subsequently be billed as their last. Clapton passed the acetate on to his close friend George Harrison, then mired in the production of The Beatles' *White Album*, a group endeavour in name only. Harrison's reaction was similar, and he made a point of visiting Woodstock that fall. By January, The Beatles were convening at Twickenham Studios in an attempt to reignite their group dynamic by playing marathon sessions of improvised songs and old rock and roll nuggets. Unfortunately, the *Get Back* experiment, or *Let It Be* as it was later called, would not be their *Big Pink*. Instead, it was the sad realization that The Beatles' unique chemistry no longer existed.

Within months, other established British groups, like Procol Harum and Traffic, were following suit in dispensing with psychedelic trappings, and amid the revolutionary rhetoric of The Rolling Stones' *Beggars Banquet* (released in November 1968), that record's stripped-down country overtones were a nod to *Big Pink*, whether consciously or not. Even the embryonic Led Zeppelin toyed with covering "Chest Fever," an idea that quickly morphed into "Your Time Is Gonna Come" on their debut album. With such obvious influence, the world seemingly rested on The Band's doorstep. Yet, as 1968 came to a close, the freedom the band members had earned nearly proved to be their undoing. Helm had already injured a leg in a motorcycle accident during a visit back to Arkansas, but it was the dangerous winding roads around Woodstock that wreaked havoc with those who had no concerns about driving while intoxicated. Manuel had tempted fate in this manner several times, and somehow always managed to escape unscathed. Danko was not so lucky. While racing with Helm (according to some) during an early winter storm, his car slid off a curve at high speed and hit a tree, breaking Danko's neck and back in four places. The damage kept him in traction for the next three months, by which time demand for the group to play live had reached a fever pitch.

However, there were few public answers as to why The Band refused to appease its fans. Grossman was closely guarded about

Danko's accident in order to avoid exposing the recklessness that ran counter to what was becoming a finely honed image. On top of that, only Robertson gave interviews — albeit reluctantly — and spent most of them downplaying the hype. In fact, the only substantial coverage the group received was Al Aronowitz's cover story in the August 24, 1968, issue of *Rolling Stone*, illustrated by an outtake from the *Big Pink* photo shoot that showed all of the band members crammed onto a bench with their backs to the camera. With it, the outlaw mythos firmly took hold, and getting The Band to emerge from its hideout was going to cost dearly.

Still, with Danko on the mend, the others focused on the next album. A recording session on September 10, 1968, at Capitol's brand-new New York studio that yielded the unique Robertson/Danko duet "Bessie Smith," as well as a rollicking cover of the blues standard "Key to the Highway," didn't possess the required feel, so a return to the *Big Pink* aesthetic appeared inevitable. But with Woodstock now containing a myriad of distractions, many of them a hindrance to the creative process, it became crucial to find the isolation that the house once offered in a different location. Someone within the Grossman organization knew of such a property north of Sunset Boulevard, owned by Sammy Davis Jr., that was available to rent. The deal was sealed when it was determined that an adjoining pool house could be turned into a studio. In early February 1969, everyone assembled in L.A. and settled in.

"The plan was for Capitol to supply recording equipment," John Simon said. "We waited for it for a month, and Robbie used the time to finish the songs. So now we had one month in which to record two months of scheduled work. We had a band meeting in the living room of the house the night after the gear arrived. Richard Manuel said, 'What we want is to get a hold of some of them high-school fat-girl diet pills.' So I called up a college buddy who was now a neurosurgeon in San Francisco and he prescribed a whole pile of these amphetamines. That's how they liked to work. I got into it and started smoking for the first time in my life because the pills made cigarettes taste so good."

Simon added, "Then I found I wasn't really there to produce the record. I was supposed to teach the guys in the band — meaning Robbie — what I did, so they could make records by themselves."

Indeed, Robertson was taking a more dominant role in the proceedings, building on what he'd done with "The Weight" by writing songs that were tailored to particular voices and crafting stories with the sweep of a Hollywood screenwriter. While Manuel and Danko had each shared over half the credit on *Big Pink*, Robertson's overall vision for the new album left little room for other interpretations. "I don't really understand how it works, it just goes that way," Robertson said in late 1969. "Everybody plays a totally different part in the group. There is no leader, nobody in the group wants to be a leader. I do a lot of the out-front stuff, but the guys do a lot of the [back-end] stuff. On the new album, I don't sing at all. I can hear it when someone else is doing it, but when I'm singing I can't hear it. That way, I can tell if it's right. I was engineering, writing, and playing guitar, and I just didn't have time. Everybody played many, many instruments on this album."

Speaking to *Melody Maker* in 1971, Robertson had gained a bit more perspective on the approach that congealed during the pool-house sessions. "The only thing that I'm consciously trying to do is to write songs that, if you listen to them in a couple of years, they're [still going to hold up]. I mean, a lot of people's records that I really liked a couple of years ago, I listen to them now and I can't understand how come I liked them so much. I'm really trying to get around the time element, so that it's got a better possibility of lasting. The only songs that we do in relation to the South at all are sung by Levon, and I write these songs for the people who sing them. Richard and Rick don't sing about the South — it works for Levon because he's from Arkansas. We're not doing something that we don't know nothing about; I'm trying to write songs that he could sing, lyrics that he can get off on, like 'The Night They Drove Old Dixie Down.'"

Robertson was certainly painting a much more substantial

picture of America than the one *Big Pink* represented on the album he intended to call *Harvest*. His ability to fuse his experiences, as well as second-hand stories, with the rest of the group's bottomless musical resources translated into a stunning pastiche of the previous century of American culture. The history itself was clearly unavoidable, but what brought the songs into a contemporary context was how each was essentially the unsentimental testimony of an average person, whether it was the ravaged post–Civil War Southern farmer Virgil Kane in "Dixie," the old salts of "Rockin' Chair," the conscientious friend coming to the aid of "The Unfaithful Servant," the carefree, Huck Finn–like optimist of "When You Awake," or the farmer struggling with the fallout of joining a union in "King Harvest (Has Surely Come)." At the same time, there was enough sly, bawdy humour in "Rag Mama Rag," "Up on Cripple Creek," and "Jemima Surrender" to keep the album firmly in line with the founding principles of rock and roll.

The only song that truly stood out from the rest was "Whispering Pines." Although Robertson claimed a co-writing credit, this was Richard Manuel's finest moment: a heartrending portrait of a man trapped within himself, unable to engage the outside world until a lost love (presumably) returns. While other songs were firmly rooted to some kind of narrative, "Whispering Pines" hung in the air, largely due to Hudson's unearthly organ tone, but also because of Manuel's unparalleled ability to convey a sense of spiritual displacement that comes from utter loneliness. This was no character singing, and the sheer beauty of the performance could not deny "Whispering Pines" a place on the album. Its sentiments were as pure as the blues could ever get.

The song was actually recorded at the Hit Factory in New York in June, along with "Up on Cripple Creek" and "Jemima Surrender," during a final session to wrap up the album, now to be called *The Band* in an effort to clear up any lingering confusion over the group's name. Only weeks earlier, on April 17, they had made their long overdue live debut at San Francisco's Winterland arena, part of promoter Bill Graham's live music empire. Coming straight off the L.A. recording sessions, the group had to quickly shift gears, and Robertson, in particular, was not ready for it. He arrived in San Francisco with a very pregnant Dominique, still unsure about the state of the album, and knowing that expectations for the concerts were ridiculously high thanks to a continuous buildup from influential *San Francisco Chronicle* music critic Ralph J. Gleason. The stress wreaked havoc on Robertson's health, leaving him bedridden with a high fever. The rest of the group rehearsed without him, and up to the Thursday opening-night show there were doubts about whether he would be able to perform. As Graham kept the audience at bay, a hypnotist worked on getting Robertson to his feet, telling him that when he heard the word "grow," his legs would feel like steel springs. "They brought in this man dressed all in black who spoke French," Robertson said. "So we start to play, and I'm in such a strange frame of mind that at one point I just get completely zoned out. I know he's at the side of the stage, so I give him this pathetic look, and he's staring straight at me. I could hear him saying 'grow' directly in my ear, louder than the music, louder than anything, and I actually started to come back. By the end of it I was feeling pretty good."

While the hypnotist may have salvaged the evening for Robertson, the crowd was on the verge of lynching the group for giving a seven-song, thirty-five-minute show after a two-hour delay. Nobody believed it could get any worse, and the next night The Band rallied, playing for over an hour by mixing in extra songs like "Little Birds," a bluegrass waltz Helm had learned as a child from his father, along with Little Richard's "Slippin' and Slidin'," a stubborn holdout from the early Hawks repertoire. Gleason, like most other critics, was glad he held his judgment back until the conclusion of the three-night stand. In his final pronouncement, published the following month in *Rolling Stone,* he wrote, "The average man is paranoid today and he has reason to be. The band was worried and nervous about playing in public again, about bringing out this music for the first time before an audience like this. But they were determined to do it right, and they worked at it, and it is a kind of ironic tribute that they first had to survive the psychic earthquake of that opening night in order to come back stronger than ever and turn everybody on. And the truth is that this is a remarkable, deeply important group of artists whose music is now firmly embedded in the American consciousness, the fruits of which are yet to be seen."

On May 9 and 10 they played four shows in two nights at Graham's Fillmore East in New York, with the *Times* calling them "coolly professional" and adding, "They appeared on stage wearing suits (of all things) and worked into a rocking fever of an intensity seen only occasionally." The genie was now out of the bottle. And with scores of rock festivals being organized all over North America that summer, all wanting The Band, they soon found it impossible to stay off the road. Choosing to start in familiar territory, they played the Toronto Pop Festival at Varsity Stadium on June 21, taking the stage in the afternoon prior to sets by, among others, The Velvet Underground. The show was proof that not being in total control of their surroundings was a handicap that was difficult for the band members to overcome. As Helm wrote in his autobiography, "Our set was a disaster, with horrendous sound problems. Those amps crackled like machine guns."

Technicalities aside, The Band's general reception in Canada was more tepid than most would have expected, especially in Toronto, where many still couldn't wrap their heads around the group's transformation. Ronnie Hawkins, in particular, seemed bemused with all the adulation being heaped upon his former proteges, and took the opportunity to vent his spleen to *Rolling Stone* that summer. The article amounted to the first tell-all of their sordid exploits together, and while Hawkins grudgingly admitted to liking *Big Pink*, he added, "I don't know what came over those boys. They never pretended they were something they're not when I was around 'em. The pure image just doesn't suit them." While Grossman pondered legal action over Hawkins' disclosures, a more pressing matter was the massive concert being planned that August in Woodstock, a site chosen largely in tribute to the mystique that Dylan and The Band had created around the area. Using the prospect of Dylan as the headliner provided organizers with the necessary leverage to book many of the leading rock and folk acts — including The Band — even as the actual location of the festival changed on a weekly basis. Dylan, in fact, wanted nothing to do with an event that disrupted the tranquility that Woodstock had come to represent for him, and instead committed to appear with The Band later that month, safely across the Atlantic at the Isle of Wight Festival.

Like the other festivals The Band had played, both of these were exercises in futility. At Woodstock, they hit the stage on the soggy Sunday night, sandwiched in between the over-the-top blues of Ten Years After and Johnny Winter. Things went marginally smoother in Britain, only because of the unwavering attention that was paid to Dylan. Still, this was a far cry from 1966. In trying to stick to the hard-line country approach of *Nashville Skyline* amid the presence of 300,000 people, it took Dylan much of the hour-long set to find his rhythm with the others. "Like a Rolling Stone" was a shadow of its former self, and only during a barnstorming version of "Highway 61 Revisited" did the sound ever seem to catch fire. However, by then the show was nearly over, leaving many scratching their heads and wondering what all the fuss had been about. The Band members themselves were among them. "I don't understand to this day why we did those things," Robertson said a few months later. "We did it in Toronto because it was Toronto. We did it in Woodstock because it was originally supposed to be in Woodstock. We thought we would just drive down the road, play, and come home. And it turned out it wasn't in Woodstock [but in Bethel]. The Isle of Wight we did because we wanted to go to Europe to visit with our musician friends, and we wanted to do it for Bob, because he really wanted to play. So that's really what it's all about. I thought [Woodstock] was kind of remarkable, but as a happening, that's all. It was a drag playing. We got even less response from the audience. The event was not the music, the event was the people. We were like muzak; it was very inappropriate for us."

But the follies of the summer were soon forgotten when *The Band* was released in late September 1969. The album quickly rose into the Top 10 on the strength of unanimously glowing reviews, with "Up on Cripple Creek" peaking in the Top 30. They played the song on *The Ed Sullivan Show* on November 2 as a kickoff to a sold-out tour that lasted until the end of the year. It picked up again after the holidays with three successive Ontario dates starting on January 16, 1970, at the University of Guelph, Massey Hall in Toronto, and McMaster University in Hamilton. That week, the media glare reached its apogee when The Band was featured on the cover of *Time*, which hailed them as leading purveyors of "The New Sound of Country Rock." The gushing profile by future screenwriter Jay Cocks balanced comments by all five members and managed to preserve a sense of communal harmony. However, by the time the gruelling tour ended in March, the influx of cash it had generated, on top of the royalties that had just been received from the previous year, suddenly brought about an entirely new set of demands.

It was the first real financial independence each band member had ever known, and for those already accustomed to certain habits and hobbies, being able to afford them without much struggle proved a dangerous situation once they resumed their lives in the Catskills. "Things went berserk," Robertson recalled in the early eighties. "Different guys went crazy. I don't know what happened, it's so difficult to understand. It was self-destructive things. It was drugs, or just a way of life, or driving fast. It's a fever, a riding of things to the limit. Maybe people think that they don't really deserve success, that they don't believe in it. So they start fucking with it, start sticking their hand in the fire. It was different for me; I had already started a family. I had a commitment that prevented me from leaping off; I had an anchor. If I hadn't had a family, I could've gotten as goofy as anybody. My family was like a protective device. The other guys' lives were just more available. I had to go home to change diapers."

With his family's well-being in mind, Robertson purchased a home in Montreal. While he knew that this could cause a major disruption to The Band's operations, he assumed that everyone would still be able to contribute whenever it was necessary. This turned out to be over-optimistic since, by his own doing, Robertson had come to be perceived as the group's leader and spokesman. "The other guys' availability was definitely an alienating factor," he admitted. "It tested our relationship, and it was scary for everyone, since we were concerned about one another. So that place of leisure turned into a snake pit, because everyone was bored. Now what? Now we're successful, now we're making money. But so what? I was afraid of someone dying; they were getting into car wrecks — I mean all the time. Rick broke his neck very, very bad. Richard had several severe accidents. It wasn't unusual to get up in the morning and hear, 'Richard's out here, upside down in a car.' Everything played a part: drugs, drinking, anything that was taboo."

It was in this environment that The Band began work on its third album in the spring of 1970. The idea was to record it as a concert at the tiny Woodstock Playhouse in a gesture to local residents who were blaming the proliferation of musicians for irreversibly altering the town's image. The plan was ultimately vetoed by town council, which, still gun-shy after the previous summer's festival, assumed that fans from nearby urban areas would once again create similar problems. In the end, The Band simply rented the theatre and set up as they would have for a normal concert, while engineer Todd Rundgren was confined to a recording truck outside. This was not the clubhouse feel that had been the group's stock-in-trade up until then, and it showed in the material. From what became the title track, "Stage Fright," on down, the bulk of the songs were undeniably locked in the present tense, reflecting from many different perspectives the effect that fame was having on the band members' psyches. Being back on the road certainly played a large role in Robertson's writing, and an overall toughness that came with being a touring band once again became the hallmark of songs such as "Strawberry Wine," "Just Another Whistle Stop," and "The Shape I'm In." Yet, coming off such an immaculately crafted record like *The Band, Stage Fright* sounded wildly uneven, causing a simple ode to their adopted home, "Time to Kill," somehow to ring hollow. Even worse, Robertson's latest attempts at creating instant mythology, "The W.S. Walcott Medicine Show" and "Daniel and the Sacred Harp," now seemed overwrought. Only on the album's closing track, "The Rumor," did any effortlessness shine through. With vocals shared by Manuel, Danko, and Helm, this remarkably constructed song, on the surface, spoke to the dark side of small-town life. But it could have also easily been inspired by the reaction The Band received at each place they visited while on tour, and would not have been out of place on either of the previous albums.

The Band was now long past the point of being a rumour, and the gap between writing songs for the band members' own amusement, as opposed to the marketplace, irrevocably expanded with *Stage Fright*. It would be the highest-charting album they would ever have; it hit number five a few weeks after its release in August, following The Band's appearances on the Festival Express tour and a string of dates along the west coast. The Band continued to tour the U.S. throughout the fall, often using a small private plane that could bring them back to Woodstock after shows in the northeast. Meanwhile, the Grossman camp had been dealt a devastating blow by the heroin-overdose death of Janis Joplin in an L.A. hotel room on October 4. It came as she was completing her next album, *Pearl*, with her all-Canadian backing band, which included Richard Manuel's Rockin' Revols partner John Till. The loss foreshadowed the impending changes in the music business, changes that would soon find many others vying for the power that was once Grossman's alone. But with his dream of working outside of the business through his own label already established, Grossman turned his energy to the next phase of his plan: building the recording studio.

Construction of the huge, wooden, barn-like Bearsville Sound was still far from finished when Grossman suggested that The Band test it out in February 1971. Robertson, for one, was reluctant, since he had not had much time to formulate any sort of concept for the next record. Still, Grossman was insistent, so as a compromise they laid down one of their live staples, Marvin

Gaye's "Don't Do It." Hearing their unique interpretation of classic Motown on tape seemed to unlock something within the group, and in short order they came up with the similarly funky "Life Is a Carnival." In this case, instead of Detroit, Robertson felt a syncopated groove directly from New Orleans, which prompted him to imagine how the song might sound in the hands of one of their seminal influences: Allen Toussaint, songwriter and arranger for Lee Dorsey, Aaron Neville, Irma Thomas, and many others. Much to Robertson's delight, Toussaint was up to the challenge, and composed a horn part that turned the song into an irresistible Mardi Gras parade march.

But in spite of everyone's excitement over "Life Is a Carnival," the rest of the sessions for *Cahoots* dragged on due to a lack of similarly styled material. Dylan had graciously offered "When I Paint My Masterpiece," a song that immediately revealed its Mediterranean essence once Hudson played it on accordion, but crafting the rest of the album was decidedly more hit-and-miss. A visit to the studio one day by recent Woodstock transplant Van Morrison inspired "4% Pantomime," a wildly spontaneous duet with Manuel, but elsewhere the general goal was to connect with the past, as they had on *The Band*. Sadly, however, it seemed that the past could no longer be retrieved. "Where Do We Go From Here" was the most obvious example of Robertson's view that he was living within a dead culture, and this notion spilled over into "Last of the Blacksmiths," "Thinking Out Loud," and "Smoke Signal," each of which expressed in one way or another the disappearance of once-flourishing aspects of life. Only on the album's closing song, "The River Hymn," was there any shred of hope that traditions could continue, although this thought was mainly conveyed through Helm's passionate vocal, one of the best he would ever record.

The group struggled to complete the album right up until leaving for their first European tour in mid-May. It turned out to be a much-needed boost of confidence, as both audiences and the press had been eagerly anticipating their arrival. The biggest surprise turned out to be the media's unending fascination with the 1966 tour, which, now accepted as a seminal moment in rock history, was the focus of most interviews. Engaging in a rare conversation, Manuel was typically recalcitrant in telling *Disc and Music Echo*, "Being with Dylan probably did help us, it would be silly to say it didn't, but I'd hate to say that we wouldn't have made it otherwise. It would have probably just taken us *longer*."

· The opportunity to play on their own in prestigious European concert halls had everyone, for once, in top form on stage. But the renewed sense of purpose was partially extinguished by the decidedly disappointing reviews *Cahoots* received upon its release in October. Even The Band's staunchest critical supporters sensed something was amiss, and the album failed to crack the Top 20, falling off the charts completely after only fourteen weeks. The simple fact was that by the end of 1971, rock fans heard The Band's blue-collar substance-over-bourgeois style everywhere. The previous year, The Grateful Dead struck gold with *Workingman's Dead* and *American Beauty*; Elton John became a star on the strength of *Tumbleweed Connection* and *Madman Across the Water* (containing lyricist Bernie Taupin's unabashed tribute "Levon"), as did Rod Stewart through *Gasoline Alley* and *Every Picture Tells a Story*; Ray Davies added his own London eccentricities to it on The Kinks' *Muswell Hillbillies*, while a group of New York musos calling themselves Steely Dan would soon burst onto the scene with *Can't Buy a Thrill*.

Robertson could feel the impending changes; the others agreed that the prospect of another studio album in the coming year would have undoubtedly led to disastrous consequences. They determined, instead, to record a live album after the fall tour for *Cahoots*. But there would be a twist: they would add a full horn section and call upon Allen Toussaint to write charts. He was once again happy to oblige, arranging eleven songs at his New Orleans home before heading to New York for rehearsals. Incredibly, the bag containing the sheet music was stolen at the airport, forcing Toussaint to hole up in Woodstock and start from scratch. It turned out to be a better situation than Toussaint could have imagined, as he explained to Rob

Bowman: "The music got so much more personal because the guys were so much more personal. Their personalities were just outstanding. I remember being at the place where they were noodling around a bit. I would hear them playing, and they would just set my heart and spirit in a place where, if I had written something before that, I would have scratched it out."

The *Rock of Ages* shows took place December 28–31 at New York's Academy Of Music, with everyone on edge about whether they could pull it off. By the end of the first night, those fears had been put to rest; both the crowd and The Band were elevated by the sheer power the horn section added. It all led up to the final night, New Year's Eve, which provided the bulk of the selections that comprised the eventual double album, from the finally fully realized version of "Don't Do It" to Hudson's extended intro to "Chest Fever," now given its own title, "The Genetic Method." Robertson had saved a trump card for that night, as well, persuading a then-reclusive Dylan to join the group for a ragged four-song encore that included two basement songs: "Down in the Flood" and "Don't Ya Tell Henry." But even as The Band convincingly tore into Chuck Willis's "(I Don't Want to) Hang Up My Rock and Roll Shoes" for the first and only time, the prevailing sense was that these shows marked the end of a part of their career they would never be able to recapture.

Released in September 1972 to wide praise and healthy sales, *Rock of Ages* effectively provided the touring break the group had desired for the past two years. But, as with their previous periods apart, each member used his time in radically different ways. While Helm took the unusual step of honing his chops at the Berklee School of Music in Boston as part of an effort to get clean, Robertson dabbled with creating an extended piece of experimental music, arbitrarily entitled *Works*, as well as exploring some film-scoring opportunities. Danko helped produce close friend Bobby Charles's much-beloved self-titled album for Bearsville, and Hudson finished constructing his Woodstock home in between various session appearances. Only Manuel seemed at loose ends, and as the year dragged on, his lack of motivation was compounded by his increasing drug and alcohol abuse. Unlike most of the others, the adjustment to life off the road came hard for Manuel. His wife, former Toronto model Jane Kristianson, whom he married shortly after the release of *The Band*, had by this time left Woodstock, taking their two children, Joshua and Paula, with her. Manuel subsequently invited his friend, destitute cult-hero writer Mason Hoffenberg, to move in, and together they proceeded to fend off their shared heroin habits through constant drinking.

When a writer for *Playboy* tracked Hoffenberg down for a profile, he unintentionally got a full view of the squalor in which the pair lived. Hoffenberg said, "I'm supposed to head off all the juvenile dope dealers up here who hang around rock stars. So I answer the phone and say Richard's not here. He's not allowed to answer the phone. And I go around privately and tell them to leave him alone because he's really going to kill himself. But if they actually come over to the house, he can't say no. He's brilliant, that guy, an incredible composer. But we just sit around watching *The Dating Game*, slurping down the juice, laughing our asses off, then having insomnia, waking up at dawn with every weird terror and anxiety you can imagine. The four other guys in The Band are serious about working, and he's really hanging them up. They can't work without him, and there's no way to get him off his ass. He feels bad about it, he's just strung out."

No one has ever been willing to admit that the idea to make an album of vintage rock and roll and R & B covers was a blatant attempt to throw Manuel a lifeline, but when the band members decided to follow this path in early 1973, their choice of material largely put him front and centre. And when given the chance to sing, Manuel didn't let the others down, turning in remarkable performances of Lee Dorsey's "Holy Cow" (a nod to Toussaint, as well), "Share Your Love" (the Bobby Blue Bland song he'd sung since the early Hawks days), the slightly ironic Leiber-Stoller faux-gospel number "Saved," and the all-too-appropriate Platters standard "The Great Pretender." However, nothing else about the *Moondog Matinee* sessions, named in honour of Alan Freed's first rock and roll radio show, out of

Cleveland, suggested The Band was exerting much of an effort beyond putting out a long-overdue new record and indulging in a few novelties like "Third Man Theme" and a radically rearranged version of the early Elvis Presley hit "Mystery Train." The album was in the can by June, just ahead of The Band's promised appearance at a massive outdoor festival in Watkins Glen, New York, along with The Grateful Dead and The Allman Brothers Band. With only three performers, the scale was intended to be much smaller than the Woodstock festival, but even more people somehow managed to find their way onto the grounds on that July 28 weekend.

Aside from setting a new concert attendance record, Watkins Glen wasn't notable for much beyond a nice payday, and for Hudson conducting the elements as he played solo through a rainstorm that briefly stopped the show. A few days later, all three groups did it again with two concerts at Roosevelt Stadium in Jersey City, New Jersey, with similarly unspectacular results. With no new material ready to record, The Band was suddenly faced with the bleak prospect of touring on the strength of their reputation alone in order to survive, especially since — like Dylan — they had severed business ties with Grossman. "[Albert] was burnt out and heartbroken," Peter Yarrow said shortly after Grossman's death on January 25, 1986, the result of heart failure while on a transatlantic Concorde flight. "He didn't want to, and couldn't any longer, do the job. But there was an additional element of adolescent rebellion on the part of some of his artists, as well, as history was forgotten and they symbolically broke with their parents by breaking with him."

The split left Robertson in a position to be easily seduced by David Geffen's offer to reunite with Dylan, and he didn't hesitate to move to the west coast to seal the deal following his fateful vacation to Paris with Joni Mitchell. Because The Band still owed Capitol several records, Geffen's focus was entirely on signing Dylan to a long-term deal, although, with The Band on board as support and Bill Graham handling the tour preparations, he insisted that everyone would make truckloads of money. Robertson duly introduced Geffen to Dylan, who cautiously agreed to a one album/one tour plan. It then became Robertson's task to get the rest of The Band together. By November 1973, they were set up in L.A. to record an album nobody seemed prepared to make.

So much emphasis was being placed on the sold-out tour, scheduled to play forty dates in twenty-one cities across North America from January 3 to February 14, that Dylan and The Band knocked out *Planet Waves* in three days amid marathon rehearsals, with many of the new songs composed in the studio, and one, "Forever Young," presented in two vastly different arrangements. "It went by so quick," Robertson said of the sessions. "I mean, *Planet Waves* was as good as we could make it in the situation. Bob really didn't have a bag of songs there, so it was just kind of a last-minute thing, and under those circumstances, I thought that it was extraordinary. There were a lot of simple songs on that album, and people don't necessarily want to hear very simple songs from him. But I really enjoyed that album, we had a lot of fun doing it. Anything you do that fast is really rewarding, I guess."

However, Robertson was not about to concur that the tour itself was just as easy. Even though Graham provided every necessity, including a converted 707 similar to those then being used by Led Zeppelin and Elton John, The Band's separate sets during the course of the evening were often received as distractions from the main event — Dylan. "It was hard work, just the intensity of the music was so high that it was really straining," Robertson added. "Whenever Bob sings with The Band he wants to get an energy level out of it. I mean, we can certainly do that, but we can do a bunch of other things, too, and we didn't get to that. I think that his anticipation and nervousness on that tour didn't allow for any laid-back stuff and we do lots of that. We didn't do any of that on Tour '74, it was really like a train going by, and I missed all those different moods."

The many who were unable to witness that energy were able to experience it when Dylan agreed to release *Before the Flood* — largely recorded during the tour's final stop in L.A. — on Asylum that July.

However, having had a taste of how Geffen's California regime operated, Dylan opted to return to the security of Columbia Records, and spent the rest of the year working on the songs that would become *Blood on the Tracks*, along with building an opulent Malibu home. Robertson was keeping his eye on the local real-estate market as well, and stumbled upon what he immediately perceived could be Big Pink West, a dilapidated bordello near Zuma Beach called Shangri-La. The ambience of the place alone was the perfect reflection of the shadowy lives that many in the L.A. music community lived at the time. As soon as The Band refurbished the building, with a twenty-four-track recording studio at its heart, Shangri-La became a common hangout for Dylan, Neil Young, Eric Clapton, the ubiquitous Ron Wood, and other close associates of the group. For some, like Danko and Manuel, the change of scenery only meant that the party carried on at a new location. Manuel, in fact, lived in an adjoining building on the Shangri-La grounds, where his drinking reached terrifying levels.

For Robertson, the return of the clubhouse atmosphere provided the impetus to write, which had been missing for much of the past few years. Over the course of several months, the songs were recorded as they came, a much more daunting process than ever before, while in between Robertson produced records at Shangri-La for Neil Diamond and an eccentric L.A. singer-songwriter named Hirth Martinez, who came highly recommended by Dylan. The decision was also made, spontaneously it seems, to release *The Basement Tapes*, a project that Robertson readily took up. The double album that hit stores in June 1975 was far from a definitive collection (several tracks of The Band on their own were *Big Pink* demos, and Robertson even added some guitar overdubs), but it received glowing reviews and satisfied the curiosity of fans, at least until the digital age, when bootleggers issued the complete tapes on CD.

Yet somehow all of these projects only pushed Robertson harder to make what became *Northern Lights–Southern Cross* an undeniable rekindling of The Band's trademark musical fire. A sense of rebirth was evident right from the opening track, "Forbidden Fruit," a thinly veiled reference to the group's drug use that showed them swinging in top form. The same could be said of the heavily New Orleans–infused "Ophelia," on which Helm turned in another fine, lascivious vocal. Hudson shone throughout, approaching every song as he had on the first two albums, with an ear to providing subtle but stunning sonic backdrops through a myriad of previously unheard keyboard effects. But the album's greatness rested on two expansive compositions. On the surface, "It Makes No Difference" was just a simple country ballad, but once sung by Danko it revealed bottomless depths of sorrow. It would come to be regarded as one of the finest vocal performances in all of rock and roll history, and, along with "Stage Fright," define his role as The Band's naive romantic, as opposed to Manuel's image as the hard-bitten loser. The other track was "Acadian Driftwood," an ambitious attempt to condense the story of the expulsion of the French from the Maritimes following the decisive British victory on the Plains of Abraham in 1759. Robertson had been interested in this crucial event in Canadian history since watching a television documentary about it a few years earlier in Montreal, and became even more fascinated when he realized that many of these refugees ended up in Louisiana, where they made crucial contributions to the state's unique culture. Robertson went to great pains to be historically accurate, as with "The Night They Drove Old Dixie Down," and the song contained many parallels with the present, in this case Robertson's own search for a culture to which he could connect. In this way, "Acadian Driftwood" was also the first real "Canadian" song he had ever successfully written. As Robertson explained in 1971, "There's no Canadian music. I mean, we did a song called 'Rag Mama Rag,' and there's a combination of some kind of music from Canada where they would use a tuba and an accordion, and we were reflecting a little bit of that. We do it instrument-wise rather than song-wise. There is no music that you can say, 'Oh, that's Canadian' — know what I mean? It's North American music — different countries, but you hear the exact same music, from blues to cowboy. So rather than talking about Calgary or Montreal, we talked about places that we'd played in."

Northern Lights–Southern Cross was released late in 1975 to generally positive reviews but disappointing sales. The question of a tour inevitably arose, and for the sake of supporting what they all agreed was an excellent album, The Band took to the road again, starting with a concert on June 26, 1976, at Stanford University. It was their first group appearance since a few forgettable opening sets on the massive Crosby, Stills, Nash & Young tour two summers earlier. The new material reinvigorated their performances, but the big question mark remained Manuel's physical state. Still despondent over his failed marriage, he had renewed ties with Cathy Evelyn Smith and coaxed her to come to Malibu to help him get through rehearsals for the tour. The others were understandably wary of her sudden reappearance in their lives, and assumed it would only be temporary, but as the first date approached, Manuel insisted that he wouldn't do the tour unless Smith came along as his "nurse." Everything proceeded more or less as planned until early September when, during a day off in Texas, Manuel injured his neck in a boating accident, forcing the cancellation of ten shows. It was during this layoff that Robertson had an epiphany.

"It is heartbreaking to see people you care about abusing themselves," he said. "I'm no saint, but I could never take it to the degree that other people could. It's just that our ideals and philosophies strayed. I just became more productive. And, eventually, I saw there was nothing I could really do about it, or wanted to. You don't want to run someone's life — these were my friends, my brothers. The best thing you can do is to walk away.

"So I told everybody I wasn't interested in going on the road anymore. I'm off the bus. I told them I was sick of [staying at] Howard Johnson's in the middle of nowhere, that I had nothing to learn anymore. And everyone said, 'Me too, me too.' Everyone really felt that way too. But we weren't breaking up, we said we'd still record, we'd write, we'd do projects. It's only later on that I think it sunk in. Everyone said, 'Well gee, does this mean that we'll never, ever do this again?' So I said, 'Yes, yes, *this* is what we've been talking about."

Once Manuel was well enough to resume the tour, there were only two more scheduled shows left, September 17 in Philadelphia, and the following night at the Palladium in New York. Both were edgy affairs, with everyone on stage keeping a close eye on the piano player. On October 19, *L.A. Times* music critic Robert Hilburn was the first to report that plans for a "farewell concert" were in motion for November 25, American Thanksgiving. On October 30, that news was broadcast nation-wide when The Band made a much-trumpeted appearance on *Saturday Night Live* (coincidentally, Chevy Chase's final show as a cast member), performing "Life Is a Carnival," "Stage Fright," and "Dixie," as well as Manuel's unsteady rendition of "Georgia on My Mind." This last song was specifically chosen as a show of support for presidential candidate Jimmy Carter, who would go on to win the election three days later. According to Smith, who remained at Manuel's side, he had mistakenly snorted heroin prior to going on the air. "Richard was splayed out in an armchair, the skin on his face ashen, his eyes rolled back and staring whitely at the ceiling. When the house doctor arrived, he gave Richard a shot to counteract the heroin. The doctor's shot may have saved his life, but it didn't exactly restore him to normalcy. As soon as he was well enough to move, he leaned over and threw up. [He] was sick to his stomach more or less continuously for the next forty-eight hours."

Undaunted, Robertson pushed ahead with preparations for the farewell concert. Bill Graham suggested that a logical loca-tion would be Winterland, the site of their first concert, and from there discussions shifted to inviting Dylan and Ronnie Hawkins to participate. But once that suggestion was raised, the list of friends potentially able to perform soon expanded to include Eric Clapton, Van Morrison, Neil Young, Dr. John, Paul Butterfield, Joni Mitchell, and Bobby Charles, along with John Simon and the *Rock of Ages* horn section. Robertson and Helm argued about adding Neil Diamond and Muddy Waters, the latter of whom Helm had just produced, and both ended up getting their way. By early November, all restrictions surrounding The Last Waltz, as it was called, were cast to the wind. As Graham organized a Thanksgiving feast for the audience, Robertson pondered how to document the event. A live recording was a given, but to do something visually Robertson went out on a limb and contacted director Martin Scorsese, whose early triumph *Mean Streets* (produced by The Band's former road manager, Jonathan Taplin) defied convention by spending a large chunk of its budget licensing songs by The Rolling Stones and Eric Clapton, which Scorsese subsequently utilized to full extent on the soundtrack. "I could tell that he had a very special knack for music," Robertson says. "He had worked on the Woodstock film. The way that he used music in his films, to me, it was above and beyond what I could see other filmmakers doing. And I was somewhat sensitive to that, too, of just how music was used in films. I was always fascinated by that. And so, when it came time to figure out who would be 'the man' who could figure out how to get this on film and capture this whole thing, he was my first choice, and actually, my only choice."

Although Scorsese was being lauded that year for *Taxi Driver*, he was immersed in assembling his next project, the uncharacteristically lavish 1940s-era musical *New York, New York*, a process hampered further by his drug-fuelled affair with co-star Liza Minnelli. But when Robertson's call came, the director couldn't turn down this once-in-a-lifetime opportunity to live out his rock and roll fantasies. Scorsese quickly assembled a two-hundred-page script for the multi-camera shoot, which would be manned by some of the most respected cinematographers in the world, and also dressed the stage with the set of the San Francisco Opera Company's production of *La Traviata*. Robertson revelled in the splendour, and in simply being around Scorsese. Others in the group immediately recognized similarities to how the guitarist had attached himself to Dylan ten years earlier, but remained focused on the music rather than the overall production. The fact was, it was all they could do.

The concert was a success overall, although many out-of-tune parts needed to be corrected during post-production, which lasted throughout the next year.★ However, the mutual attraction that had brought Robertson and Scorsese together would go on to shape the film into something no one was prepared for. Predominantly, it was Robertson who, upon realizing that Scorsese was someone who could stimulate him creatively as Dylan once did, suddenly saw that the film could give him the power to construct a mythology around the group —and himself — in much the same way as he had done with historical subjects in his songs.

Scorsese, being merely a fan with a desire to make a groundbreaking film, ate up Robertson's ideas with a spoon, and gave little thought to anyone else's input. The most crucial of these ideas was the inclusion of interview segments to provide context to the performances, as well as give the film a loose narrative structure. However, instead of having someone with a critical knowledge of The Band conduct the interviews, Robertson gave the task to Scorsese, a calculated move that essentially put the guitarist in total control of the group's story. The pair also decided to film two set pieces after the fact, one with Emmylou Harris, who was unable to appear at the concert, and a dramatic version of "The Weight" with the Staple Singers, both of which fit seamlessly into the reverential tone the film had taken on. Indeed, most viewers were awed by the confidence and magnetism Robertson exuded during his ample screen time, although those who knew the group also recognized that it was coming at the expense of the others.

But Robertson, as he had always done since he determined to play with Ronnie Hawkins, had seen his chance and taken it, and was no longer feeling responsible for keeping whatever was left of The Band together. "It was a crazy period," Robertson said of the year he and Scorsese lived together in Hollywood while finishing *The Last Waltz*. "Marty and I were the 'misunderstood artists,' and

---

★The Band also completed a final contractual album for Capitol, the odds-and-sods (and roundly ignored) *Islands*, released in March 1977 in order to secure the rights to the three-album soundtrack to *The Last Waltz* for the film's financier, Warner Brothers.

our wives threw us out. We were just kind of lost in the storm and we ran amok. There was a magazine article that said something like, 'I went to Martin Scorsese's house. He and Robbie Robertson are having these wild parties with women and drugs that make Hugh Hefner's place look like kindergarten.' So Marty sees this and goes crazy. He starts breaking glasses, smashing things, talking with lawyers, ripping phones out. He says, 'Look at this! Read it! I'm suing these people!' And I looked at it and I said, 'Marty, the only thing inaccurate here is that we don't live in Bel Air.'"

On the strength of *The Last Waltz*, Robertson did get to star in a feature, an appropriate role as a midway hustler in 1980's *Carney*, before assuming a regular job as Scorsese's musical consultant.★ He also resumed his family life, along with a sporadic solo career. But Robertson kept his word, even as the rest of The Band was forced to regroup in 1983 for financial reasons. Without Robertson's guiding presence, they were relegated to the nostalgia touring circuit, a circumstance that proved too much for Manuel, who committed suicide following a show in Winter Park, Florida, on March 4, 1986.

"One day in the early eighties I got a call from Levon," Harold Kudlats remembers. "I guess he was in Toronto putting some finishing touches on the music for *Coal Miner's Daughter*. We met upstairs at the old Friar's Tavern and he started to tell me what had been happening. I'd assumed that every member of the group were multi-millionaires, and when he told me the actual financial condition they were all in, it was sickening. At that time business was slow, so when he asked me to book him again, I agreed, and after a while we got the brainwave to get everyone back together because everybody had such financial problems. So we salvaged the old Band and we were doing

---

★Robertson's later influence on Scorsese was apparent in more subtle ways, as well, mainly whenever the film in question portrayed a scrappy street kid trying to make a name for himself. In fact, after several viewings, Ray Liotta's performance in *Goodfellas* starts to eerily evoke Robertson's monologues in *The Last Waltz*.

good, we were getting top dollar. But when we did the last tour of Japan, my wife came down sick and I quit the road. Before that, I remember taking Richard to a music store in Washington, where I bought him a new portable piano. He was happier than hell. After I quit, my wife and I were in Florida when I heard he'd hung himself, and I found out later that the guy who was handling them then wouldn't let them travel with their own instruments. I said to my wife, 'I bet that's one of the reasons, amongst others, that he decided there was no use going on.'

"But to tell you the truth, I never knew that these boys were into drugs, and yet I was with them for twenty-five or thirty years. At the time I blamed it on the piano bit, but then I found out that that was maybe just part of it. Even when The Band got back together, there wasn't a city that they went into where someone didn't come up and offer everyone, including me, whatever I wanted. Of course, I never touched the stuff, but it was always available."

Yet, just like the content of the songs, the music itself somehow acquired the importance of history in how it continued to inspire successive generations of musicians to put songs before solos, feeling before perfection, and, above all, group loyalty before fame. Garth Hudson, who got through it all without a hint of complaint, summed it up best in 2005 upon the release of the comprehensive box set *A Musical History*. "The material is still good, so I wanted to emphasize that, rather than how some of us had too much fun from time to time in our personal lives. What was most important to me was that we preserved the sense of family that we all shared growing up in Canada."

DISCOGRAPHY

Caveat: For nearly all of the artists discussed in this book, the CD era brought with it myriad attempts to compile "complete" or "definitive" collections of their work. While in some cases this has been accomplished, this section will try to focus on releases that remain essential on their own, and will hopefully provide the most value for the unfamiliar listener.

WILF CARTER

Carter recorded as many as seventy-five "sides" (songs) for RCA-Victor (and its Bluebird subsidiary) up until the 1940 car accident that set him back for most of the war years. These ranged from his trademark yodels to topical subjects like the Hindenburg disaster and infamous bank robber John Dillinger. The company's 1941 catalogue lists thirty-three of his records available to order, although by then virtually all of them were western-themed, given the popularity of singing cowboys. His return to full-time performing brought with it a reissuing of almost everything he had recorded, which was a further reflection of Carter's unparalleled popularity at that moment.

However, it would not be until this material starting appearing on LPs in the early sixties that Carter would once again see such sales figures. The first of these LPs have everything most would want: *Wilf Carter/Montana Slim* (RCA-Camden, 1962) contains a standard sampling of favourites, among them "There's a Love Knot in My Lariat," "It Makes No Difference Now," and "You Are My Sunshine." The next release, *Reminiscin' With Wilf Carter* (U.S. title: *Reminiscin' With Montana Slim*) (RCA-Camden, 1963) has aged slightly better due to the inclusion of his first recording, "My Swiss Moonlight Lullaby," "The Fate of the Old Strawberry Roan," "(There's a) Bluebird on Your Windowsill," and "The Blue Canadian Rockies." From there, RCA's repackaging of the old songs continued unabated. Those wanting nearly all of the RCA recordings can seek out the eight-CD set *Cowboy Songs* (Bear Family, 1997).

Carter's stint with Decca in the mid-fifties, which saw him working in Nashville with renowned producer Owen Bradley, is compiled on the thirty-track CD *The Dynamite Trail: The Decca Years* (Bear Family, 1990). Here, Carter's traditional sound is accentuated by the work of session stars like Chet Atkins and Buddy Emmons, with an occasional passing nod to rock and roll. Following that period, Carter recorded sporadically and licensed the material for such releases as *Songs of the Calgary Stampede* (Apex, 1964). The most convenient way to find these selections is on the four-CD *A Prairie Legend* (Bear Family, 1999), which also includes the balance of his post-accident RCA sessions. The most obscure item from this period appears to be the *Living Legend* album, recorded for Nashville label Starday in 1965. It is notable mostly for the new composition "Grandad's Yodelling Song," written to mark the birth of Carter's first grandchild. Carter's last major release was the album *Have a Nice Day*, issued by RCA in 1976, although it has been out of print since. His final original recording was the cassette-only *That's the Bottom Line*, issued on his approval through his booking agency, Rocklands Entertainment, just prior to his death.

HANK SNOW

With his unmatched forty-five-year relationship with RCA, the sheer amount of Hank Snow product is staggering, especially given that once he had the chance to record, Snow took the demands of the marketplace extremely seriously. The easiest point of entry is *The Best of Hank Snow* (RCA-Victor, 1965) — RCA's *The Essential* (1997) is the CD version — which marks the peak of his career. Almost identical is *Souvenirs* (RCA-Victor, 1961), a worthy attempt to re-record his best-loved early American singles. Better still, though (if it can be found), is *Country Classics* (RCA-Victor, 1956), containing the original versions of "I'm Moving On," "I Don't Hurt Anymore," "A Fool Such As I," "The Rhumba Boogie," "The Golden Rocket," and others. Released at the height of the rockabilly revolution, Snow doesn't sound far off with his approach on these takes.

Also mandatory is *The Old and Great Songs* (RCA-Camden, 1964), the first LP collection of Snow's most successful Canadian recordings dating back to 1937's "The Blue Velvet Band." Also containing the original take of "Brand on My Heart," these songs reveal that Snow and Hank Williams were clearly on the same path. However, following his U.S. breakthrough, Snow covered a lot of territory with his many themed albums. Of these, *When Tragedy Struck* (RCA-Victor, 1958) and *Sings Jimmie Rodgers Songs* (RCA-Victor, 1960) hold up the best, but his love for train songs almost always yielded interesting results, as well — see *Railroad Man* (RCA-Victor, 1963). Canadian fans also welcomed the release of *My Nova Scotia Home* (RCA-Camden, 1968), notable for the title track and the Maritime favourite "Squid Jiggin' Ground."

By the end of the sixties, Snow was largely confined to the margins, and the ensuing decade produced little that added to his legacy, apart from his last number-one hit, "Hello Love," available on *Hello Love* (RCA-Victor, 1974) which made him (at that point) the oldest artist to have a chart-topping single. It also gave him the distinction of having the longest number-one hit-spanning period (twenty-four years). He continued to make records for RCA until an acrimonious split in 1981 over unpaid royalties, although the collaboration with Willie Nelson on *Brand on My Heart* (Columbia, 1985) allowed Snow to bow out of his recording career gracefully. As might be expected, Bear Family has gone to great lengths to provide the full overview of Snow's work, with its extensive four-volume, twenty-nine-CD *Singing*

Ranger collection, its five-CD *Yodelling Ranger* companion set, along with several other boxed collections.

Among the many covers of "I'm Moving On," the most notable are by Ray Charles (*The Birth of Soul 1952–1959*, Atlantic, 1991), The Rolling Stones (*December's Children*, London, 1965, reissued by ABKCO, 2002), Elvis Presley (*From Elvis in Memphis*, RCA, 1969, also *From Nashville to Memphis: The Essential '60s Masters*, RCA, 1993), and Johnny Cash (*Unearthed*, American, 2003).

Snow's son Jimmie's rare single "It Won't Do No Good" b/w "Milk Cow Blues" (RCA, 1956), done just before he realized that rock and roll was the devil's music, can be heard on *That'll Flat Git It, Vol. 1* (Bear Family, 1993).

BOB NOLAN & THE SONS OF THE PIONEERS

In their first two years with Decca, The Sons of the Pioneers recorded thirty-two songs, a good chunk of them Nolan originals like "Tumbling Tumbleweeds," "Cool Water," and "Way Out There." In 1937, they moved to Columbia, where they recorded a further thirty-two sides that were also the last to feature Leonard Slye before he became Roy Rogers, America's favourite cowboy. In 1941 they signed their own movie deal with Republic Pictures, and were billed as Bob Nolan & The Sons of the Pioneers. In 1944 they signed with RCA and focused solely on music. With the label persuading them to expand their sound, this period produced many of their best recordings, such as the immortal "Ghost Riders in the Sky."

Although Nolan left the group in 1949, the group carried on for the next several decades — often re-recording the same material ad nauseum — making it a challenge to search out versions of Nolan singing his own songs. A safe bet is *Tumbling Tumbleweeds* (MCA, 1987, reissued 1995) containing the classic Decca hits. *Columbia Historic Edition* (Sony, 1988, reissued 1990) offers seven more little-known Nolan songs, while *RCA Country Legends: Sons of the Pioneers* (RCA/BMG, 2004) provides a good sampling of their work with that label. Of further interest is *Symphonies of the Sage* (Bloodshot, 2001), which compiles radio transcription recordings made in Chicago in 1940. Completists will once again want to turn to the Bear Family box sets *Songs of the Prairie* and *Memories of the Range.*

Nolan's only widely known post-retirement recording is *The Sound of a Pioneer* (Elektra, 1979), made at the urging of his close friend, producer Tommy "Snuff" Garrett, two years before Nolan's death. Although it contains new versions of "Tumbleweeds" and "Cool Water," Nolan was free to choose the rest of the songs, and turned in fine renditions of Billy Joe Shaver's "Ride Me Down Easy," and Marty Robbins' "Man Walks Among Us."

Covers of "Tumbleweeds" and "Cool Water" by others are too numerous to mention, although Robbins' take on the latter on his *Gunfighter Ballads & Trail Songs* (Columbia, 1959) is as close to a definitive version as any.

RONNIE HAWKINS ET AL.

For someone whose career stretches over fifty years, it's incredible that there is barely enough material to fill up the only necessary release bearing his name, *The Best of Ronnie Hawkins and the Hawks* (Rhino, 1990). This is simply because, while some artists are ahead of their time, Hawkins was undeniably of his time — a painful fact that sank in far too late. This collection is virtually the same as the live show he put on since the early sixties, but for all of Hawkins' obvious musical shortcomings, the material continues to prove (partly through his own stubbornness to keep playing it) that he could indeed hold his own with any of his rockabilly peers.

Hawkins certainly was the real deal compared to attempts by native Canadians to produce rockabilly. *Shakin' Up North* (Bear Family, 1997) is a fascinating collection of little-known tracks of the time by the likes of future Motown songwriter and solo artist R. Dean Taylor and pianist-turned-politician Ray St. Germain. The deliberately toned-down approach they all shared makes the sound that Hawkins and his (mostly) all-Canadian Hawks achieved on the 1963 version of "Who Do You Love" even more terrifying. Some of Hawkins' lesser-known recordings prior to this can be found on the British releases *The Roulette Years* (Sequel, 1994), and the hard-to-find LP *RRRacket Time* (Charly, 1979), which contains the 1958 Quality Records release of "Hey Bo Diddley." The two 1961 Paul London and the Capers/Kapers singles featuring Garth Hudson have not been reissued on any compilation to this point.

In 1964, Hawkins created his own Hawk label to put his records out in Canada. During its five-year run, it also released singles by up-and-coming Canadian bands such as Robbie Lane & The Disciples, and Buddy Carlton & The Stratones. Unfortunately, Hawkins's own sales during that time couldn't keep the company going, despite much fanfare surrounding a U.S. deal with Atlantic that resulted in the albums *Ronnie Hawkins* (Cotillion, 1970) and *The Hawk* (Cotillion, 1971), both recorded in Muscle Shoals, Alabama, with a band that included Duane Allman. Hawkins took one final shot with Monument Records, churning out *Rock 'n' Roll Resurrection* (Monument, 1972) and *Giant of Rock 'n' Roll* (Monument, 1974), before ultimately living off his legend.

It proved to be a savvy move, leading to film roles — notably *Heaven's Gate* and, to a lesser degree, Bob Dylan's *Renaldo and Clara* — along with periodic high-profile concerts that reaffirmed his place as Canada's torchbearer for rock and roll. Always good for a quote, Hawkins was never far from the media spotlight, and drew more attention in 2004 than he had in years when he claimed that a bout with cancer was cured by a teenaged mystical healer from Vancouver. As it has always been, in Ronnie Hawkins' world, anything is possible.

The best Dale Hawkins compilation available is undoubtedly the thirty-track *Rock 'n' Roll Tornado* (Ace, 1998), while the rockabilly side of Conway Twitty can be heard on *The Best of Conway Twitty Vol. 1: The Rockin' Years* (Polygram Country, 1991), which compiles his Mercury recordings along with "It's Only Make Believe" and other early MGM hits. The consistently wide-ranging work of Jack Scott is collected on the five-CD *Classic Scott* (Bear Family, 1993), with a sufficient single-disc alternative being *The Best of Jack Scott 1957–60* (Stardust, 1995).

Robbie Robertson's guitar mentor, Roy Buchanan, remained a well-kept secret for most of the sixties after leaving The Hawks, rarely venturing outside of the club scene in his home state of Maryland. But by 1970, his legend had grown to the point where rumours circulated that he had turned down offers to join The Rolling Stones and Derek and the Dominos. The following year, he finally embarked on a widely varied solo recording career that, sadly, never lived up to his abilities. All the best moments from it (aside from his last three albums in the 1980s for Chicago blues label Alligator) are on *Sweet Dreams: The Anthology* (Polydor, 1992). The title track, Buchanan's stunning instrumental interpretation of the Patsy Cline standard, is also heard to great effect over the closing credits of Martin Scorsese's 2006 Oscar-winning film *The Departed*.

IAN & SYLVIA

The Complete Vanguard Studio Recordings (Vanguard, 2001) is a convenient four-CD set of all seven albums the duo made for the label, although the twenty-five-track *The Best of the Vanguard Years* (Vanguard, 1998) is a more affordable option. Their two albums for MGM, *Lovin' Sound* and *Full Circle*, can be heard together on *Movin' On* (Mercury, 1999). Of the two albums for Columbia, only 1971's *Ian & Sylvia* has been officially issued on CD, though under the misleading title *The Beginning of the End* (Bear Family, 1996), which adds four previously unreleased tracks. Also of note is *Live at Newport* (Vanguard, 1996), a fine sampling of the couple's performances at the festival in 1963 and 1965, some of which had previously appeared on earlier Newport compilation LPs. *Great Speckled Bird* was finally given a proper release in 1994 by Canadian label Stony Plain, with a bonus live take of "New Trucker's Café" from *Nashville North*, but this landmark record still requires a complete overhaul to put it in its rightful context alongside work by The Byrds and The Flying Burrito Brothers.

In 2003, Stony Plain also reissued Ian Tyson's first solo album, *Ol' Eon* (originally A & M, 1973), a more standard country record that was made while he was still regularly seen on television. Nothing further appeared until *One Jump Ahead of the Devil* (Boot, 1979) featuring the modest Canadian hit "Half Mile of Hell." He would not emerge again until *Old Corrals and Sagebrush* (Columbia, 1983), although by then Tyson was fully devoted to keeping the tradition of cowboy songs and cowboy poetry alive. New albums in this style appeared at regular intervals from that point on, and the best of these can be heard on *All the Good 'Uns* (Stony Plain, 1996) or *Live at Longview* (Stony Plain, 2002). Tribute album *The Gift* (Stony Plain, 2007) offers a glimpse of Tyson's contemporary influence on artists like Blue Rodeo, Corb Lund, and Tom Russell. Such a gesture undoubtedly motivated Tyson to record again — at age 75 — resulting in *Yellowhead to Yellowstone and Other Love Stories* (Stony Plain, 2008), an album on which he bravely refused to hide the ravaging effect that time had taken on his voice. This gave the performances even greater emotional depth.

It was Sylvia Tyson who initially had the more productive solo career of the couple, making two albums in quick succession, *Woman's World* (Capitol, 1975) and *Cool Wind From the North* (Capitol, 1976), both produced by Ian. From there, she established her own label and a new band that included a then-unknown guitarist from Hamilton named Daniel Lanois. Two more albums resulted, *Satin on Stone* (Salt, 1978) and *Sugar for Sugar, Salt for Salt* (Salt, 1979), before she took an extended hiatus. An offer from Stony Plain brought Sylvia back for *Big Spotlight* (Stony Plain, 1986) and *You Were on My Mind* (Stony Plain, 1989). Soon after releasing *Gypsy Cadillac* (Sony, 1992), she formed the group Quartette with three other distinguished female Canadian singer-songwriters; this remained her primary musical outlet from then on. *The Very Best Of Sylvia Tyson* (Varese Sarabande, 2001) sufficiently covers her contemporary work.

Of the dozens of renditions of "Four Strong Winds," the best known is still probably Neil Young's, heard on *Comes a Time* (Reprise, 1978), and now on the expanded *The Last Waltz* (Warner, 2002). A poignant version (alongside Gordon Lightfoot's "If You Could Read My Mind") can also be heard on Johnny Cash's final recording, *American V: A Hundred Highways*

(Lost Highway, 2006). The We Five's "You Were on My Mind" is on *Two Classic Albums: You Were on My Mind/Make Someone Happy* (Collector's Choice, 1998) and the box set *Love Is the Song We Sing: San Francisco Nuggets 1965–1970* (Rhino, 2007). Covers of "Someday Soon" by various sixties folk-rock-era artists abound, as well, but one of the most accurate representations of how quickly folk, pop, and country converged during that period is the comprehensive Gene Clark anthology *Flying High* (A & M, 1998), which includes his excellent 1967 take of "The French Girl."

ED MCCURDY, BONNIE DOBSON, ET AL.

Existent pre-war Canadian folk recordings are extremely rare and mostly feature Québecois artists. This only re-emphasizes the relevance of Edith Fowke's groundbreaking work, including *Folk Songs of Canada* (1954) and *Canada's Story in Song* (1960). These, along with the rest of Fowke's legacy, are readily available in most libraries. Sam Gesser's efforts for Folkways are best heard on *Classic Canadian Songs* (Smithsonian Folkways, 2006), which includes recordings by Alan Mills, Karen James, and Jean Carignan of such material as "Un Canadien Errant," "When the Ice Worms Nest Again," and "Anti-Confederation Song." Complementing this release is The Travellers' *This Land Is Your Land 1960–1966* (Sony, 2004), which displays the pioneering Canadian folk group's Weavers-esque approach to homegrown songs, as well as folk-revival standards.

Ed McCurdy's history has been partly preserved by Warner/ Elektra Records, which reissued some of his varied releases. Although all of them remain hopelessly dated, *The Best of Dalliance* (Elektra, 2003) possesses a unique charm in terms of McCurdy's penchant for sexually risqué material. His work with more standard forms can be found on *A Ballad Singer's Choice: The Traditional Years* (Empire, 2006). "Last Night I Had the Strangest Dream" is most easily found on Simon and Garfunkel's *Wednesday Morning, 3 A.M.* (Columbia, 1964), although other versions from that period are common.

Similarly, while covers of Bonnie Dobson's "Morning Dew"

remain plentiful, hearing her actually sing it requires some searching. *Bonnie Dobson at Folk City* (Prestige, 1962), the album on which it first appeared, has long been out of print. However, this version can be found on the varied compilation *The Music Never Stopped: Roots of the Grateful Dead* (Shanachie, 1995), and also the five-CD set *The Best of Broadside: 1962–1988* (Smithsonian Folkways, 2000). *Bonnie Dobson* (Nimbus 9/RCA, 1969), containing a fully fleshed-out "Morning Dew," is easily her best album, and has, thankfully, been reissued by U.K. label Rev-Ola, along with its weaker follow-up *Good Morning Rain* (RCA, 1970). She recorded the song once more for her last official album, the U.K.-only release Morning Dew (Polydor, 1976). Fred Neil's "Morning Dew" is on the combined edition of *Tear Down the Walls/Bleecker & MacDougal* (WEA International, 2001). Perhaps the most underrated figure of the Greenwich Village scene, the bulk of Neil's excellent non-Elektra catalogue is gathered on *The Many Sides of Fred Neil* (Collector's Choice, 1998). Tim Rose's 1967 "Morning Dew" (as well as his "Hey Joe," which he always claimed Jimi Hendrix copied) is available on *Tim Rose/Through Rose Colored Glasses* (Beat Goes On, 1998), which couples his two Columbia albums.

BUFFY SAINTE-MARIE
The Best of the Vanguard Years (Vanguard, 2003) is a reissue of 1970's *The Best of Buffy Sainte-Marie* that adds two tracks ("Bird on the Wire," "God Bless the Child") from an aborted live album from Carnegie Hall. This release is augmented by *Up Where We Belong* (EMI Canada, 1996), which presents the best of her contemporary material with new recordings of older songs. *Performance* (Warner Brothers, 1970, reissued 1991) remains one of the essential film soundtracks, and Sainte-Marie's tracks exemplify producer Jack Nitzsche's paranoiac vision at the time.

Her relationship with Nitzsche is also briefly explored on *Hearing Is Believing: The Jack Nitzsche Story 1962–1979* (Ace, 2005), containing "Helpless," backed by Neil Young & Crazy Horse, originally released on *She Used to Wanna Be a Ballerina* (Vanguard, 1971). Donovan's "Co'dine" and "Universal Soldier" can both be found on his two-CD *Troubadour: The Definitive Collection 1964–1976* (Sony, 1992). Quicksilver Messenger Service's hard-rock version of "Co'dine" is on the two-CD anthology *Sons of Mercury 1968–1975* (Rhino, 1991) and the aforementioned *Love Is the Song We Sing* box set. Elvis Presley's "Until It's Time for You to Go" is on *Elvis Now* (RCA, 1972) or the five-CD *Walk a Mile in My Shoes: The Essential '70s Masters* (RCA, 1995).

DENNY DOHERTY AND ZAL YANOVSKY

The two albums by Doherty's first group have been compiled on *The Complete Halifax Three* (Collector's Choice, 2002), with minimal bonus tracks. The much-ballyhooed sessions with The Mugwumps came next, and were belatedly released as *An Historic Recording* (Warner Brothers, 1967, reissued by Collector's Choice, 2007). Although the short-lived group also included Yanovsky and Cass Elliott, the material is demo quality at best. Other early group efforts are found on *The Magic Circle: Before They Were The Mamas and the Papas* (Varese Vintage, 1999). The standard M & P compilation is still the two-CD *Creeque Alley: A History of The Mamas and the Papas* (Teldec, 1991), although several more condensed best-of albums have appeared since, with improved sound.

Likewise, Yanovsky's tenure with The Lovin' Spoonful is most readily heard on the many available compilations of the group. The most comprehensive is probably the twenty-six-track *Greatest Hits* (Buddha, 2000). In 2002, Buddha started reissuing the band's full catalogue with bonus material, beginning with the much-loved albums that feature Yanovsky: *Do You Believe In Magic* (originally Kama Sutra, 1965), *Daydream*, and *Hums of the Lovin' Spoonful* (both originally Kama Sutra, 1966), and, to a lesser extent, the soundtrack to Woody Allen's *What's Up Tiger Lily* (originally Kama Sutra, 1966). However, a worthwhile curiosity from that period is *What's Shakin'* (Elektra, 1966, reissued 1995), which finds the Spoonful busting out some Stones-ish garage rock to keep pace with tracks by The Paul Butterfield Blues Band and The Powerhouse, a recording session that brought Eric Clapton, Jack Bruce, and Steve Winwood together for the first time. Needless to say, Yanovsky asserts himself on lead guitar extremely well in the face of this stiff competition. Then again, Clapton has never hidden the fact that he lifted the distinctive descending chord progression for Cream's "Tales of Brave Ulysses" directly from the similar one in the Spoonful's "Summer in the City."

Doherty released only two solo albums, *Whatcha Gonna Do* (ABC-Dunhill, 1971) and *Waiting For A Song* (Ember, Canada/U.K. only, 1974, reissued on Varese Sarabande, 2001) before devoting most of his time to keeping The Mamas and the Papas' name alive on the oldies touring circuit. His last release was *Dream a Little Dream: The Nearly True Story of The Mamas and the Papas* (Lewlacow/CBC, 1999), a pure nostalgia trip interspersed with some of Doherty's always engaging storytelling.

Yanovsky's *Alive and Well in Argentina* (Buddha, 1968), his only solo outing, has taken on much more of a mystique, mainly because it is a landmark slice of unhinged sonic surrealism from an era dominated by studio experimentation. The single "As Long as You're Here," is found on *Hard Workin' Man: The Jack Nitzsche Story Vol. 2* (Ace, 2006). A few years later, Yanovsky quit music for good in favour of running a restaurant in Kingston, Ontario, and making occasional appearances on Canadian television.

GORDON LIGHTFOOT

Like the man himself, Lightfoot's catalogue is orderly and generally accessible, with the exception of his earliest recordings. The Two Tones' *Live at the Village Corner* (Chateau, 1962) has never been issued on CD, and all of his solo singles for Chateau can still only be found on the unauthorized *Early Lightfoot* (AME, 1971). The comprehensive career overview is the four-CD *Songbook* (Warner/Rhino, 1999), which includes "Remember Me (I'm the One)," "It's Too Late, He Wins," and several revealing outtakes such as "Stone Cold Sober."

Still necessary, however, is *The Original Lightfoot: The United Artists Years* (United Artists, 1992), which packages the first five albums. While, for many, this was Lightfoot's most vital period, United Artists' decision to flood stores with cheap compilations after Lightfoot signed with Warner/Reprise prompted him to retaliate with *Gord's Gold* (Reprise, 1975, reissued by Rhino, 2005), a mix of hits from *Sit Down Young Stranger* to *Cold on the Shoulder* and re-recordings of early classics. It still stands as his best-selling North American release. *Gord's Gold 2* (Warner Brothers, 1988, reissued by Rhino, 2005) gathered the best from *Summertime Dream* on, and racked up similarly impressive sales.

Although Lightfoot's post-1976 original output became increasingly sporadic, each album proved to be a minor event in itself, and a model of consistency in the face of prevailing trends. Even *Harmony* (Linus, 2004), made in the aftermath of a near-fatal stomach ailment, showed that Lightfoot's gifts were intact and he was continuing to age gracefully.

Peter, Paul & Mary's "Early Morning Rain" and "For Lovin' Me" are on *The Very Best Of* (Warner/Rhino, 2005), while Marty Robbins's "Ribbon Of Darkness" is on *The Essential* (Sony, 2005). Any George Hamilton IV compilation will include at least one of the many Lightfoot songs he recorded, but worth searching out is his *Lightfoot Country* (U.S. title: *Early Morning Rain*) (RCA, 1970), which contains nearly all of them. Bob Dylan's "Early Morning Rain" is, unfortunately, on the best-forgotten covers album *Dylan* (Columbia, 1973), released out of spite after his temporary defection to Asylum. Elvis Presley's version of the song, along with his "For Lovin' Me," can be heard on *Elvis: A Canadian Tribute* (RCA, 1978, reissued 1999), an intriguing glimpse of his whirlwind 1957 appearances in Toronto, Ottawa, and Vancouver through interviews and press conferences, interspersed with tracks written by Canadians that Presley recorded throughout his career.

Nico's "I'm Not Sayin'" is found on *The Classic Years* (Polydor, 1998) and also *Jimmy Page: Hip Young Guitarslinger* (Castle/Sanctuary, 2000), while The Grateful Dead's primitive 1965 demo of "Early Morning Rain" is on *Birth of the Dead* (Rhino, 2003). For more recent Lightfoot interpretations by the Cowboy Junkies, Ron Sexsmith, and Blue Rodeo, see the excellent Canadian-produced *Beautiful: A Tribute to Gordon Lightfoot*

(Borealis, 2003). As well, The Rheostatics' brilliant update of "The Wreck of the Edmund Fitzgerald" on their landmark *Melville* (DROG, 1991) remains a worthy testament to the song's lasting power. And, of course, the disco version of "If You Could Read My Mind" by Stars on 54 is available on *54: Music From the Motion Picture Vol. 2* (Rhino/Ada, 1998).

LEONARD COHEN

Cohen's first appearance on record, *Six Montreal Poets* (Folkways, 1957), was reissued on CD in 1991, and the eight selections (all from *Let Us Compare Mythologies*) can now also be individually downloaded. Another little-known spoken-word recording is *Canadian Poets 1* (CBC Publications, 1966), featuring seven Cohen poems drawn from his four collections, along with readings by Irving Layton, Earle Birney, and Gwendolyn MacEwen. The 1965 documentary *Ladies And Gentlemen . . . Mr. Leonard Cohen* was released on DVD by the National Film Board of Canada in 1999. The package includes the short films *Angel*, *A Kite Is a Victim*, and *Poen*, made in the mid-sixties. *Angel* is also the most readily available evidence of The Stormy Clovers performing Cohen's songs, although demos by the group remain hidden.

In early 2007, *Songs of Leonard Cohen*, *Songs From a Room*, and *Songs of Love and Hate* were all freshened up with bonus outtakes, making previous CD editions redundant. Of this material, "Store Room" and "Blessed Is the Memory" are early considerations for Cohen's first album, when John Hammond was still producing it, and "Like a Bird" and "Nothing to One" are a snapshot of David Crosby's ultimately discarded groundwork for *Songs From a Room*. *Live Songs* (Columbia, 1973) was intended to accompany the 1972 tour film *Bird on a Wire*, and to possibly be Cohen's last recording. The live atmosphere and spoken passages certainly add an entirely different emotional element, although the thirteen-minute "Please Don't Pass Me By (A Disgrace)" fully encapsulates Cohen's schizophrenic poet/troubadour persona.

However, the next year he was back with *New Skin for the Old Ceremony* (Columbia, 1974), a title that virtually proclaimed the fact that Cohen was struggling to find new things to say musically.

The ironically titled *Greatest Hits* (Columbia, 1975) was well-received, and set the stage for Cohen's next original album, *Death of a Ladies' Man* (Columbia, 1977), a legendary mess produced by Phil Spector in L.A. and featuring a cameo by Bob Dylan. Partly as a reaction, *Recent Songs* (Columbia, 1979) returned to a more traditional sound, but did not garner much attention.

Cohen would not re-emerge until *Various Positions* (Columbia, 1984), an album built on a slick contemporary sound, but also a damaged grandeur that firmly connected with the new generation of disillusioned post-punks. "Hallelujah" became their "Suzanne," and also an imposing challenge to dozens of interpeters from that point on. It is hard to say that anyone has topped Jeff Buckley's version on *Grace* (Columbia, 1994). It also appears on his *Mystery White Boy* as a medley with the Smiths' "I Know It's Over" (Columbia, 2000), and *Live At L'Olympia* (Columbia, 2001). The closest was probably k.d. lang on her all-Canadian covers album *Hymns of the 49th Parallel* (Nonesuch, 2004), but heard even more dramatically in a stunning performance at the 2005 Juno Awards in Winnipeg available on iTunes.

Cohen came back just as strong with *I'm Your Man* (Columbia, 1988), which included further instant standards such as "Tower of Song," "Everybody Knows," "First We Take Manhattan," and "Ain't No Cure for Love." The stylishly grim *The Future* (Columbia, 1992) firmly solidified Cohen's place within the new "alternative music" environment, allowing subsequent releases to take a more toned-down approach.

Covers by Cohen's earliest champion, Judy Collins, are found on *Democracy: Judy Collins Sings Leonard Cohen* (Elektra, 2004), which adds the more recent recordings of the title track, "A Thousand Kisses Deep," and "Night Comes On." The great British vocalist Sandy Denny's takes on "Suzanne" and "Bird on the Wire" are on Fairport Convention's *Heyday: The BBC Sessions 1968–1969 Extended* (Island, 2002), and Joe Cocker's excruciating version of the latter is on *Joe Cocker!* (A & M, 1969) or *Mad Dogs and Englishmen* (A & M, 1970). In a similar vein, part of Cohen's infamous performance at the 1970 Isle of Wight festival is in the BBC documentary *Message to Love* (Castle Video, 1995).

Although Cohen was back in form by the mid-eighties, this renaissance was also partly boosted by his one-time backup singer Jennifer Warnes's widely praised *Famous Blue Raincoat* (BMG, 1987), an album that opened the floodgates for subsequent Cohen tributes. The twentieth anniversary edition, released on Shout Factory, adds four bonus tracks. Other available tributes are *I'm Your Fan* (Atlantic, 1991) featuring some of Cohen's natural offspring, like Nick Cave and Lloyd Cole, and the hopelessly bland *Tower of Song: The Songs of Leonard Cohen* (A & M, 1995). Most riveting is the Hal Willner–organized tribute documentary *I'm Your Man* (Lion's Gate DVD, 2006) with gut-wrenching performances by Cave, Antony Hegarty, Rufus Wainwright, and others.

JONI MITCHELL

Remarkable footage of Mitchell (or Joni Anderson as she was then known) on Oscar Brand's *Let's Sing Out* program, shot at the University of Manitoba in Winnipeg on October 4, 1965, is easily found online, and shows confident performances of the unreleased "Born to Take the Highway," the civil rights–themed "Favourite Colour," John Phillips' "Me & My Uncle" (later a staple of The Grateful Dead), as well as an uncomfortably stilted duet with Brand on "Blow Away the Morning Dew." *A Let's Sing Out* appearance from the following year, probably shot at Laurentian University in Sudbury, Ontario, on October 24, features another unreleased song, "Just Like Me," as well as a chilling "Urge for Going." Stellar coffee-house and radio recordings of much of this material, as well as all of her best early songs from 1967, are found on the long-circulated bootleg *Second Fret Sets*.

By that year, Tom Rush was widely performing Mitchell's material, giving her a formal introduction to U.S. audiences. He later released the acclaimed *The Circle Game* (Elektra, 1968), and both its title track and "Urge for Going" are on *No Regrets: The Very Best of Tom Rush* (Columbia Legacy, 1999). Next came Judy Collins doing "Both Sides, Now" and "Michael From Mountains" on *Wildflowers* (Elektra, 1967). Collins' 1969 "Chelsea Morning" single turned up later on *Living* (Elektra, 1971). Fairport Convention's versions of that song, as well as "I Don't

Know Where I Stand," are on their self-titled debut (Polydor, 1968, reissued on Universal, 2003), and their take of the otherwise unreleased "Eastern Rain" is on *What We Did on Our Holiday* (Island, 1969, reissued on Universal, 2003).

Unlike most of her peers, Mitchell has never seemed concerned about dredging up her past. The arrival of the companion retrospectives *Hits* and *Misses* (both Warner Brothers, 1996) therefore caught many by surprise, but together they accurately reflected the image dilemma Mitchell had faced since she began expanding her musical range with *Court and Spark* (Asylum, 1974). That said, the trio of studio albums that came immediately after — *The Hissing of Summer Lawns* (Asylum, 1975), *Hejira* (Asylum, 1976), and *Don Juan's Reckless Daughter* (Asylum, 1977) — have all received positive critical reassessment and are worth exploring apart from her first six essential albums.

She seemed to find rejuvenation with *Turbulent Indigo* (Warner, 1994). By maintaining a consistent, if less active, creative drive from that point on, Mitchell became one of the most lauded musicians in the world by the turn of the century. It also led her to embrace her past in a way similar to the *Hits/Misses* concept, with the release of *The Beginning of Survival* (Geffen, 2004), a personally selected compilation of her most politically motivated material. This was quickly followed by *Dreamland* (Rhino/WEA, 2004), a more standard collection of favourites, and *Songs of a Prairie Girl* (Elektra/WEA, 2005) comprised of material inspired by her upbringing. On top of that were the symphonic excursions *Both Sides Now* (Warner, 2000) and *Travelogue* (Nonesuch, 2002), both of which displayed her full musical maturity. Mitchell's often challenging eighties material is best sampled on the four-CD *Complete Geffen Recordings* (Geffen, 2003).

Part of Mitchell's emotional performance at the Isle of Wight festival is also included in *Message to Love*. Her official live albums, *Miles of Aisles* (Asylum, 1974) and *Shadows and Light* (Elektra, 1980) are largely for fans of her overt jazz work. Speaking of which, Mitchell's prowess in that field was acknowledged in a most unexpected way when Herbie Hancock won the 2008 Grammy for album of the year with *River: The Joni Letters* (Verve, 2007), shocking virtually every music fan under the age of sixty in the process.

At last count, there were over 550 known covers of "Both Sides, Now," two hundred of "Big Yellow Taxi," over one hundred each of "Woodstock," "River," "The Circle Game," and "A Case of You," and over fifty each of "Chelsea Morning," "Urge for Going," and "All I Want." And, of course, there is Nazareth's incomprehensibly popular rock version of "This Flight Tonight." See *Greatest Hits* (A & M, 1996), or simply tune into your local classic rock radio station.

ANNE MURRAY

As the vast majority of her catalogue is the ultimate representation of middle-of-the-road blandness, it's a shame that Murray's debut album, *What About Me* (Arc, 1968) was given only a limited CD release on the Quebec-based budget reissue label Unidisc in 2004. Although not a complete artistic triumph, the album shows Murray and Brian Ahern attempting things they never would again, making it a fascinating glimpse at several musical paths not taken. Things fell into place on the next two records, *This Way Is My Way* (Capitol, 1969) and *Honey Wheat & Laughter* (Capitol, 1970), and Murray never looked back. These were reissued together as *The Signature Series Vol. 1* (EMI, 1998). The U.S. breakthrough compendium *Snowbird* (Capitol, 1970) is long out of print.

After three more releases, Murray hit her easy-listening stride with *Danny's Song* (Capitol, 1974), the title track for which was her biggest North American hit since "Snowbird." A sufficient sampling of her best material up to that point is found on the three-CD set *Now and Forever* (EMI, 1994), but few will have the stamina to sit through the schmaltz on the bulk of this collection.

DAVID WIFFEN ET AL.

With both 1965's *David Wiffen Live at the Bunkhouse* and his first olo album, *David Wiffen* (Fantasy, 1971), nearly impossible to find, the best place to start discovering his work is the CD reissue of 1973's *Coast to Coast Fever* (EMI Canada, 1997). Due to high demand for all those records, Wiffen was persuaded to make *South of Somewhere* (True North, 1999), comprised of new recordings of "Lost My Driving Wheel," "Skybound Station," "Lucifer's Blues," and "Smoke Rings," and the rest of his best material. Although his voice was still in fine form, the arrangements and production were merely adequate, making the album really only a last resort if the earlier releases can't be turned up.

Tom Rush's 1970 cover of "Lost My Driving Wheel" is on *No Regrets: The Very Best of Tom Rush* (Columbia Legacy, 1999). The post-*Sweetheart Of The Rodeo* Byrds cut the song in 1972, although it wasn't heard until it surfaced as a bonus track on the reissued *Farther Along* (Sony Legacy, 2000). Roger McGuinn instead re-recorded it for his first solo album, *Roger McGuinn* (Columbia, 1973, reissued on Sundazed, 2004). A later, extremely affecting cover was done by the Cowboy Junkies on *200 More Miles: Live Performances 1985–1994* (RCA/BMG, 1995), and also on *Studio: Selected Studio Recordings 1986–1995* (RCA/BMG, 1996).

Wiffen's other frequently covered song is "More Often Than Not," best heard by Jerry Jeff Walker on *Bein' Free* (Atco, 1970, reissued on Wounded Bird, 2000), and by Eric Andersen on *Blue River* (Columbia, 1972, reissued on Sony, 1999). The 3's a Crowd album *Christopher's Movie Matinee* (ABC-Dunhill, 1968) has not been reissued on CD to date. However, band member Trevor Veitch went on to have to have an interesting career as a pop songwriter and session musician, penning/producing the massive hits "Gloria" for Laura Branigan and "Mickey" for Toni Basil. No recordings by Wiffen's subsequent group, The Children, appear to exist, although many from the Ottawa folk community revisited those glory years on *Dancing Alone: Songs of William Hawkins* (True North, 2008), a tribute to the scene's prominent poet/lyricist.

BRUCE COCKBURN AND MURRAY MCLAUCHLAN

The reputed 1967 recordings by Cockburn's psychedelic rock band The Flying Circus, prior to his brief stint with The Children, have yet to see the light of day, undoubtedly at

Cockburn's urging. However, two of his songs from this period, "Flying Circus" and "Frankly Stoned," later turned up on *Mapleoak* (Decca, 1971, reissued on Decca Japan, 2004), the eponymous album from a British-based group formed by former Flying Circus members Marty Fisher and Gordon McBain. "Morning Hymn," a third song recorded but not included on that album, was ultimately recorded by Cockburn for the B-side of his 1972 single "It's Going Down Slow."

In association with Rounder Records, True North has begun to reissue Cockburn's catalogue in expanded editions, although his charming 1970 self-titled debut album is so far not among them. The most convenient compilation is still the two-CD *Waiting for a Miracle: Singles 1970–1987* (True North, 1987; the Canadian edition includes ten extra tracks), which is complemented by *Anything Anytime Anywhere: Singles 1979–2002* (True North, 2002). The latter shows more concisely Cockburn's transformation from his only real brush with U.S. pop charts, "Wondering Where the Lions Are," originally on *Dancing in the Dragon's Jaws* (True North, 1979), to the defiance of songs like "If I Had a Rocket Launcher" and "Call It Democracy," which put him at the forefront of the resurgence of political activism in rock and roll during the early eighties. The stretch of albums on which these latter tracks originally appeared, from 1980's *Humans* to 1988's *Big Circumstance*, mark Cockburn's most engaging period as a songwriter, although the subsequent releases *Nothing but a Burning Light* (True North, 1991) and *Dart to the Heart* (True North, 1994) have much to offer musically.

Cockburn's relevance to the new generation of Canadian musicians of this period was wholeheartedly displayed on *Kick at the Darkness: Songs of Bruce Cockburn* (Intrepid/Capitol, 1991), best remembered for the Barenaked Ladies' version of "Lovers in a Dangerous Time." Cockburn also entered Deadhead culture through Jerry Garcia's cover of "Waiting for a Miracle" from *Jerry Garcia Band* (Arista, 1991). Bizarrely, electro-pop act Primitive Radio Gods lifted the title "(Standing) Outside a Broken Phone Booth With Money in My Hand" for its only hit — see *Rocket* (Sony, 1996) — although this track had nothing to do with Cockburn's own song bearing that title, heard on *Further Adventures Of* (True North, 1978).

The film *Goin' Down the Road*, featuring Cockburn's score and the songs "Another Victim of the Rainbow" and "Goin' Down the Road," was released by Warner as a Signature Collection DVD in 2002.

Murray McLauchlan's career has been sufficiently summed up with the two-CD *Songs From the Street* (True North, 2007). It divides his work almost evenly between the country/folk of his first five albums and a more rock-influenced sound beginning with *Boulevard* (True North, 1976), which debuted his band The Silver Tractors. More of a songwriter than a performer, McLauchlan ventured into other media by the eighties, while releasing albums mainly for his diehard Canadian fan base. "Child's Song" is (again) heard on Tom Rush's *No Regrets*, although it, along with "Old Man's Song" and David Wiffen's "Lost My Driving Wheel" were all originally on *Tom Rush* (Columbia, 1970). And while Waylon Jennings and Kris Kristofferson each performed "Honky Red" live, the only notable recorded cover of that song is by Dylan sidekick Bob Neuwirth on *Bob Neuwirth* (Asylum, 1974).

KATE AND ANNA MCGARRIGLE ET AL.

Their classic 1976 debut album has been available on CD since 1993, and is undoubtedly due for an update. The follow-up, *Dancer With Bruised Knees* (Warner Brothers, 1977), didn't capture as many imaginations, but was still a worthy effort, notable for several more songs in French. *Pronto Monto* (Warner Brothers, 1978) was marred by attempts to give the sisters more of a pop sheen, and the label dropped them soon after its release. It remains their only recording that has not been issued on CD. They regrouped by self-releasing *Entre la Jeunesse et la Sagesse* in 1980, an homage to their roots, in collaboration with lyricist Philippe Tatartcheff. The album also marked a reunion with producer Joe Boyd. It was reissued as *The French Record* (Hannibal, 1981).

That album seemed to directly inspire the next, *Love Over and Over* (Hannibal, 1983), which recaptured some of the homey spirit of the first album, while at the same time incorporating a more contemporary rock sound through guests like guitarist Mark Knopfler. The McGarrigles would not make another album until *Heartbeats Accelerating* (Private/Atlantic, 1990), a thoroughly modern folk recording, thanks to producer Pierre Marchand, best known for his work with Sarah McLachlan. Another long interval preceded their next release, *Matapedia* (Hannibal, 1996), but its more traditional folk approach reconnected with a broad audience that had all but forgotten about them. Of particular note was Anna's "Goin' Back to Harlan," recorded earlier by Emmylou Harris on her mesmerizing collaboration with Daniel Lanois, *Wrecking Ball* (Elektra, 1995). Their next project saw them truly coming full circle. *The McGarrigle Hour* (Hannibal, 1998) allowed listeners to sit in on a gathering of the entire family, including the Wainwrights and close friends Tatarcheff, Harris, Linda Ronstadt, and Chaim Tannenbaum. With a mix of originals and a selection of whimsical covers that included Sonny James's 1956 country smash "Young Love" and Irving Berlin's "What'll I Do," the album exuded a rare sense of intimacy. Continuing at their own pace, the McGarrigles then took several years to complete a second album in French, *La Vache Qui Pleure* (La Tribu, 2003).

Maria Muldaur's first two solo albums containing McGarrigle songs, *Maria Muldaur* (Reprise, 1973) and *Waitress in a Donut Shop* (Reprise, 1974) are both on CD, as is Linda Ronstadt's *Heart Like a Wheel* (Capitol, 1974). Almost any Loudon Wainwright III album contains insights into his family life, but a good introduction to his unique approach is the live *Career Moves* (Virgin, 1993). More confrontational is *Unrequited* (Columbia, 1975), made in the midst of his breakup with Kate, notable for the ode to breastfeeding, "Rufus Is a Tit Man."

The careers of Rufus and Martha Wainwright deserve more consideration than can be afforded here; suffice it to say that both rank among the most engaging songwriters of their generation. See especially *Rufus Wainwright* (Dreamworks, 1998) and his sprawling dual opus *Want One* (Dreamworks, 2003) and *Want Two* (Geffen, 2004).

EARLY SEVENTIES ADDENDUM: STOMPIN' TOM CONNORS, WILLIE P. BENNETT, STAN ROGERS, ET AL.

The immediate post-1967 cultural awakening inspired many Canadian songwriters to suddenly see the potential in cultivating a purely homegrown fan base, and nobody was more successful at this than Stompin' Tom Connors. Coming from the east coast like an amalgamation of Woody Guthrie, Johnny Cash, and Popeye the Sailor, Connors' simple, direct songs were steeped in his years of travelling around the country, living hand to mouth. However, his image as an unpolished rube was slightly deceiving. After starting his own label, Boot Records, in 1971 as a deliberate response to foreign control of the Canadian recording industry, Connors cranked out a steady stream of albums that celebrated working-class life in all corners of Canada, and in the process became a bona fide folk hero. That status was affirmed in 1979 when, in a fit of protest over the continuing obstacles facing Canadian musicians, Connors announced his retirement and returned his six Juno awards. He was lured back in 1988 by EMI Canada, which also agreed to reissue his Boot catalogue, and he resumed writing new songs that were, not surprisingly, embraced by a generation hungry to feel a sense of national pride. Most of Connors' career-defining moments are found on the compilation *A Proud Canadian* (Capitol/EMI, 1990).

Toronto native Willie P. Bennett first came to prominence as a songwriter when David Wiffen recorded "White Line" on *Coast to Coast Fever*. After that, Bennett stayed close to home, making a trio of albums, *Trying to Start Out Clean* (Woodshed, 1975), *Hobo's Taunt* (Woodshed, 1977), and *Blackie and the Rodeo King* (Woodshed, 1978) that put a decidedly Canadian slant on the new school of impressionistic folk-based songwriting that was then associated with the Texas school of Townes Van Zandt, Guy Clark, and Steve Young. While few paid much attention to Bennett at the time, these albums remained influential, and would be reintroduced at the urging of fellow Canadian singer-songwriters Tom Wilson, Colin Linden, and Stephen Fearing, who named their late nineties "supergroup" Blackie and the Rodeo Kings in Bennett's honour. Further, they launched the band with a tribute album, *High or Hurtin'* (True North, 1996). Bennett had made one more album in the meantime, *The Lucky Ones* (Duke Street, 1989), but the renewed interest in his work prompted the release of *Heartstrings* (Bnatural, 1998), which won a Juno award. However, by this time Bennett had chiefly devoted himself to working as a sideman for Fred Eaglesmith, whose own fine work ironically owed a lot to Bennett's hard-nosed storytelling. Some of Eaglesmith's best songs can be heard on his essential triumvirate, *Drive-In Movie* (Vertical, 1995), *Lipstick, Lies & Gasoline* (Vertical, 1997), and *50-Odd Dollars* (Razor & Tie, 1999). Sadly, Bennett died on February 15, 2008, in the midst of once again rejuvenating his solo career.

Although born in Hamilton, Ontario, Stan Rogers' obsession with his Maritime heritage eventually made him one of the most beloved figures in Canadian folk music. His songs helped establish a distinct contemporary musical voice for that part of the country. After recording several forgettable singles for RCA in the early seventies, Rogers started his own label, Fogarty's Cove, in 1976. Its first release was an album of the same name. Consisting of yarns about fishermen, shipwrecks, and the east coast's rugged terrain, *Fogarty's Cove* was immediately hailed as a Canadian folk milestone. Rogers followed it up with *Turnaround* (Fogarty's Cove, 1978) and *Between The Breaks . . . Live!* (Fogarty's Cove, 1979) before hitting another peak with *Northwest Passage* (Fogarty's Cove, 1981). That album focused on the constant westward migration of Maritimers, and the title track quickly became Rogers' signature song. However, this was the last release he saw in his lifetime, as he died on June 2, 1983, during a fire on board his flight from Dallas to Toronto. Subsequent posthumous releases appeared regularly, and his younger brother Garnet Rogers carried on his spirit with his own career as a singer-songwriter.

NEIL YOUNG

When Young's fall 2007 tour unexpectedly included airings of "The Sultan" — the first song he ever recorded, in 1963 — along with several other unreleased tracks, it seemed a clear indication that his long-awaited *Archives* set was about to be released. In fact, accumulating and recycling the sheer volume of unreleased material for *Archives* provided Young with an almost parallel career by the turn of the twenty-first century, when the idea of *Archives* was first leaked. Young was actually scooped when *The Complete Motown Singles Vol. 6: 1966* (Hip-O, 2006) was released, and offered the only known Mynah Birds recordings of "It's My Time" and "Go On and Cry," finally shedding some light on that previously foggy moment in Young's career. Harder to find still are the seven Elektra demos from November 1965, best heard on *Ancient History Up Close* (Scorpio bootleg). As far as Buffalo Springfield's catalogue goes, *Box Set* (Warner/Rhino, 2001) has virtually everything the band recorded during its two-year existence in chronological order and pristine sound, making any other release unnecessary.

Although *Decade* (Reprise, 1977) is still a useful overview of Young's first golden era, the previously unheard live recordings that preceded *Archives* painted an entirely different picture of that time. *Fillmore East 1970* (Reprise, 2006) caught a rare glimpse of the original Crazy Horse in full flight, just before their crash, and *Massey Hall 1971* (Reprise, 2007) was Young at his absolute solo best, in full command of his muse and his audience. A more innocent glimpse of him as a fledgling solo performer was revealed on *Sugar Mountain: Live at Canterbury House 1968* (Reprise, 2008), the complete tape from which the long-cherished recording of the title track was originally drawn.

The belated 2003 CD release of *On the Beach* (Reprise, 1974) was proof of its lasting impact, but *Time Fades Away* (Reprise, 1973) is still, inexplicably, only available in its original vinyl form. This will undoubtedly be rectified at some point, and it can rightfully be assumed that future live *Archive* releases will include something from the *Tonight's the Night* tour, or the powerful May 16, 1974, Bottom Line solo performance. The soundtrack to *Journey Through the Past* (Reprise, 1972) can also only be found in its original vinyl package, and, in this case, is better left that way.

Young's sporadic work with Crosby, Stills & Nash is best left to the curious, especially the dreadful later-period albums *American Dream* (Warner, 1988) and *Looking Forward* (Warner,

1999). The same can be said for the Stills–Young Band's *Long May You Run* (Warner, 1976). On the other hand, Young's post-*Decade* seventies releases, *Comes A Time, Rust Never Sleeps*, and *Live Rust*, are all mandatory.

The eighties brought the legendary standoff with David Geffen after Young was persuaded to join Joni Mitchell, Elton John, and other high-profile artists on the roster of his new label. Geffen subsequently sued Young after the initial sequence of genre-hopping albums *Trans* (Geffen, 1982), *Everybody's Rockin'* (Geffen, 1983), *Old Ways* (Geffen, 1985), and *Landing on Water* (Geffen, 1986) all tanked, both critically and commercially. Young responded to this unprecedented accusation of not sounding like himself with the caustic "Prisoners of Rock 'n' Roll," recorded with Crazy Horse on his next album, *Life* (Geffen, 1987). He ultimately re-signed with Reprise, and after indulging in some novelty R & B on *This Note's for You* (Reprise, 1988), Young moved from strength to strength, starting with the glorious *Freedom* (Reprise, 1989) and the anthem "Rockin' in the Free World."

Perhaps not surprisingly, few of Young's peers were able to put personal stamps on his material. Most successful were his backup singers; Nicolette Larson hit number eight on *Billboard*'s pop chart with "Lotta Love" — see *Nicolette* (Warner Brothers., 1978) — and Linda Ronstadt hit number five on the country chart with "Love Is a Rose" — see *Greatest Hits* (Asylum, 1976).

It wasn't until the post-punk generation connected with Young's uncompromising style that new interpretations suddenly became plentiful. Much of this reassessment began with *The Bridge: A Tribute to Neil Young* (Caroline, 1989), featuring Sonic Youth, the Pixies, Dinosaur Jr., Flaming Lips, Soul Asylum, and others. A year later, Young reunited with Crazy Horse and recorded *Ragged Glory* (Reprise, 1990). Soon after, he was hailed as the godfather of grunge, and yet another new era began.

THE BAND

Of the several attempts to fully compile the group's entire career in a single package, the one that has come closest is the six-

CD/DVD *A Musical History* (Capitol, 2005). Containing all the crucial Hawkins recordings, Levon & The Hawks singles, live tracks with Bob Dylan, and a treasure trove of demos, it possesses a sweeping narrative that clearly bears Robbie Robertson's personal touch. A truncated version, *The Best of a Musical History* (Capitol, 2007), containing only one CD, along with a DVD, is for those who merely want something to accentuate a "best-of" release, the most up-to-date of which is *Greatest Hits* (Capitol, 2000).

Indeed, the story never seems to be complete. The pre-Dylan sessions with John Hammond Jr. are still available on the CD reissue of *So Many Roads* (Vanguard, 1993), and the subsequent *Mirrors* (Vanguard, originally released in 1967) includes two supposedly leftover takes of Billy Boy Arnold's "I Wish You Would" and Robert Johnson's "Travelling Riverside Blues." Hammond's *I Can Tell* (Atlantic, 1967) features further guest appearances by Robertson and Danko during their pre–Big Pink downtime. The first flash of the unparalleled freedom that Woodstock provided is captured on the soundtrack to *You Are What You Eat* (Columbia, 1968, reissued on Sony Japan, 1997). On it, the group (minus Helm) backs up Tiny Tim on predictably outrageous takes of "Be My Baby" and "I Got You Babe," which make their spontaneous work with Dylan at Big Pink sound utterly reserved by comparison.

The appearance of the full basement tapes on bootleg during the nineties made the official *The Basement Tapes* (Columbia, 1975) suddenly unnecessary. The best source for these at present seems to be the four-CD *A Tree With Roots* (Wild Wolf bootleg, 2001). While on the subject, another useful collection is *Crossing The Great Divide — Genuine Bootleg Series, Take 4* (Wild Wolf bootleg, 1997), a career-spanning three-CD set that fills in some of the gaps from *A Musical History*, notably some unreleased samples from the Woodstock and Isle of Wight festivals and a healthy amount of *Rock of Ages* outtakes. Still the only place to find all three songs performed with Dylan at the Woody Guthrie memorial is *A Tribute to Woody Guthrie Part One* (Columbia, 1972, reissued on a single CD with *Part Two* on

Warner Brothers, 1989). Some of their 1965–66 recordings with Dylan are scattered over his various *Bootleg Series* releases and the box set *Biograph* (Columbia, 1985), but the seminal document of that period remains *Bob Dylan Live 1966: The "Royal Albert Hall" Concert* (Columbia Legacy, 1998). See also Martin Scorsese's documentary *No Direction Home* (Paramount Pictures, 2005) for previously unseen (and truly shattering) live footage from the tour.

All of The Band's eight albums for Capitol were remastered and reissued with bonus tracks in 2000, thereby securing the group's legacy for all time. *The Last Waltz* was expanded from its original three LPs to four CDs for its re-release on Warner/Rhino in 2002 to coincide with the film's restoration. After a decade of touring without Robertson, and without Manuel after his death in 1986, The Band released *Jericho* (Pyramid, 1993), a noble attempt to rekindle the spirit of the group while updating the overall sound in subtle ways. Sadly, bridging that gap proved an insurmountable task, and two more largely ignored albums in the same vein, *High on the Hog* (Pyramid, 1996) and *Jubilation* (River North, 1998), followed before Danko's death ultimately put an end to the group.

Robertson's much-hyped solo debut, *Robbie Robertson* (Geffen, 1987), produced by Daniel Lanois and featuring guest appearances by U2 and Peter Gabriel, as well as Danko and Hudson, showed promise — for whatever it was worth — that he could survive in the modern corporate world of rock and roll, but after his disappointing paean to New Orleans, *Storyville* (Geffen, 1991), his interests turned to exploring indigenous North American music almost exclusively. This resulted in the innovative, if challenging, releases *Music for the Native Americans* (Cema/Capitol, 1994), and the techno-driven *Contact From the Underworld of Red Boy* (Cema/Capitol, 1998).

Danko and Helm were actually the first to go solo, the former releasing the guest-packed *Rick Danko* (Arista, 1977), and the latter *Levon Helm and the RCO All-Stars* (ABC, 1977), while the group was still officially together. Danko would not release anything again until the unusual collaboration with Eric Andersen and Norwegian singer-songwriter Jonas Fjeld, which spawned two albums, *Danko/Fjeld/Andersen* (Mercury/Polygram, 1991) and *Ridin' the Blinds* (Rykodisc, 1997), although some aborted late seventies sessions turned up on the posthumous *Crying Heart Blues* (OPM, 2005). *Live on Breeze Hill* (Woodstock, 1999) captured Danko's timeless innocence for the last time. Helm remained prolific into the early eighties, as he balanced film roles in *Coal Miner's Daughter* and *The Right Stuff*, although the only release of any significance during this period was *American Son* (MCA, 1980), a well-chosen selection of hard-edged country material recorded in Nashville with former Hawks guitarist Fred Carter, Jr. With The Band's final demise, Helm stuck close to Woodstock, performing mainly at his weekly Midnight Ramble sessions even as he suffered through treatment for throat cancer. In what can only be called a miracle, he released *Dirt Farmer* (Vanguard, 2007) with the aid of his daughter Amy and multi-instrumentalist extraordinaire Larry Campbell. *Dirt Farmer* was a profound collection of songs recalled from his childhood, including "Little Birds," a staple of The Band's early repertoire. It's as moving as anything in Johnny Cash's *American* series.

The ever-enigmatic Hudson kept a relatively low profile throughout the eighties while at the same time staying busy as a session musician. Notable turns included Leonard Cohen's *Recent Songs*, Don Henley's *I Can't Stand Still* (Asylum, 1982), Tom Petty's *Southern Accents* (MCA, 1985), Marianne Faithfull's *Strange Weather* (Island, 1987), The Northern Pikes' *Snow in June* (Virgin, 1990), and several albums by California band The Call. However, something of a renaissance took place for Hudson after he and Helm did guest appearances on Mercury Rev's *Deserter's Songs* (V2, 1998), an album that, for a new generation, brimmed with all the magic and mystery contained on *Big Pink*. Hudson suddenly made himself available as never before to young admirers such as Norah Jones, Neko Case, Martha Wainwright, and even The Lemonheads on their 2006 "reunion" album. Of particular interest is Toronto band The Sadies' *In Concert Vol. 1* (Outside, 2006), on which Hudson sits in on a blistering version of the old Levon & The Hawks nugget

"Leave Me Alone." The increased activity also inspired Hudson to put out his own records for the first time, too, in collaboration with his wife Maud, *The Sea to the North* (OPM, 2001) and *Live at the Wolf* (OPM, 2005). As he said of his situation in 2001, "It's been like another lifetime." While the spectre of The Band will forever hang over him, Hudson deserves an equal place alongside Glenn Gould and Oscar Peterson as one of the greatest musicians ever born in Canada.

ACKNOWLEDGEMENTS

I am greatly indebted to the many people who personally shared their stories for this book. Some interviews were conducted over the course of my fifteen years as a music journalist, but most were done specifically for this project, and for that reason I also humbly acknowledge here the efforts of those who helped facilitate them.

Thank you to Robbie Robertson, Garth Hudson, Brian Ahern, Mary Martin, Murray McLauchlan, Ronnie Hawkins, Harold Kudlats, Greil Marcus, Jared Levine, Maud Hudson, Frazier Mohawk, Walter Sobczak, Larry LeBlanc, Alan Kates, David Fougere, David Lewis, Frank Dodman, Jim Dean, and Gerry Taylor (for his invaluable Wilf Carter research).

Thanks also to Michael Barclay, Rob Bowman, Rick Klaver, David Booth, and Glenn Smith.

Most of all, I am forever grateful to Wendy Rofihe for the care and wisdom she put into this book. Thank you with all of my heart.

Barr, Steven C. *History of Recorded Sound in Canada*. Canadian Antique Phonograph Society, 2000. www.capsnews.org.

Batten, Jack. "Leonard Cohen: The Poet as Hero — His Songs & His Followers." *Saturday Night* (June 1969).

BBC Radio 1. Transcript of interview with Leonard Cohen on "Suzanne" (1994). www.globalpoet.com/cohen.

Bernstein, Joel, ed. Booklet for Buffalo Springfield, *Box Set* (Elektra/Warner, 2001).

Black, Johnny. "The Madness of King Bob." *Mojo* (January 2007).

—. "Hallelujah, We Love Him So: Leonard Cohen's Comeback." *Audience* (September 2008).

Black, Johnny, with Andy Gill. "Judas Christ Superstar." *Mojo* (November 1998).

Boucher, Caroline. "The Band — Or When The Booing Ended." *Disc and Music Echo* (May 29, 1971).

Bowman, Rob. Liner note to The Band, *A Musical History* (Capitol, 2005).

Brennan, Brian. "Wilf Carter: A Fan's Fan," *Calgary Herald*, December 11, 1996.

Bunting, Findlay, dir. *Robbie Robertson: Going Home* (DVD). Cherry Lane Productions Inc./LaserLight Digital, 1995.

Caffin, Carol. "Goin' Electric: Mickey Jones Talks About Dylan's 1966 World Tour and His (Mostly Fond) Memories of The Band." *BandBites* 1, no. 6 (May 1, 2007).

Carter, Wilf. *The Yodelling Cowboy: Montana Slim from Nova Scotia.* Toronto: The Ryerson Press, 1961.

Carter, Wilf. Liner note to *Wilf Carter/Montana Slim* (RCA-Camden, 1962).

The Citizen (Amherst, Nova Scotia), "Church Still Active 153 Years After Its Founding," July 12, 1997.

Clark, Larry Wayne. "Gordon Lightfoot Portrait Of A Painter." International Songwriters Association newsletter (2002).

Clark, Rick. "Brian Ahern: A Rare Interview With Country's Great 'Natural' Producer." *Mix* 20, no. 7 (1996).

—. Liner note to Emmylou Harris, *Pieces of the Sky.* Remastered edition (Warner/Reprise/Rhino, 2004).

Cocks, Jay. "Down To Old Dixie And Back." *Time* (January 12, 1970).

Collins, Maynard. *Lightfoot: If You Could Read His Mind.* Toronto: Deneau, 1988.

Cooke, Stephen. "Scrapbook Captures Murray Memories." *Halifax Chronicle Herald,* July 27, 2000.

Cray, Ed. *Ramblin' Man: The Life and Times of Woody Guthrie.* New York: W. W. Norton, 2004.

Crowe, Cameron. "The Rolling Stone Interview: Joni Mitchell." *Rolling Stone* (July 26, 1979).

—. Liner note to Bob Dylan, *Biograph* (Columbia, 1985).

Cullingham, James. "Love on the Tracks." *Mojo* (June 2000).

Dalen, Brenda. Liner note to *Classic Canadian Songs from Smithsonian Folkways* (Smithsonian Folkways, 2006).

Dannen, Frederic. *Hit Men: Power Brokers and Fast Money Inside the Music Business.* New York: Vintage, 1991.

Davis, Chuck. *The History of Metropolitan Vancouver.* Vancouver: Harbour, 2007.

Dorman, Loranne S., and Clive L. Rawlins. *Leonard Cohen: Prophet of the Heart*. New York: Omnibus, 1990.

Escott, Colin. Liner note to Wilf Carter, *Cowboy Songs* (Bear Family, 1997).

Flanagan, Bill. *Written in My Soul: Conversations With Rock's Great Songwriters*. Chicago: Contemporary, 1987.

Fowke, Edith. Liner note to The Travellers, *A Century of Song* (Arc, 1967).

Gabites, Lee. "The Whole Truth and Nothing but the Truth: An Interview With John Simon." http://theband.hiof.no.

Gilbert, Jerry. "Kate & Anna McGarrigle: Sisters in Song." *Sounds* (April 10, 1976).

Gladstone, Howard. "The Robbie Robertson Interview." *Rolling Stone* (December 27, 1969).

Gleason, Ralph J. "The Band at Winterland." *Rolling Stone* (May 1969).

Goddard, John, and Richard Crouse. *Rock and Roll Toronto: From Alanis to Zeppelin*. Toronto: Doubleday, 1997.

Goldberg, Michael. "The Second Coming of Robbie Robertson." *Rolling Stone* (November 19, 1987).

Goldstein, Richard. "Beautiful Creep." *Village Voice* (December 28, 1967).

Goodman, Fred. *The Mansion on the Hill: Dylan, Young, Geffen, Springsteen, and the Head-On Collision of Rock and Commerce*. New York: Vintage, 1998.

Grundy, Stuart, and John Tobler. *The Record Producers*. London: BBC Books, 1982.

Gunderson, Lee. "Ian Tyson: High Plains Balladear." *Alberta Beef Magazine* (October 2007).

Guralnick, Peter. *Lost Highway: Journeys and Arrivals of American Musicians*. Boston: Back Bay, 1999.

—. *Last Train to Memphis: The Rise of Elvis Presley.* Boston: Little, Brown, 1994.

Hajdu, David. *Positively 4th Street: The Lives and Times Of Joan Baez, Bob Dylan, Mimi Baez Farina, and Richard Farina.* New York: Farrar, Straus & Giroux, 2001.

Hank And Jimmie: A Story of Country, directed by John Martin (Triad Film Productions Ltd., 2000).

Helm, Levon, with Stephen Davis. *This Wheel's on Fire: Levon Helm and the Story of The Band.* New York: William Morrow and Co., 1993.

Hilburn, Robert. "The Mojo Interview: Joni Mitchell." *Mojo* (February 2008).

Hoskyns, Barney. *Across the Great Divide: The Band and America.* Toronto: Random House, 1993.

—. *Hotel California.* Hoboken, NJ: John Wiley & Sons, 2005.

Huftig, Stacy, ed. *The Joni Mitchell Companion: Four Decades of Commentary.* New York: Schirmer, 2000.

Jackson, Randy. Interview with Bonnie Dobson, 1993. www.taco.com/roots.

Jahn, Mike. "The Band Breathes Fresh Country Air Over Fillmore East." *New York Times*, May 12, 1969.

James, Gary. Interview with Ian Tyson. www.classicbands.com.

Jennings, Nicholas. *Before the Gold Rush.* Toronto: Viking, 1997.

Johnson, L.A. "Interview with Stephen Stills and Neil Young" (video). September 15, 1995. www.youtube.com.

Joseph, Hugh A. Liner note to *Reminiscin' With Montana Slim* (RCA-Camden, 1963).

Kelton, Jim. "Farther On Up the Road." *Arkansas Times* (January 26, 2006).

Kienzle, Rich. Liner note to *RCA Country Legends: The Bristol Sessions Vol. 1.* (RCA/BMG Heritage, 2002).

Kiersh, Edward. *Where Are You Now, Bo Diddley? The Artists Who Made Us Rock and Where They Are Now*. New York: Doubleday, 1986.

Kirby, Allan. "What Ordinary People Do Is Important: Edith Fowke's Life and Publications." *Canadian Journal for Traditional Music* 26, no. 1 (1998).

Krewen, Nick. "Lightfoot at 54: 'I'm Not Worthy.'" *Hamilton Spectator*, November 6, 1993.

—. "Summers At Six Nations." *Hamilton Spectator*, March 12, 1998.

Kubernick, Harvey. "Across the Great Divide With Robbie Robertson." *Crawdaddy* (March 1976).

Lazar, Barry. "Sam Gesser, Friend to the Superstars." *Montreal Gazette*, November 30, 1997.

Lederman, Marsha. "Tyson Comes Clean." *Globe and Mail*, March 28, 2008.

Lightfoot, Gordon. Liner note to *Songbook* (Warner, 1999).

Lightfoot, Gordon, and Terry Whelan. Liner note to *The Two Tones Live at The Village Corner* (Chateau, 1962).

Long, Pete. "A Brief History of Buffalo Springfield." Liner note to Buffalo Springfield, *Box Set* (Elektra/Warner, 2001).

"Looking Back at One Knight of a Cowboy." *Wyoming Tribune-Eagle*, July 17, 2004.

MacFarlane, John. "Lightfoot: The Lyrical Loner." *Globe and Mail*, June 18, 1966.

Macklem, Katherine, with Charlie Gillis. "Leonard Cohen Goes Broke." *Maclean's* (August 22, 2005).

MacLeod, Meredith. "Making Music One Act at a Time." *Hamilton Spectator*, June 10, 2006.

Malone, Bill. C. *Country Music, U.S.A.* 2nd rev. ed. Austin: University of Texas Press, 2002.

Marcus, Greil. *Mystery Train: Images of America In Rock 'n' Roll Music.* 3rd rev. ed. New York: Plume, 1990.

—. *Invisible Republic: Bob Dylan's Basement Tapes.* New York: Henry Holt, 1997.

Martin, Sandra. "Obituary: Denny Doherty, 66." *Globe and Mail,* January 19, 2007.

Mayes, Alison. "Wilf Carter Never Forgot His Fans." *Calgary Herald,* December 7, 1996.

McDonald, Elizabeth Drake. "Bob Nolan: The Myth and the Man" (2000). Elizabeth Drake McDonald Collection, Manuscripts Department, Library of the University of North Carolina at Chapel Hill. www.bobnolan-sop.net/Biographies.

McDonough, Jimmy. *Shakey: Neil Young's Biography.* Toronto: Random House, 2002.

McLauchlan, Murray. *Getting Out of Here Alive.* Toronto: Viking, 1998.

Merrill, Sam. "Mason Hoffenberg Gets in a Few Licks." *Playboy* (November 1973).

Mock, Freida Lee, and Terry Sanders, co-directors. *American Experience* presents: "Return With Honor." PBS/Warner Video, 2001.

Morris, John. Review of Neil Young live at Waterloo Lutheran University. *The Chevron,* November 2, 1973.

Nadel, Ira B. *Various Positions: A Life of Leonard Cohen.* Toronto: Random House, 1996.

Naglin, Nancy. "After *Sundown* Gordon Lightfoot Makes Up for Lost Time." *Crawdaddy* (April 1975).

Noble, Douglas J. Interview with Nils Lofgren. *Broken Arrow* no. 62 (January 1996).

O'Brien, Karen. *Joni Mitchell: Shadows and Light.* London: Virgin Books, 2001.

O'Connor, Rory. "Albert Grossman's Ghost." *Musician* (June 1987).

Oermann, Robert K. *A Century of Country: An Illustrated History of Country Music.* New York: TV Books, 1999.

O'Malley, Martin. "Hank Snow: A Profile." *Globe Magazine* (July 10, 1971).

Palmer, Robert. "The Rolling Stone Interview: Robbie Robertson." *Rolling Stone* (November 14, 1991).

Patrick, Mick. Liner note to *The Jack Nitzsche Story: Hearing Is Believing 1962–1979* (Ace, 2005).

Perusse, Bernard. "Q & A With Gordon Lightfoot." *Montreal Gazette*, November 6, 2006.

Quill, Greg. "Family Reunion." *Toronto Star*, February 28, 2008.

Ransom, Kevin. "The Band." *Guitar Player* (May 1995).

Robertson, Robbie. "Interview with Bob Santelli for the Experience Music Project (Seattle)." Broadcast on KUOW Seattle, July 4, 2006 (Ross Reynolds, producer).

Ruhlmann, William. "The Stranger Music of Leonard Cohen." *Goldmine* (February 19, 1993).

—. "Joni Mitchell: From Blue to Indigo." *Goldmine* (February 17, 1995).

—. "Peter, Paul & Mary: A Song to Sing All Over This Land." *Goldmine* (April 12, 1996).

Schama, Simon. "The High Priest Of Minimalism." *Guardian*, June 28, 2008.

Scoppa Bud. "Neil Young: Time Fades Away." *Rolling Stone* (January 1974).

Sharp, Debra. "Mariposa: How Times Have changed." *For What Time I Am In This World* ed. Bill Usher and Linda Page-Harpa. Toronto: Peter Martin Associates Ltd., 1977.

Shelton, Robert. *No Direction Home: The Life and Music of Bob Dylan.* New York: William Morrow, 1986.

Silverstein, Richard. *Folk & Blues: An Encyclopedia.* New York: St. Martin's, 2001.

Simmons, Sylvie. "Felonious Monk." *Mojo* (November 2001).

Sloman, Larry. *On the Road With Bob Dylan.* Rev. Ed. New York: Three Rivers Press, 2002.

Smith, Cathy Evelyn. *Chasing the Dragon.* Toronto: Key Porter, 1984.

Snow, Clarence Eugene, Jack Ownbey, and Robert Burris. *The Hank Snow Story.* Champaign: University of Illinois Press, 1994.

Sounes, Howard. *Down The Highway: The Life of Bob Dylan.* New York: Grove, 2001.

Steen, Margaret. Interview with Bob Dylan. *Toronto Star,* January 29, 1966.

www.thecoolgroove.com. Entry for "The Ian Tyson Show."

This Hour Has Seven Days. Interview with Leonard Cohen (May 1, 1966). www.archives.cbc.ca.

Tosches, Nick. *Country: The Twisted Roots of Rock 'n' Roll.* New York: Da Capo, 1996.

——. *Where Dead Voices Gather.* Boston: Little, Brown, 1999.

Turner, Steve. "The Boys in the Band." *Beat Instrumental* (July 1971).

Unterberger, Richie. Interview with Sylvia Tyson. ww.richieunterberger .com/tyson.

Valentine, Penny. "Exclusive Joni Mitchell Interview." *Sounds* (June 3–10, 1972).

Van Rijn, Nicolaas. "Rocker Worked a Lifetime of Magic: Lovin' Spoonful Guitarist Dies at 58." *Toronto Star,* January 13, 2003.

Wallis, Ian. *The Hawk: The Story of Ronnie Hawkins & The Hawks.* Kingston: Quarry, 1996.

Warburton, Nick. "Mynah Birds." unpublished, 2006. human-high-way.com/pages/stories/Mynah-Birds_Nick-W1.pdf.

—. "Early Bruce Cockburn — The Flying Circus and Olivus." www.cockburnproject.net.

Wenner, Jann. "The Rolling Stone Interview: Bob Dylan." *Rolling Stone* (November 29, 1969).

Williams, Richard. "The Band: A *Melody Maker* Breakdown." *Melody Maker* (May 29, 1971).

Windolf, Jim. "Songs in the Key of Lacerating." *Vanity Fair* (May 2007).

Wolfe, Charles K. Liner note to Hank Snow, *The Yodelling Ranger: The Canadian Years 1936–1947* (Bear Family, 1993).

—. *Classic Country: Legends of Country Music.* New York: Routledge, 2001.

Woliver, Robbie. *Hoot! A Twenty-Five-Year History of the Greenwich Village Music Scene.* New York: St. Martin's, 1994.

Yorke, Ritchie. *Axes, Chops & Hot Licks: The Canadian Rock Music Scene.* Edmonton: M.G. Hurtig, 1971.

Young, Scott. *Neil and Me.* Toronto: McClelland & Stewart, 1997.